JUJUTSU KAISEN

14

THE SHIBUYA INCIDENT
—RIGHT AND WRONG—

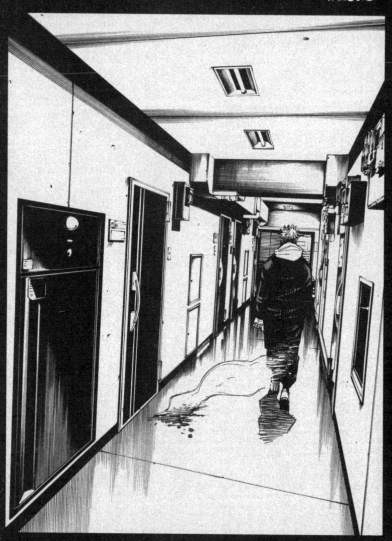

STORY AND ART BY **GEGE AKUTAMI**

JUJUTSU KAISEN
CAST OF CHARACTERS

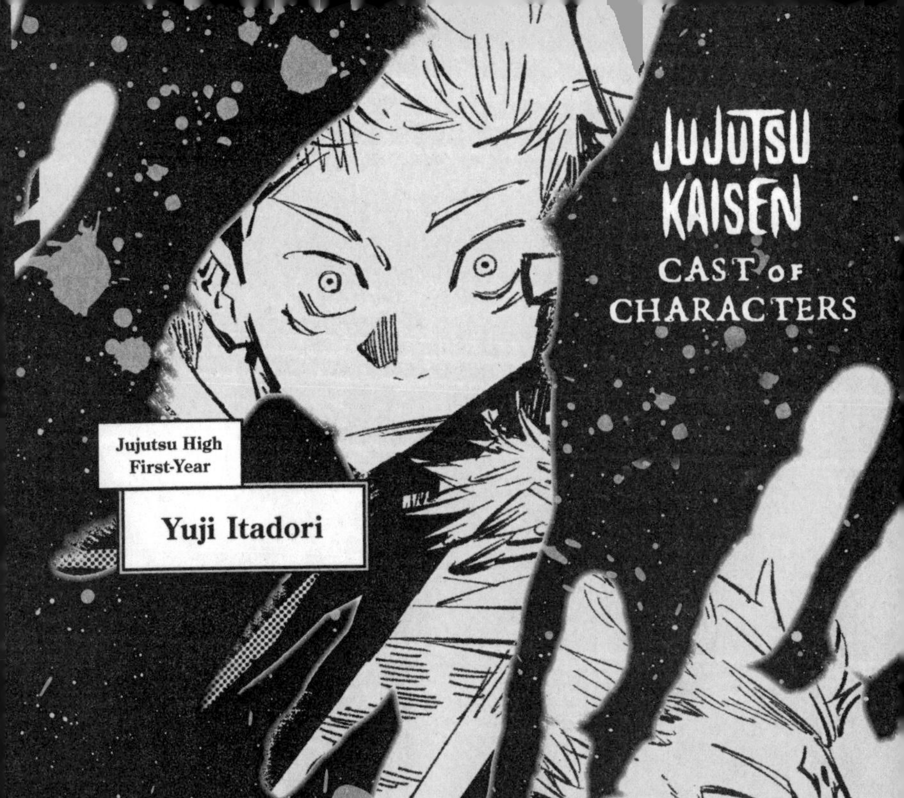

Jujutsu High First-Year

Yuji Itadori

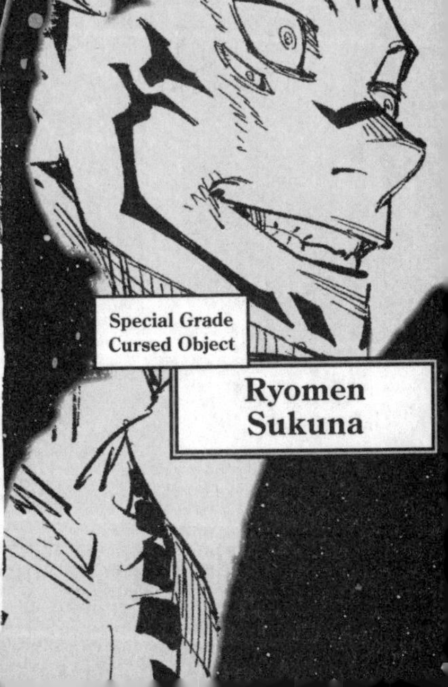

Special Grade Cursed Object

Ryomen Sukuna

—CURSE—

Hardship, regret, shame… The misery that comes from these negative human emotions can lead to death.

On October 31, cursed spirits seal off Shibuya and ensnare Gojo. As the jujutsu sorcerers frantically try to rescue Gojo, Toji Zen'in bursts in and defeats Dagon, allowing Fushiguro and the others to return from Dagon's domain. However, soon after their return, Jogo's flame burns Nanami, Maki, and Naobito. A curse user severely wounds Fushiguro, and Toji kills himself. Meanwhile, Yuji Itadori has been fed numerous fingers, and Sukuna has awakened. He squares off against Jogo, who summons help…

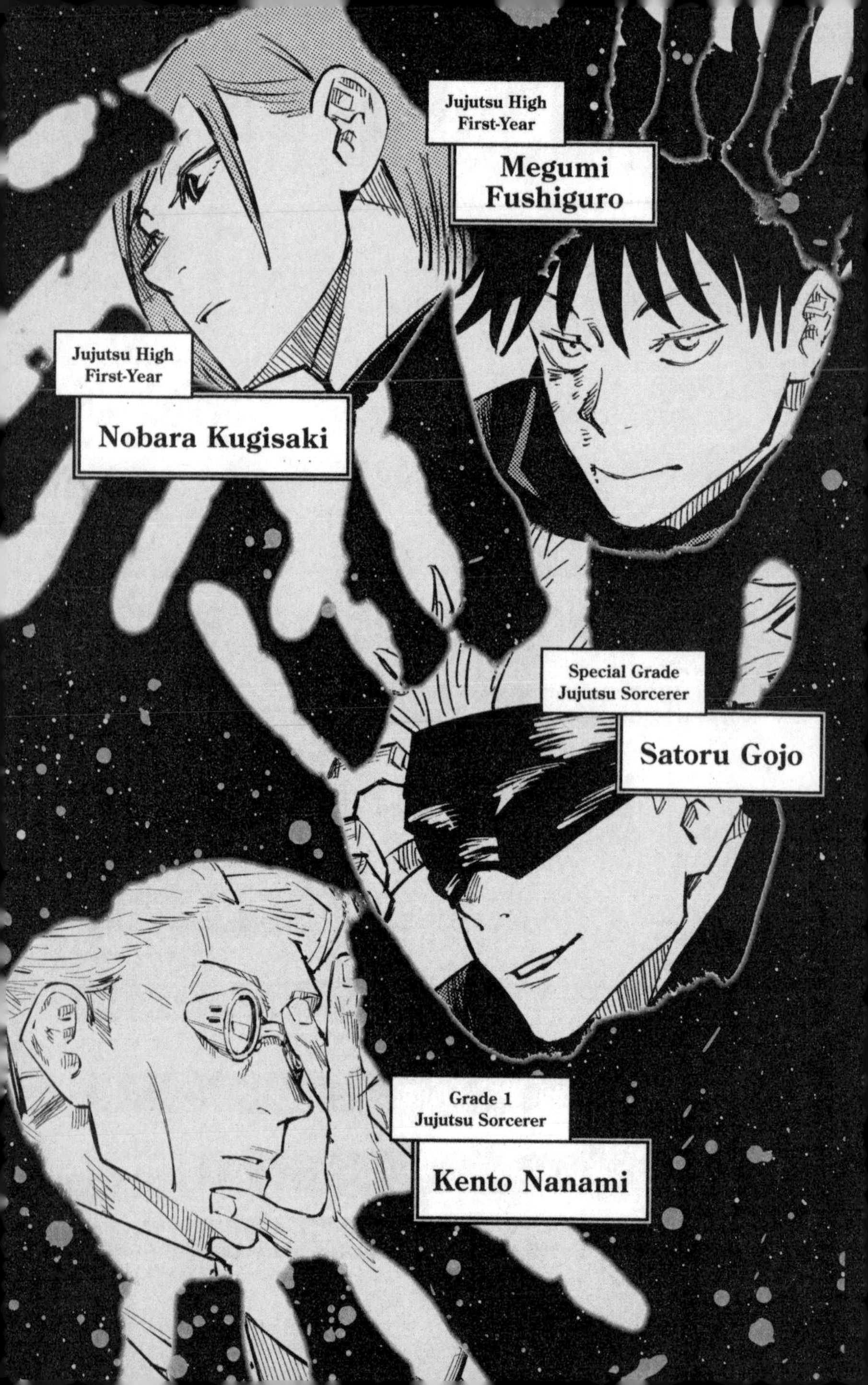
Jujutsu High
First-Year
Megumi
Fushiguro
Jujutsu High
First-Year
Nobara Kugisaki
Special Grade
Jujutsu Sorcerer
Satoru Gojo
Grade 1
Jujutsu Sorcerer
Kento Nanami

JUJUTSU KAISEN

14

THE SHIBUYA INCIDENT —RIGHT AND WRONG—

CHAPTER 116: THE SHIBUYA INCIDENT, PART 34

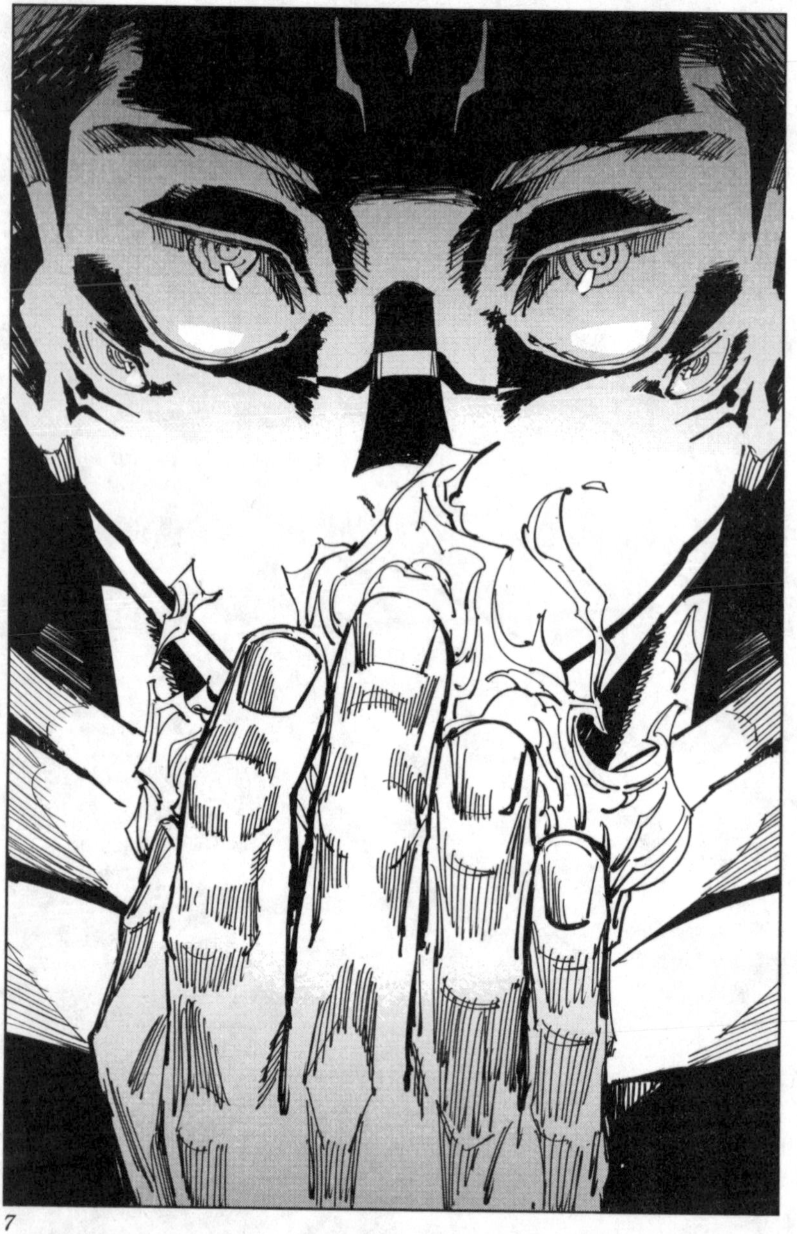

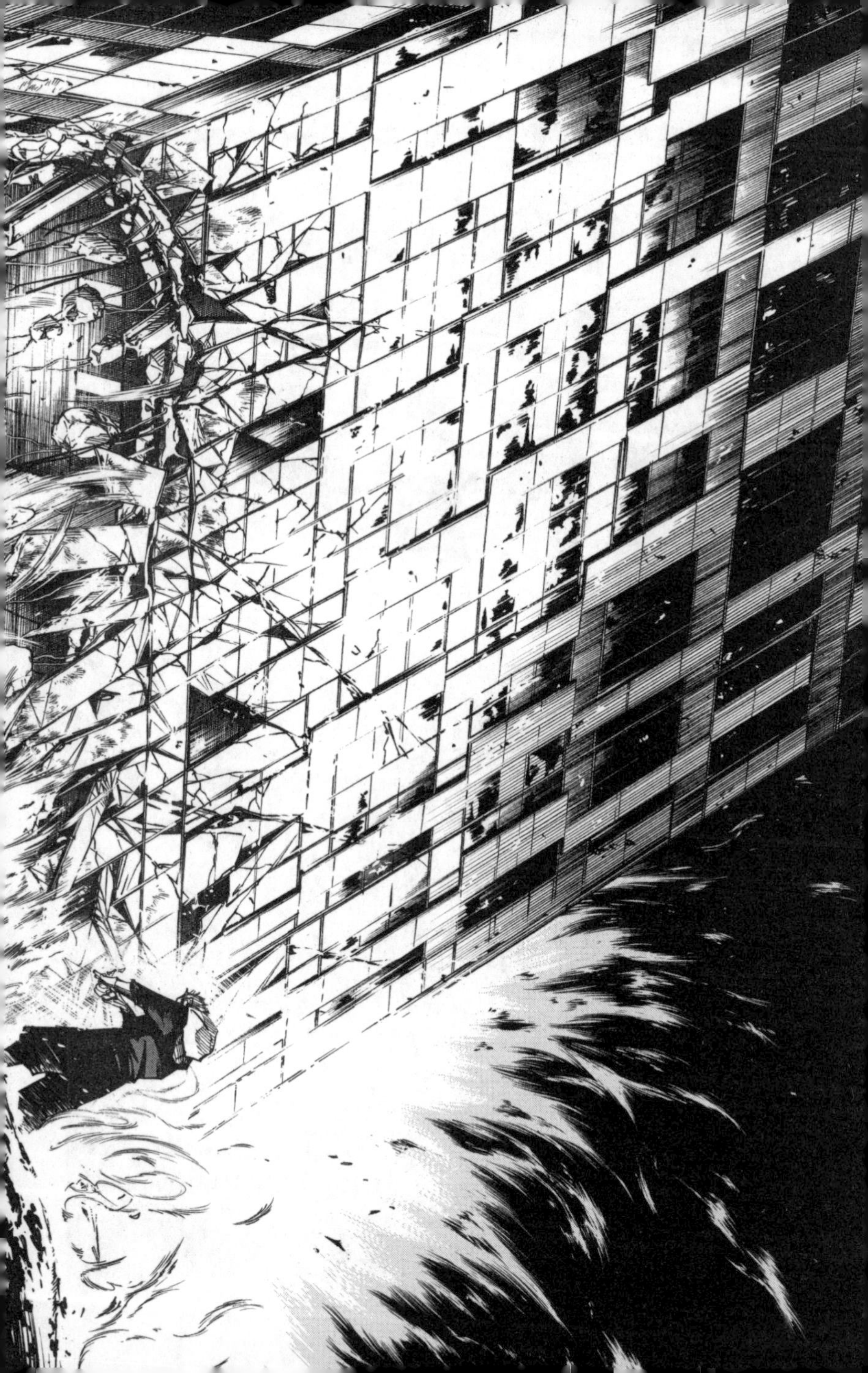

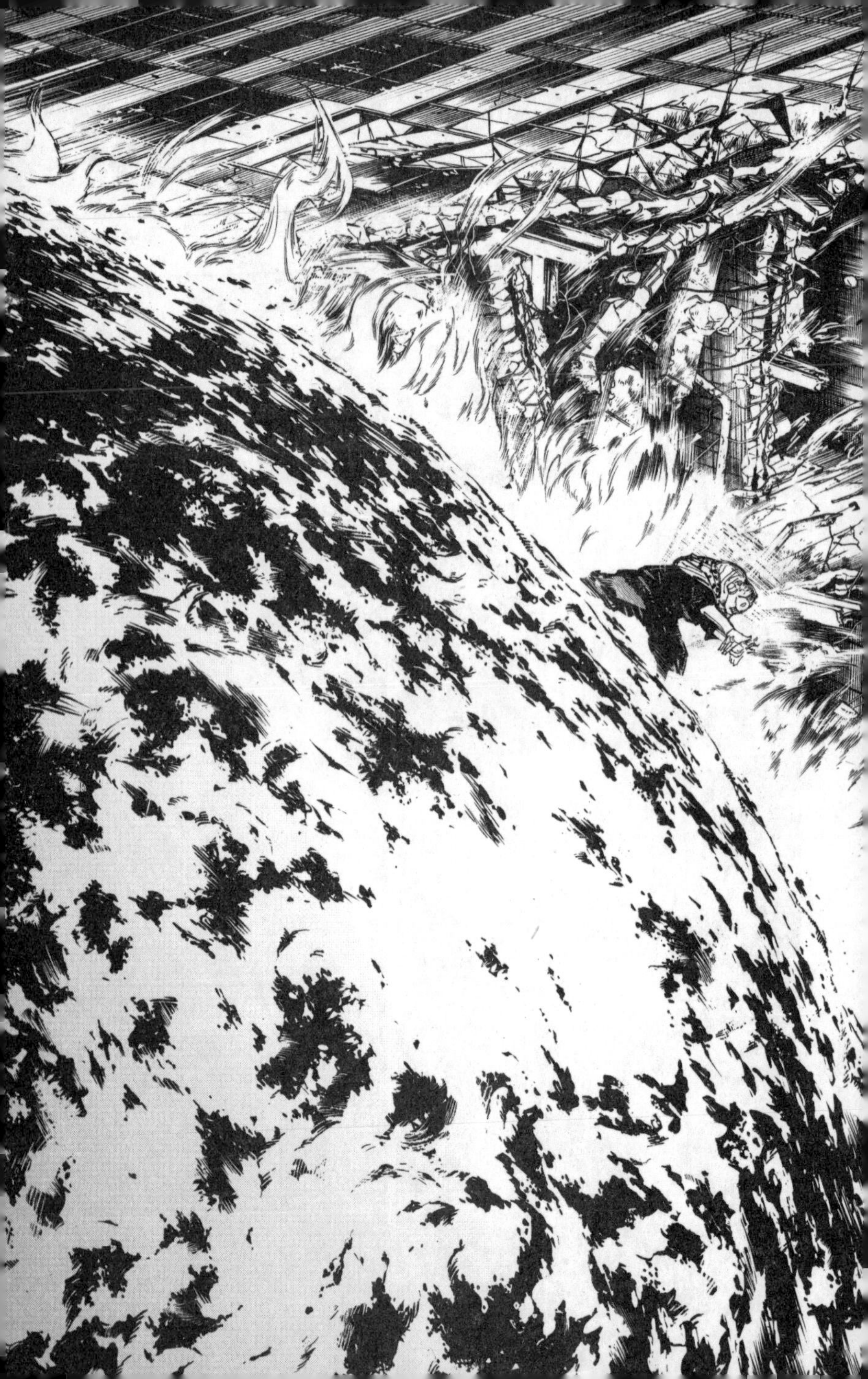

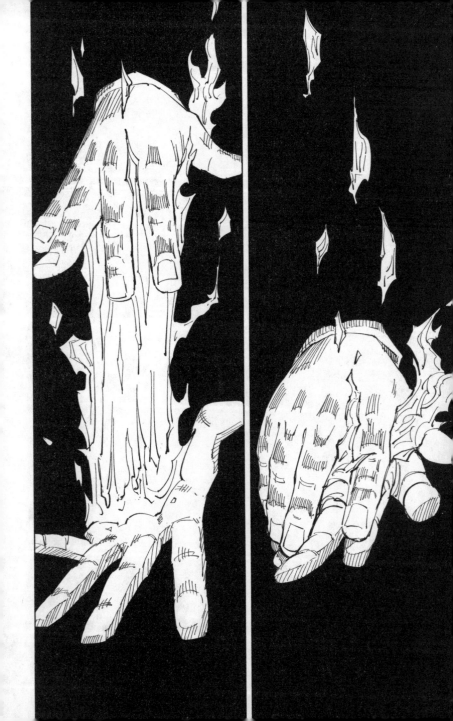

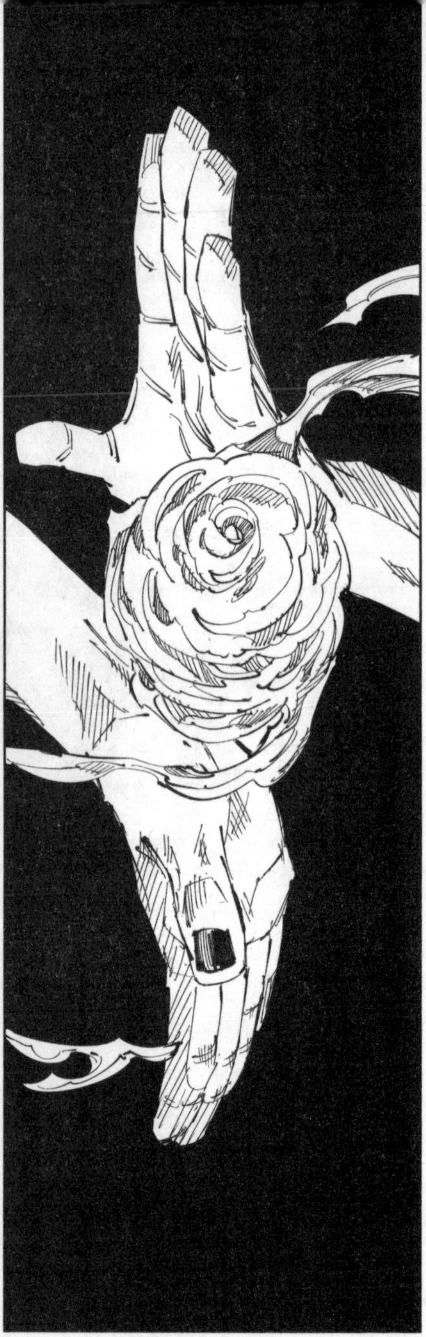
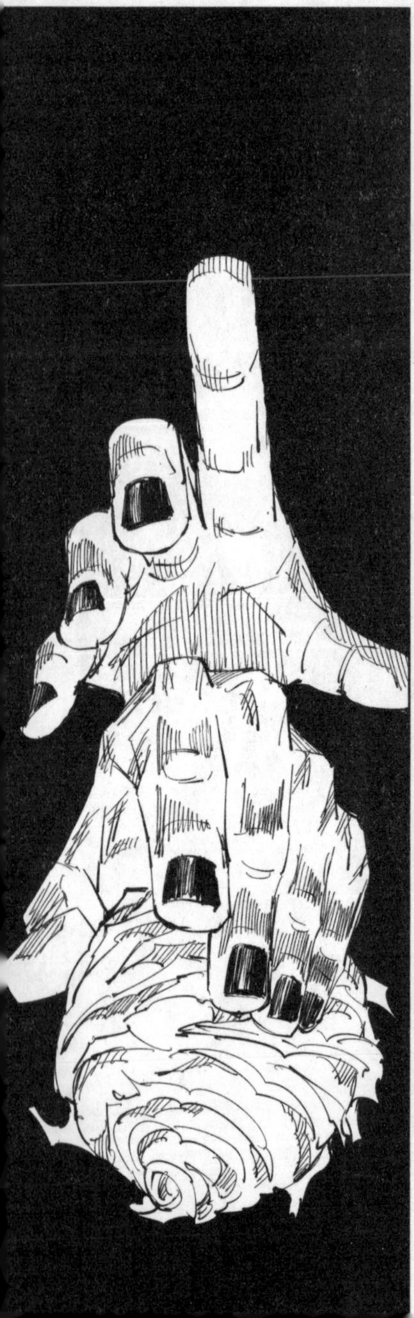

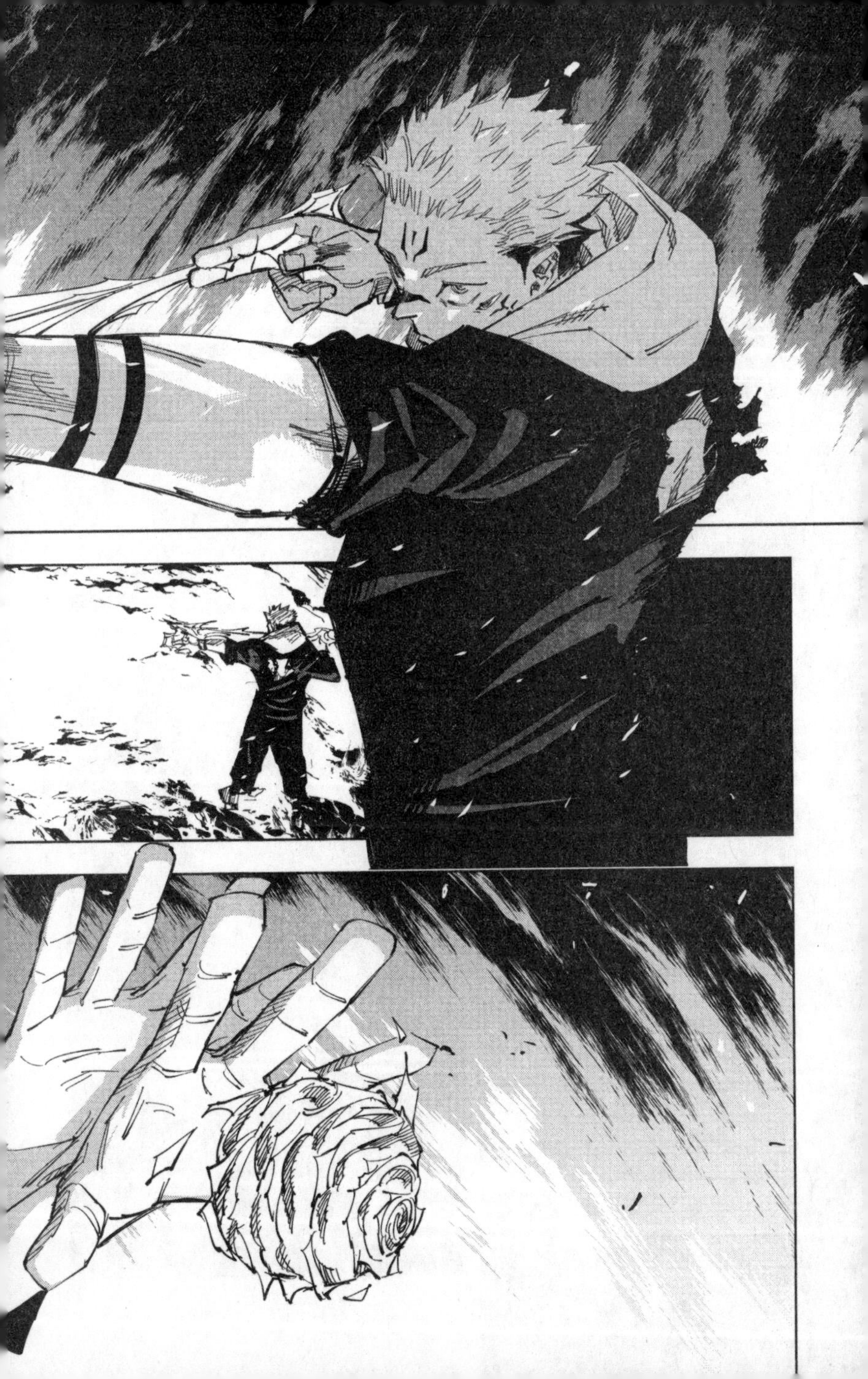

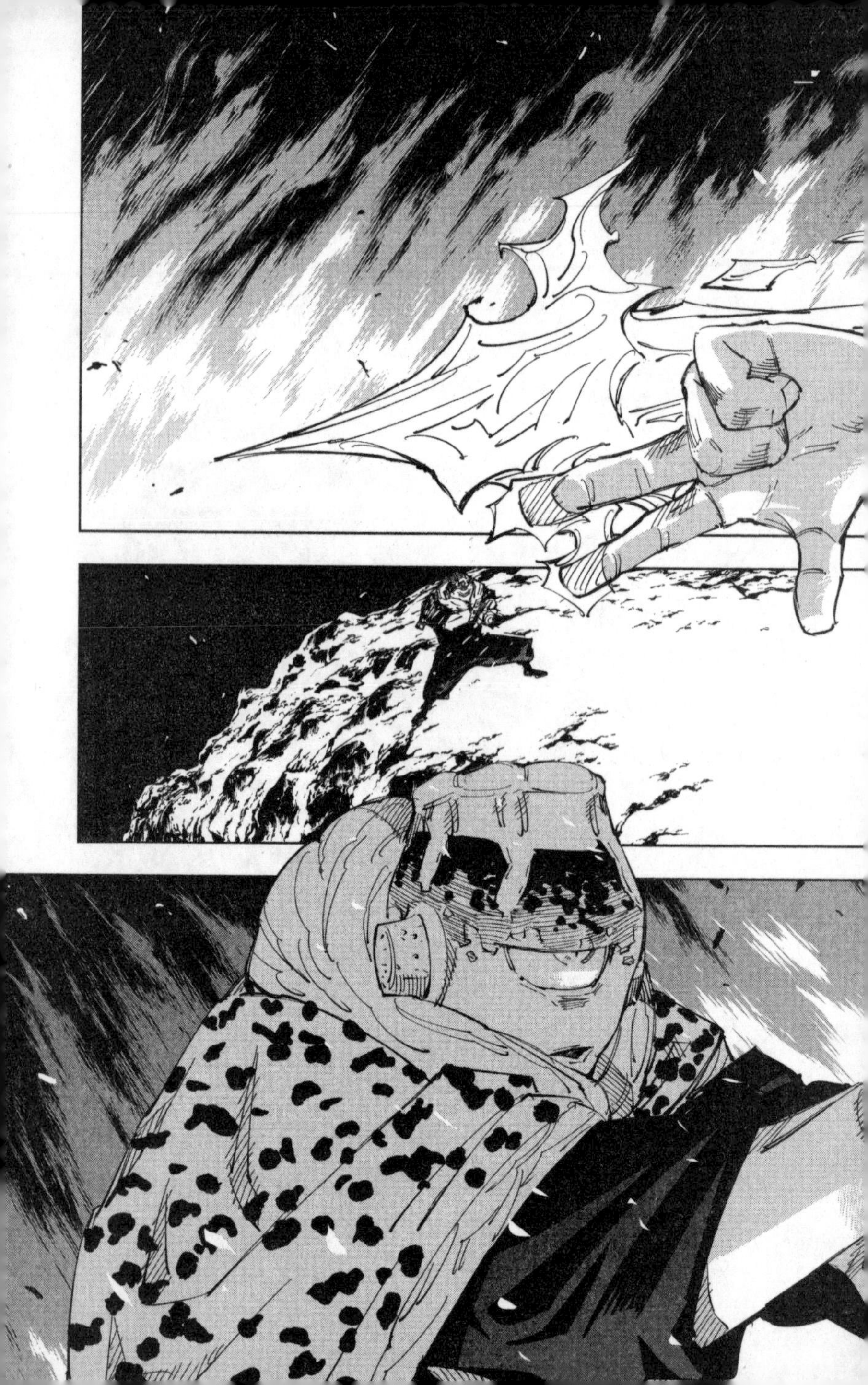

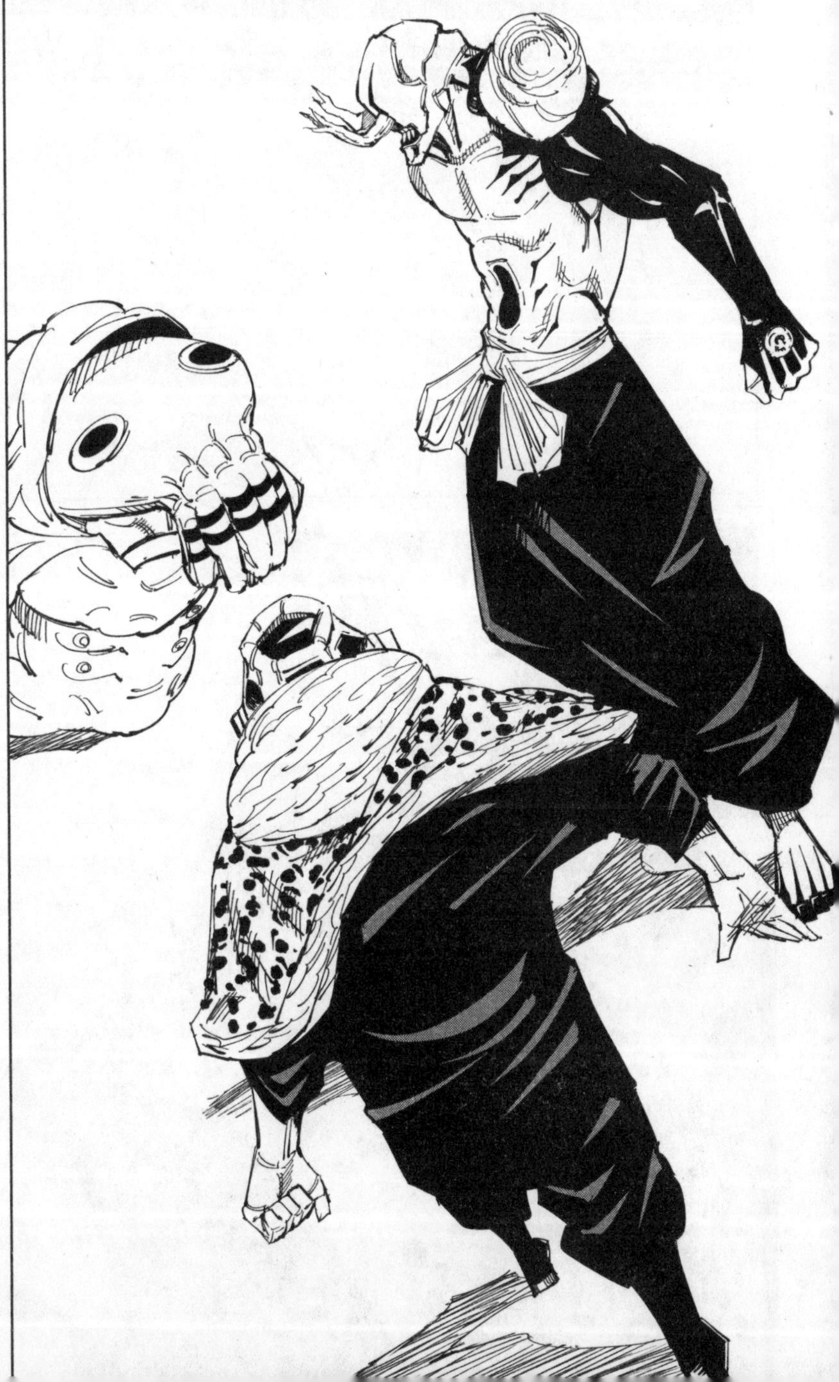

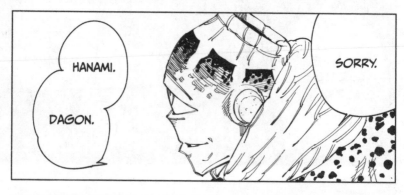

HANAMI.

DAGON.

SORRY.

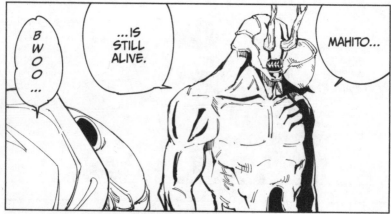

B
W
O
O
...

...IS STILL ALIVE.

MAHITO...

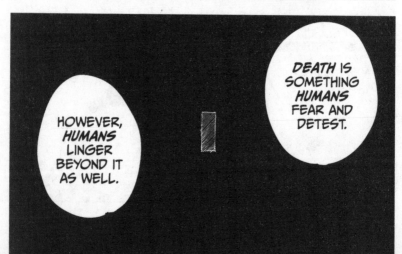

DEATH IS SOMETHING *HUMANS* FEAR AND DETEST.

HOWEVER, *HUMANS* LINGER BEYOND IT AS WELL.

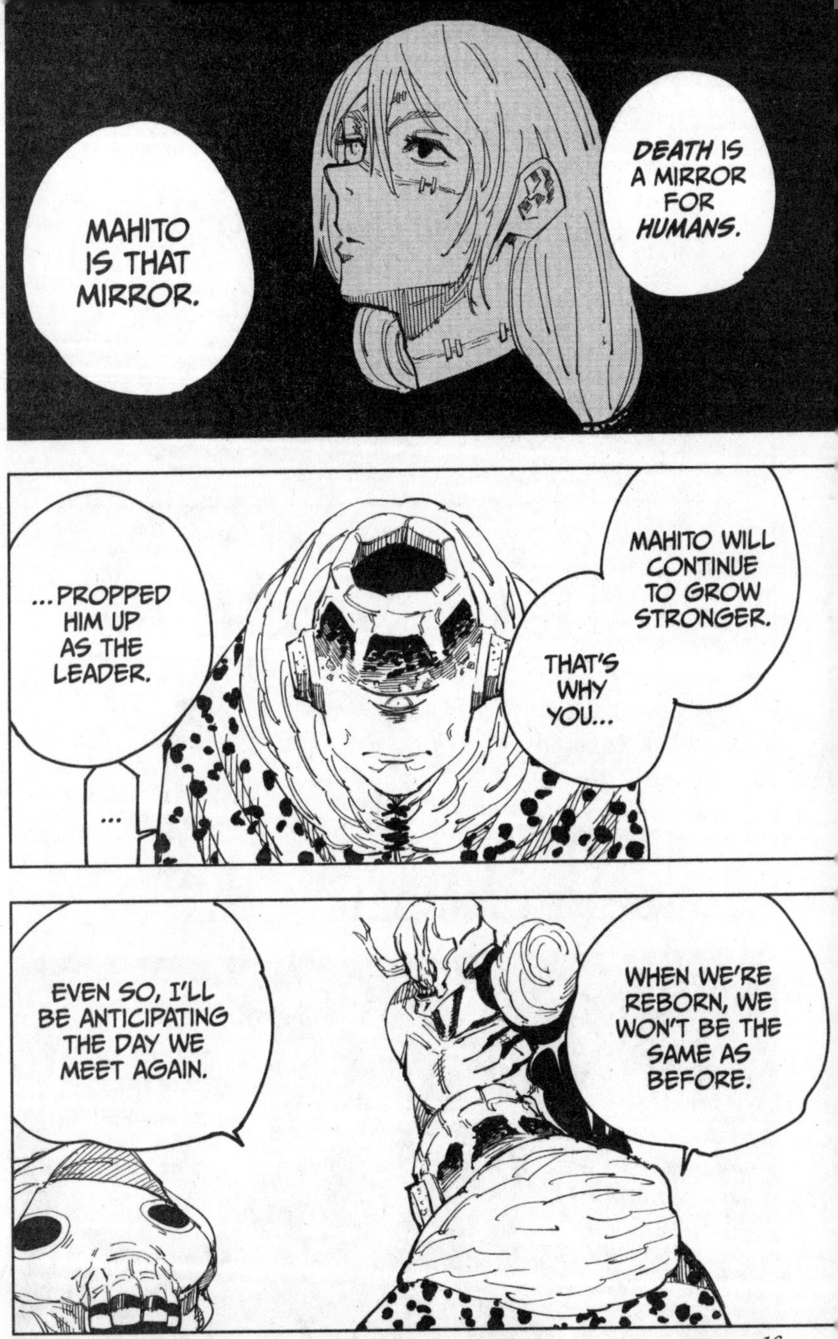
DEATH IS A MIRROR FOR HUMANS.
MAHITO IS THAT MIRROR.
MAHITO WILL CONTINUE TO GROW STRONGER.
THAT'S WHY YOU...
...PROPPED HIM UP AS THE LEADER.
...
WHEN WE'RE REBORN, WE WON'T BE THE SAME AS BEFORE.
EVEN SO, I'LL BE ANTICIPATING THE DAY WE MEET AGAIN.

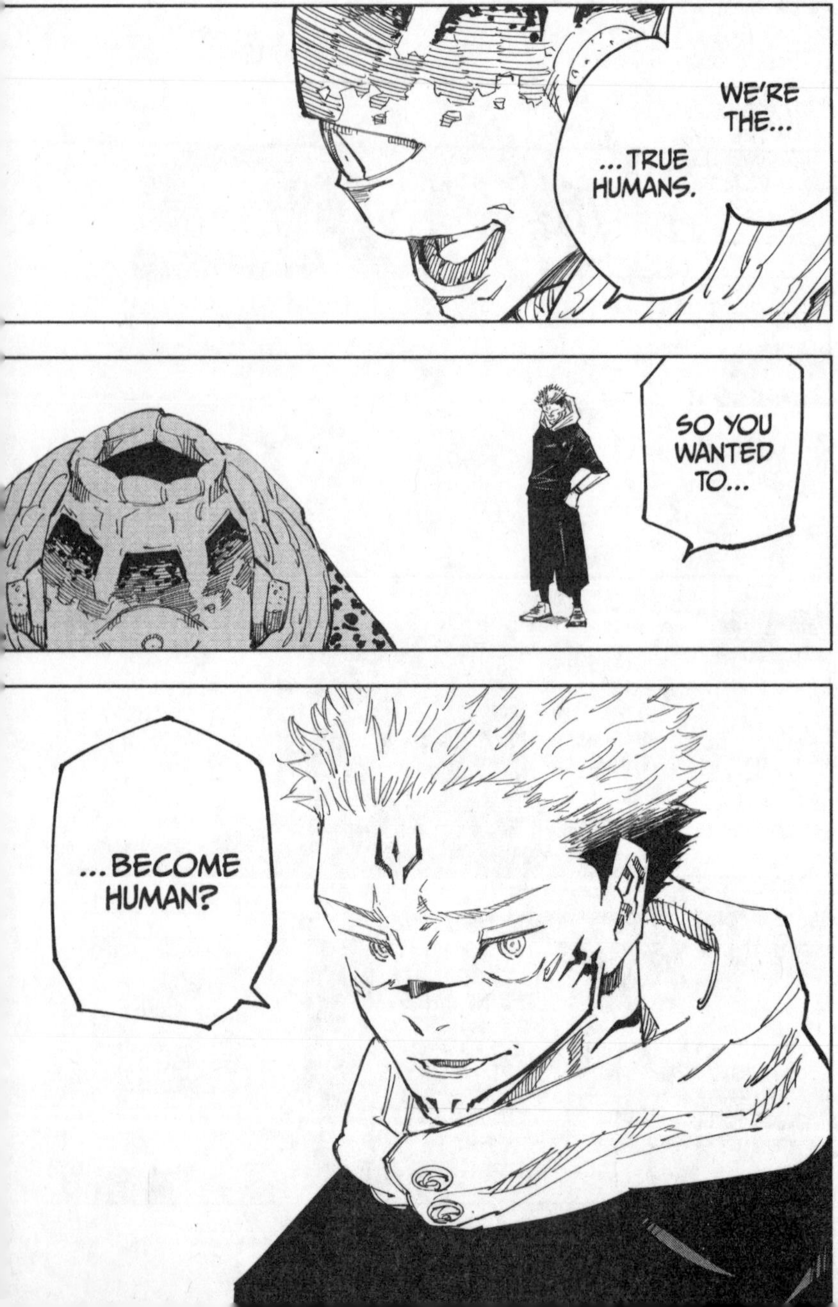
WE'RE THE...
...TRUE HUMANS.
SO YOU WANTED TO...
...BECOME HUMAN?

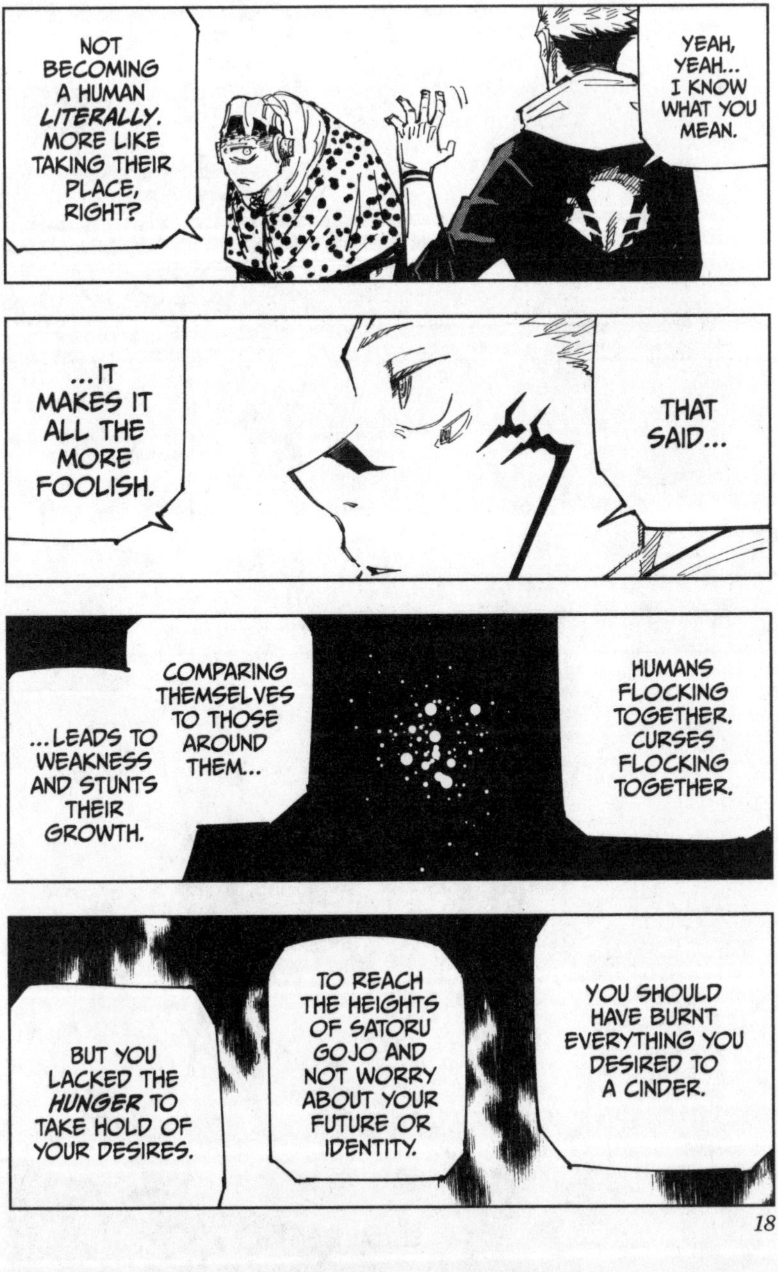
YEAH, YEAH... I KNOW WHAT YOU MEAN.
NOT BECOMING A HUMAN LITERALLY. MORE LIKE TAKING THEIR PLACE, RIGHT?
THAT SAID...
...IT MAKES IT ALL THE MORE FOOLISH.
HUMANS FLOCKING TOGETHER. CURSES FLOCKING TOGETHER.
COMPARING THEMSELVES TO THOSE AROUND THEM...
...LEADS TO WEAKNESS AND STUNTS THEIR GROWTH.
YOU SHOULD HAVE BURNT EVERYTHING YOU DESIRED TO A CINDER.
TO REACH THE HEIGHTS OF SATORU GOJO AND NOT WORRY ABOUT YOUR FUTURE OR IDENTITY.
BUT YOU LACKED THE HUNGER TO TAKE HOLD OF YOUR DESIRES.

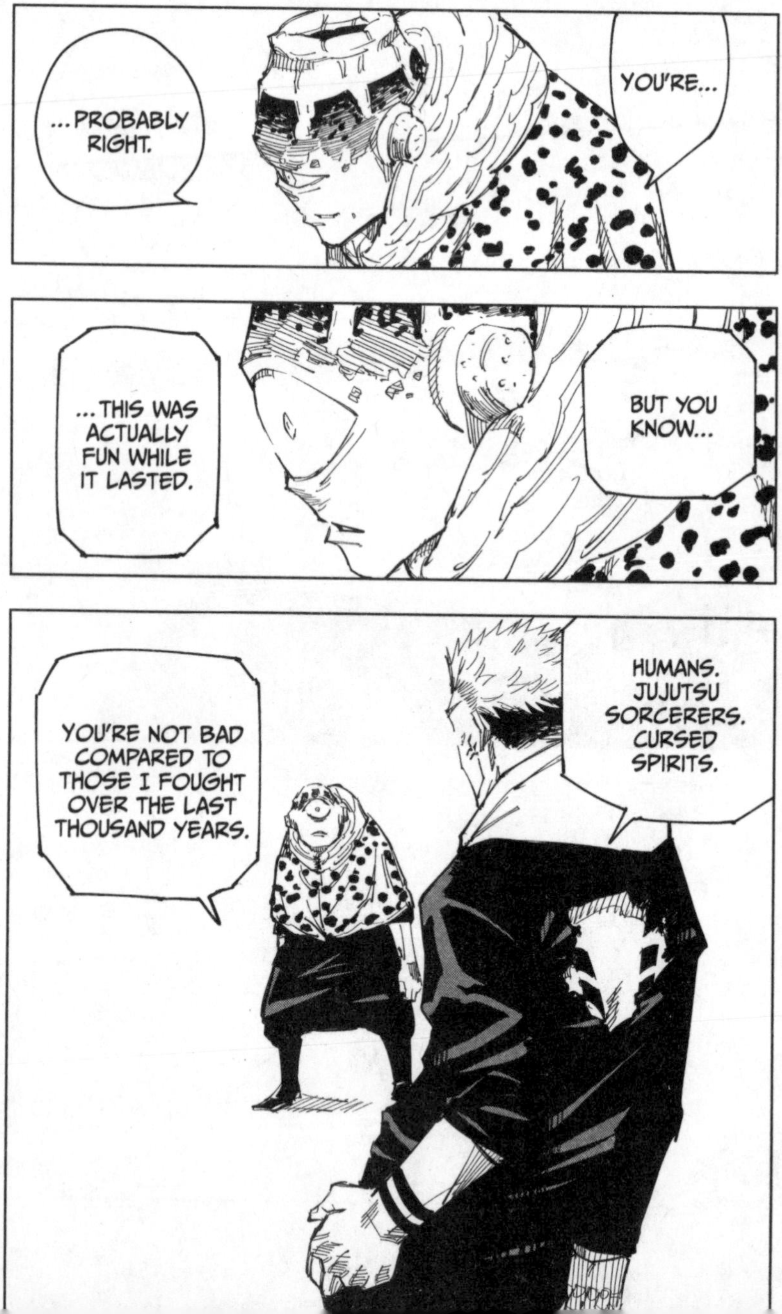
YOU'RE...
...PROBABLY RIGHT.
BUT YOU KNOW...
...THIS WAS ACTUALLY FUN WHILE IT LASTED.
HUMANS. JUJUTSU SORCERERS. CURSED SPIRITS.
YOU'RE NOT BAD COMPARED TO THOSE I FOUGHT OVER THE LAST THOUSAND YEARS.

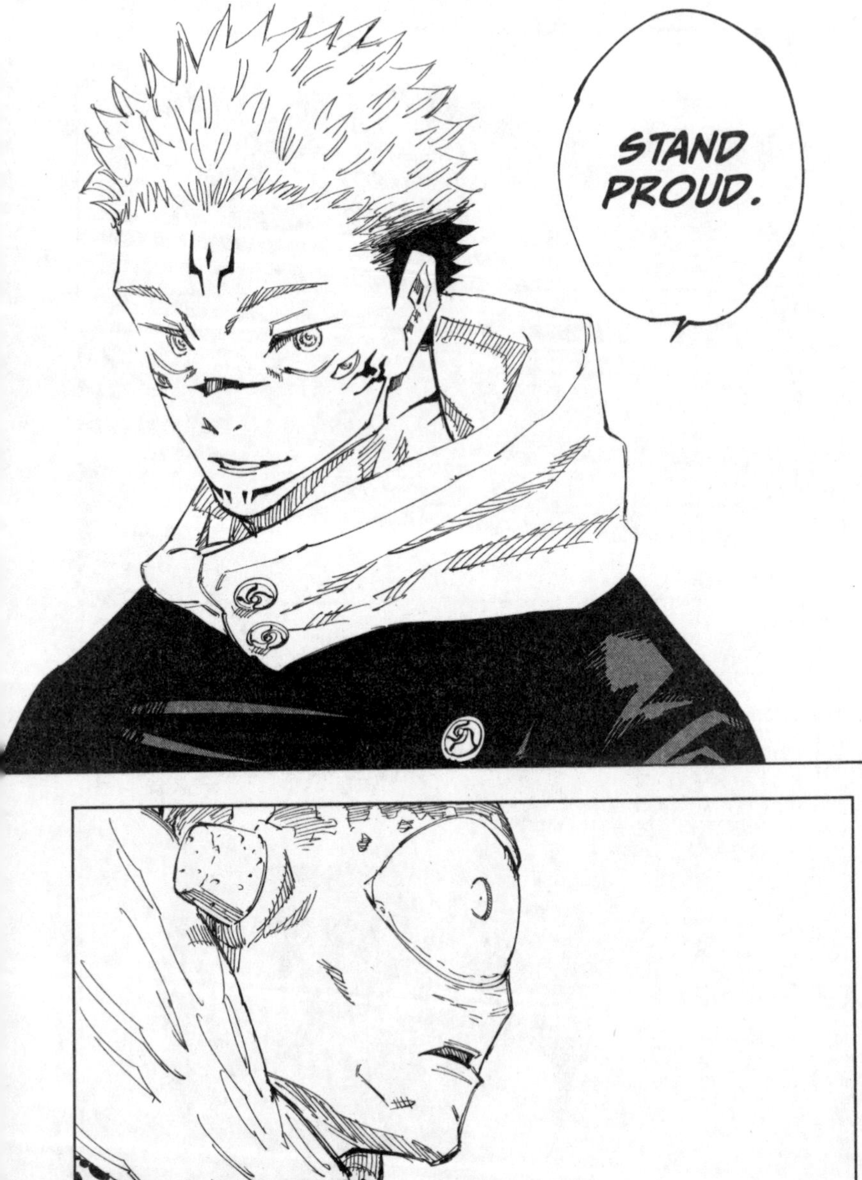
STAND PROUD.

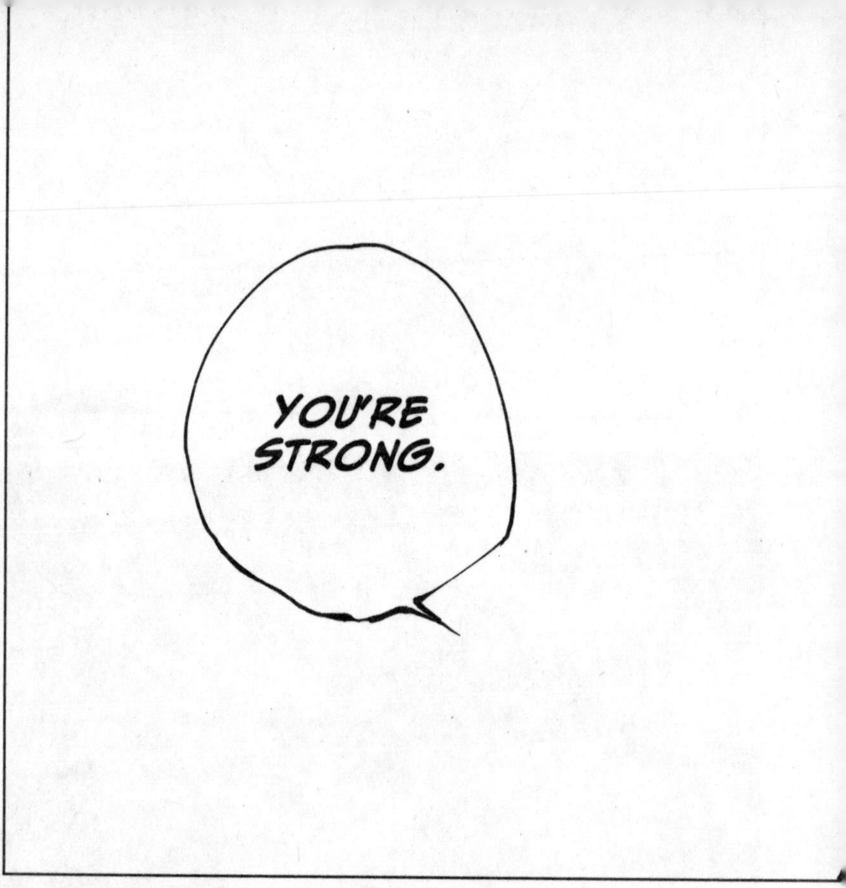
YOU'RE STRONG.

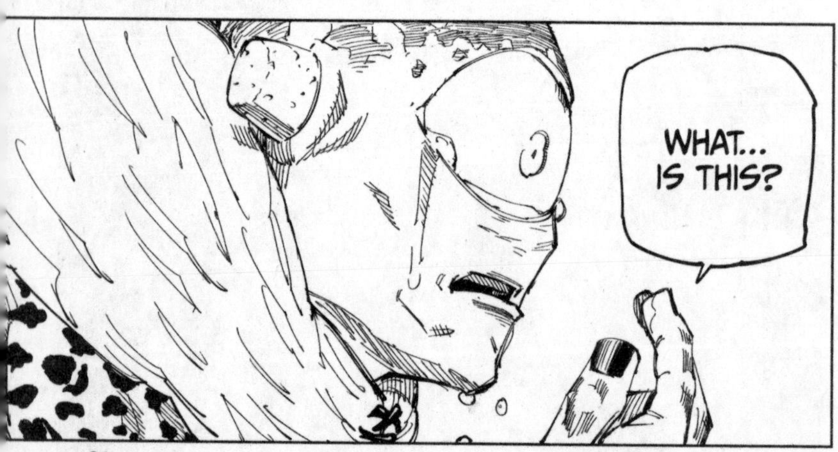
WHAT... IS THIS?

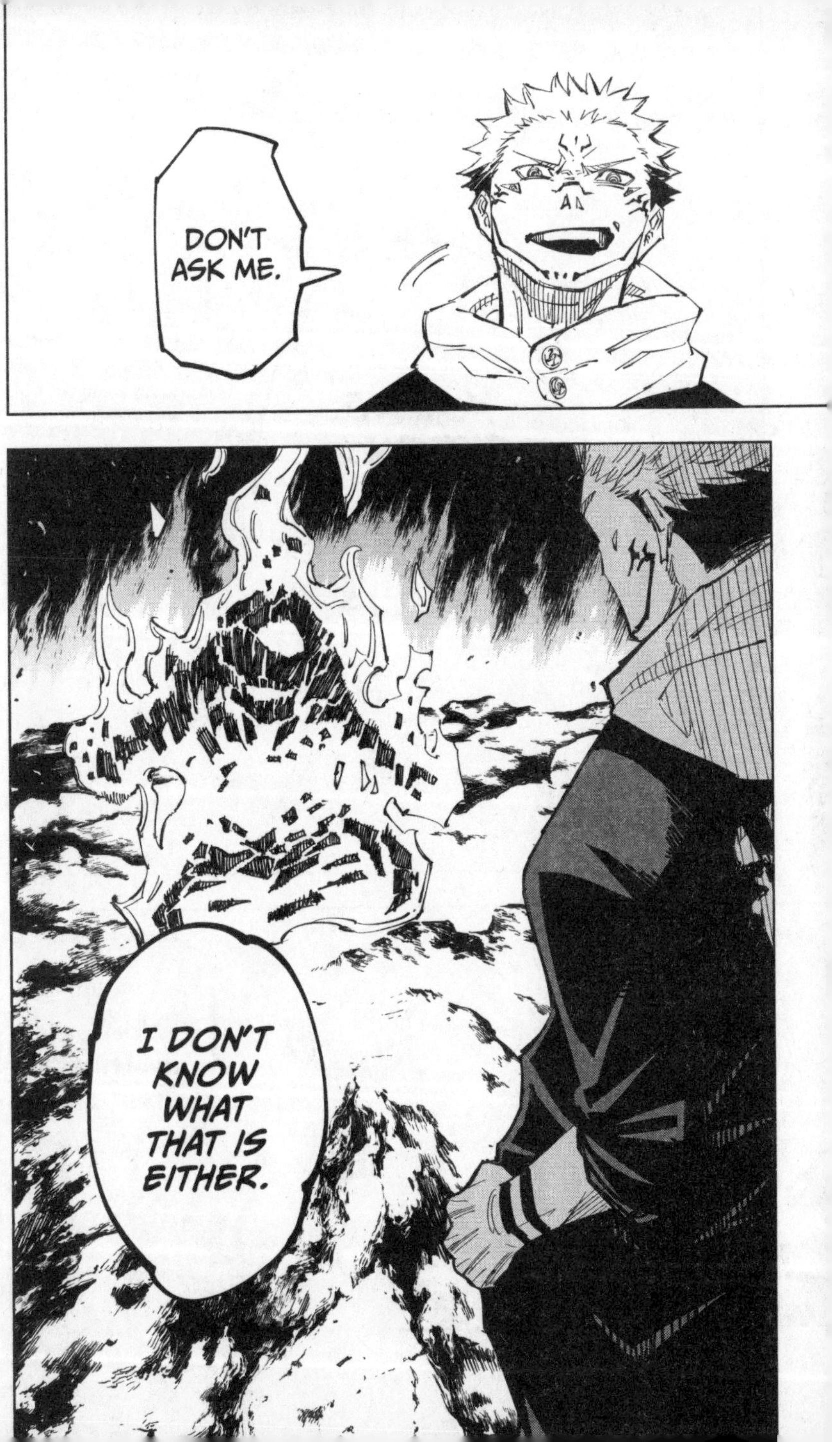
DON'T ASK ME.
I DON'T KNOW WHAT THAT IS EITHER.

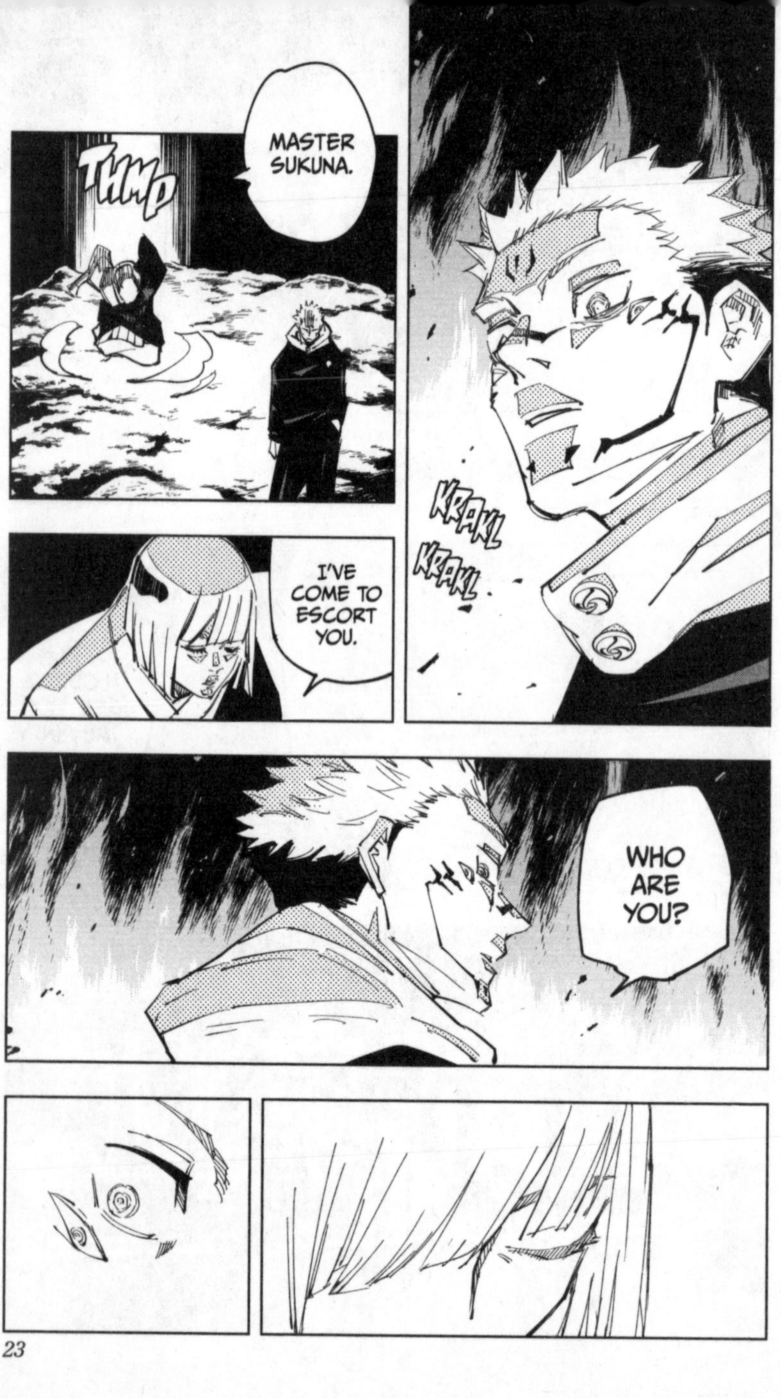
KRAKL
KRAKL
MASTER SUKUNA.
THMP
I'VE COME TO ESCORT YOU.
WHO ARE YOU?

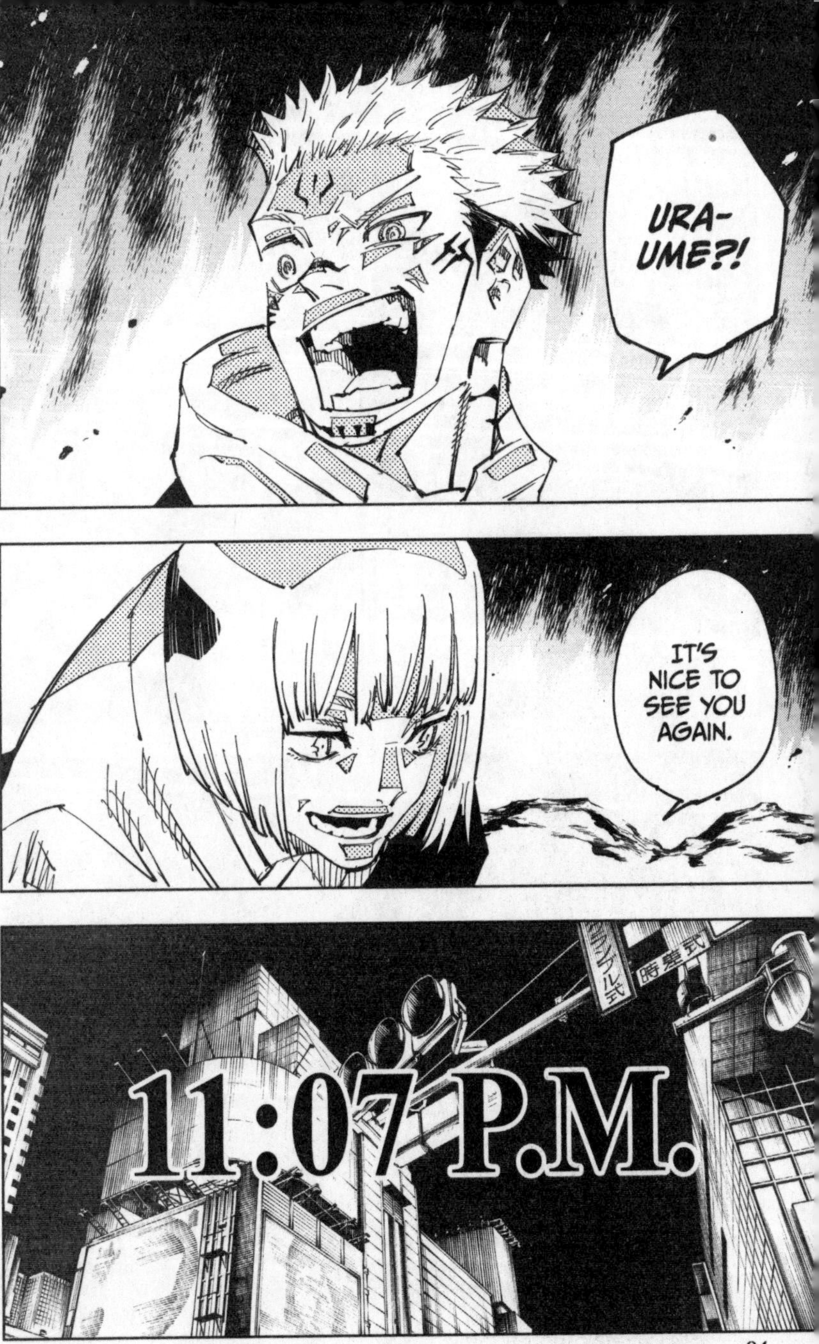
URA-UME?!
IT'S NICE TO SEE YOU AGAIN.
11:07 P.M.

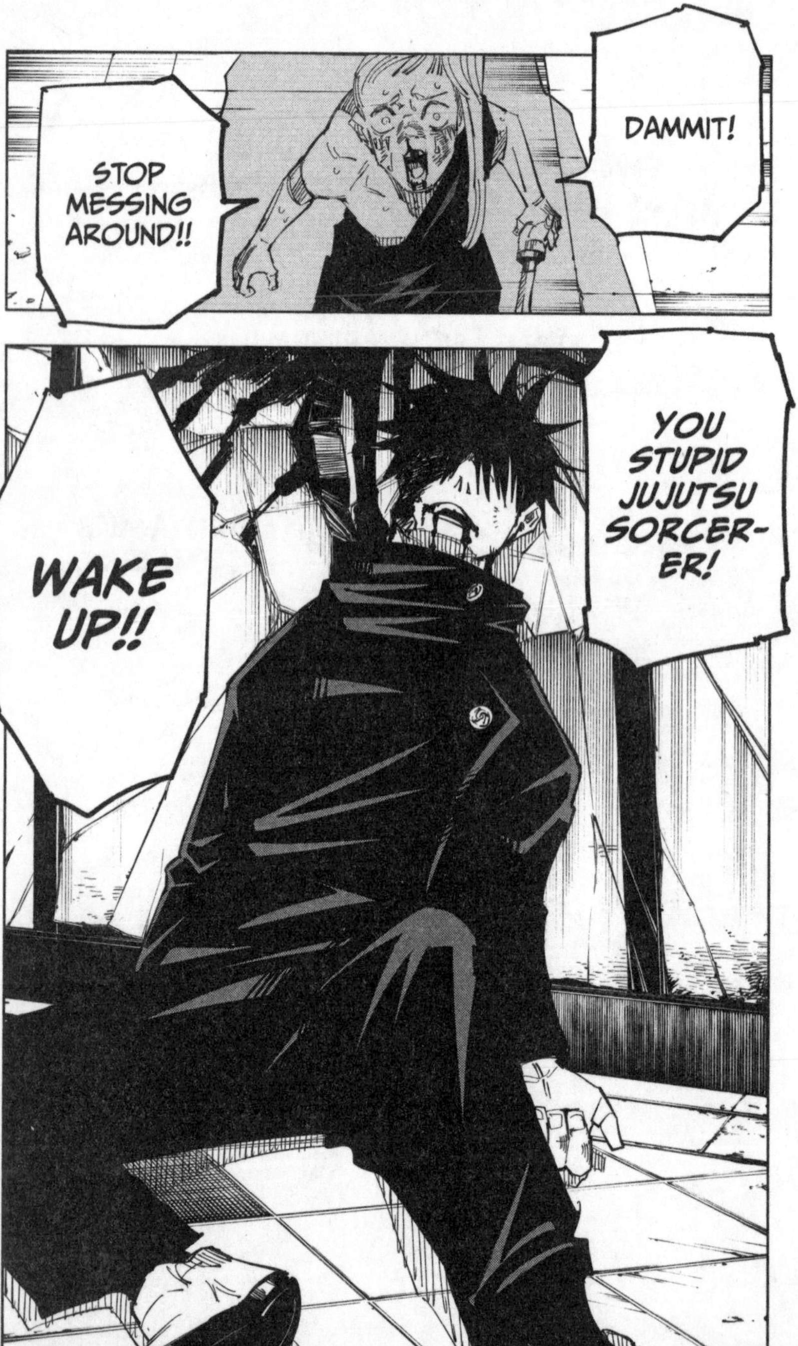
DAMMIT!
STOP MESSING AROUND!!
YOU STUPID JUJUTSU SORCERER!
WAKE UP!!

1/4

THE 2020 VALENTINES RANKINGS THAT I SERIOUSLY ALMOST FORGOT

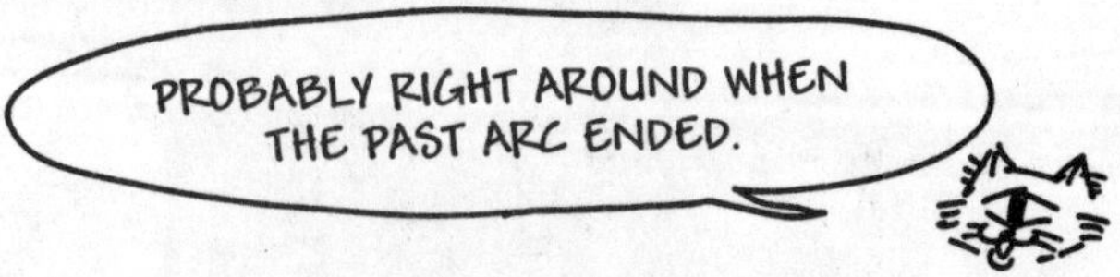
PROBABLY RIGHT AROUND WHEN THE PAST ARC ENDED.

RANKINGS (VALENTINES RECEIVED)	CHARACTER	AKUTAMI'S COMMENT
1 (54)	GOJO	OKAY, I GET IT ALREADY...
2 (30)	GETO	NOT TOO BAD.
3 (23)	FUSHIGURO	YOU NEED TO TRY A LITTLE HARDER.
4 (22)	ITADORI	SQUEAKING BY AS THE MAIN CHARACTER.

Chapter 117: The Shibuya Incident, Part 35

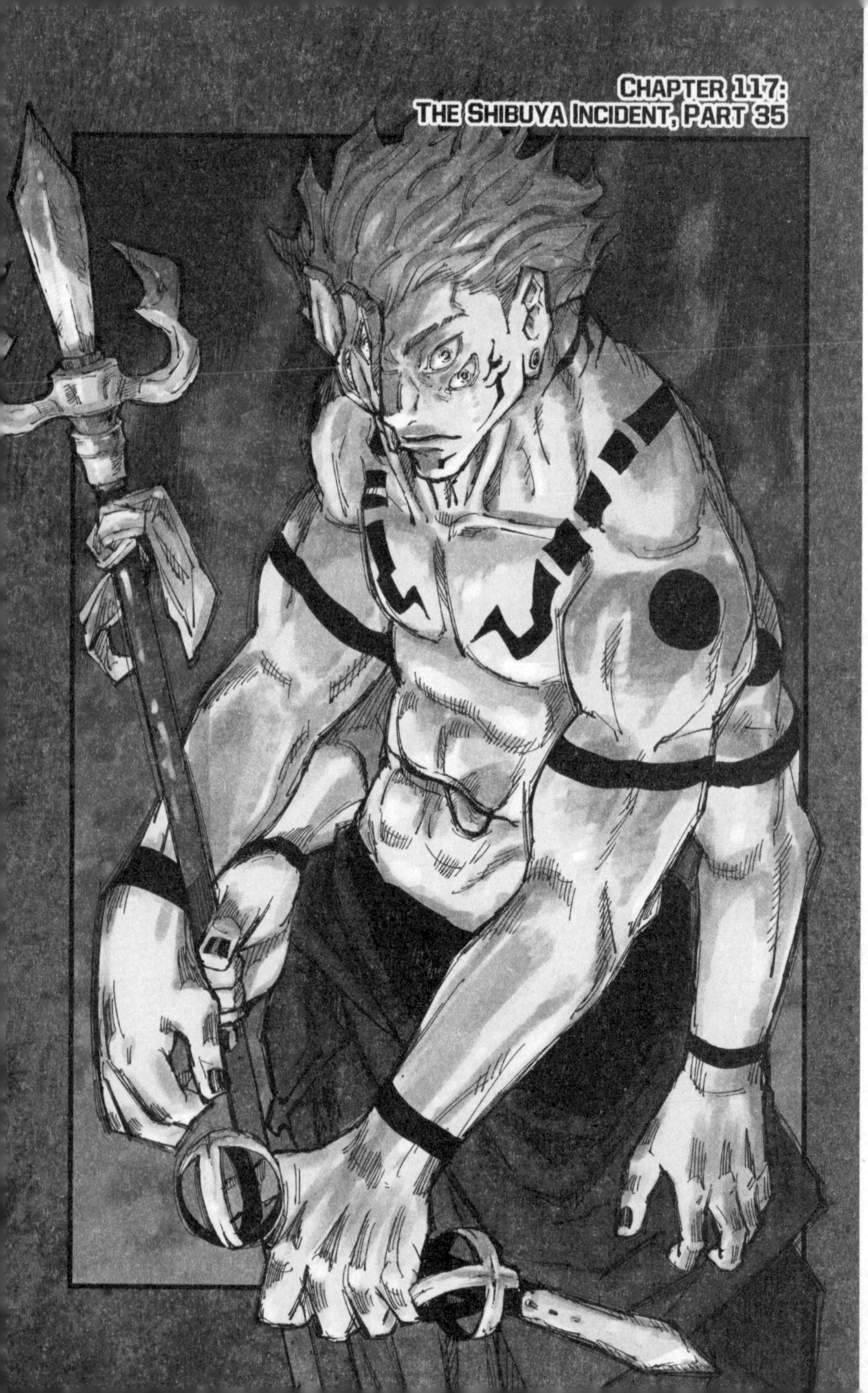

JUJUTSU KAISEN

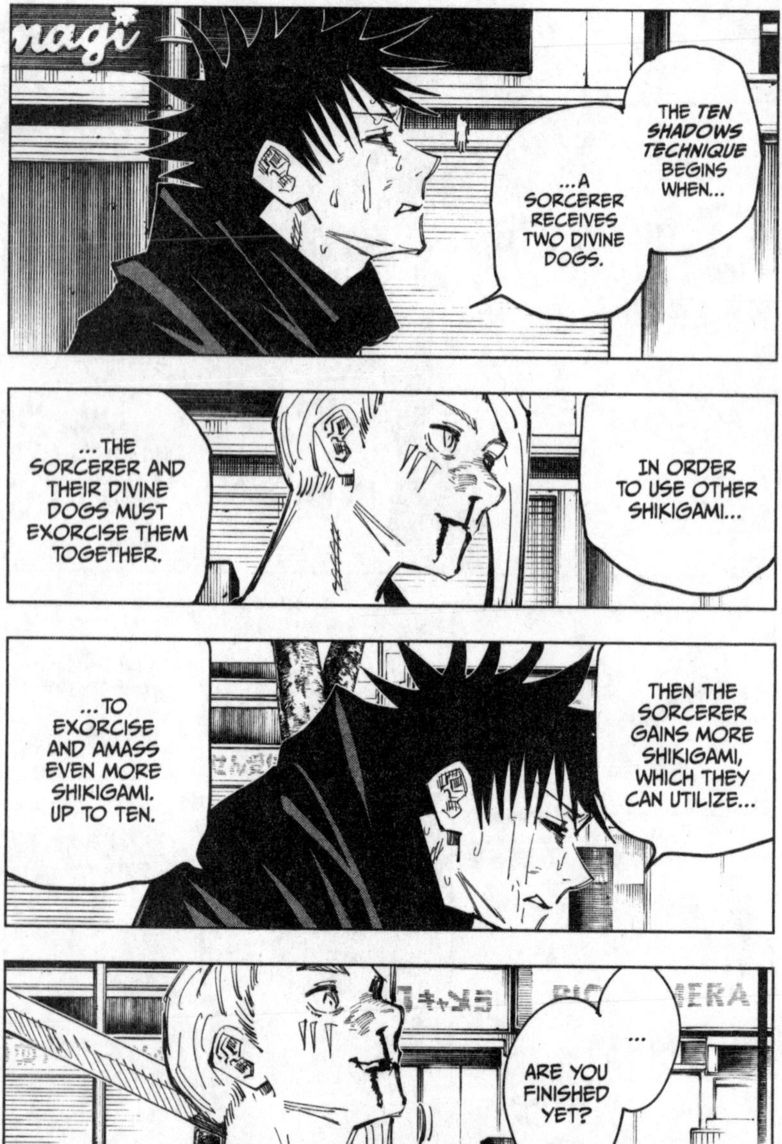
THE TEN SHADOWS TECHNIQUE BEGINS WHEN...
...A SORCERER RECEIVES TWO DIVINE DOGS.
IN ORDER TO USE OTHER SHIKIGAMI...
...THE SORCERER AND THEIR DIVINE DOGS MUST EXORCISE THEM TOGETHER.
THEN THE SORCERER GAINS MORE SHIKIGAMI, WHICH THEY CAN UTILIZE...
...TO EXORCISE AND AMASS EVEN MORE SHIKIGAMI. UP TO TEN.
... ARE YOU FINISHED YET?

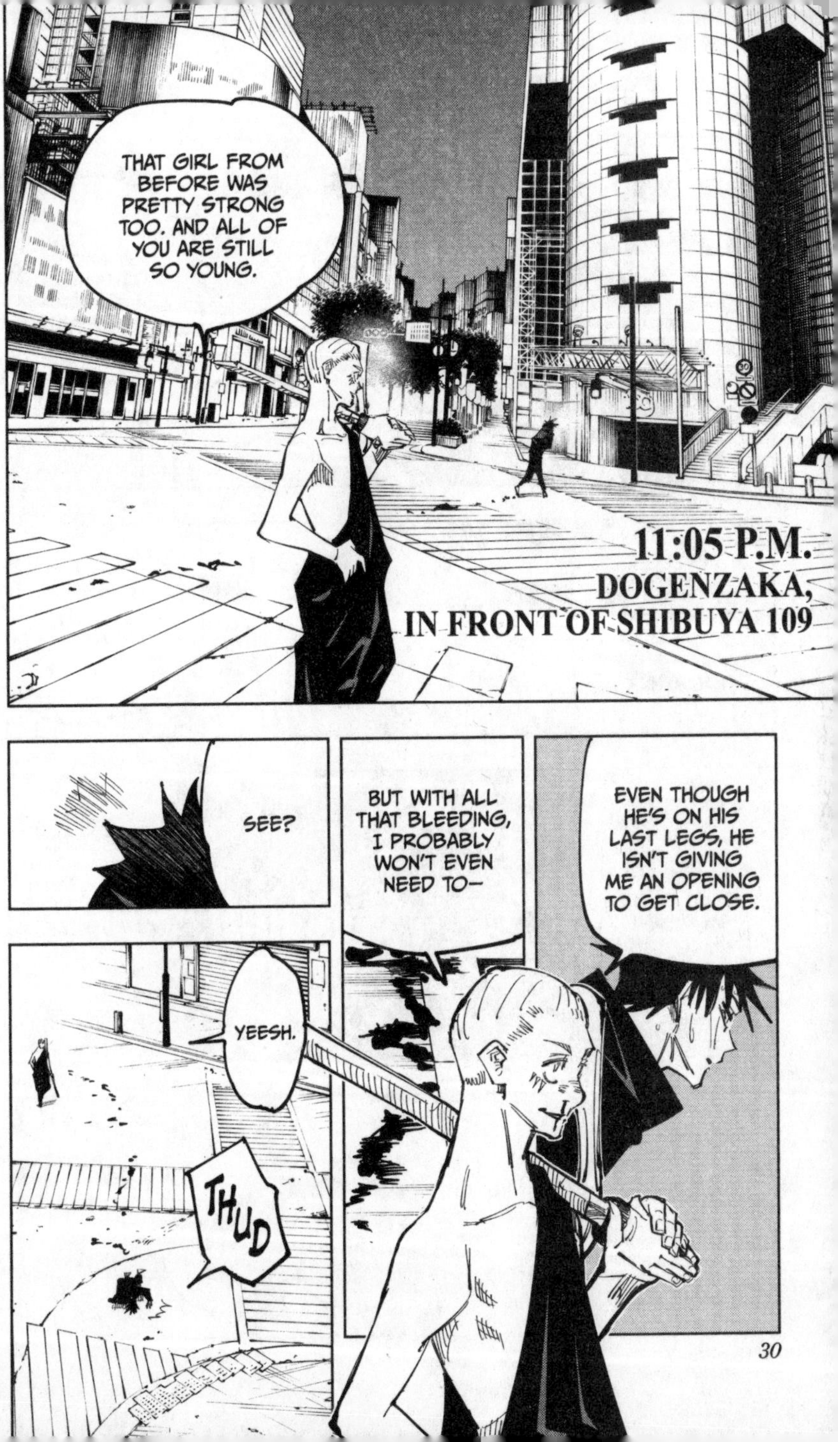
11:05 P.M.
DOGENZAKA, IN FRONT OF SHIBUYA 109
THAT GIRL FROM BEFORE WAS PRETTY STRONG TOO. AND ALL OF YOU ARE STILL SO YOUNG.
EVEN THOUGH HE'S ON HIS LAST LEGS, HE ISN'T GIVING ME AN OPENING TO GET CLOSE.
BUT WITH ALL THAT BLEEDING, I PROBABLY WON'T EVEN NEED TO—
SEE?
YEESH.
THUD

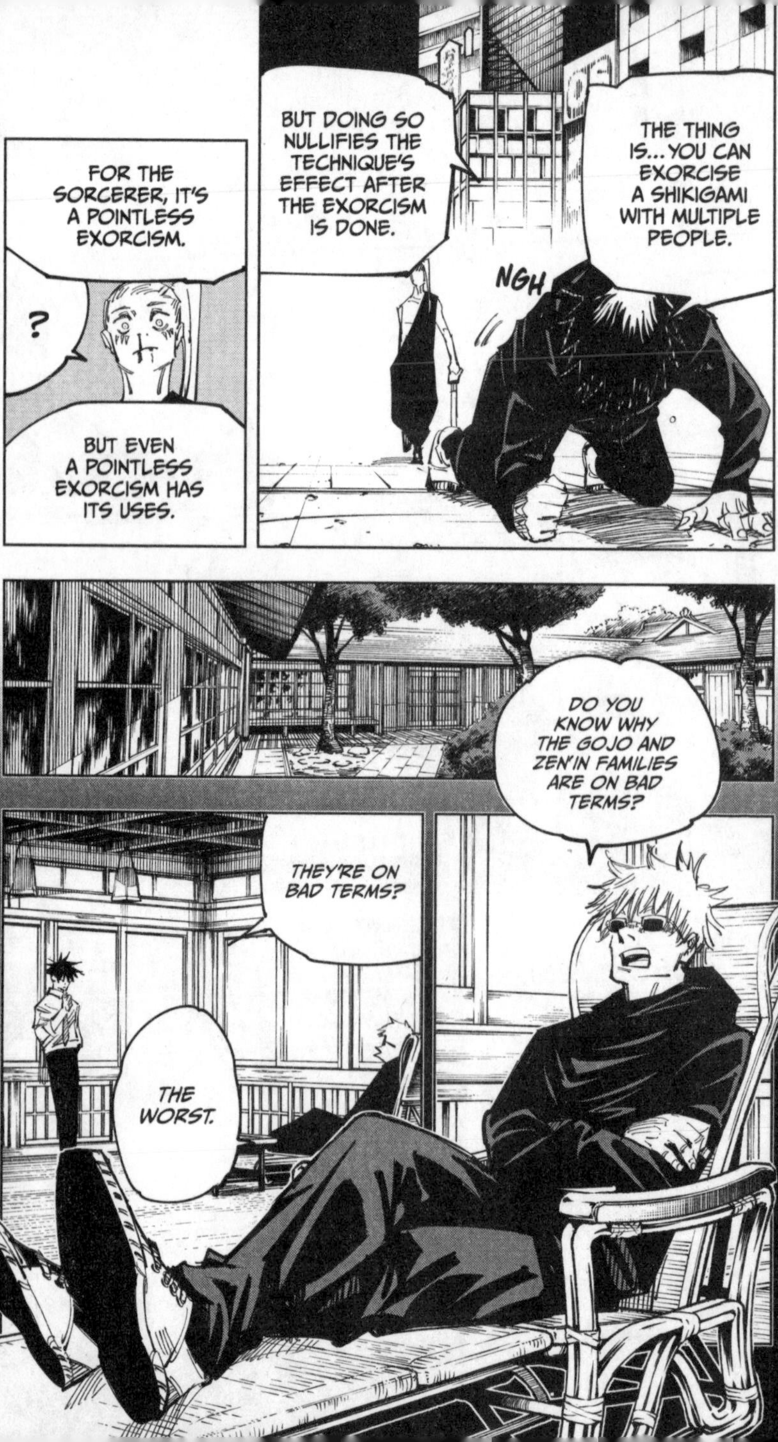
THE THING IS... YOU CAN EXORCISE A SHIKIGAMI WITH MULTIPLE PEOPLE.
BUT DOING SO NULLIFIES THE TECHNIQUE'S EFFECT AFTER THE EXORCISM IS DONE.
NGH
FOR THE SORCERER, IT'S A POINTLESS EXORCISM.
?
BUT EVEN A POINTLESS EXORCISM HAS ITS USES.
DO YOU KNOW WHY THE GOJO AND ZEN'IN FAMILIES ARE ON BAD TERMS?
THEY'RE ON BAD TERMS?
THE WORST.

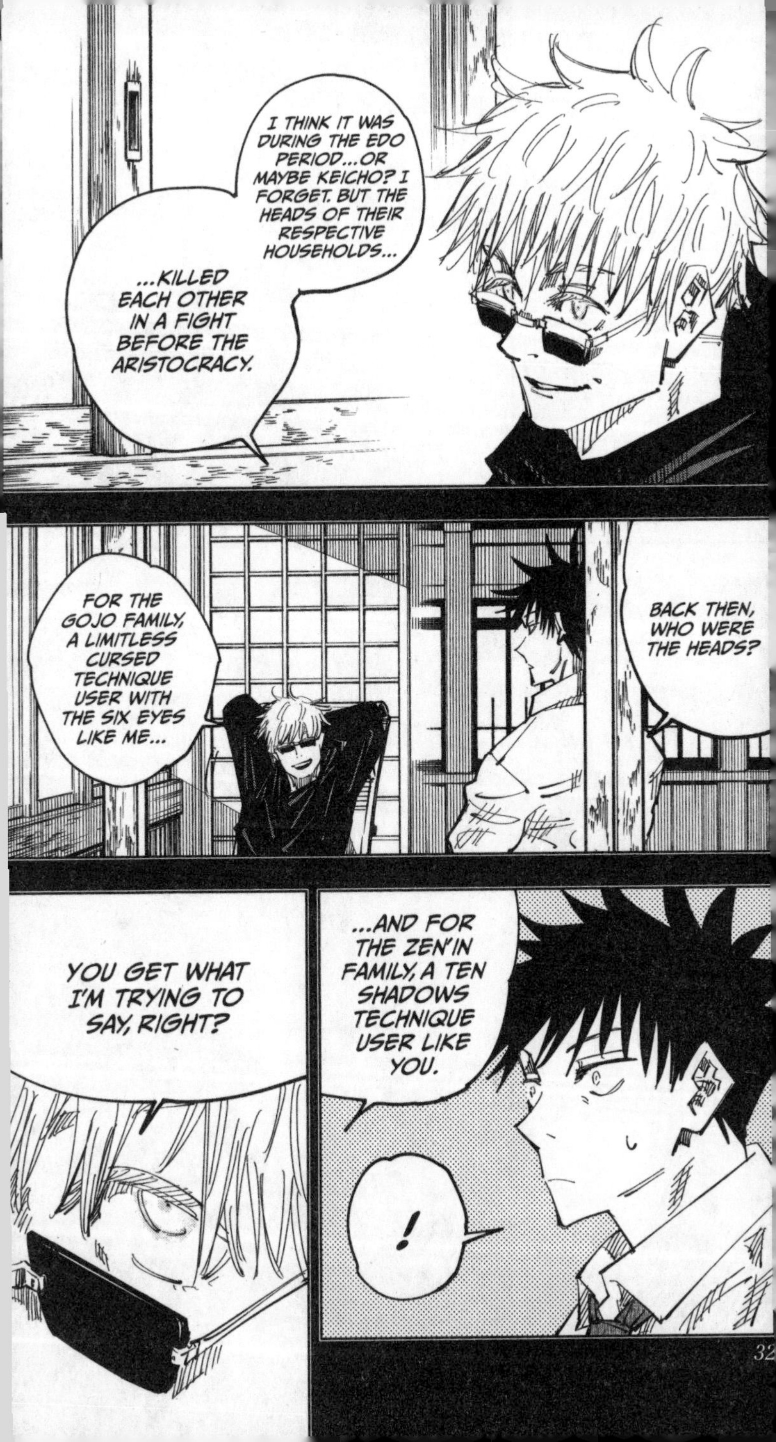
I THINK IT WAS DURING THE EDO PERIOD...OR MAYBE KEICHO? I FORGET. BUT THE HEADS OF THEIR RESPECTIVE HOUSEHOLDS...
...KILLED EACH OTHER IN A FIGHT BEFORE THE ARISTOCRACY.
BACK THEN, WHO WERE THE HEADS?
FOR THE GOJO FAMILY, A LIMITLESS CURSED TECHNIQUE USER WITH THE SIX EYES LIKE ME...
...AND FOR THE ZEN'IN FAMILY, A TEN SHADOWS TECHNIQUE USER LIKE YOU.
!
YOU GET WHAT I'M TRYING TO SAY, RIGHT?

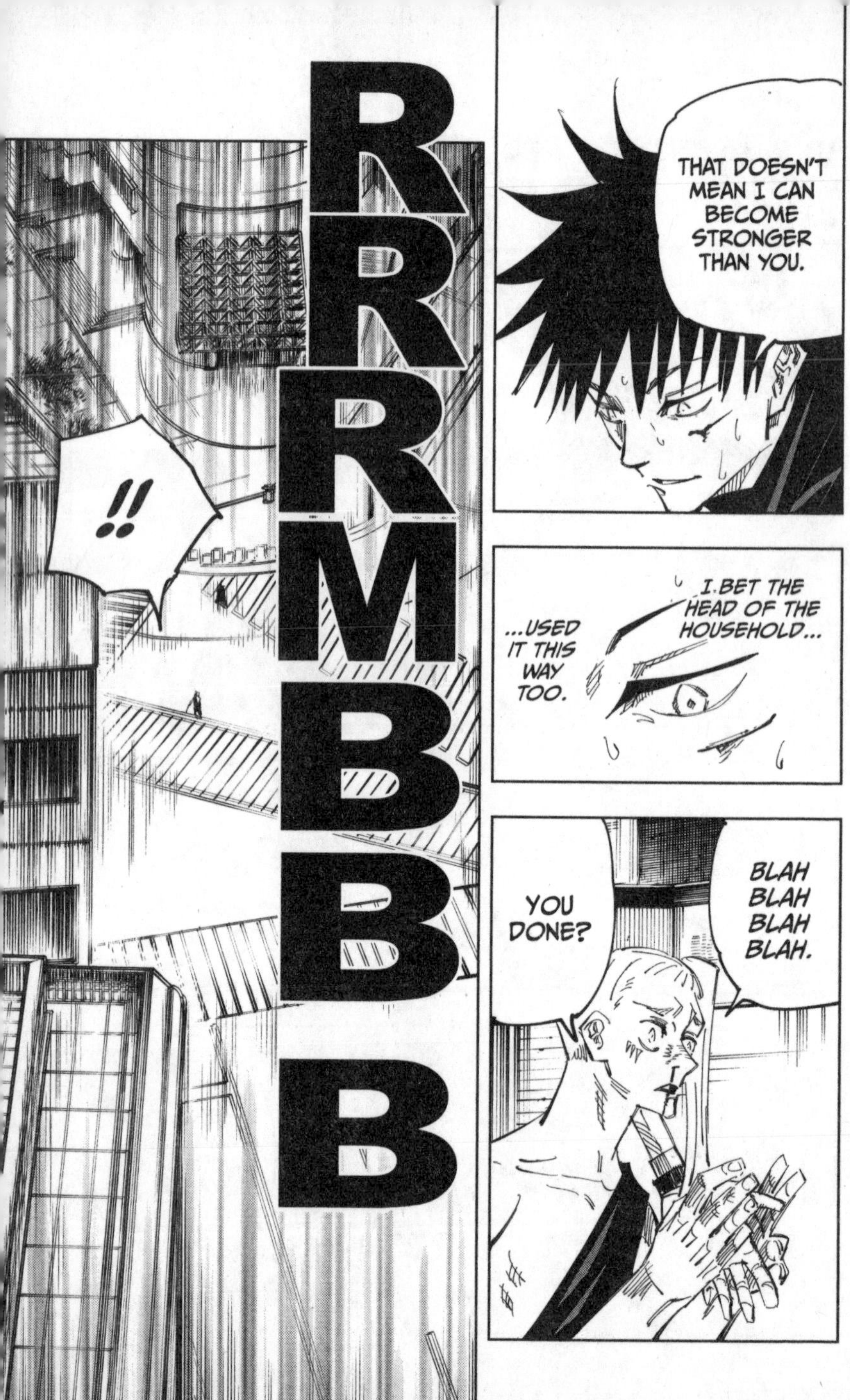
THAT DOESN'T MEAN I CAN BECOME STRONGER THAN YOU.
I BET THE HEAD OF THE HOUSEHOLD...
...USED IT THIS WAY TOO.
BLAH BLAH BLAH BLAH.
YOU DONE?
RRMBBB
!!

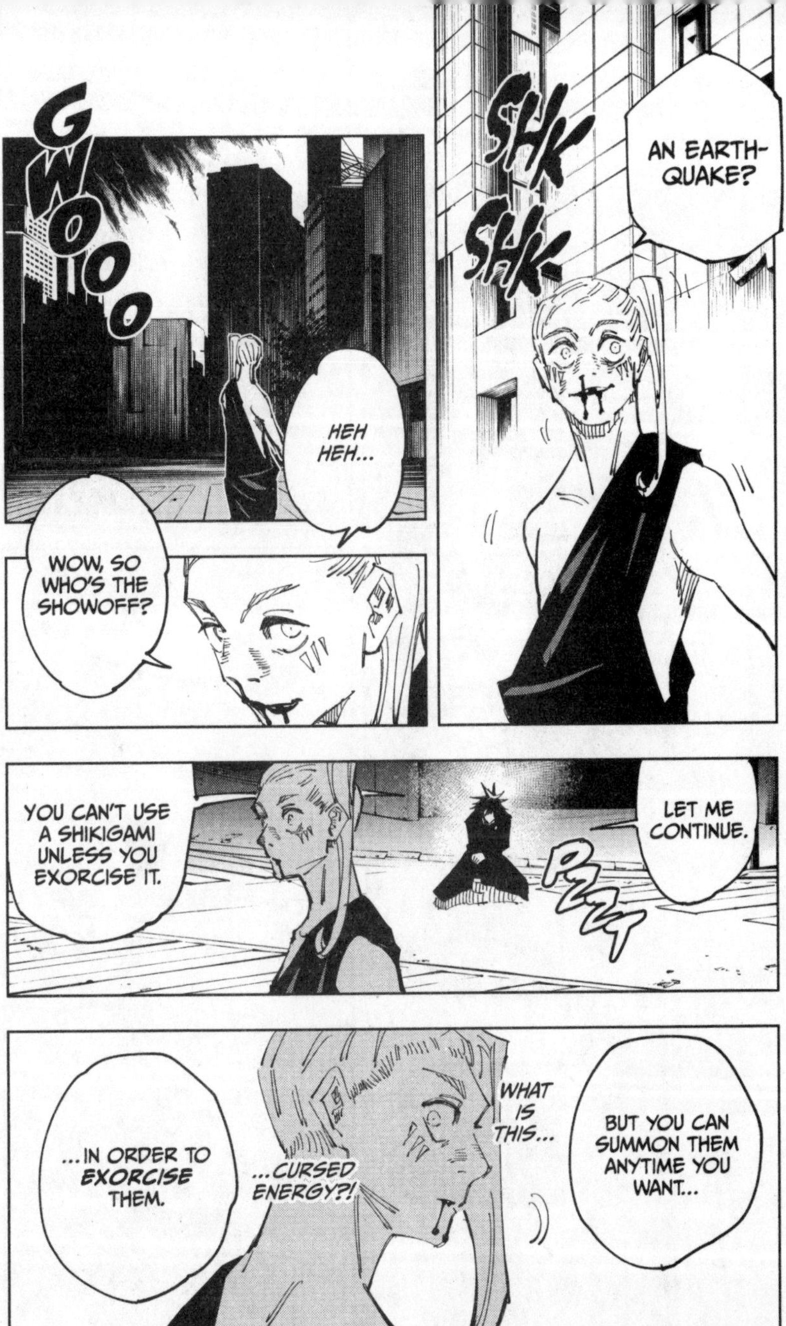
SHK SHK
AN EARTHQUAKE?
GWOOOO
HEH HEH...
WOW, SO WHO'S THE SHOWOFF?
LET ME CONTINUE.
PZZT
YOU CAN'T USE A SHIKIGAMI UNLESS YOU EXORCISE IT.
BUT YOU CAN SUMMON THEM ANYTIME YOU WANT...
WHAT IS THIS...
...CURSED ENERGY?!
...IN ORDER TO EXORCISE THEM.

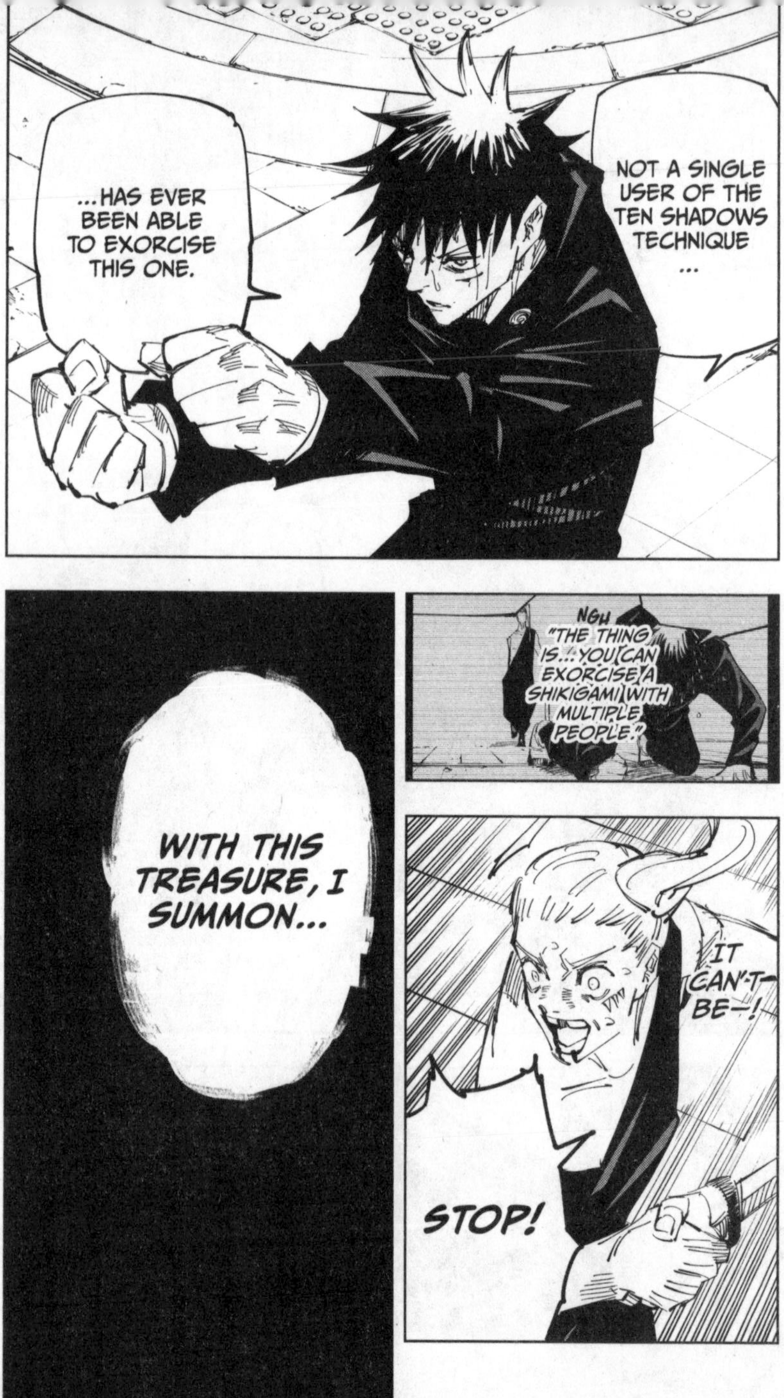
NOT A SINGLE USER OF THE TEN SHADOWS TECHNIQUE ...
...HAS EVER BEEN ABLE TO EXORCISE THIS ONE.
NGH
"THE THING IS... YOU CAN EXORCISE A SHIKIGAMI WITH MULTIPLE PEOPLE."
IT CAN'T BE—!
STOP!
WITH THIS TREASURE, I SUMMON...

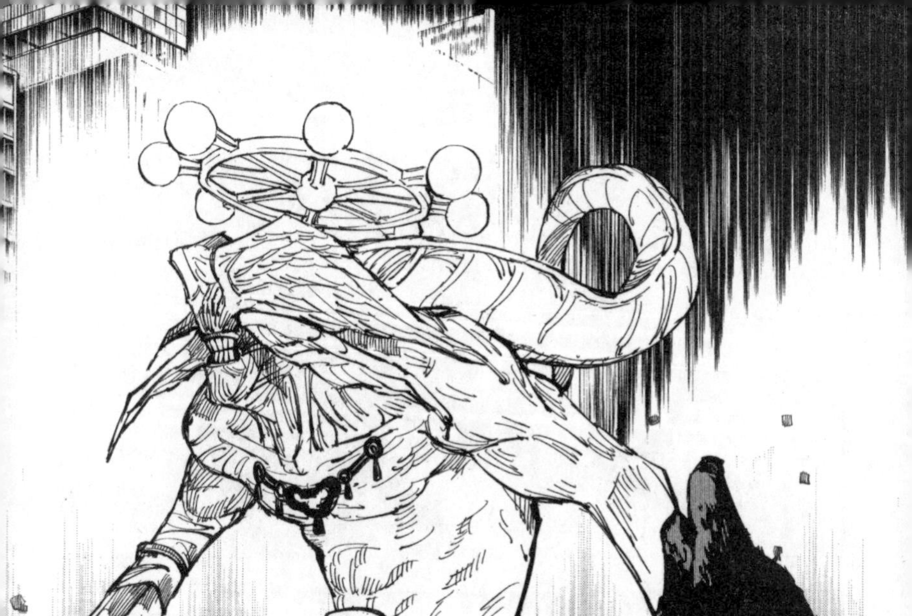

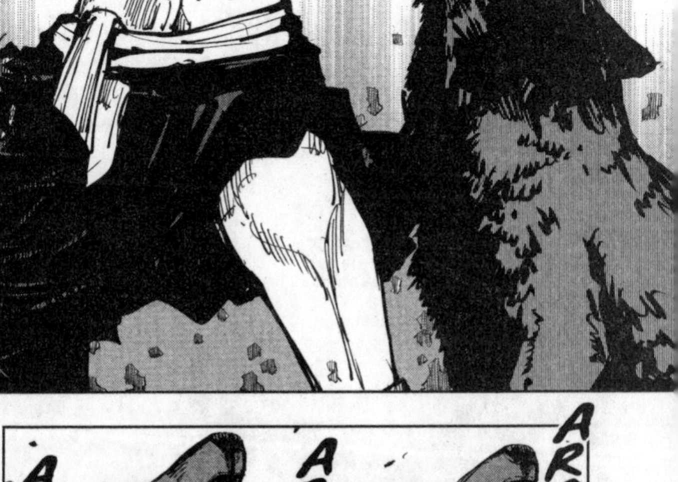
AROOOO
AROOOOO
AROOO

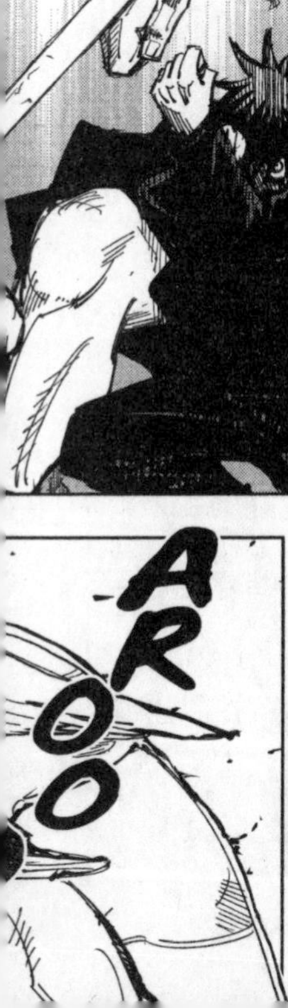
AROO

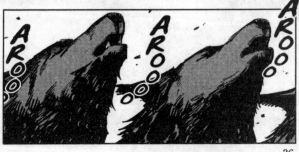

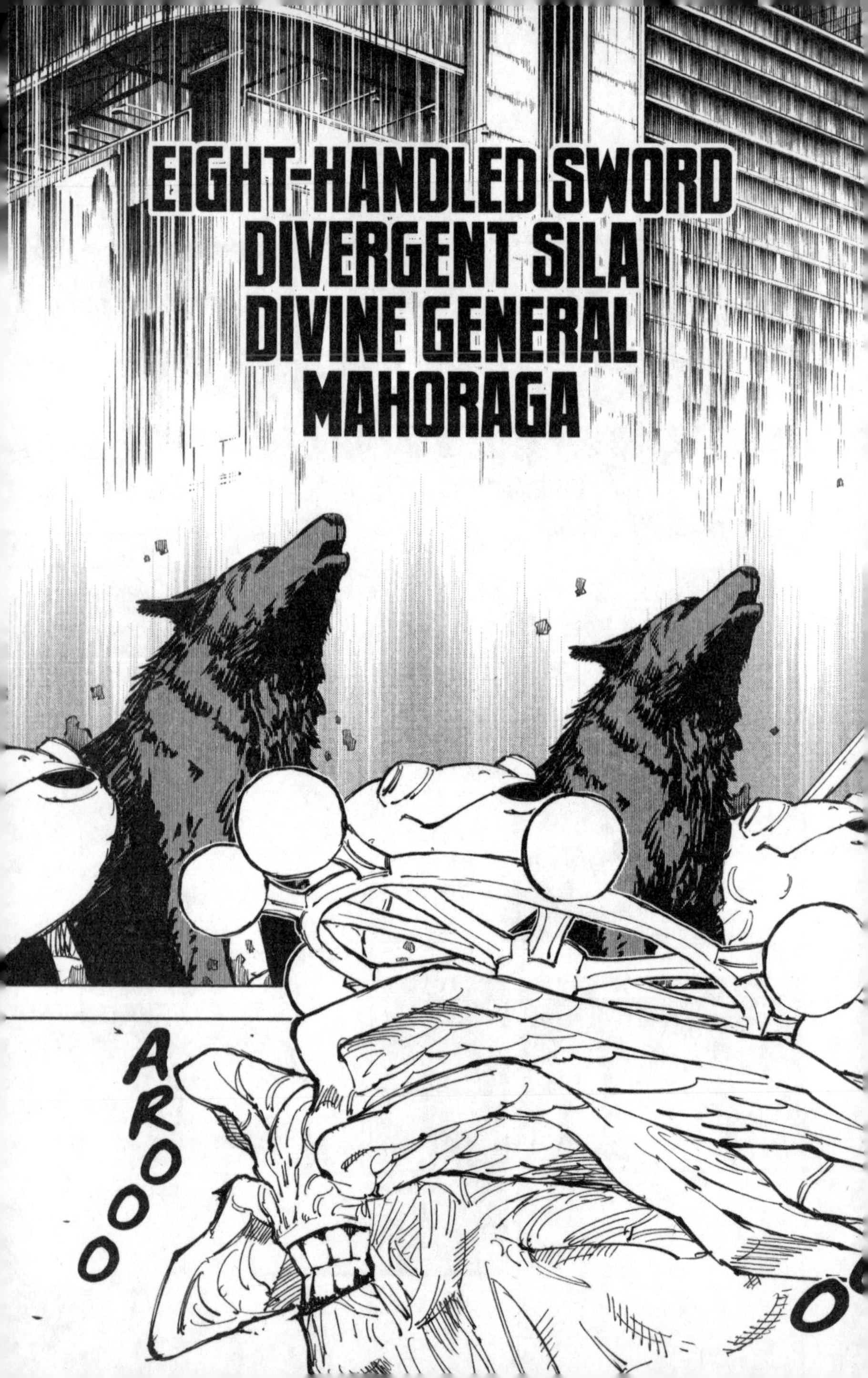
EIGHT-HANDLED SWORD DIVERGENT SILA DIVINE GENERAL MAHORAGA
AROOOO

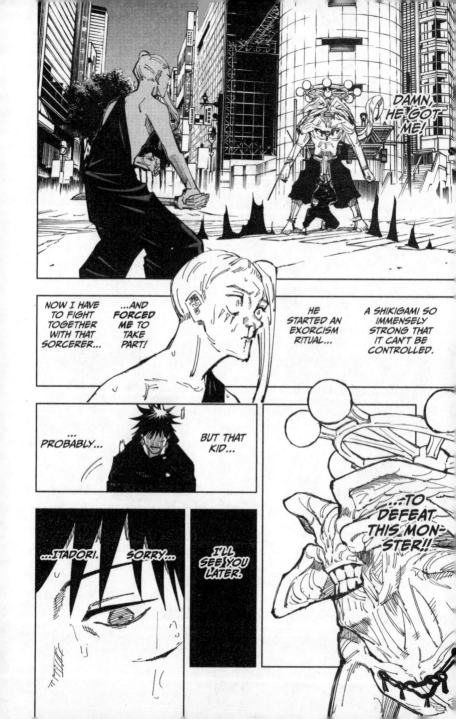

DAMN, HE GOT ME!

NOW I HAVE TO FIGHT TOGETHER WITH THAT SORCERER...

...AND FORCED ME TO TAKE PART!

HE STARTED AN EXORCISM RITUAL...

A SHIKIGAMI SO IMMENSELY STRONG THAT IT CAN'T BE CONTROLLED.

...PROBABLY...

BUT THAT KID...

...TO DEFEAT THIS MONSTER!!

...ITADORI.

SORRY...

I'LL SEE YOU LATER.

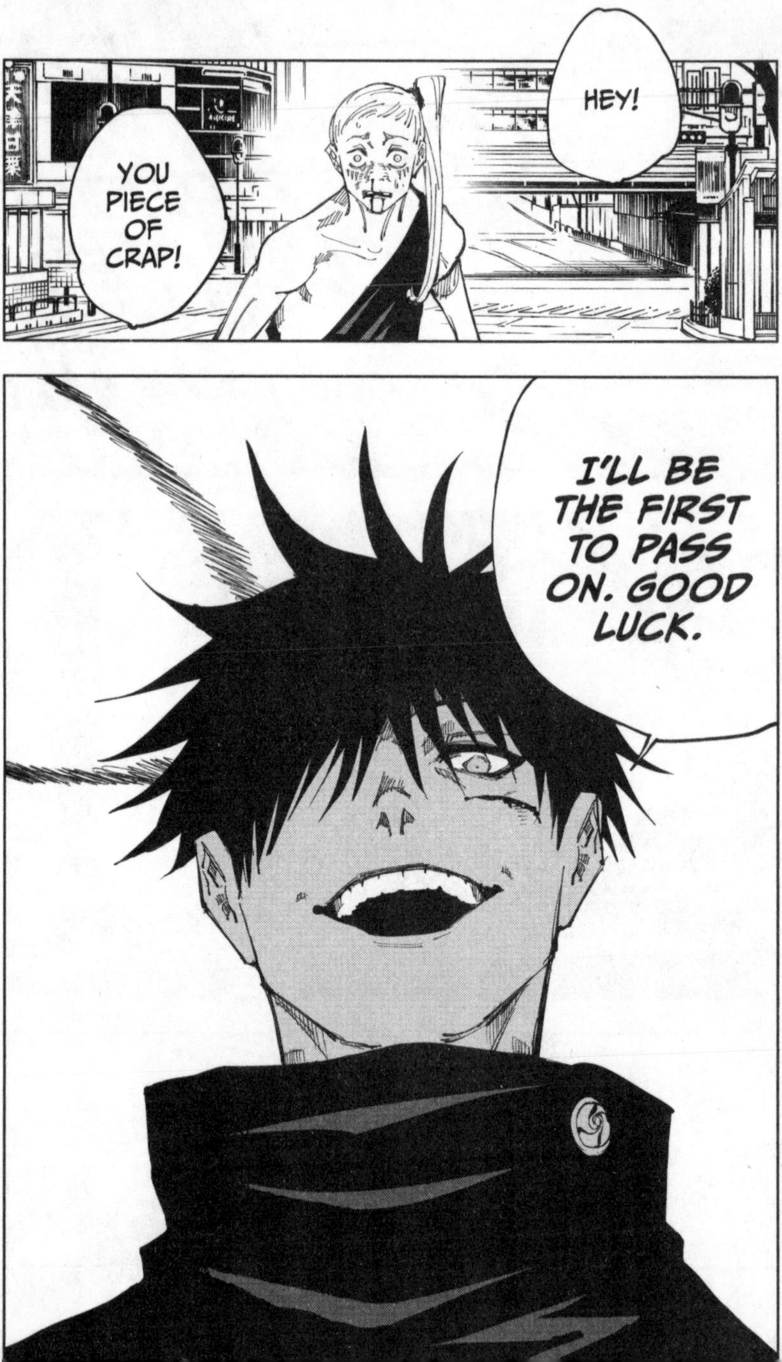
HEY!
YOU PIECE OF CRAP!
I'LL BE THE FIRST TO PASS ON. GOOD LUCK.

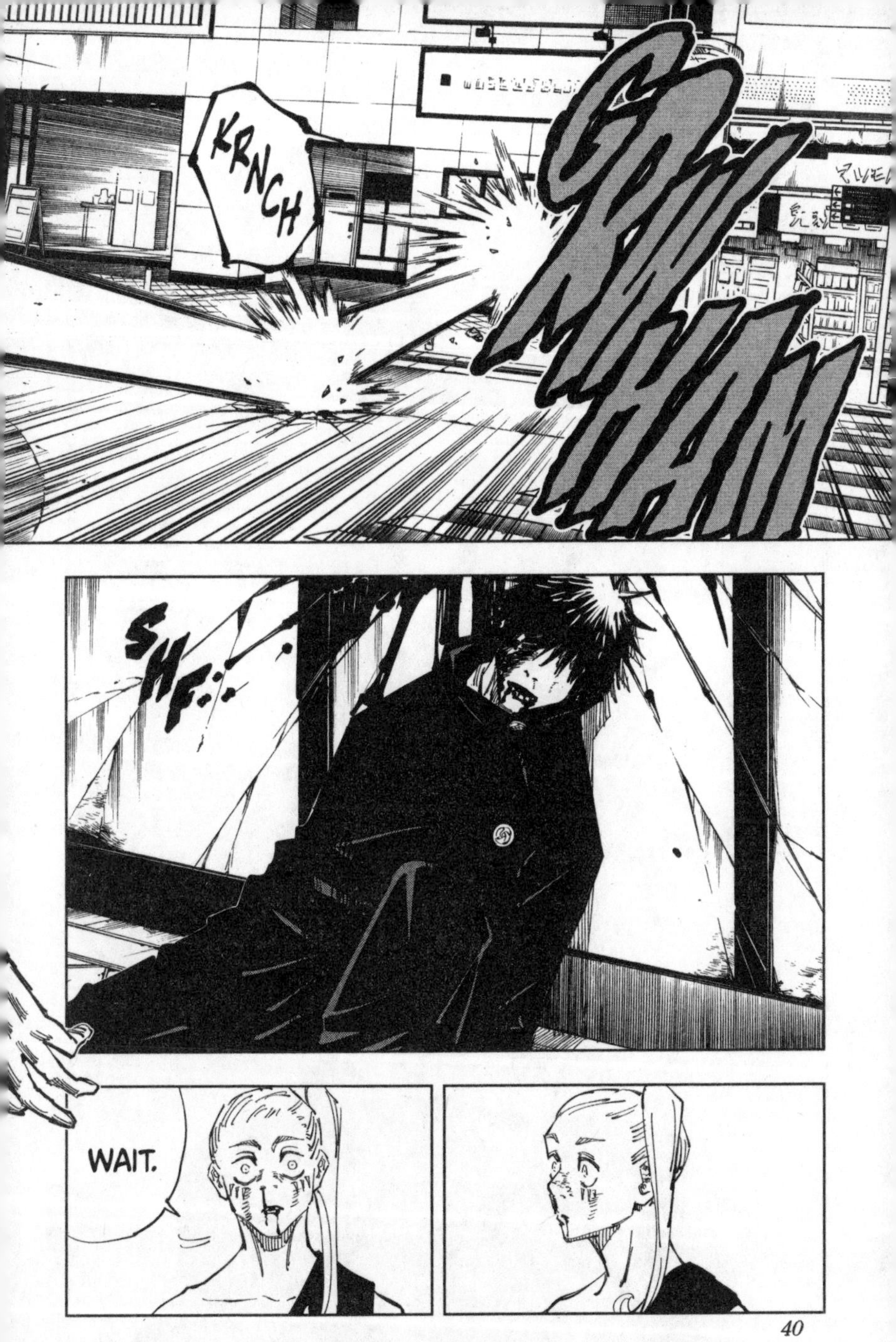
KRNCH
SHF...
WAIT.

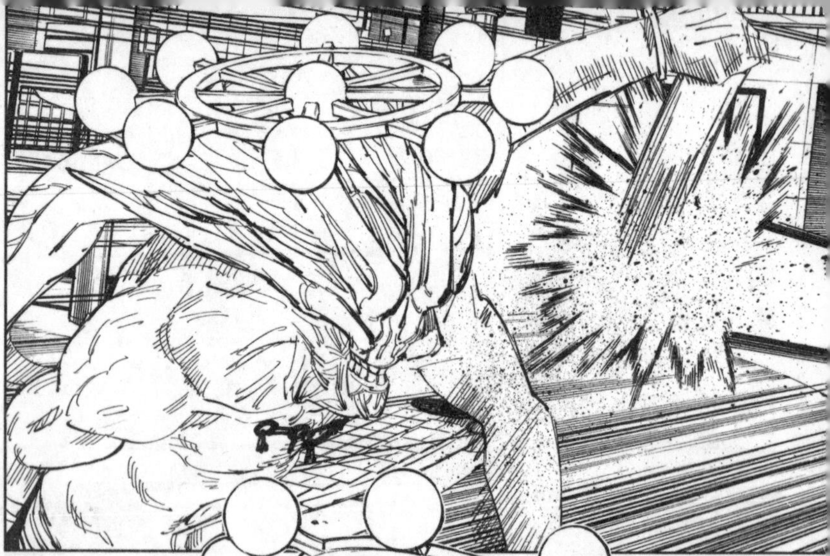

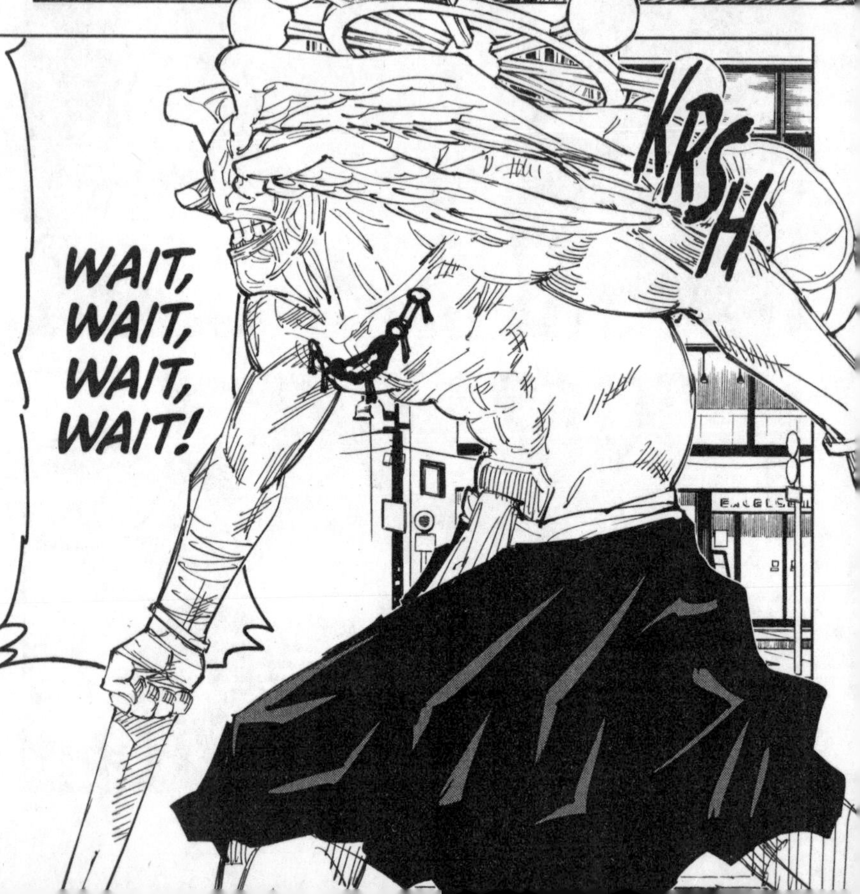
KRSH
WAIT, WAIT, WAIT, WAIT!

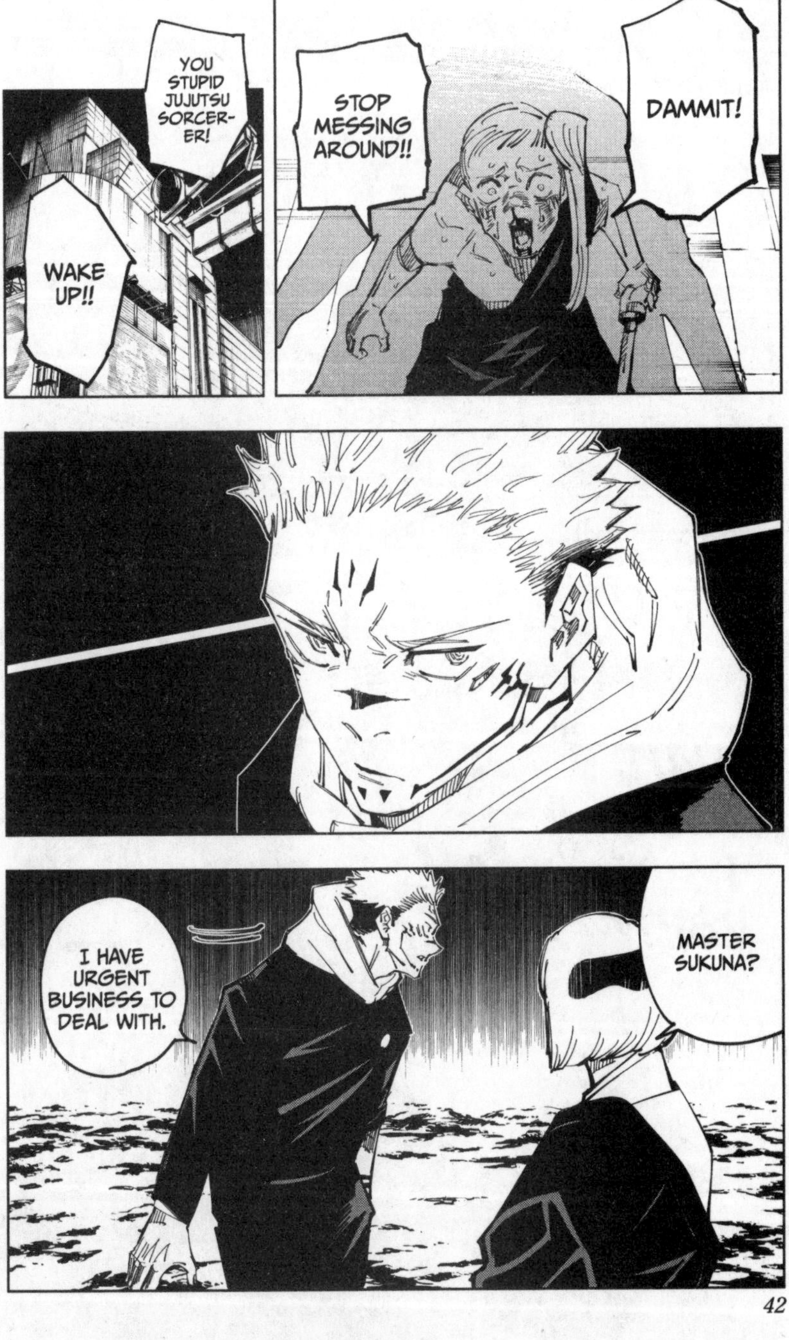
DAMMIT!
STOP MESSING AROUND!!
YOU STUPID JUJUTSU SORCERER!
WAKE UP!!
MASTER SUKUNA?
I HAVE URGENT BUSINESS TO DEAL WITH.

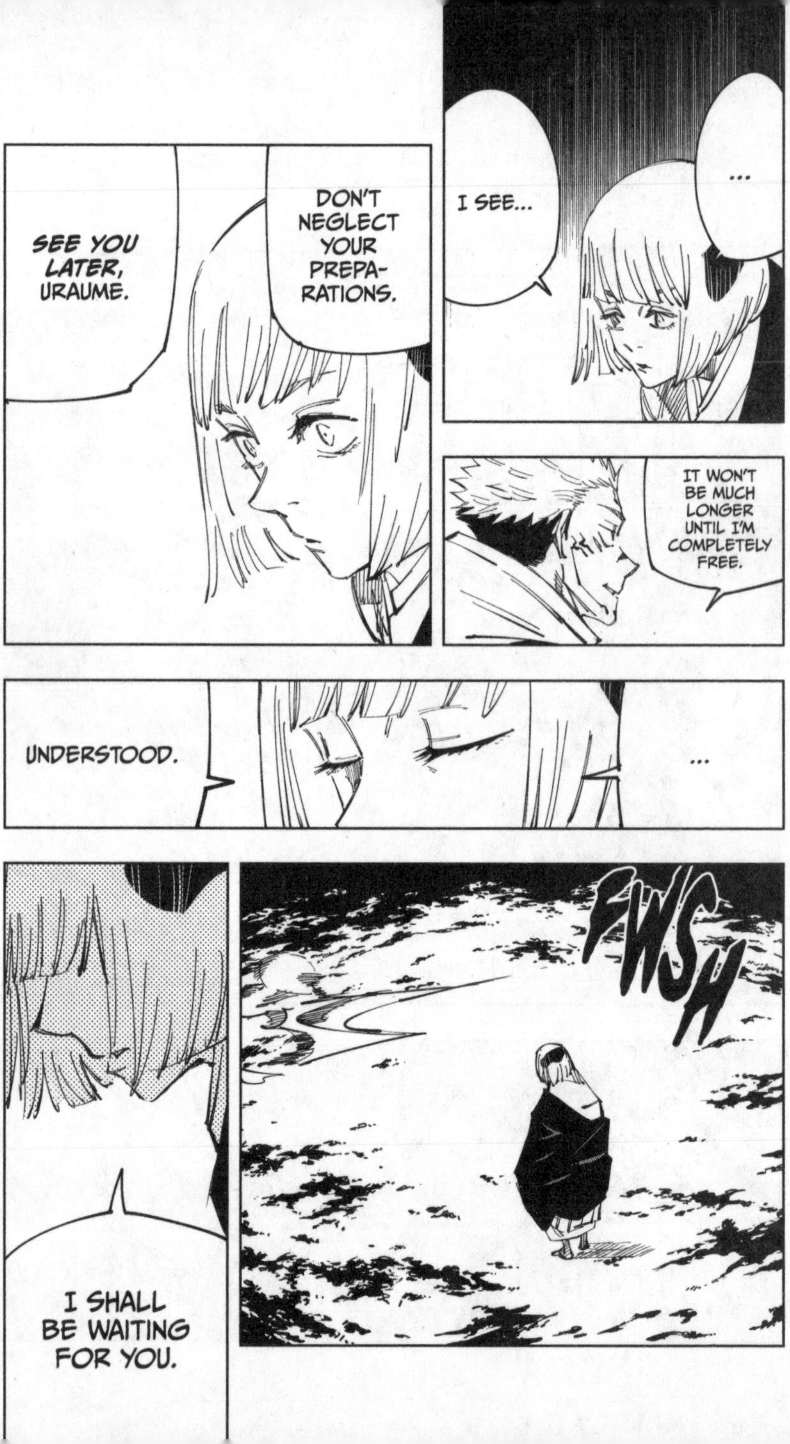
...
I SEE...
IT WON'T BE MUCH LONGER UNTIL I'M COMPLETELY FREE.
DON'T NEGLECT YOUR PREPARATIONS.
SEE YOU LATER, URAUME.
...
UNDERSTOOD.
FWSH
I SHALL BE WAITING FOR YOU.

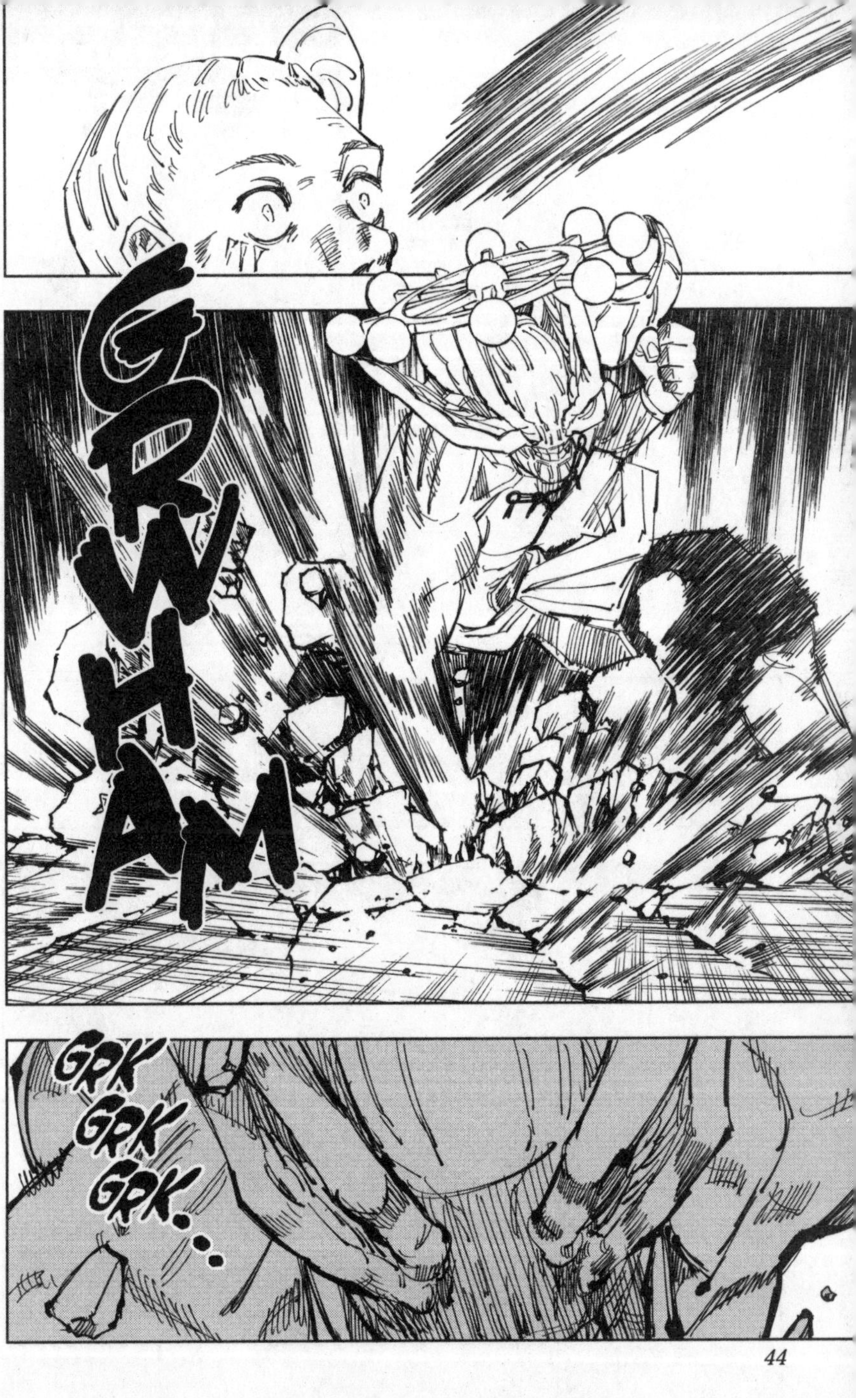
GRWHAM
GRK GRK GRK...

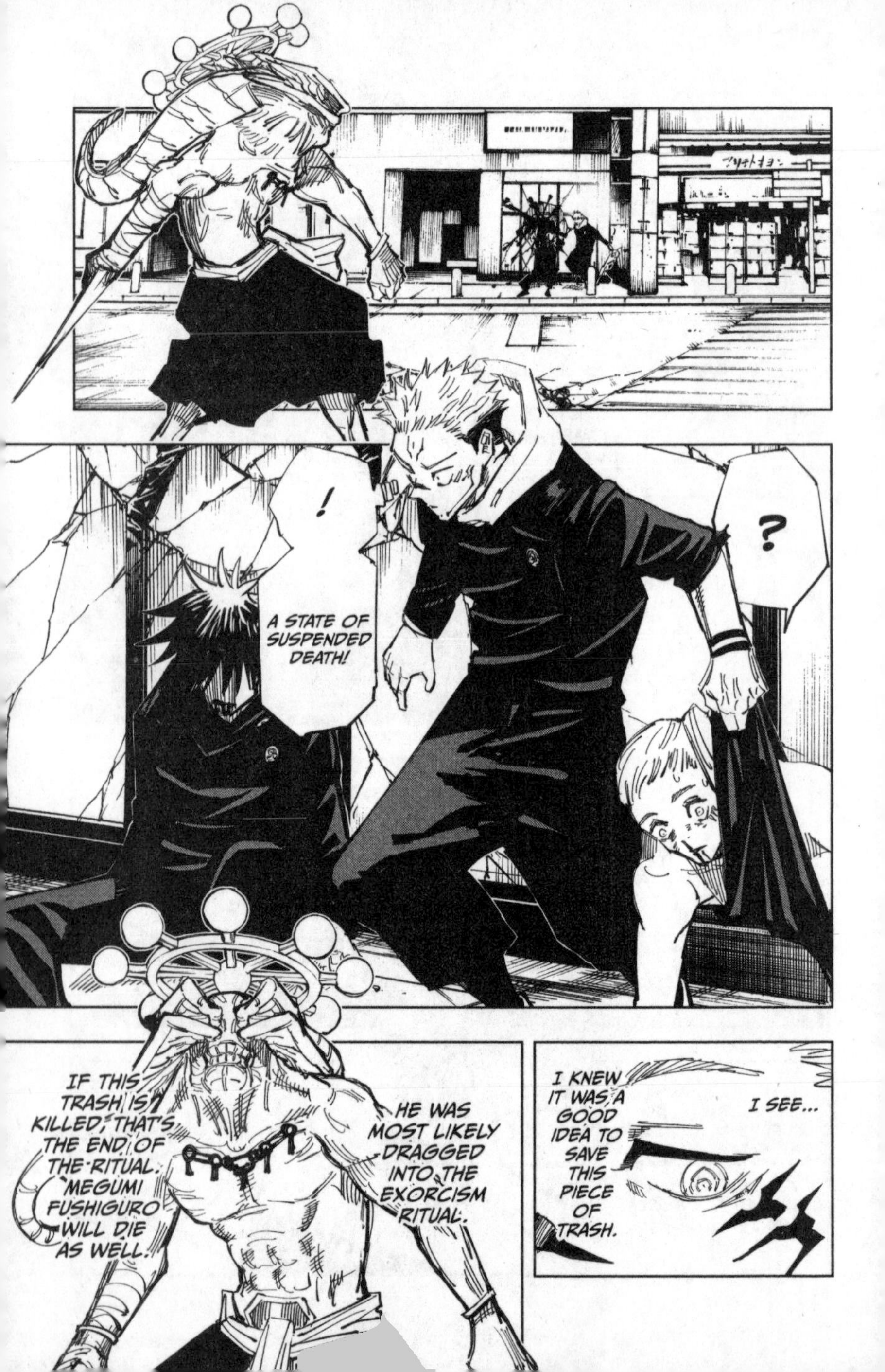
?
!
A STATE OF SUSPENDED DEATH!
I SEE...
I KNEW IT WAS A GOOD IDEA TO SAVE THIS PIECE OF TRASH.
HE WAS MOST LIKELY DRAGGED INTO THE EXORCISM RITUAL.
IF THIS TRASH IS KILLED, THAT'S THE END OF THE RITUAL. MEGUMI FUSHIGURO WILL DIE AS WELL.

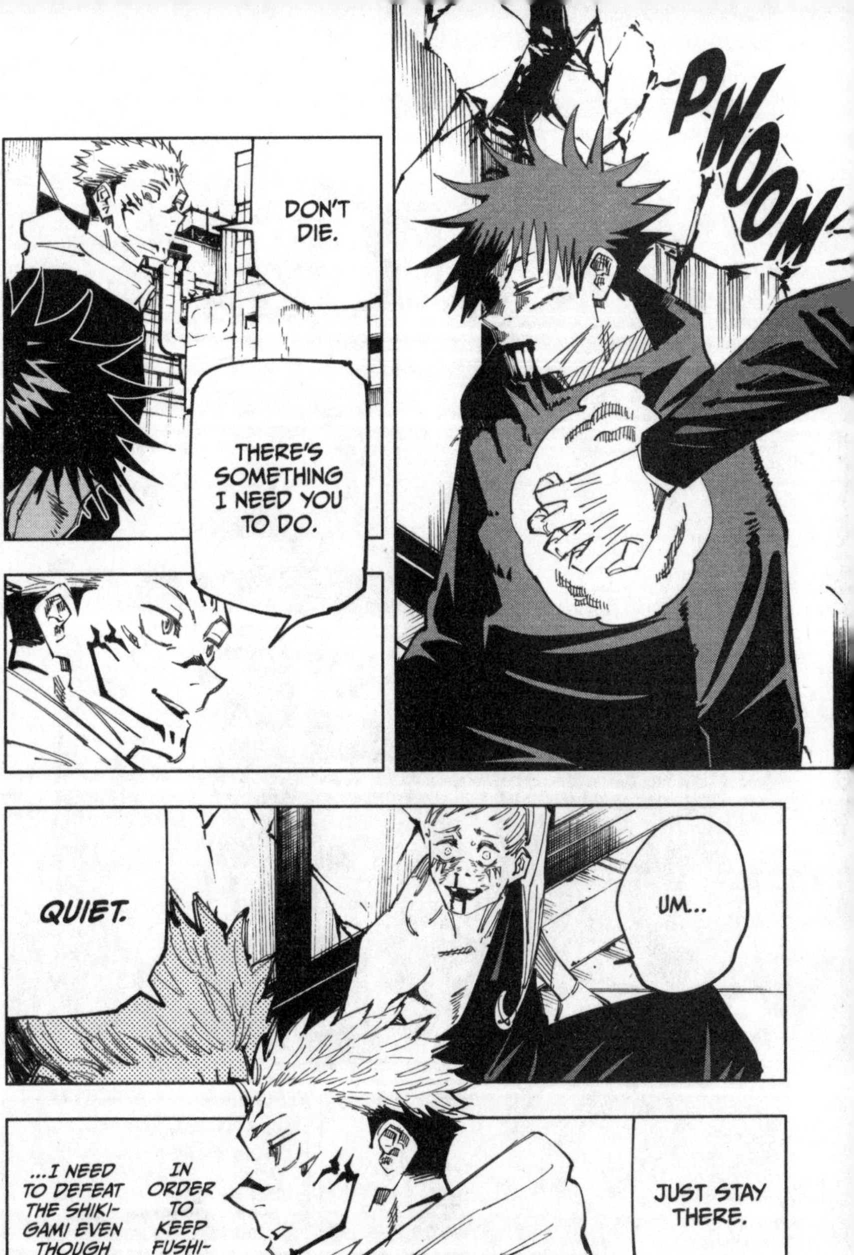
PWOOM
DON'T DIE.
THERE'S SOMETHING I NEED YOU TO DO.
UM...
QUIET.
JUST STAY THERE.
IN ORDER TO KEEP FUSHIGURO ALIVE...
...I NEED TO DEFEAT THE SHIKIGAMI EVEN THOUGH I'M AN OUTSIDER.

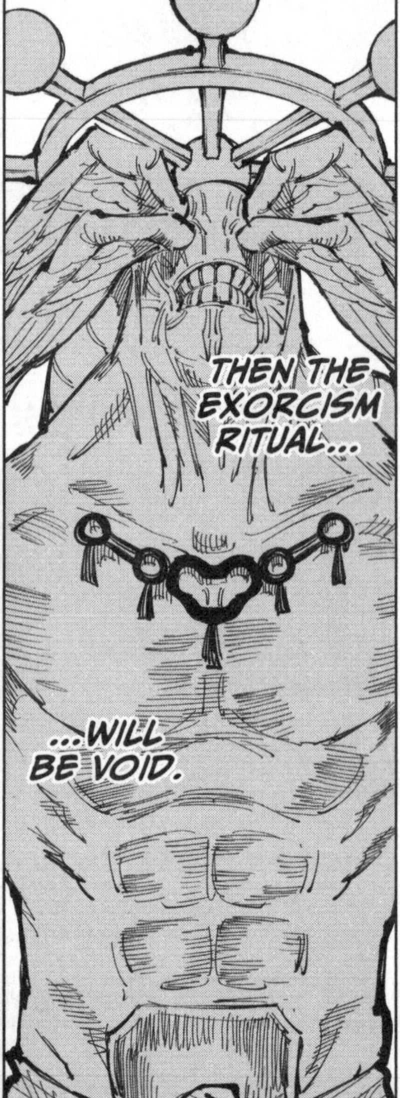
THEN THE EXORCISM RITUAL...
...WILL BE VOID.

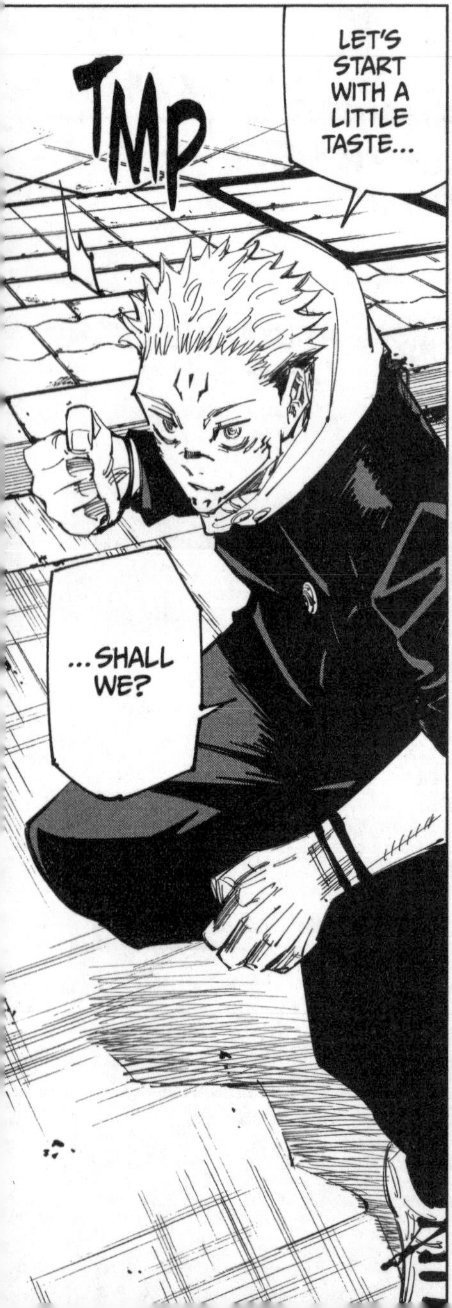
LET'S START WITH A LITTLE TASTE...
TMP
...SHALL WE?

THE 2020 VALENTINES RANKINGS THAT I SERIOUSLY ALMOST FORGOT

RANKINGS (VALENTINES RECEIVED)	CHARACTER	AKUTAMI'S COMMENT
5 (19)	NANAMI	FIFTH IS FIRST.
6 (13)	KUGISAKI	NICE!
7 (7)	CHOSO	HE HASN'T BEEN SHOWING UP MUCH, HAS HE?
8 (6)	INUMAKI	EVEN THOUGH I'VE BARELY EXPLORED HIM...
9 (5)	MAKI	MAYBE I'LL CHANGE HER HAIRSTYLE...

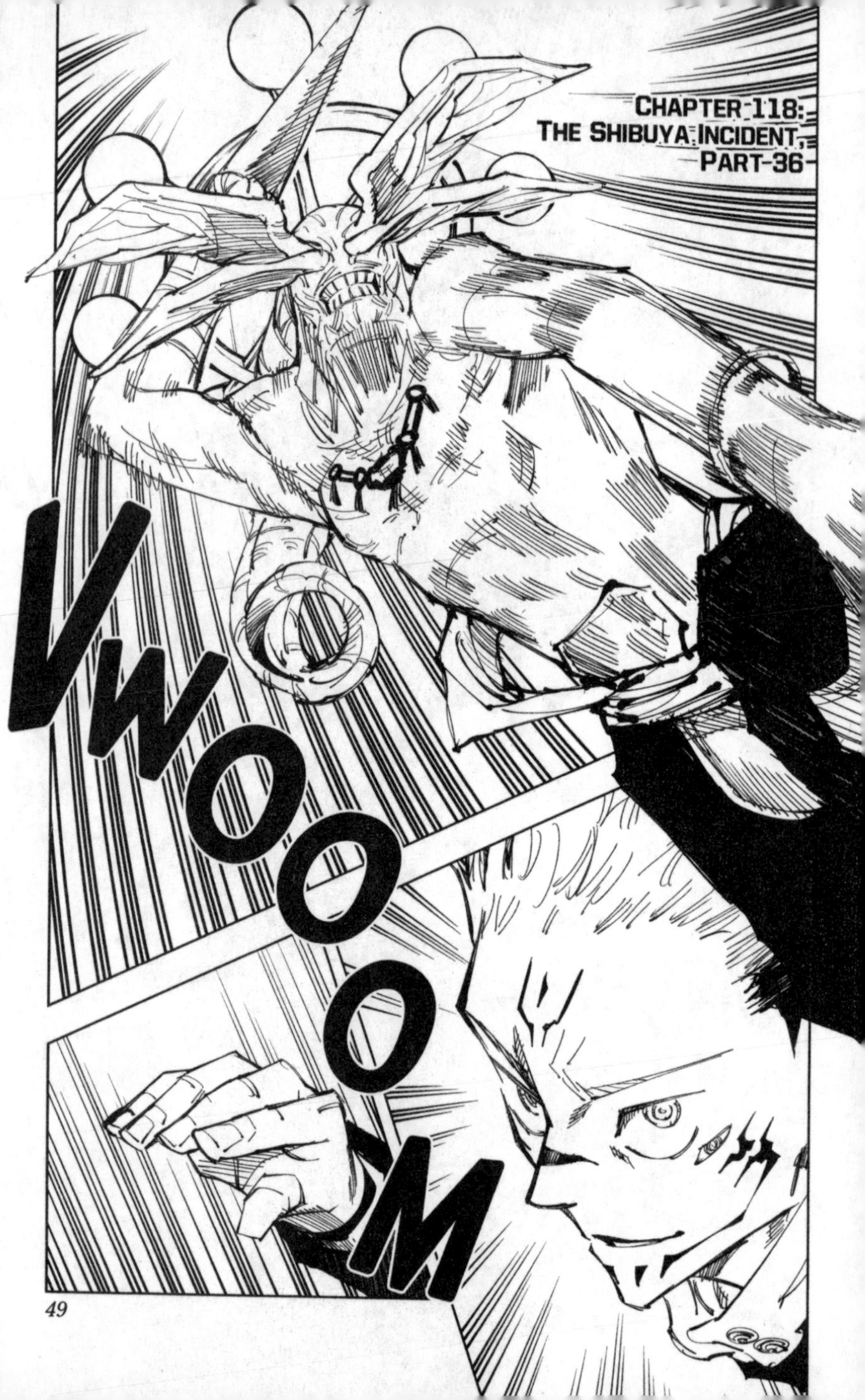
CHAPTER 118:
THE SHIBUYA INCIDENT,
PART 36
VWOOOOM

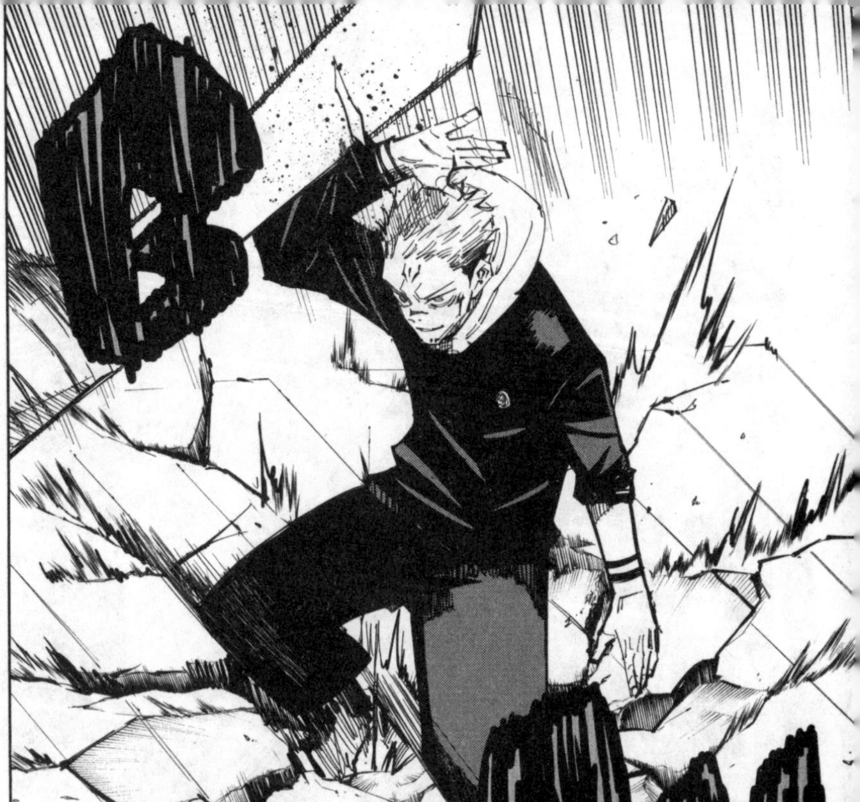
BAM
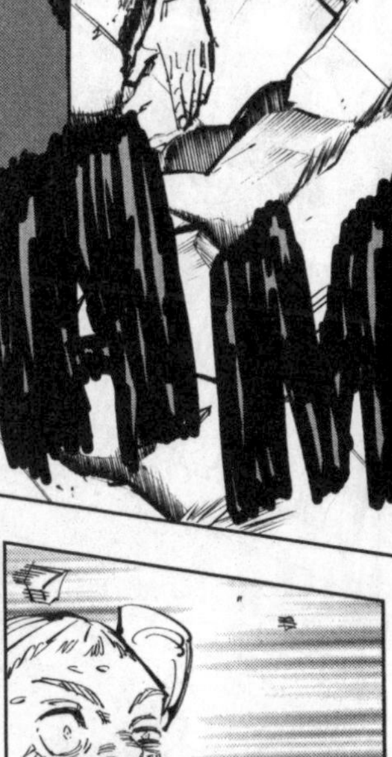
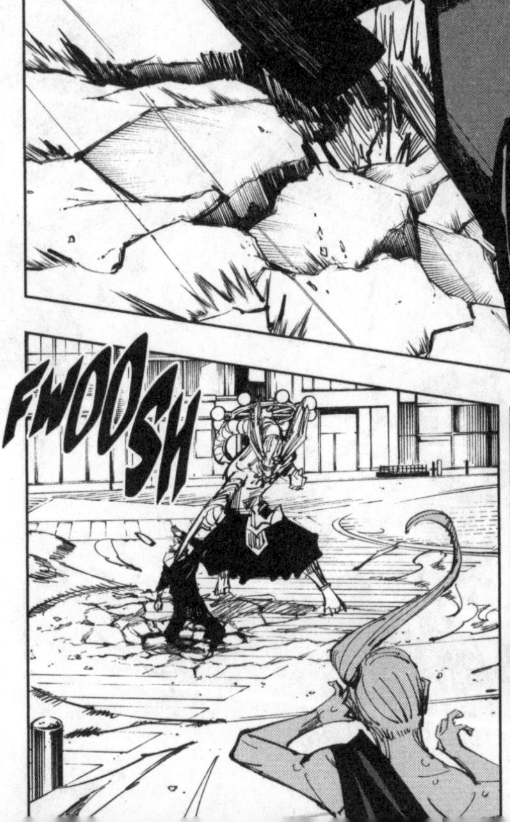
FWOOSH

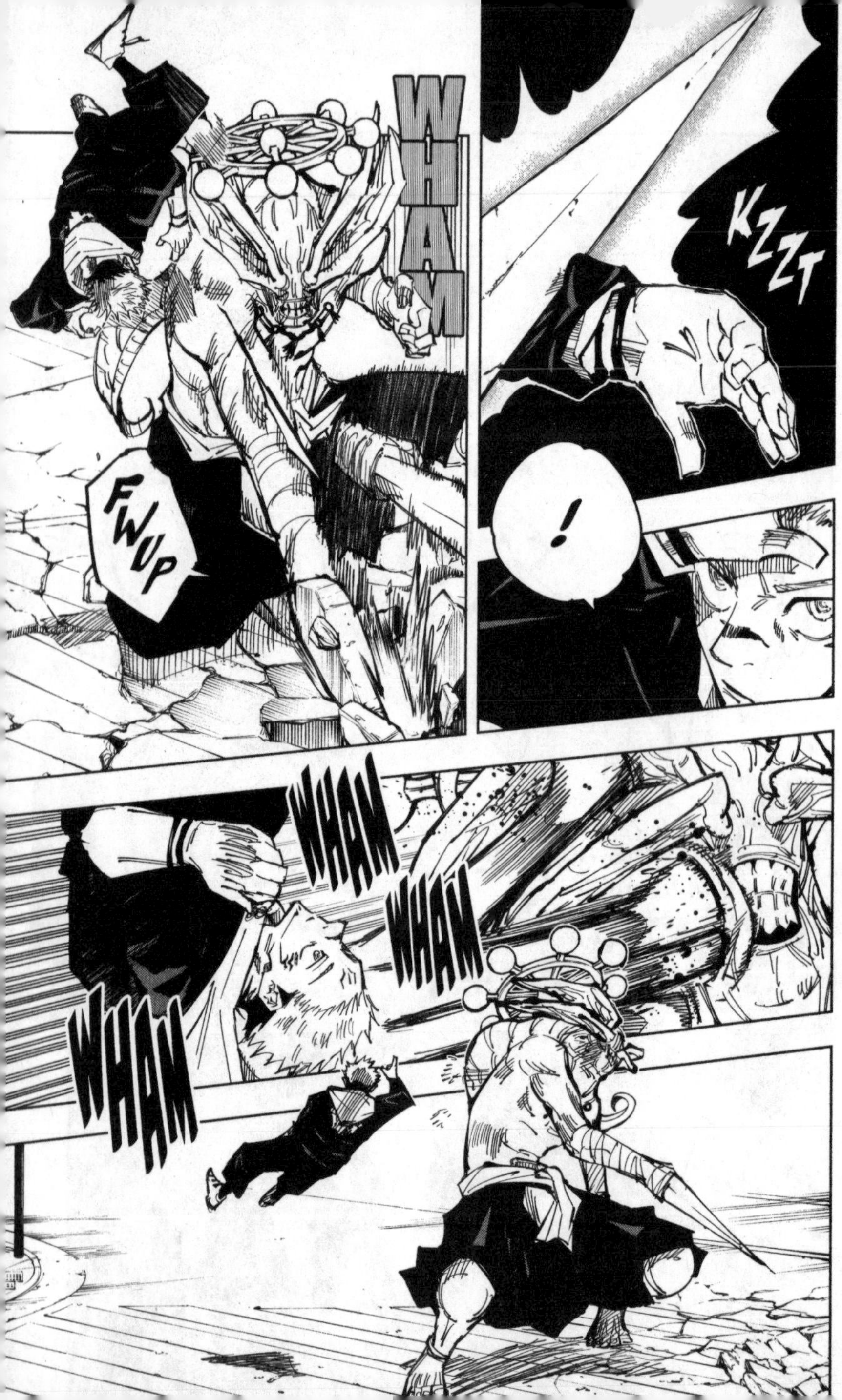
KZZT
!
WHAM
FWUP
WHAM
WHAM
WHAM

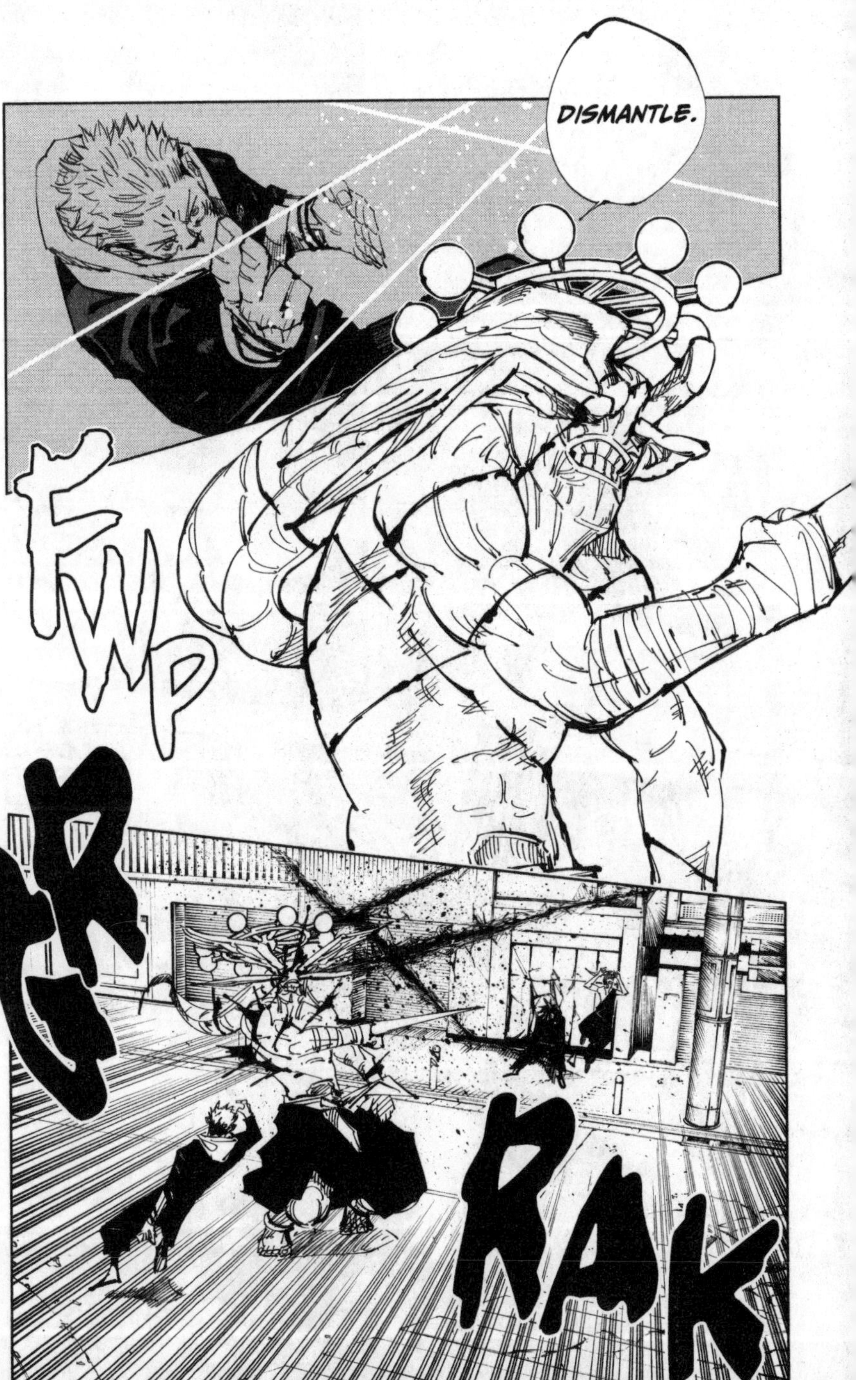
DISMANTLE.
FWP
KRAK

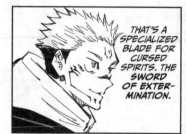

THAT'S A SPECIALIZED BLADE FOR CURSED SPIRITS. THE SWORD OF EXTERMINATION.

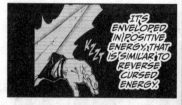

IT'S ENVELOPED IN POSITIVE ENERGY, THAT IS SIMILAR TO REVERSE CURSED ENERGY.

KZZT

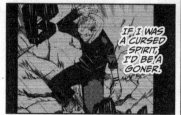

IF I WAS A CURSED SPIRIT, I'D BE A GONER.

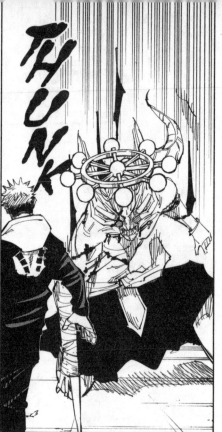

THUNK

KTNK

GRK GRK GRK...

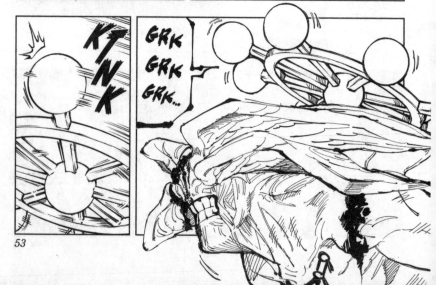

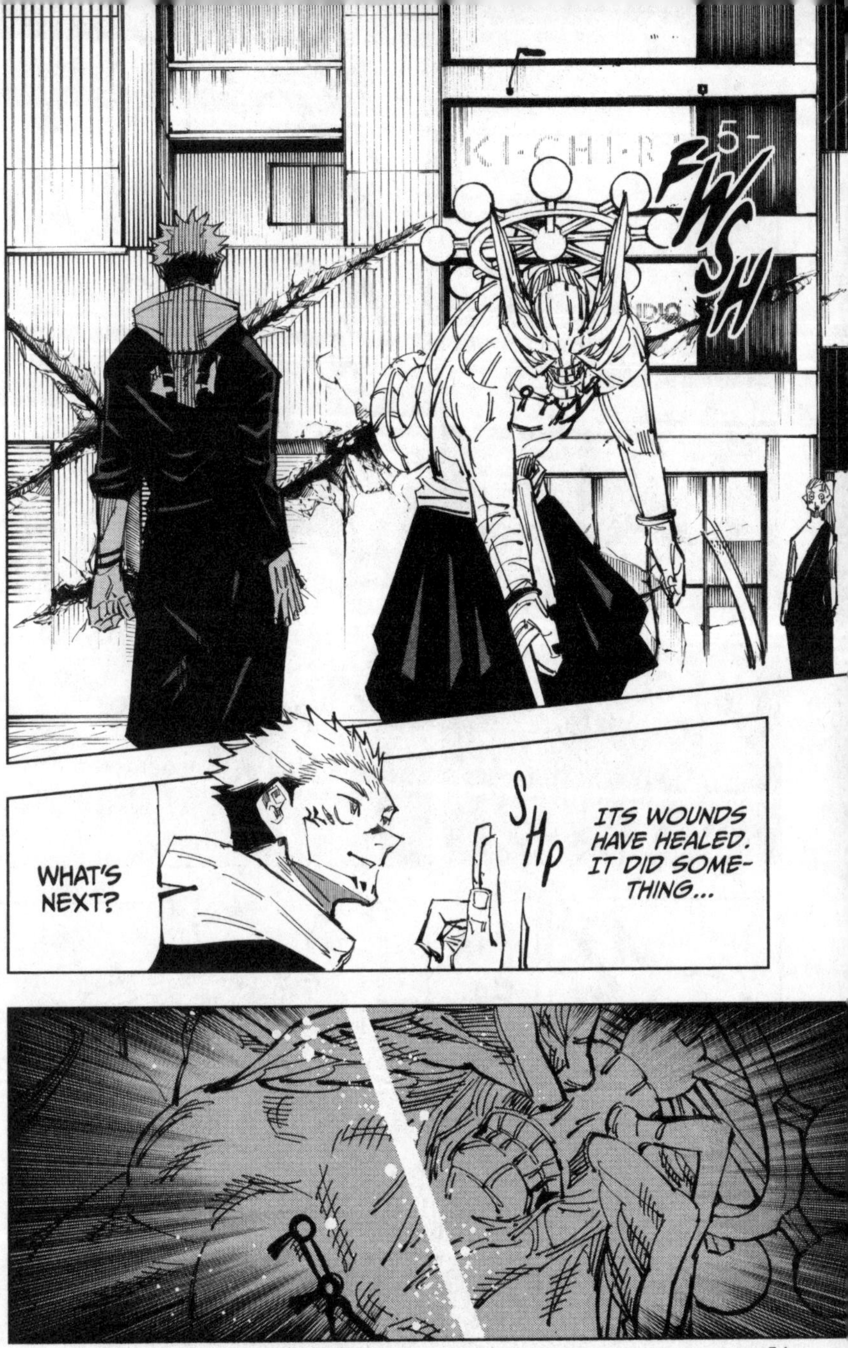
FWSH
ITS WOUNDS HAVE HEALED. IT DID SOME-THING...
SHP
WHAT'S NEXT?

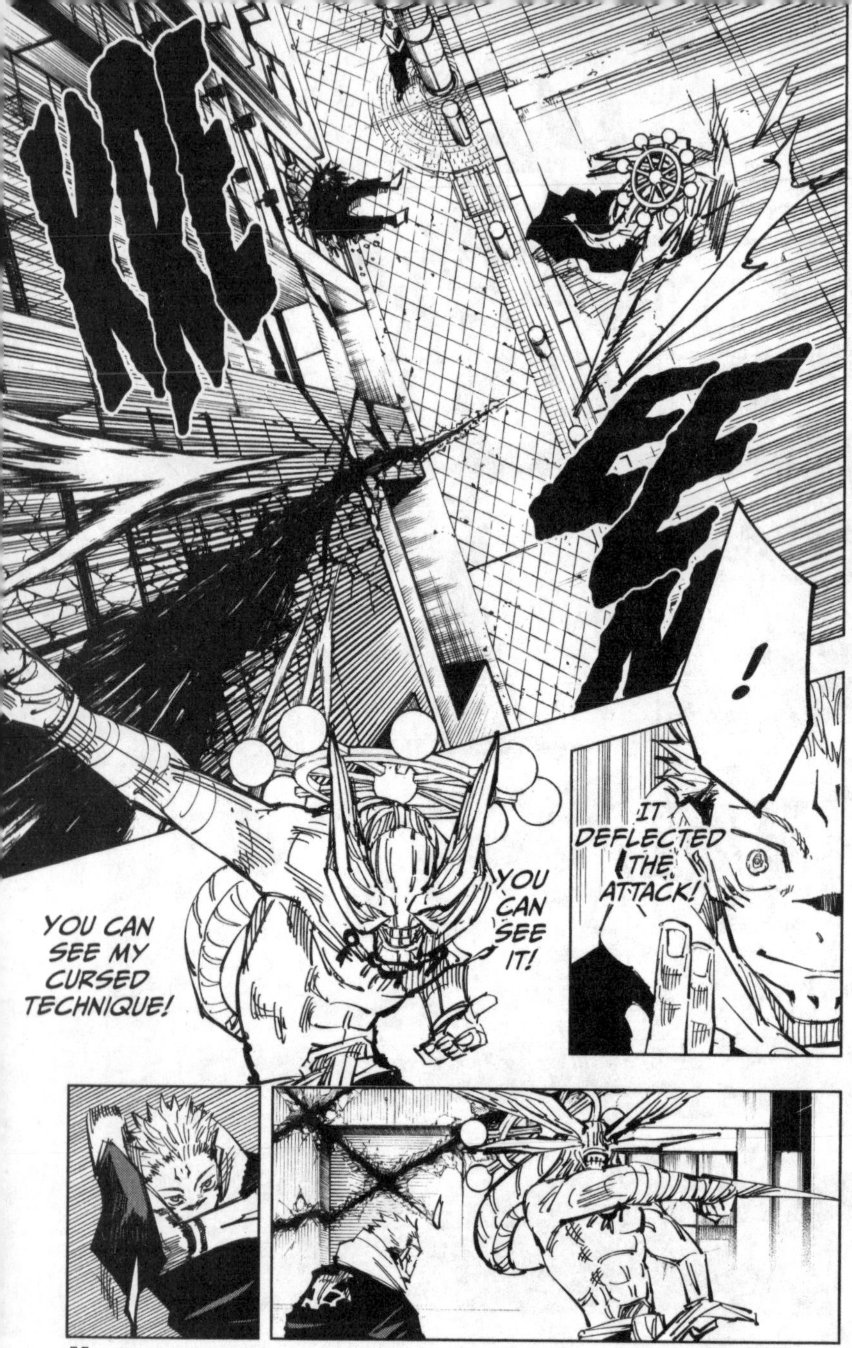
!
IT DEFLECTED THE ATTACK!
YOU CAN SEE IT!
YOU CAN SEE MY CURSED TECHNIQUE!

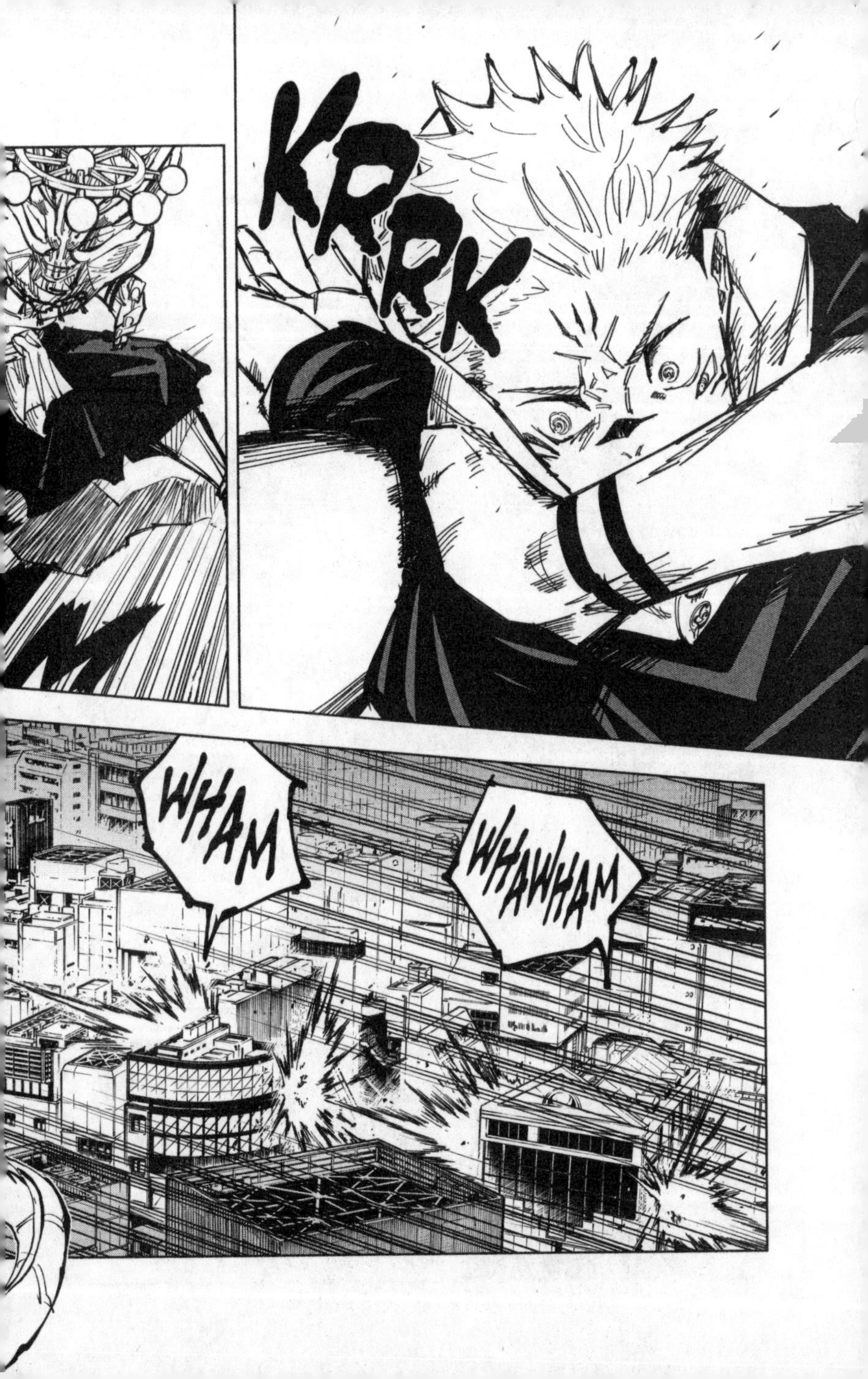
KRRK!
WHAWHAM
WHAM

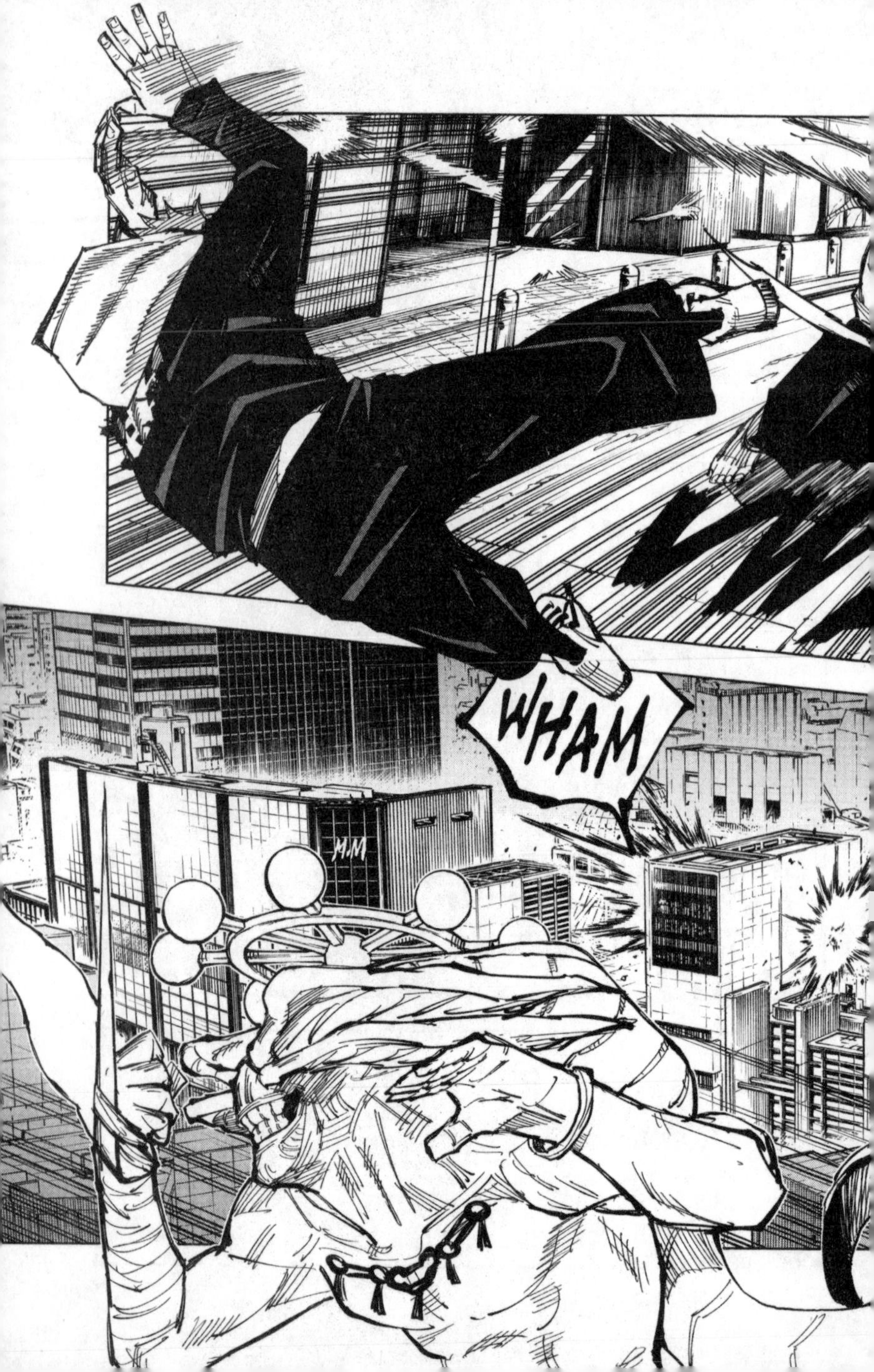
WHAM

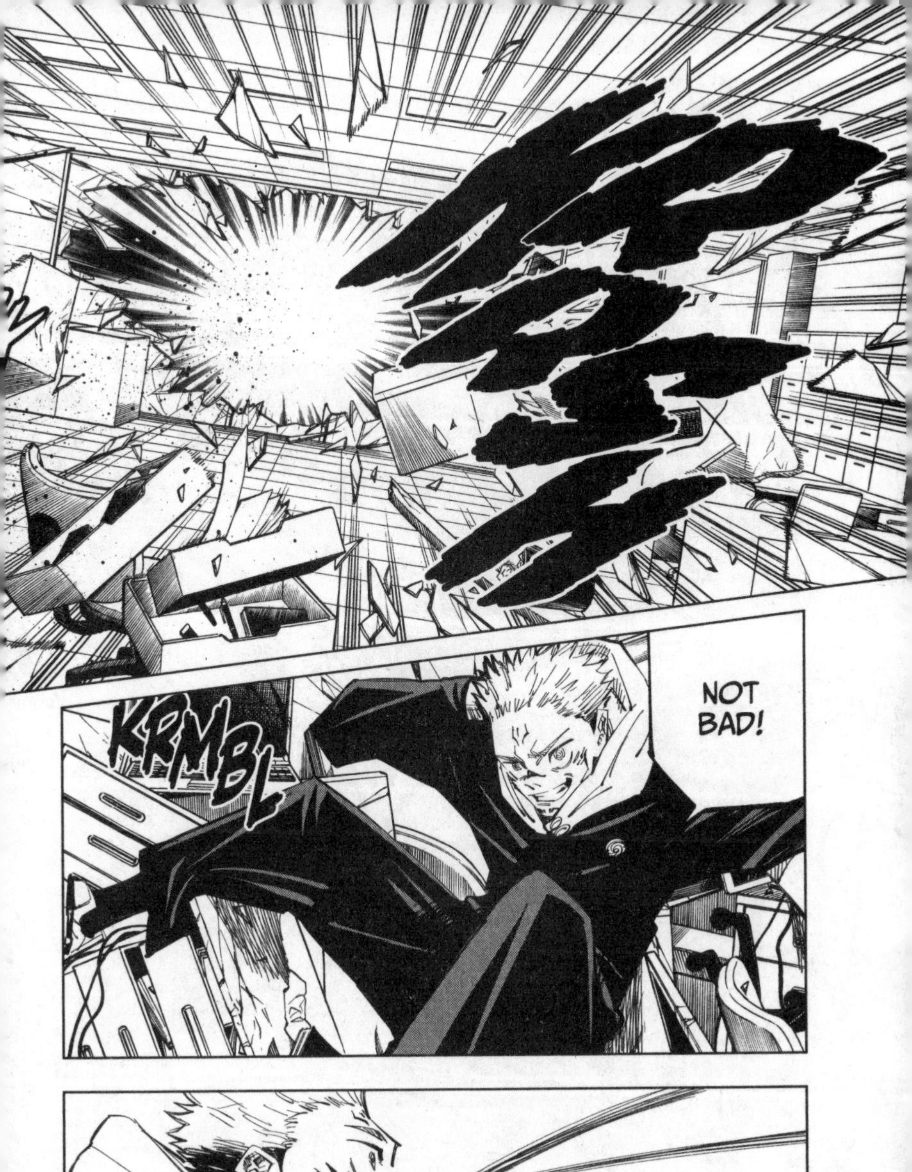
NOT BAD!
KRMBL

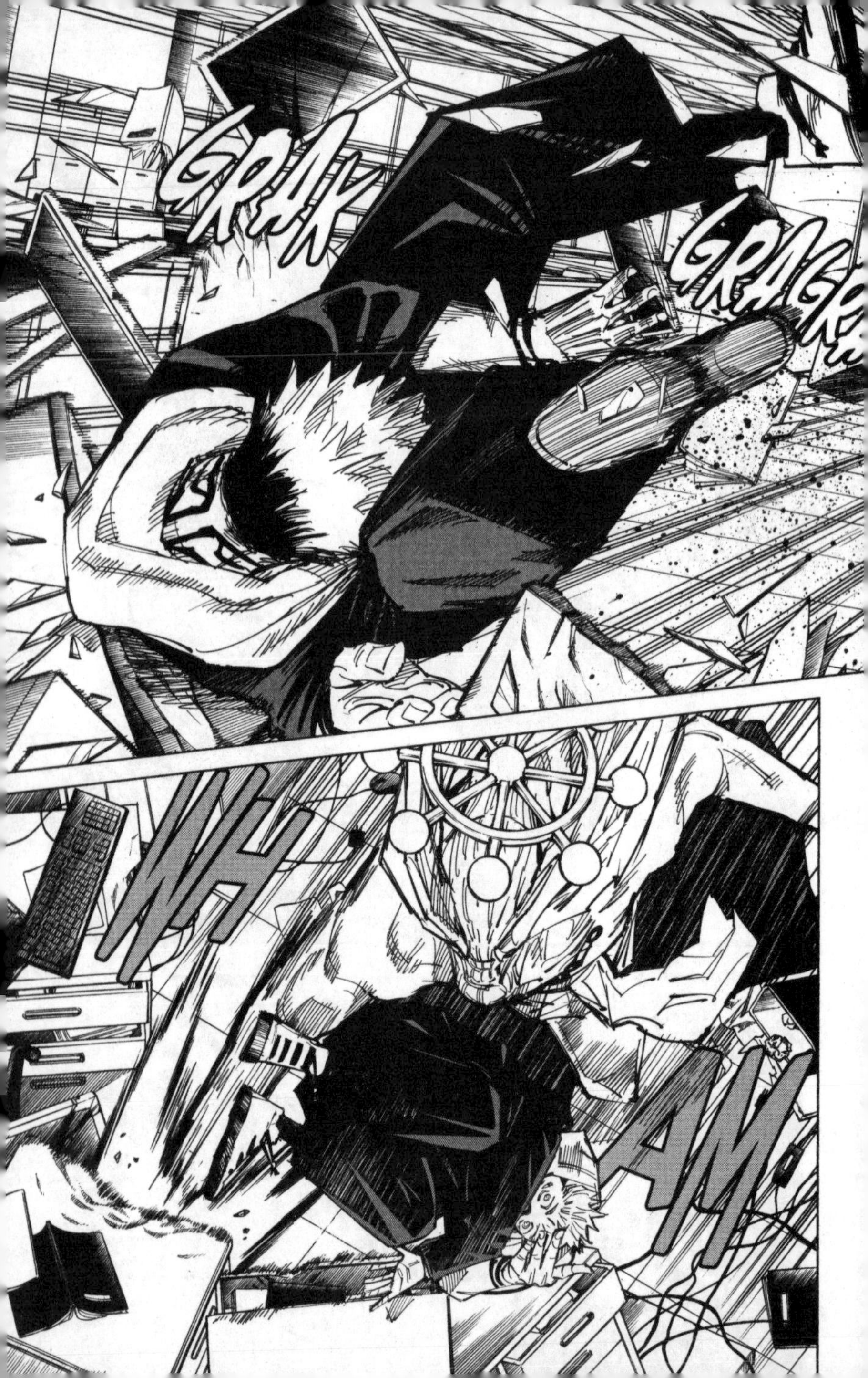
GRAK
GRAC
WHAM

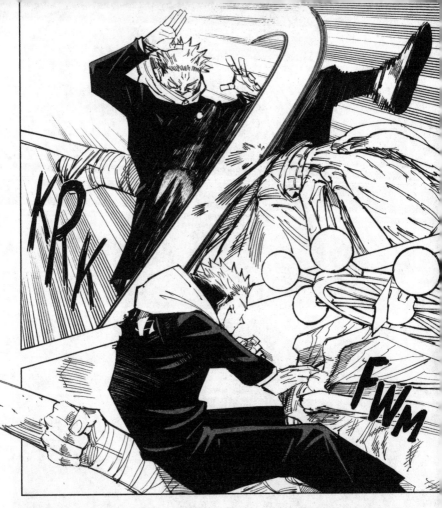

KRK

FWM

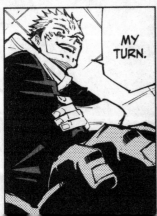

MY TURN.

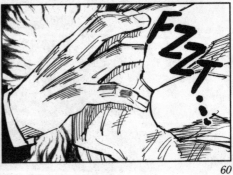

FZZT...

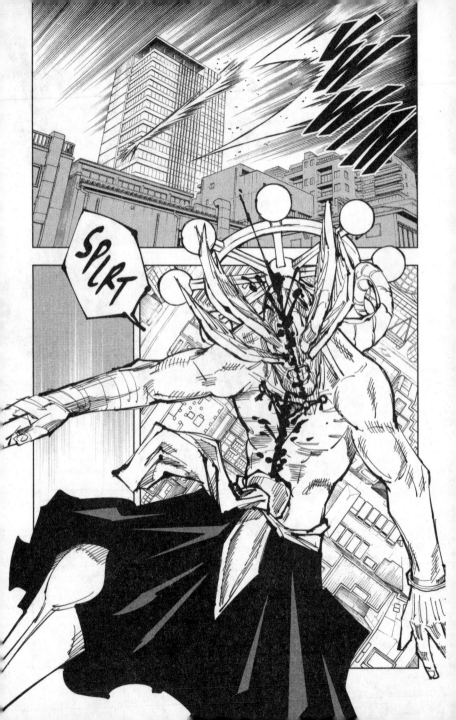

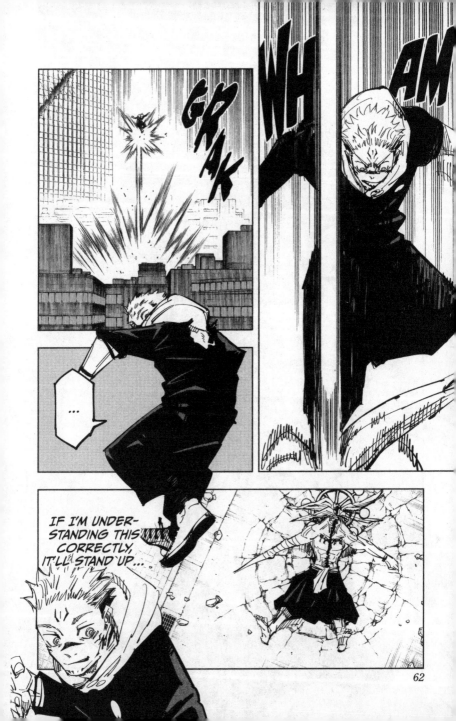

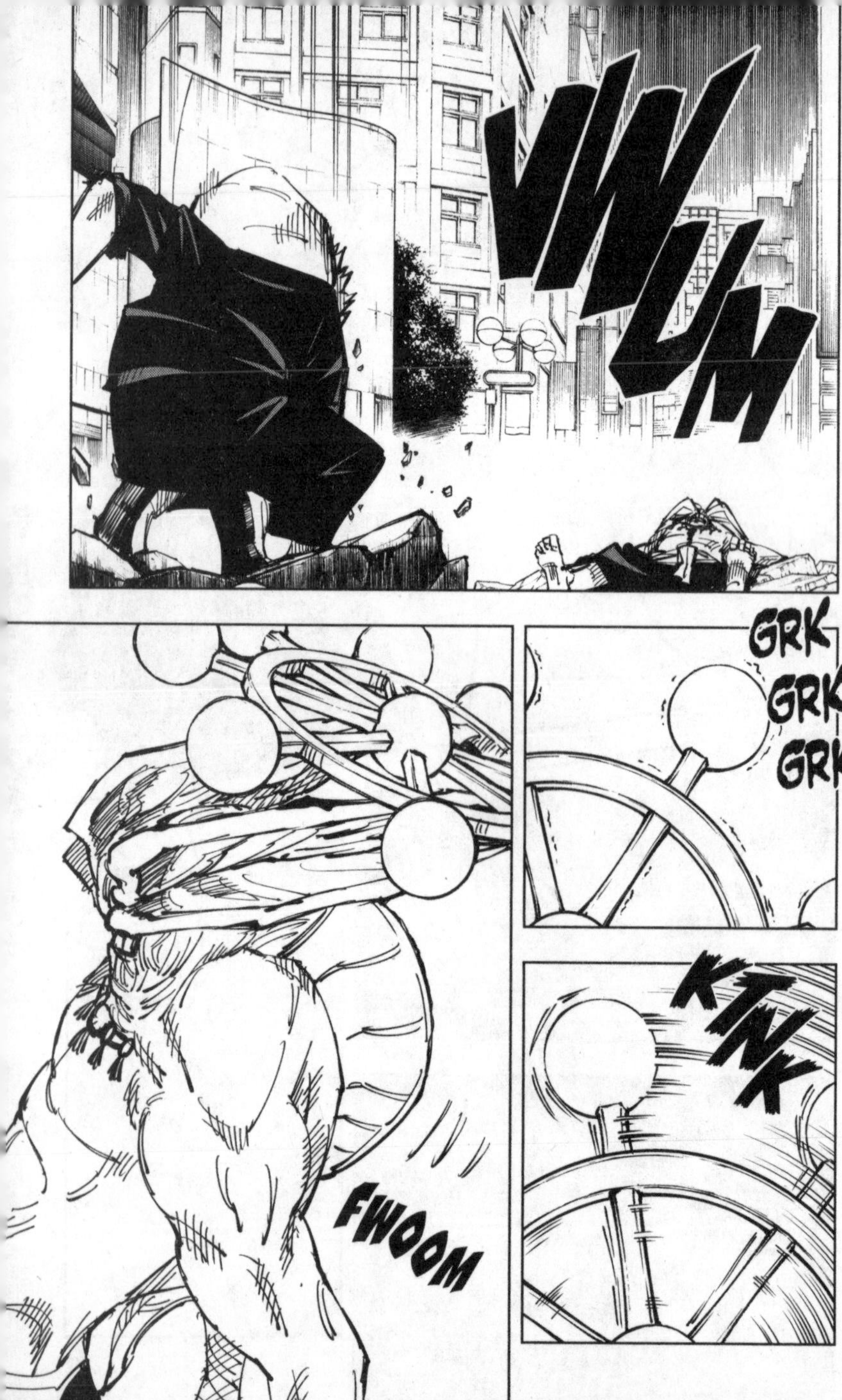
VWUM
GRK
GRK
GRK
KTNK
FWOOM

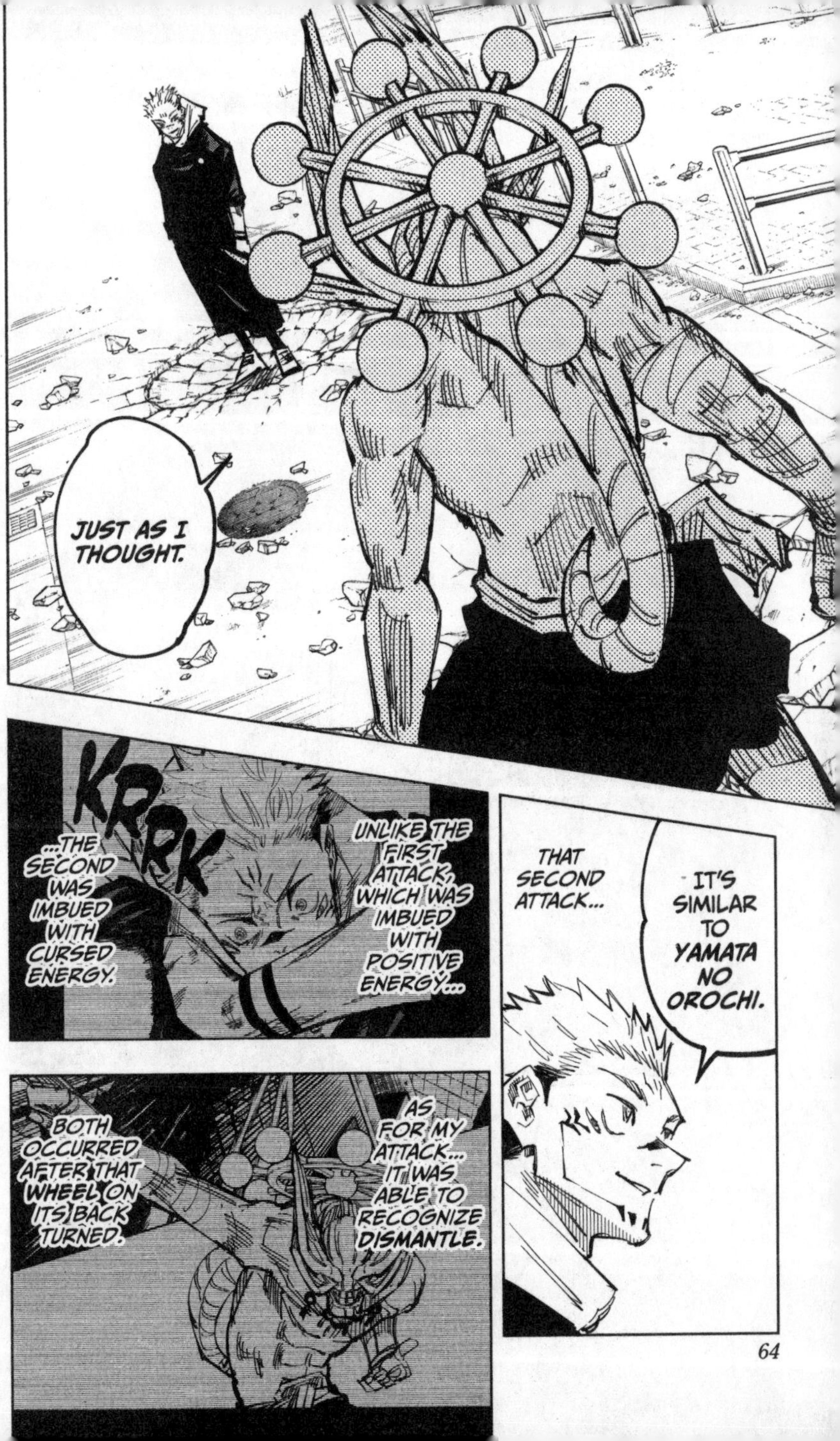
JUST AS I THOUGHT.
IT'S SIMILAR TO YAMATA NO OROCHI.
THAT SECOND ATTACK...
UNLIKE THE FIRST ATTACK, WHICH WAS IMBUED WITH POSITIVE ENERGY...
KRRRK
...THE SECOND WAS IMBUED WITH CURSED ENERGY.
AS FOR MY ATTACK... IT WAS ABLE TO RECOGNIZE DISMANTLE.
BOTH OCCURRED AFTER THAT WHEEL ON ITS BACK TURNED.

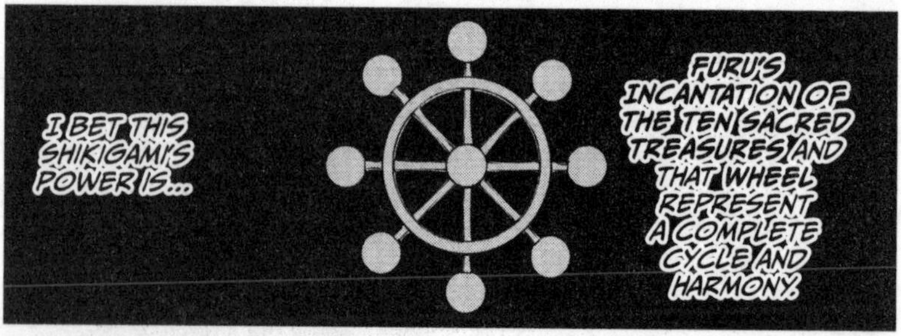
FURU'S INCANTATION OF THE TEN SACRED TREASURES AND THAT WHEEL REPRESENT A COMPLETE CYCLE AND HARMONY.
I BET THIS SHIKIGAMI'S POWER IS...
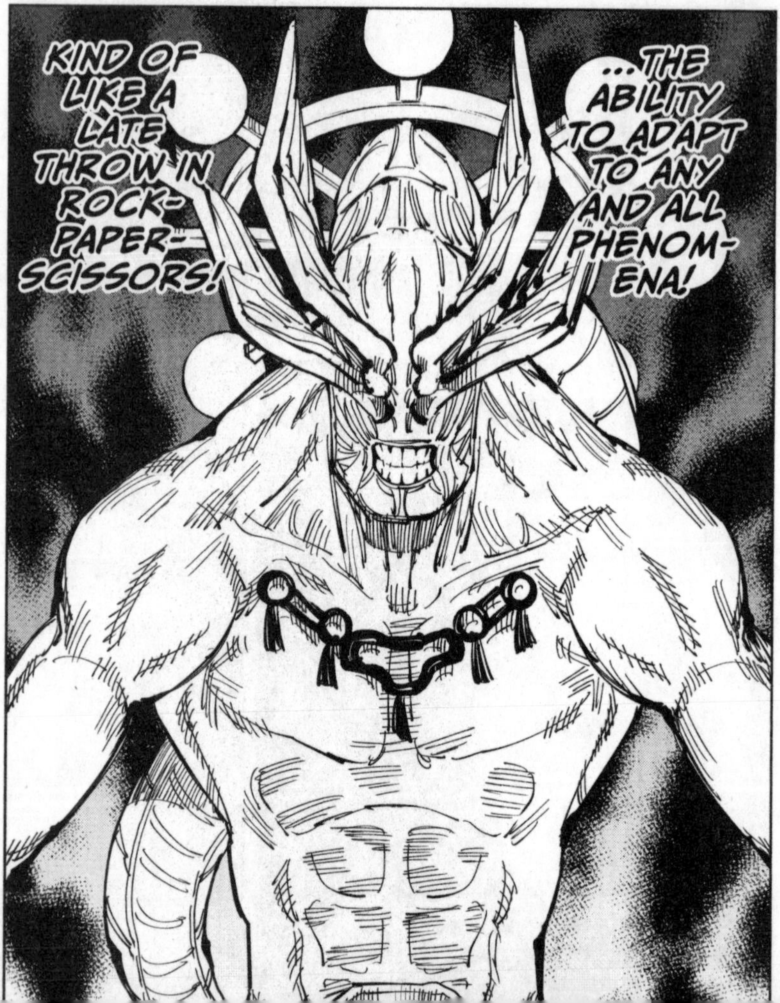
...THE ABILITY TO ADAPT TO ANY AND ALL PHENOM-ENA!
KIND OF LIKE A LATE THROW IN ROCK-PAPER-SCISSORS!

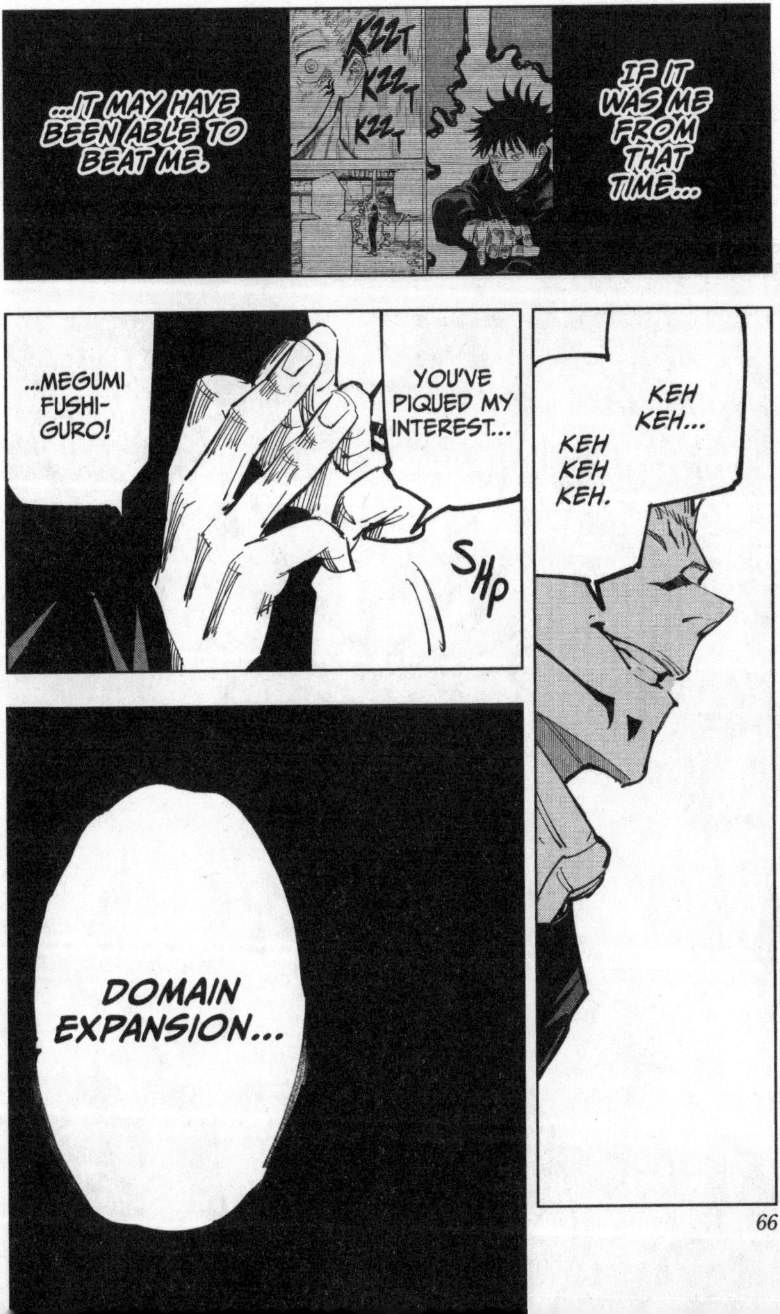
IF IT WAS ME FROM THAT TIME...
KZZT
KZZT
KZZT
...IT MAY HAVE BEEN ABLE TO BEAT ME.
KEH KEH...
KEH KEH KEH.
YOU'VE PIQUED MY INTEREST...
...MEGUMI FUSHI-GURO!
SHP
DOMAIN EXPANSION...

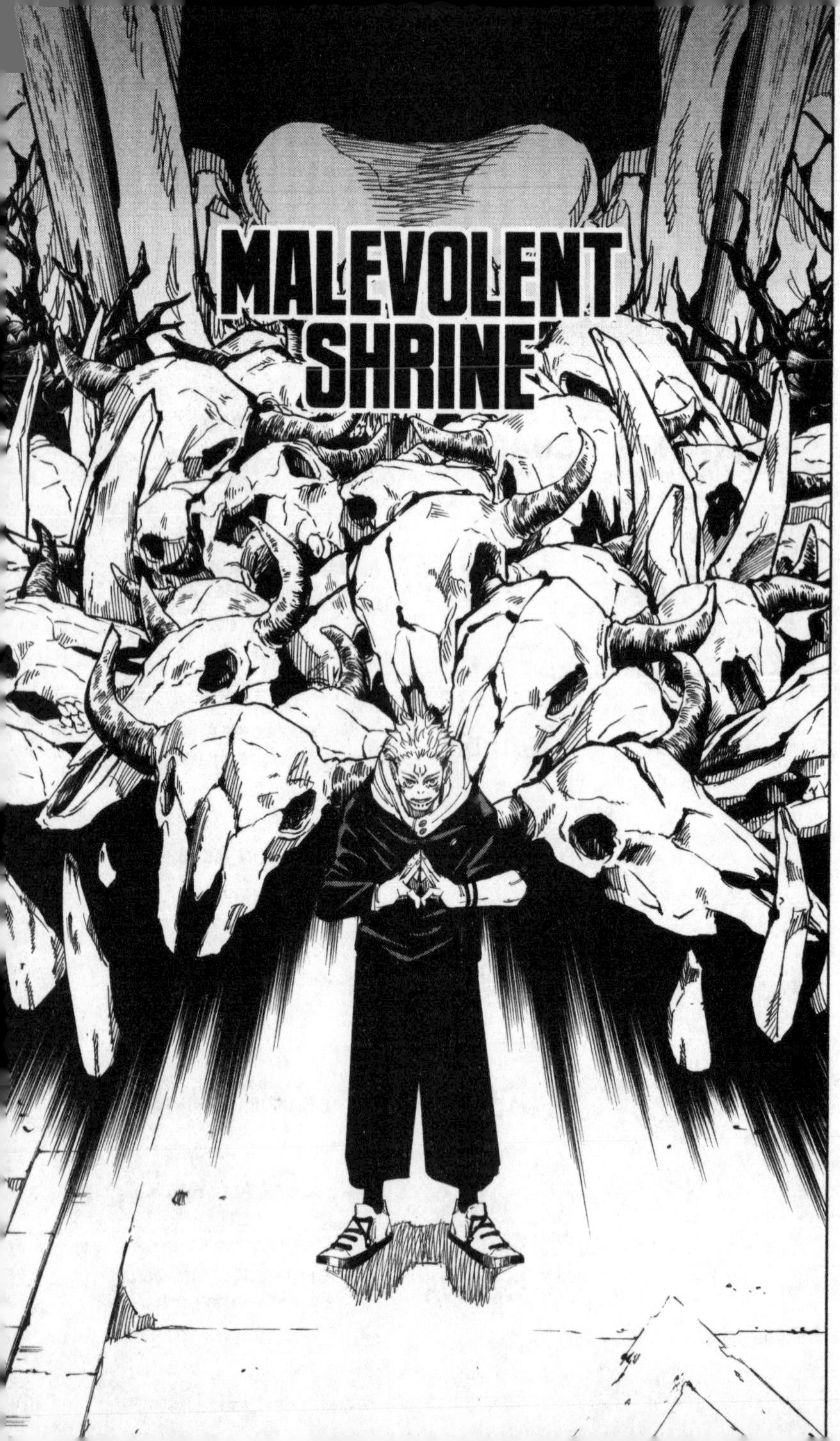
MALEVOLENT SHRINE

THE 2020 VALENTINES RANKINGS THAT I SERIOUSLY ALMOST FORGOT

RANKINGS (VALENTINES RECEIVED)	CHARACTER	AKUTAMI'S COMMENT
10 (4)	INO	MAYBE THE INCIDENT WAS STARTING ABOUT THAT TIME?
11 (3)	IEIRI	MACROSS F IN A SET WITH GOJO.
	IJICHI	COME ON, TETSUO!
	KAMO	HE LOST TO CHOSO... HA HA!
14 (2)	MEI MEI	AGE INDETERMINATE.
	MIWA	AFTER ALL, SHE'S CUTE!
	OZAWA	EVEN THOUGH SHE JUST BRIEFLY POPPED IN?

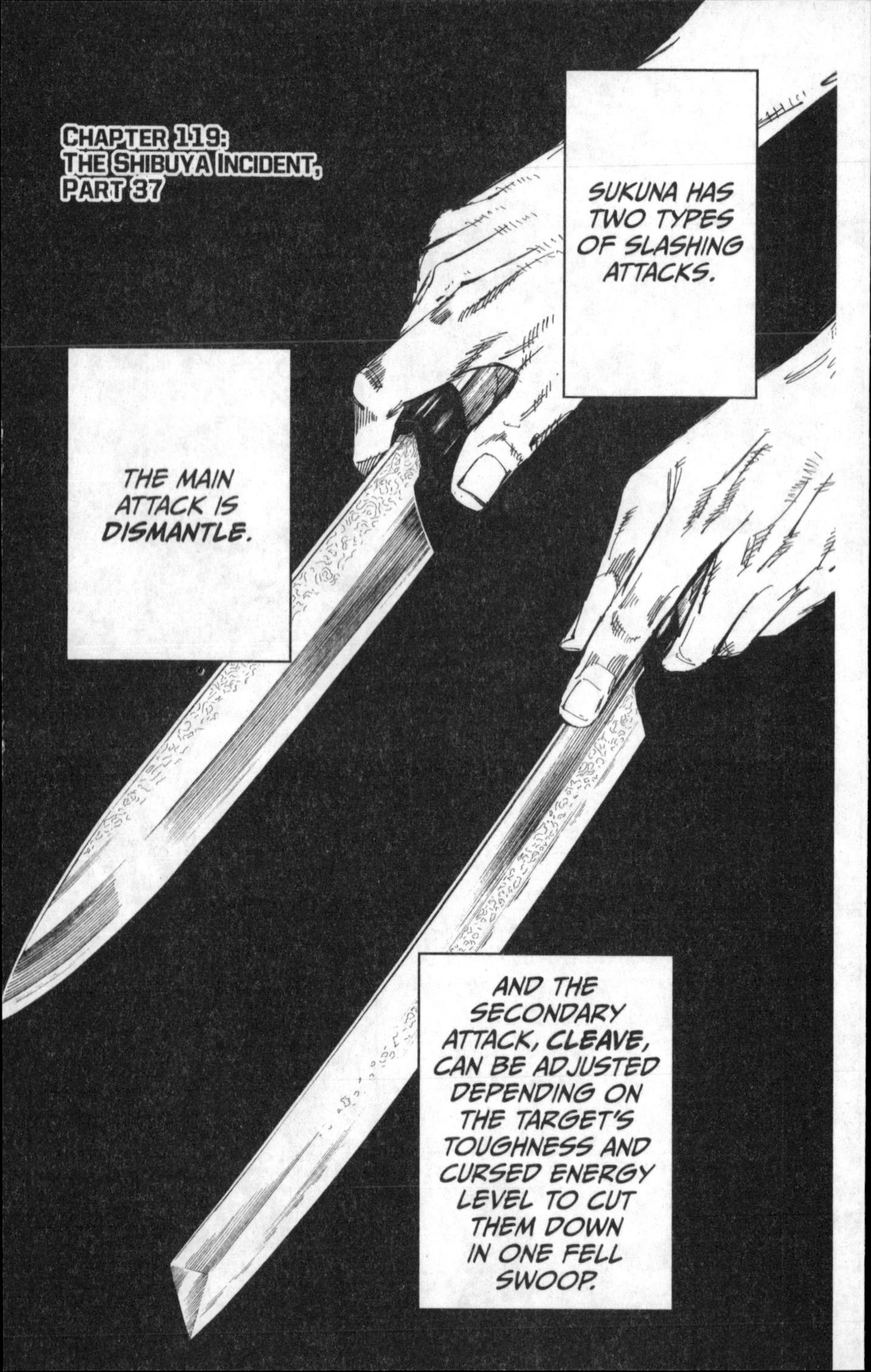
CHAPTER 119:
THE SHIBUYA INCIDENT,
PART 37
SUKUNA HAS TWO TYPES OF SLASHING ATTACKS.
THE MAIN ATTACK IS DISMANTLE.
AND THE SECONDARY ATTACK, CLEAVE, CAN BE ADJUSTED DEPENDING ON THE TARGET'S TOUGHNESS AND CURSED ENERGY LEVEL TO CUT THEM DOWN IN ONE FELL SWOOP.

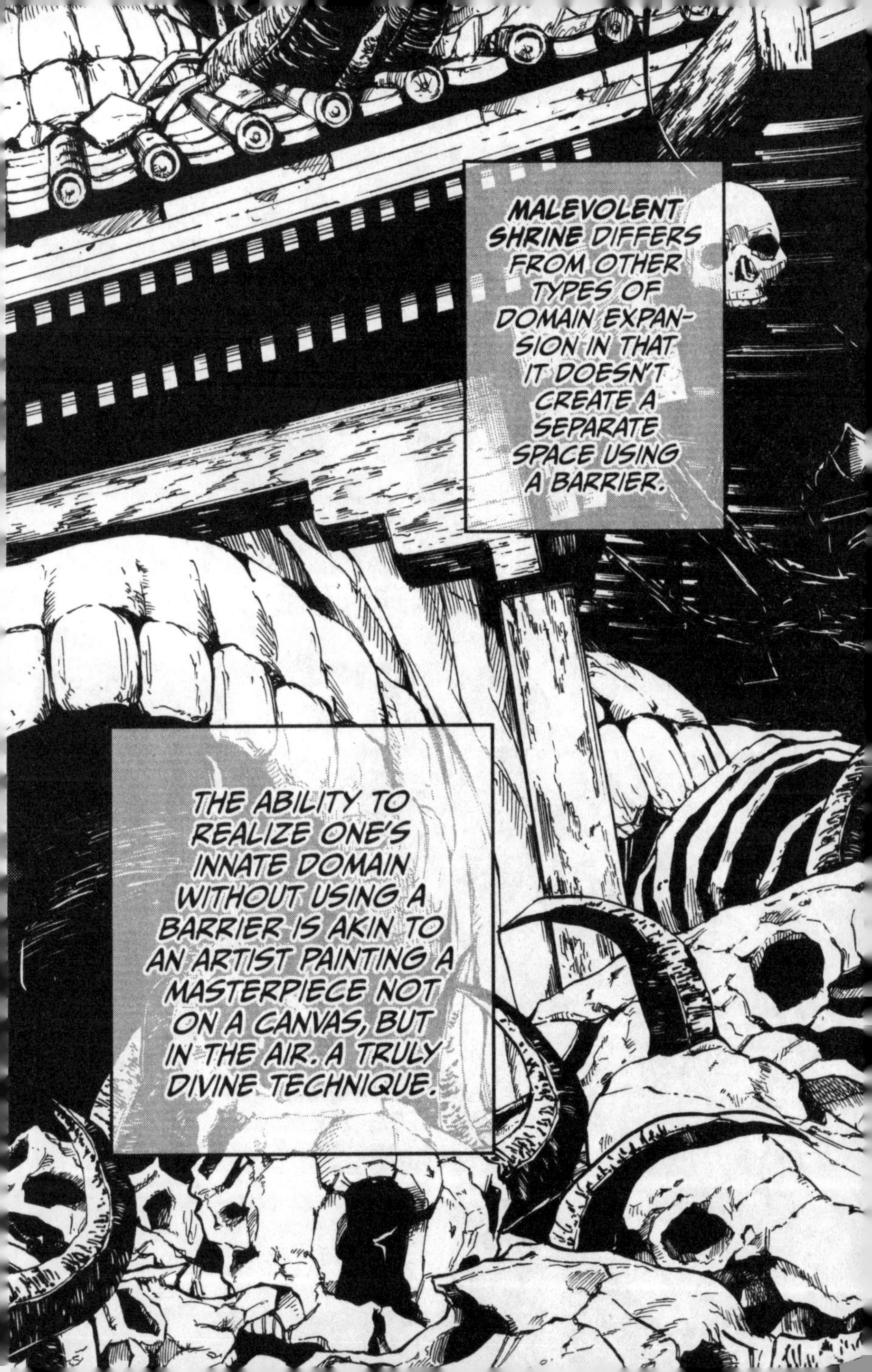
MALEVOLENT SHRINE DIFFERS FROM OTHER TYPES OF DOMAIN EXPANSION IN THAT IT DOESN'T CREATE A SEPARATE SPACE USING A BARRIER.
THE ABILITY TO REALIZE ONE'S INNATE DOMAIN WITHOUT USING A BARRIER IS AKIN TO AN ARTIST PAINTING A MASTERPIECE NOT ON A CANVAS, BUT IN THE AIR. A TRULY DIVINE TECHNIQUE.

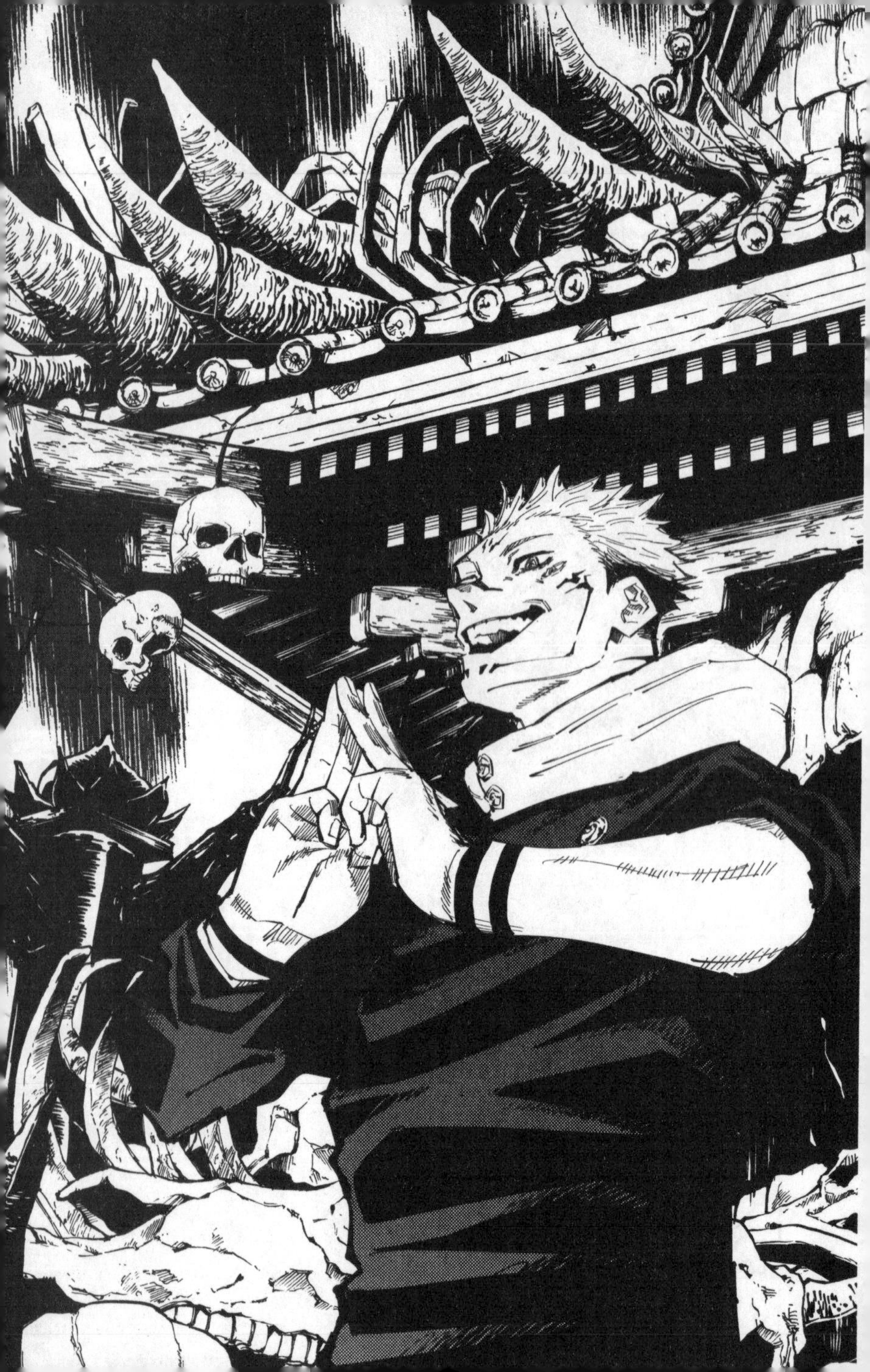

...TO A MAXIMUM RADIUS OF NEARLY 200 METERS.

FURTHERMORE, BY ALLOWING AN ESCAPE ROUTE, A **BINDING VOW** IS FORMED, WHICH VASTLY INCREASES THE GUARANTEED HIT'S EFFECTIVE AREA...

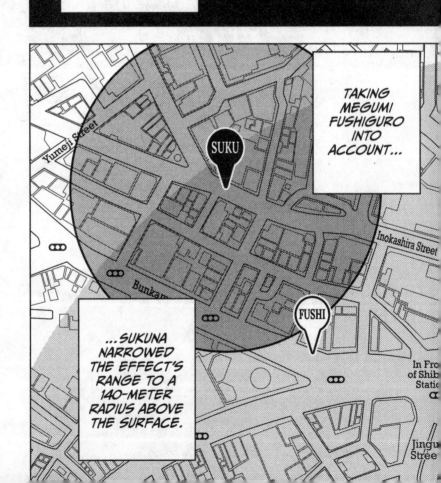

TAKING MEGUMI FUSHIGURO INTO ACCOUNT...

...SUKUNA NARROWED THE EFFECT'S RANGE TO A 140-METER RADIUS ABOVE THE SURFACE.

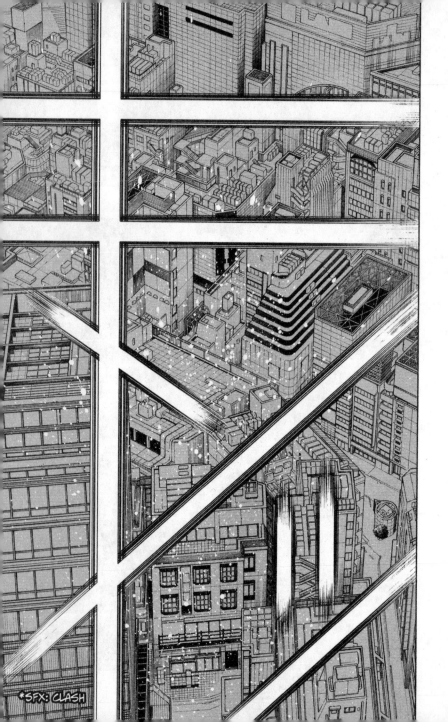

*SFX: CLASH

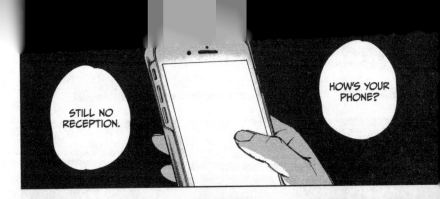

HOW'S YOUR PHONE?

STILL NO RECEPTION.

BUT...I DON'T THINK WE NEED TO WORRY ANYMORE.

HUH?

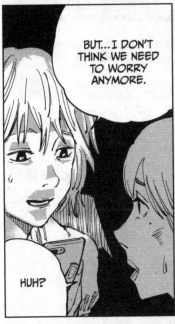

IT'D BE BAD IF BOTH OF OUR PHONES RAN OUT OF POWER.

DON'T USE YOURS TOO MUCH, KEIKO.

ME NEITHER...

TRUE...

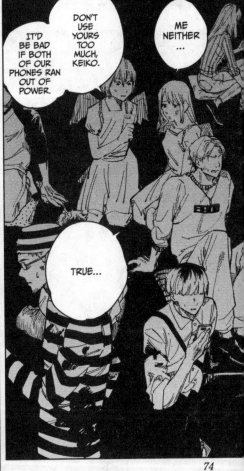

THAT MEGA-PHONE GUY IS HERE.

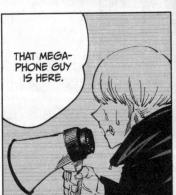

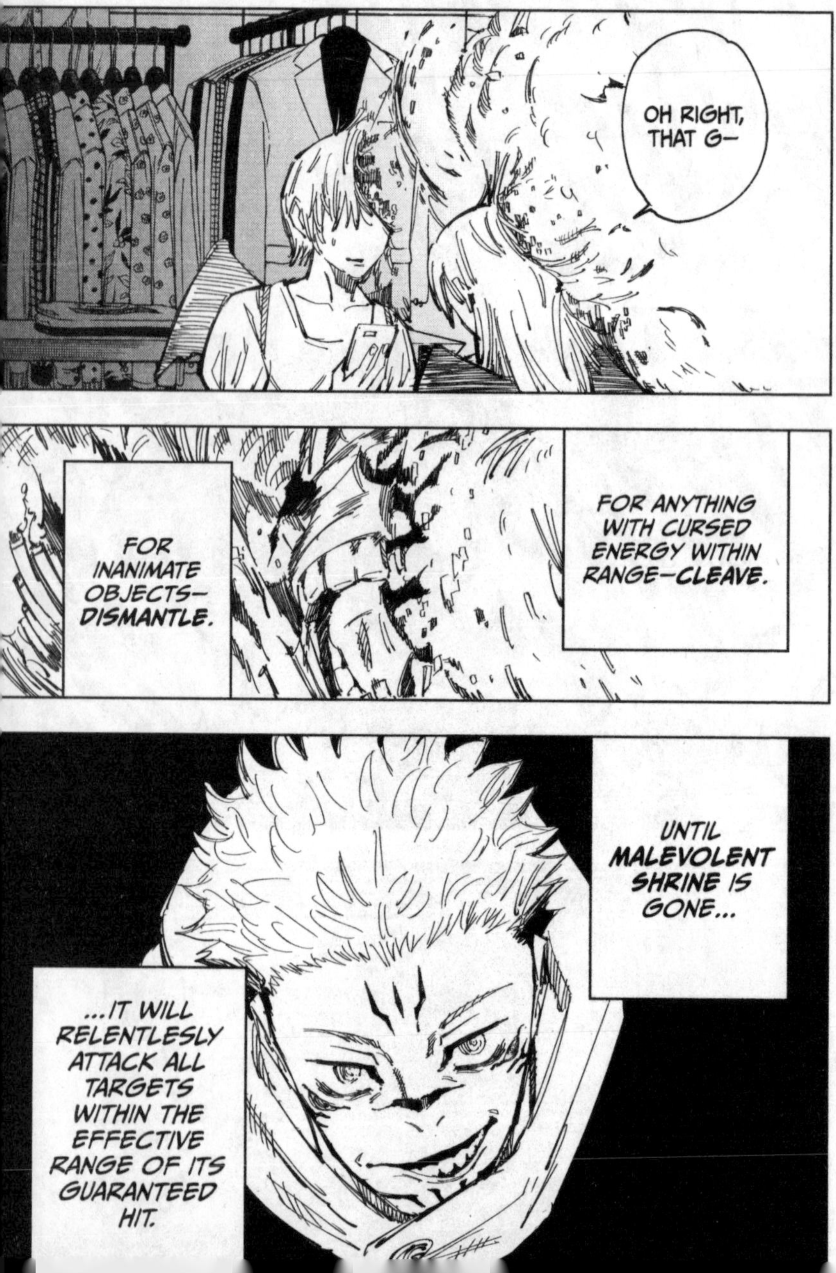
OH RIGHT, THAT G—
FOR ANYTHING WITH CURSED ENERGY WITHIN RANGE—CLEAVE.
FOR INANIMATE OBJECTS— DISMANTLE.
UNTIL MALEVOLENT SHRINE IS GONE...
...IT WILL RELENTLESSLY ATTACK ALL TARGETS WITHIN THE EFFECTIVE RANGE OF ITS GUARANTEED HIT.

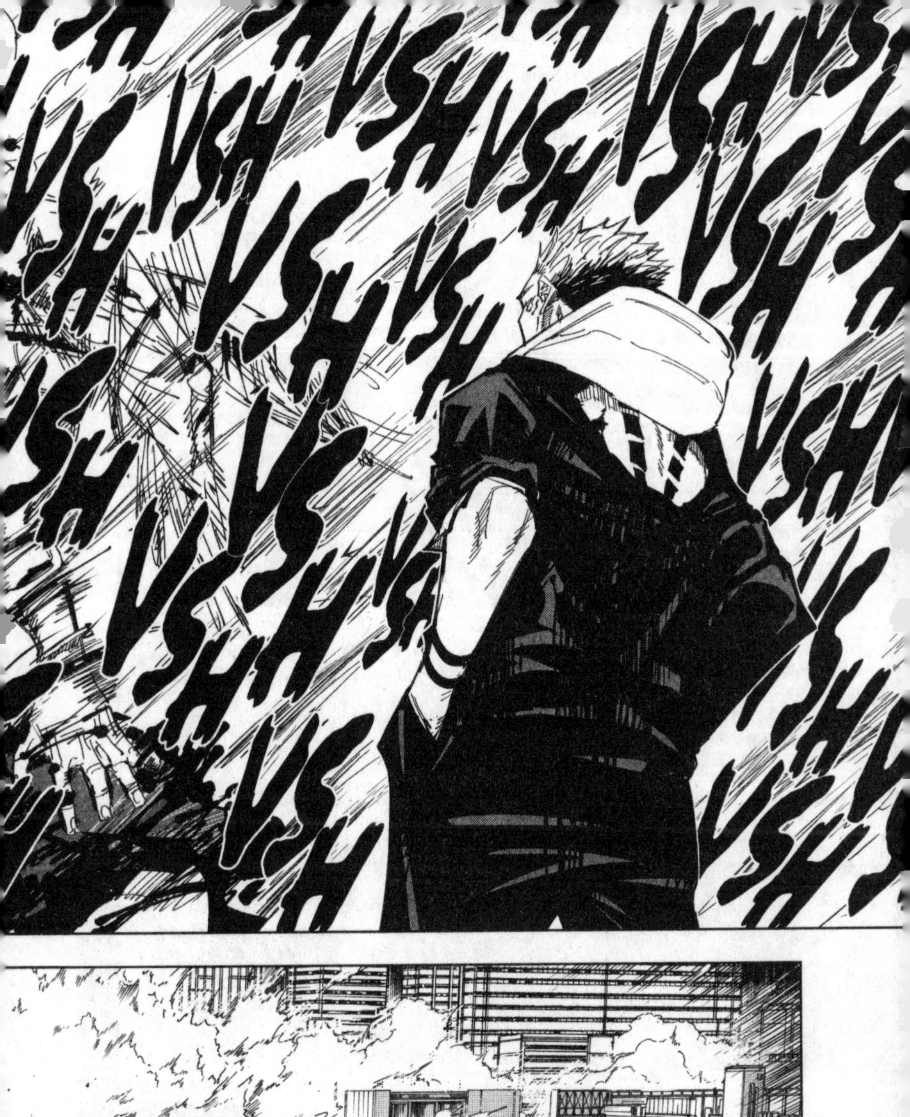
VSH VSH VSH VSH VSH VSH VSH VSH VSH VSH
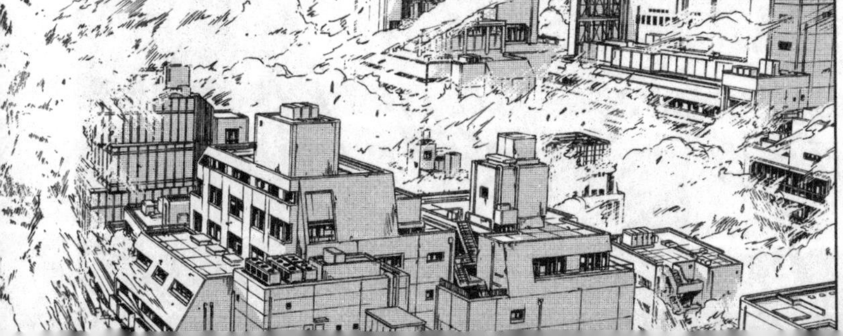

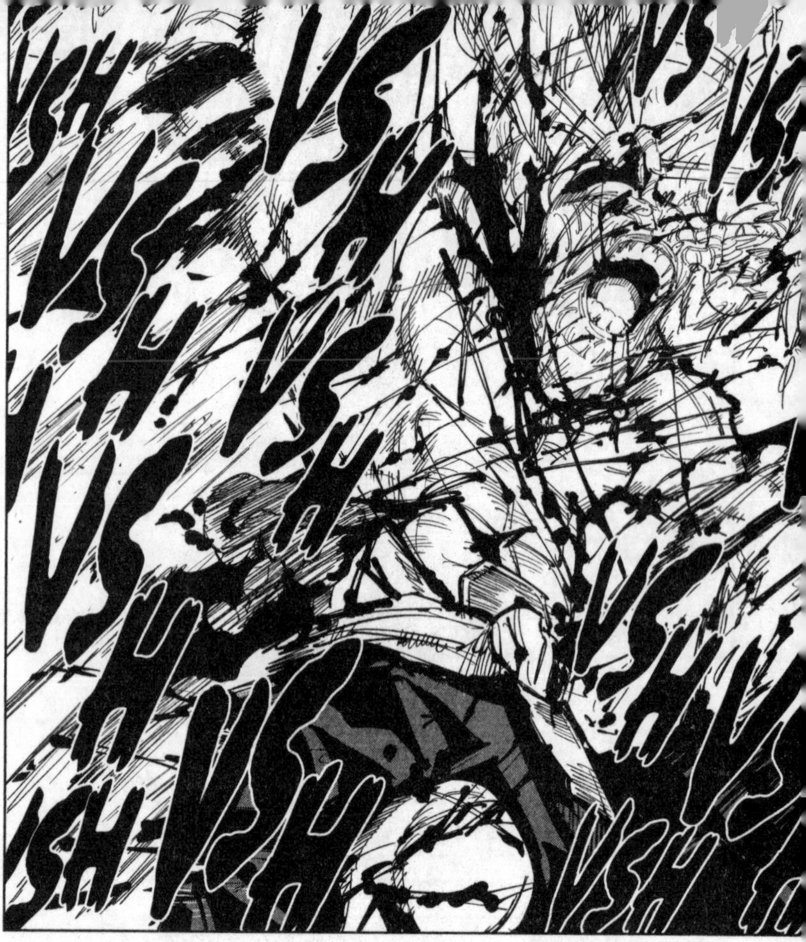
VSH
VSH
VSH
VSH
VSH
VSH
VSH
VSH
VSH
VSH
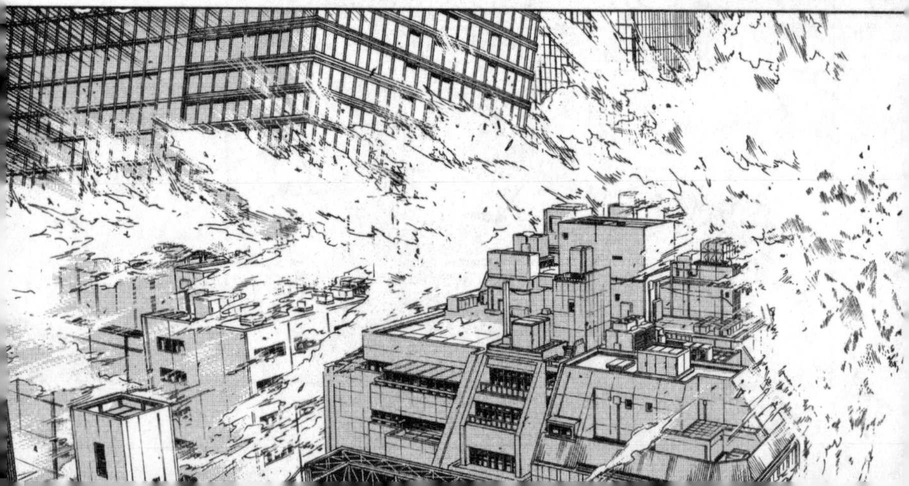

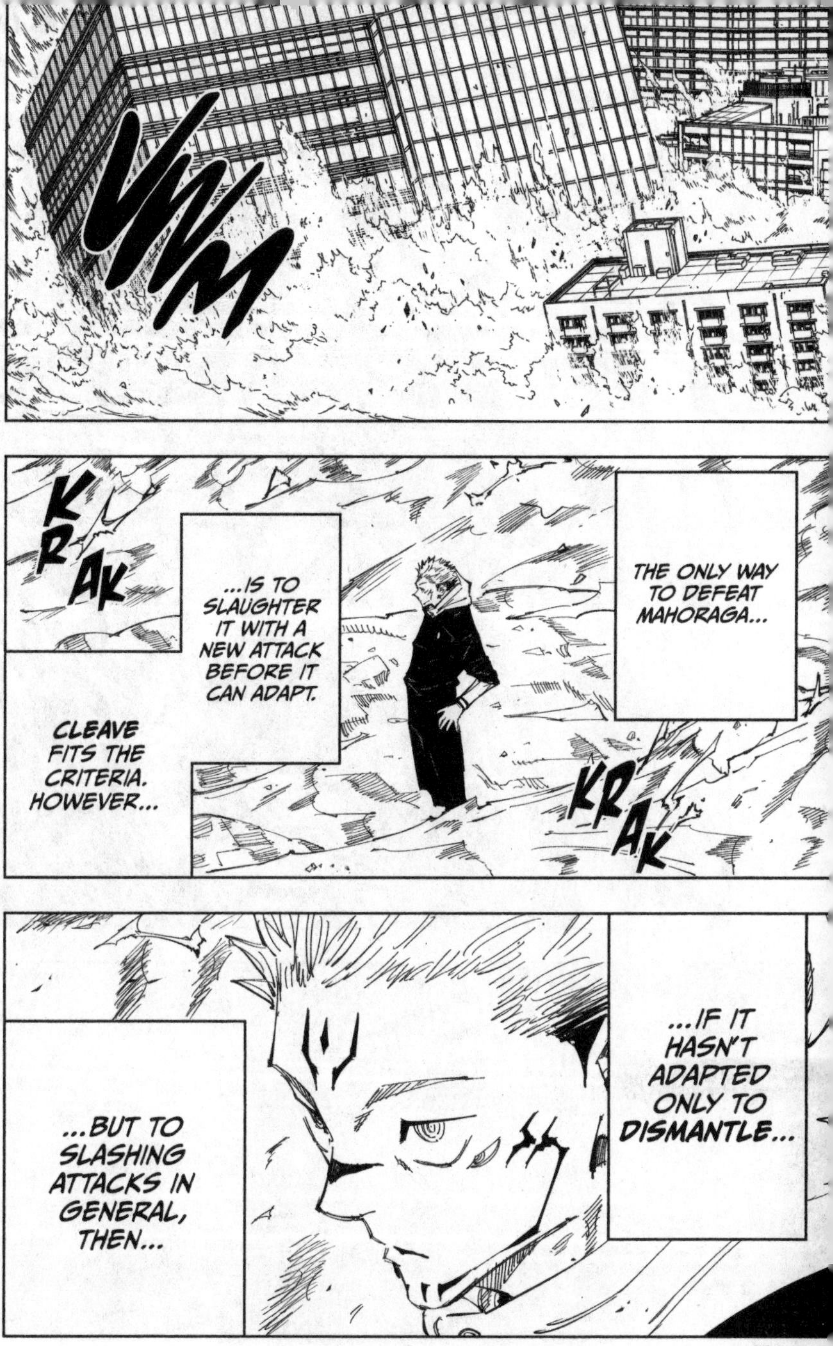
VWM
THE ONLY WAY TO DEFEAT MAHORAGA...
KRAK
...IS TO SLAUGHTER IT WITH A NEW ATTACK BEFORE IT CAN ADAPT.
KRAK
CLEAVE FITS THE CRITERIA. HOWEVER...
...IF IT HASN'T ADAPTED ONLY TO DISMANTLE...
...BUT TO SLASHING ATTACKS IN GENERAL, THEN...

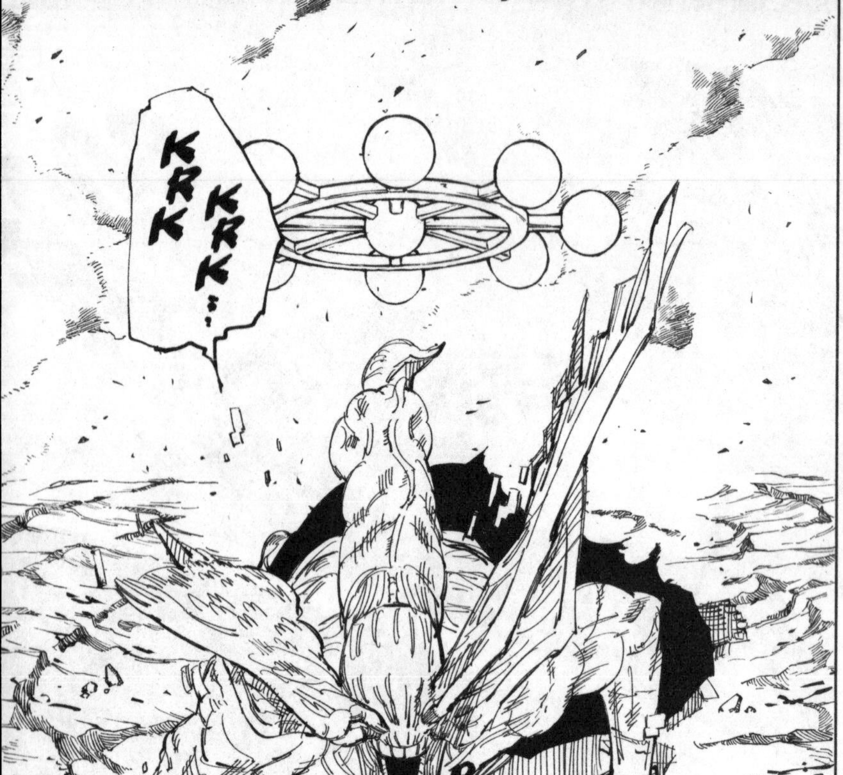
KRK KRK...
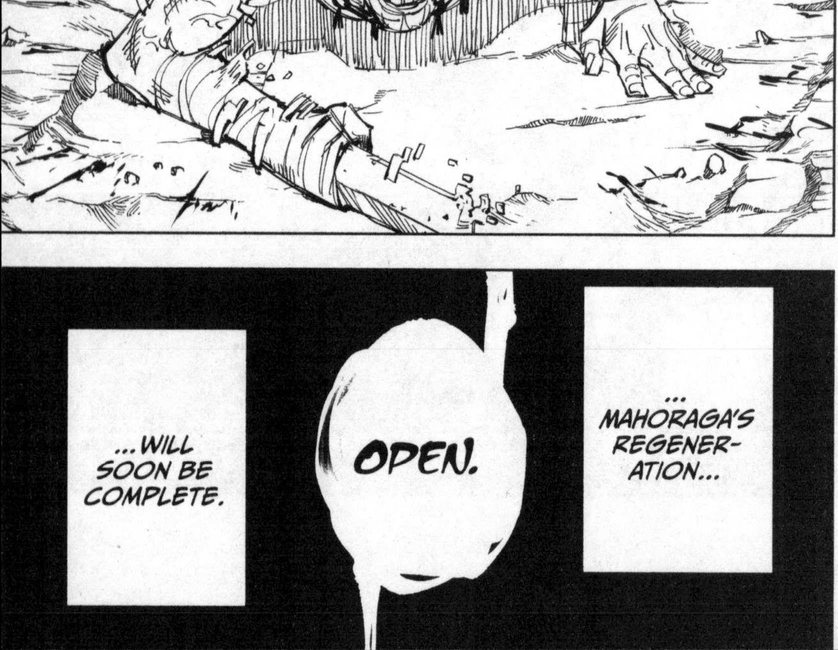
... MAHORAGA'S REGENER-ATION...
OPEN.
...WILL SOON BE COMPLETE.

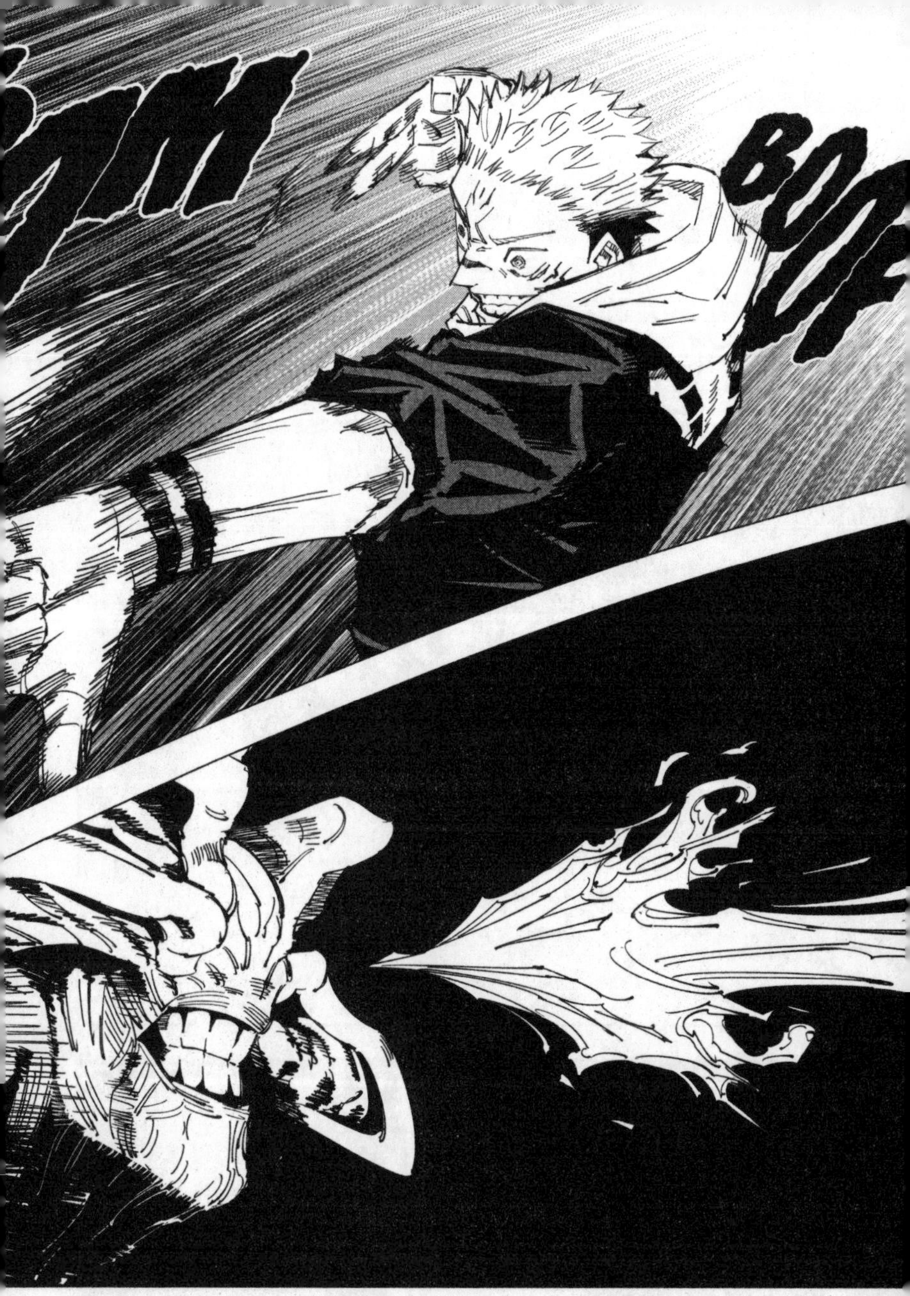

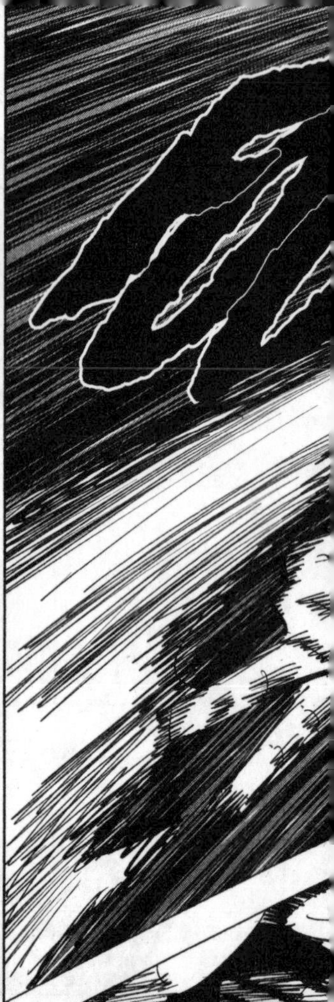
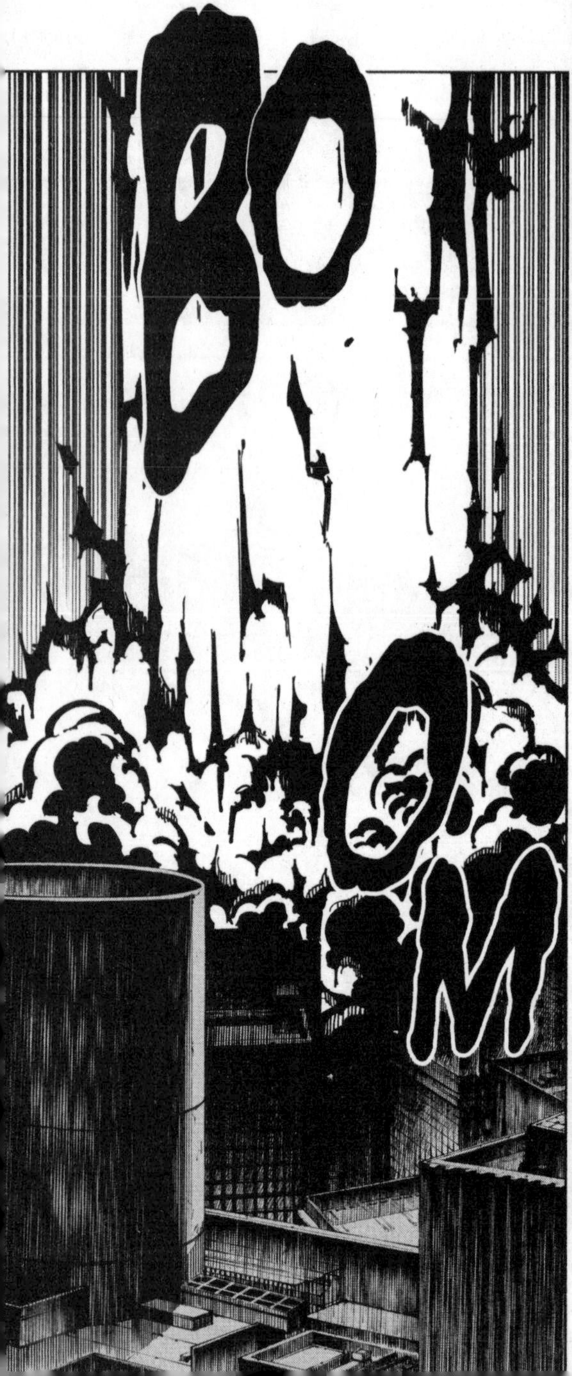
BOOM

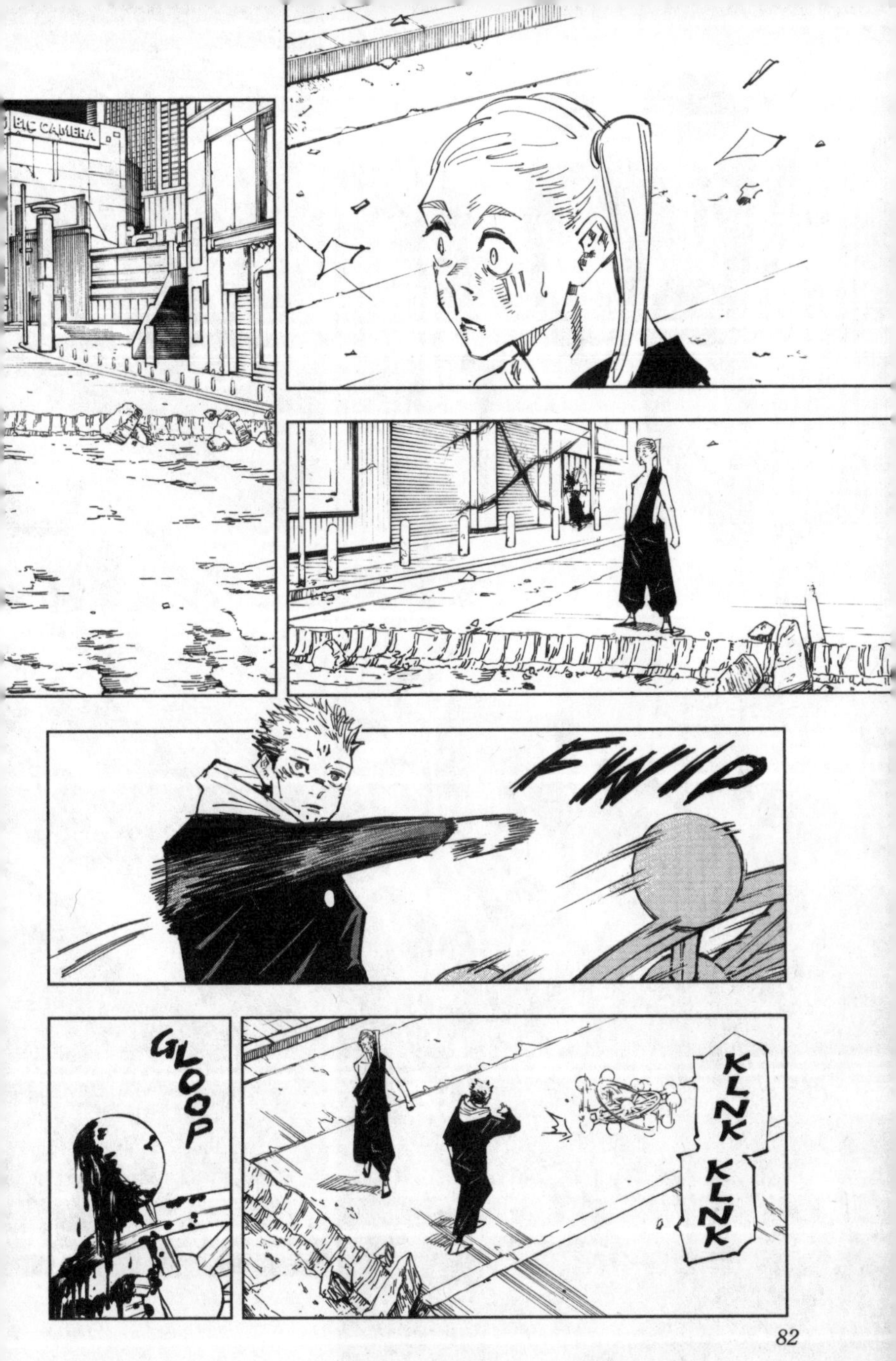
BIC CAMERA
FWIP
KLNK KLNK
GLOOP

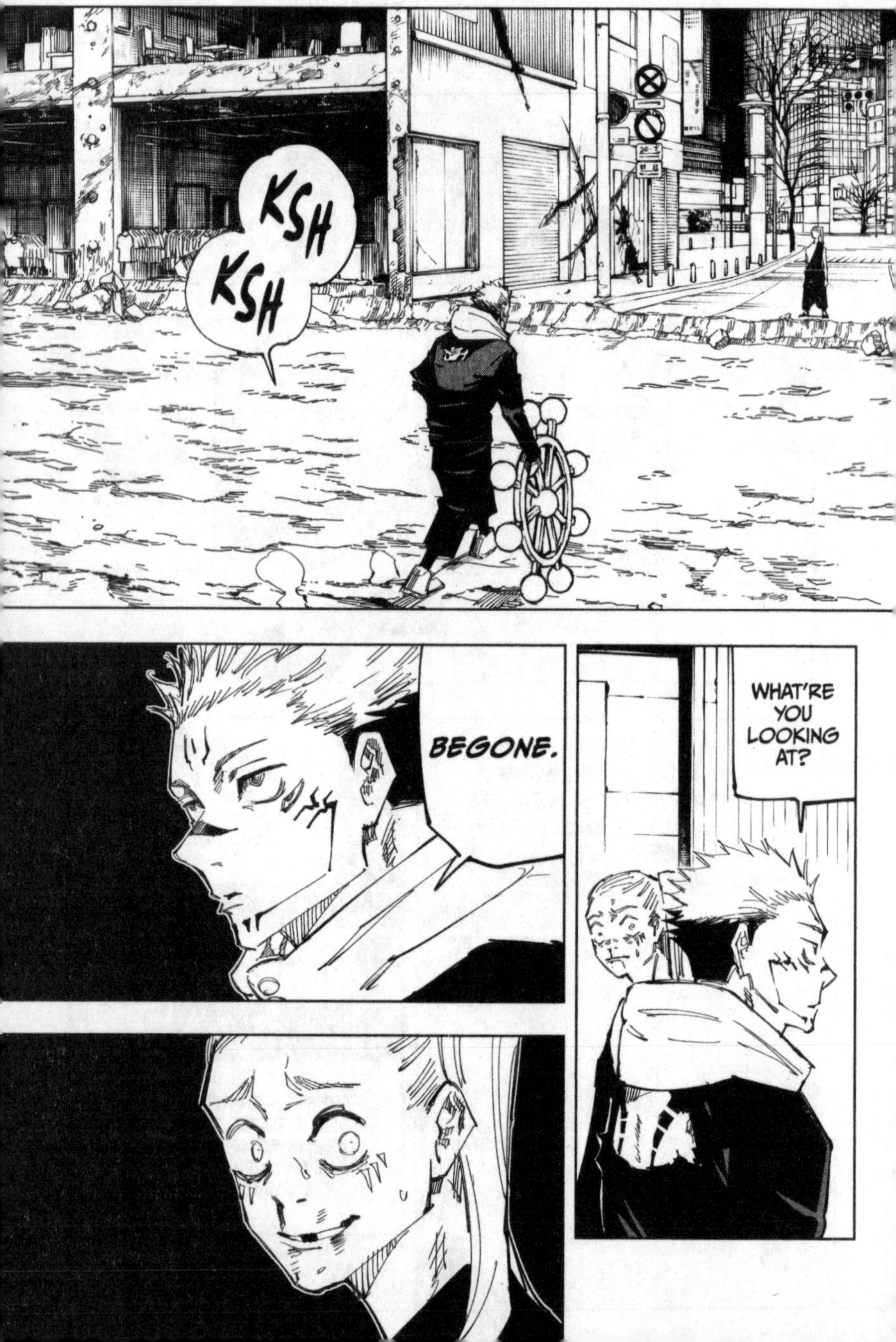
KSH KSH
WHAT'RE YOU LOOKING AT?
BEGONE.

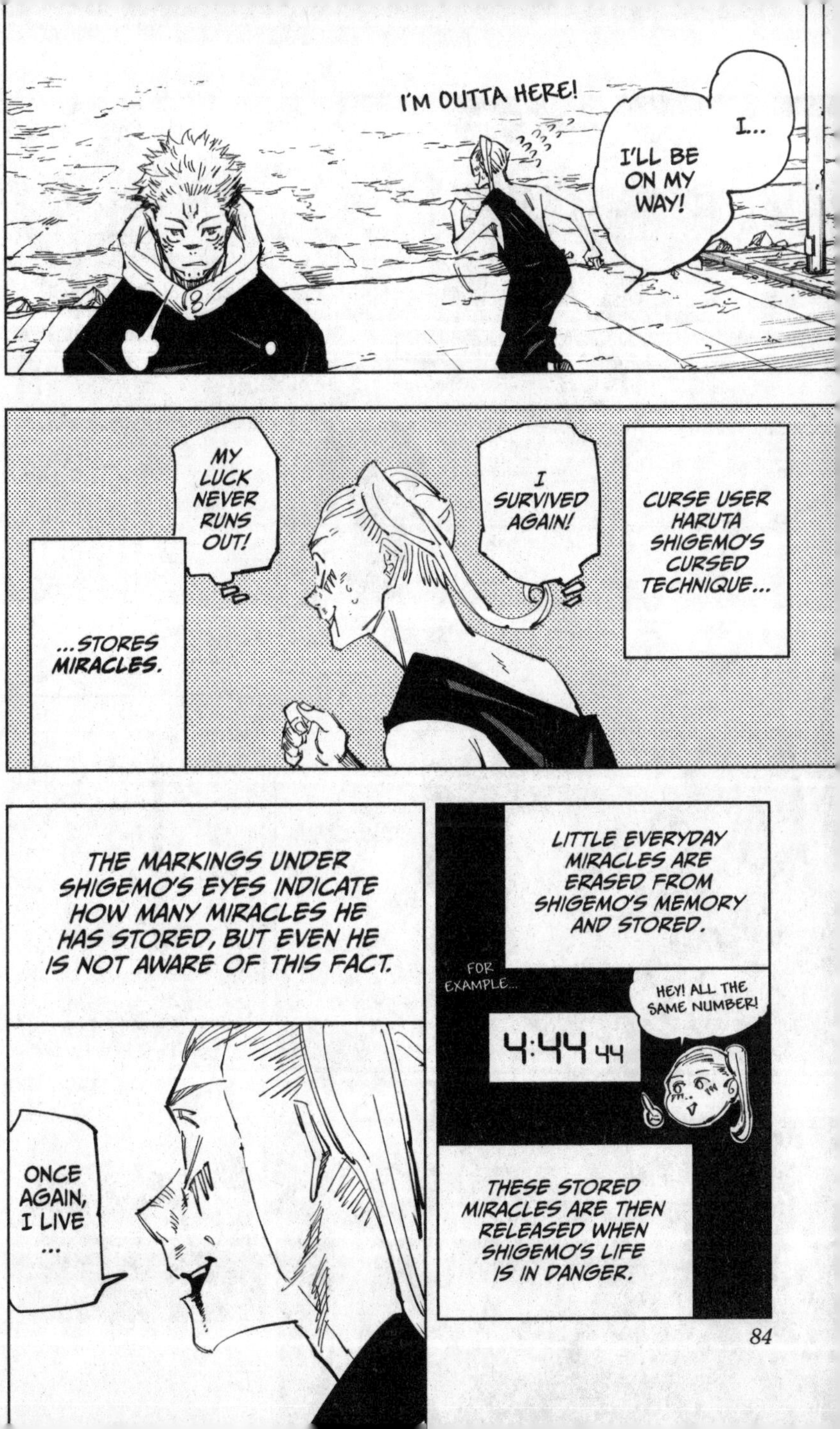
I... I'LL BE ON MY WAY!
I'M OUTTA HERE!
CURSE USER HARUTA SHIGEMO'S CURSED TECHNIQUE...
I SURVIVED AGAIN!
MY LUCK NEVER RUNS OUT!
...STORES MIRACLES.
LITTLE EVERYDAY MIRACLES ARE ERASED FROM SHIGEMO'S MEMORY AND STORED.
FOR EXAMPLE...
HEY! ALL THE SAME NUMBER!
4:44 44
THESE STORED MIRACLES ARE THEN RELEASED WHEN SHIGEMO'S LIFE IS IN DANGER.
THE MARKINGS UNDER SHIGEMO'S EYES INDICATE HOW MANY MIRACLES HE HAS STORED, BUT EVEN HE IS NOT AWARE OF THIS FACT.
ONCE AGAIN, I LIVE ...

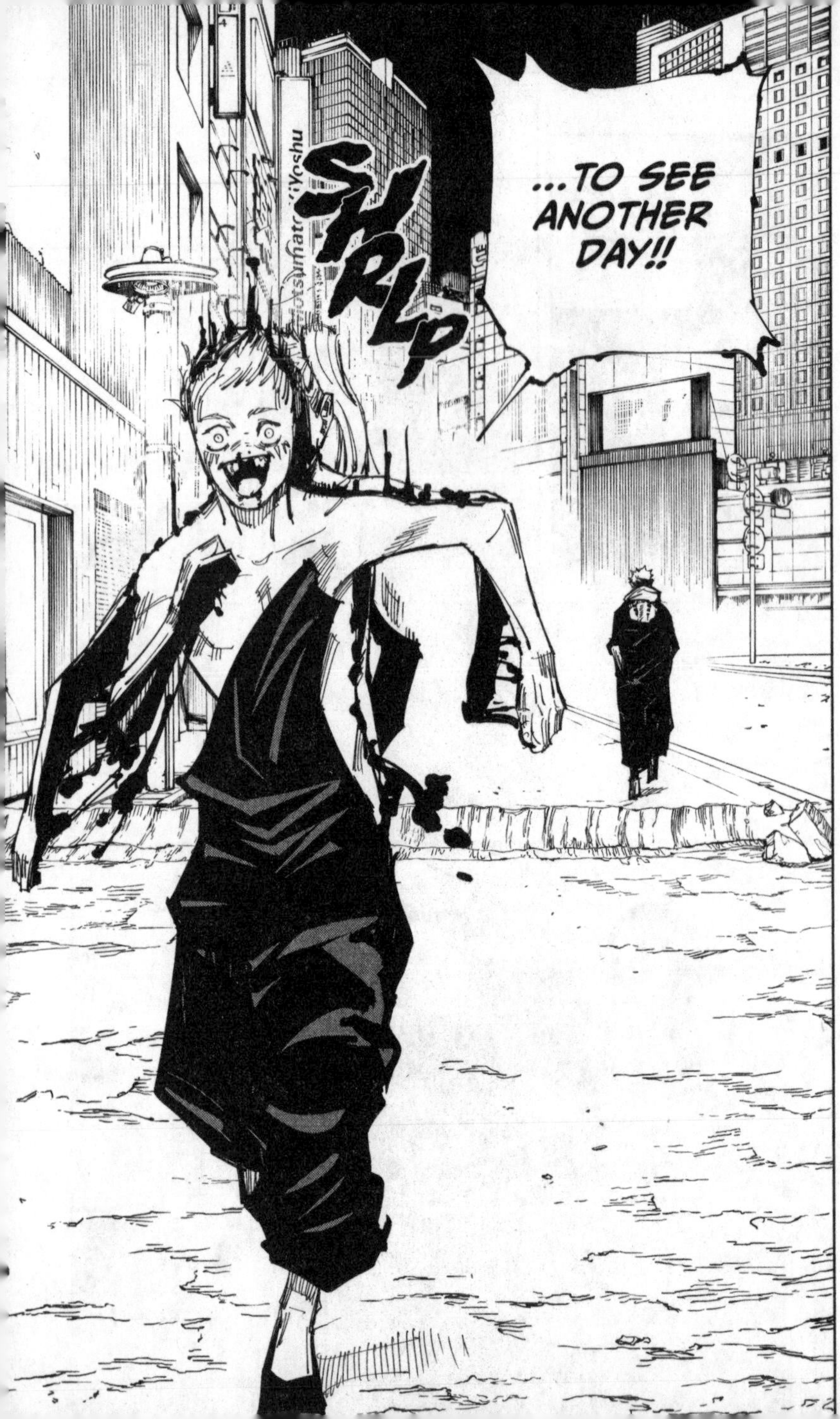
SHRLP
...TO SEE ANOTHER DAY!!

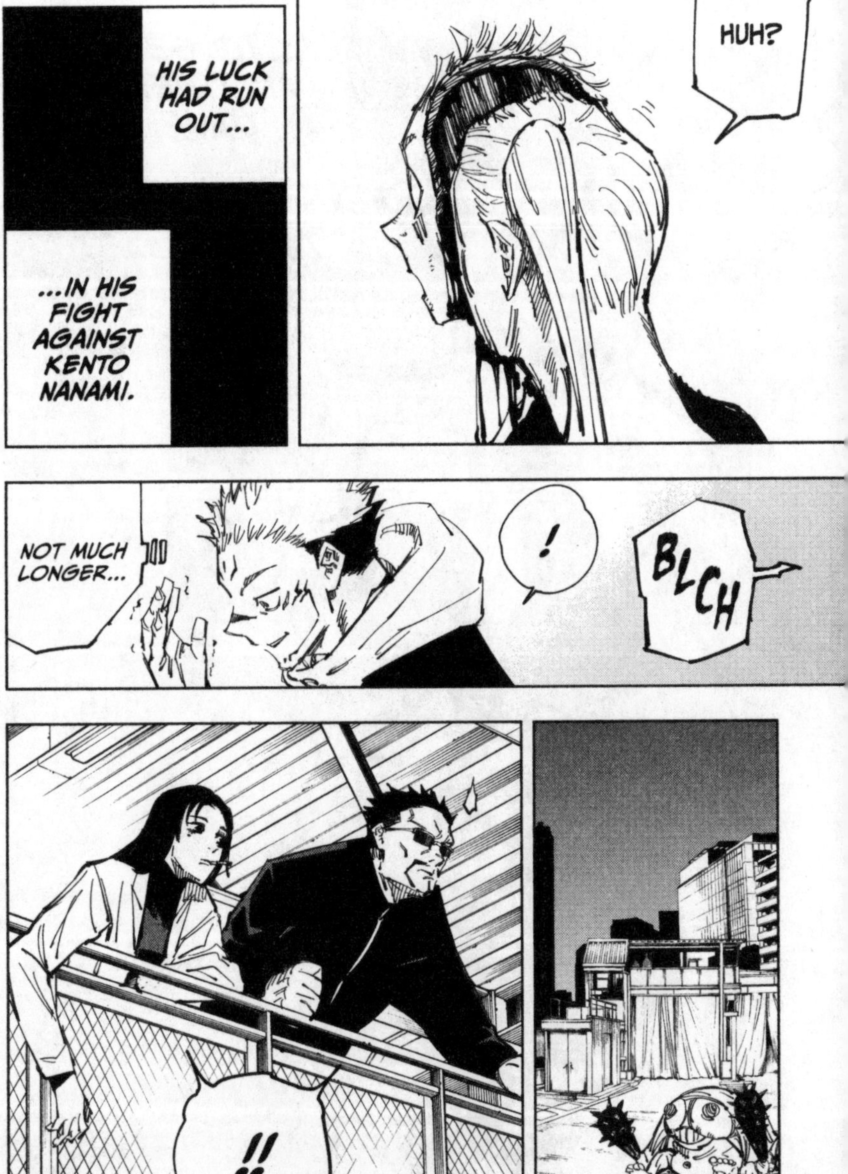
HUH?
HIS LUCK HAD RUN OUT...
...IN HIS FIGHT AGAINST KENTO NANAMI.
BLCH
!
NOT MUCH LONGER...
!!

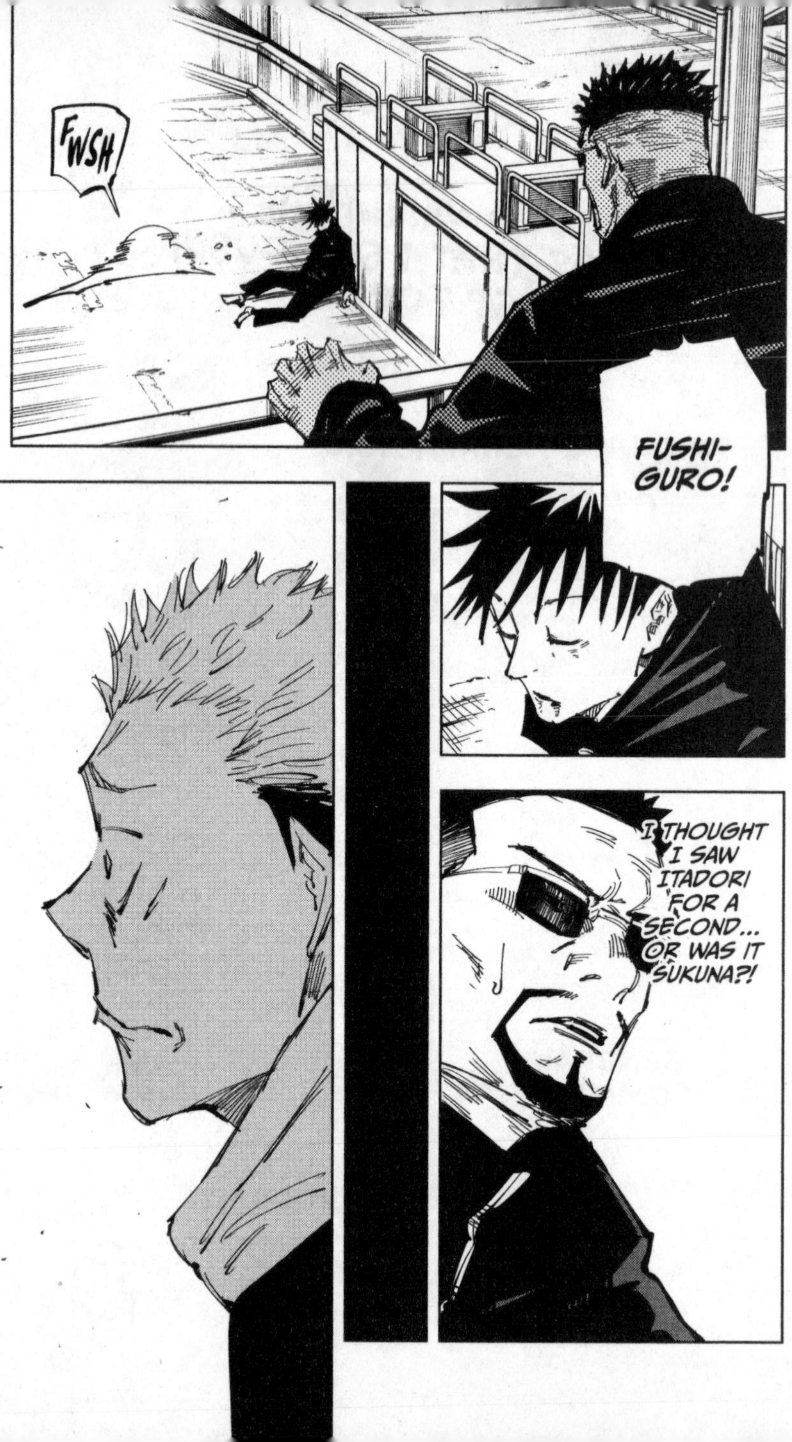
FWSH
FUSHI-GURO!
I THOUGHT I SAW ITADORI FOR A SECOND... OR WAS IT SUKUNA?!

THE 2020 VALENTINES RANKINGS THAT I SERIOUSLY ALMOST FORGOT

RANKINGS (VALENTINES RECEIVED)	CHARACTER	
17 (1)	OKKOTSU	SUKUNA
	PAPAGURO	HAIBARA
	PANDA	JUNPEI
	HANAMI	KAMO (NORITOSHI)

GENERAL COMMENT

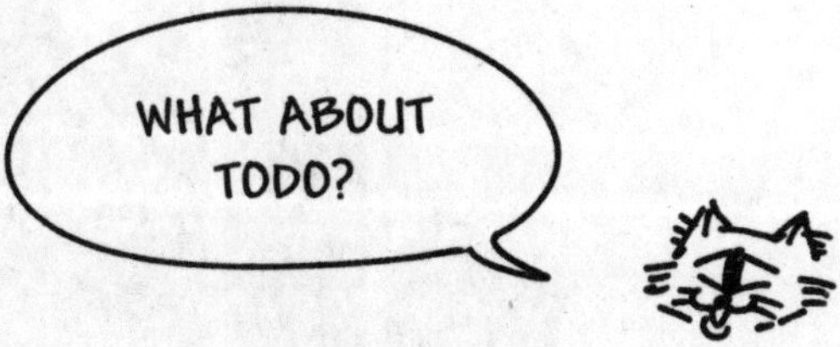
WHAT ABOUT TODO?

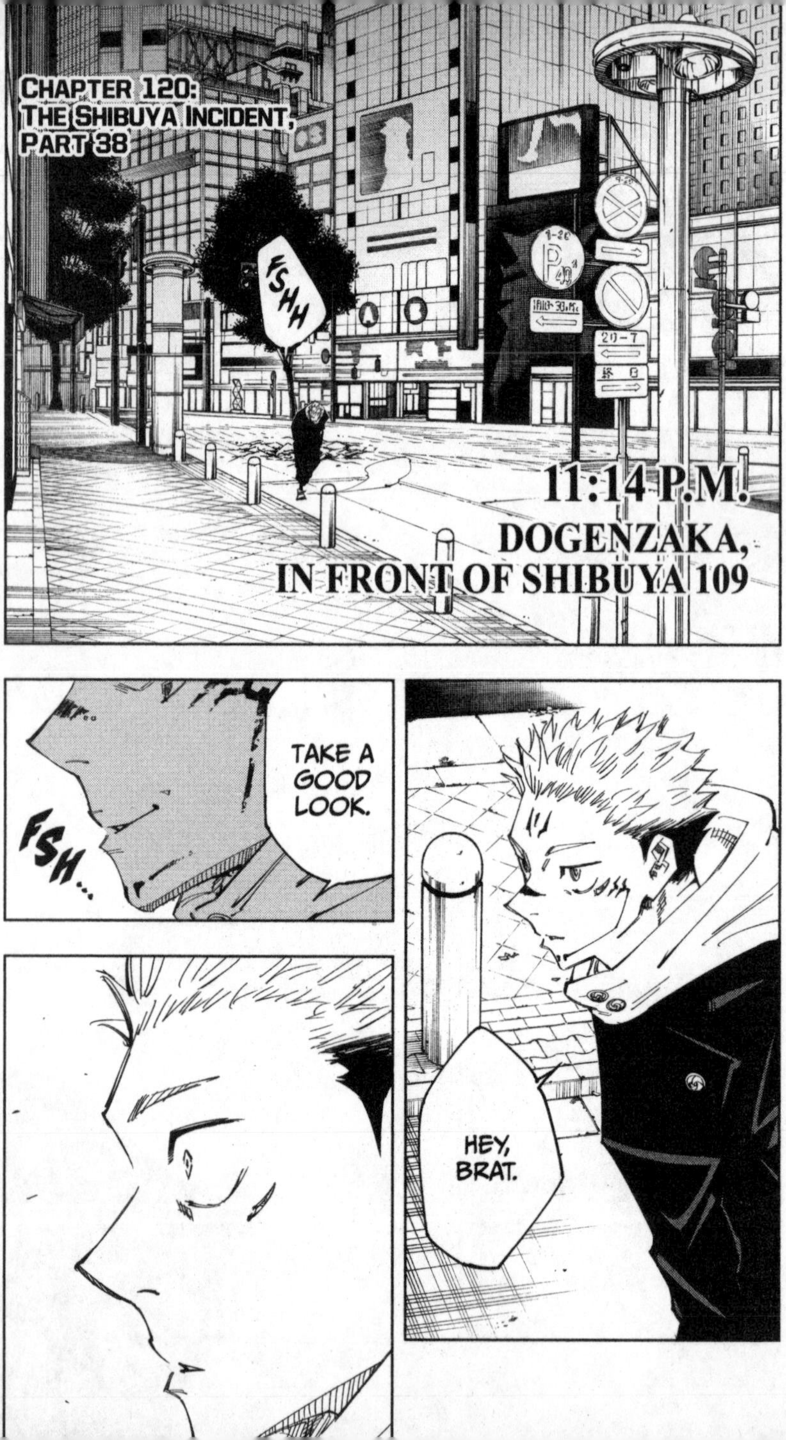
CHAPTER 120: THE SHIBUYA INCIDENT, PART 38
FSHH
11:14 P.M.
DOGENZAKA, IN FRONT OF SHIBUYA 109
HEY, BRAT.
TAKE A GOOD LOOK.
FSH...

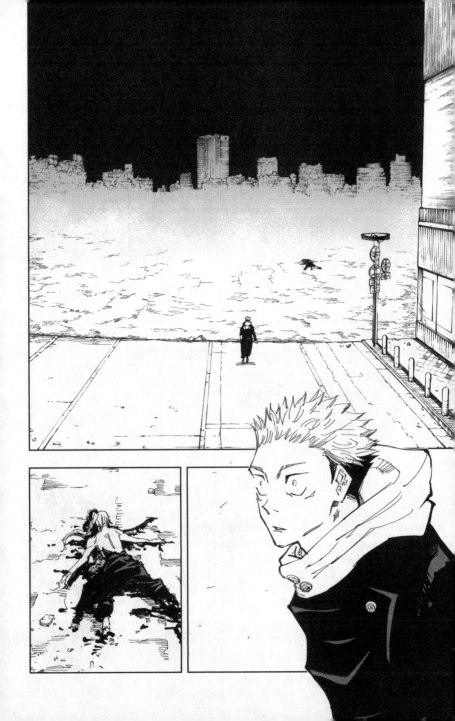

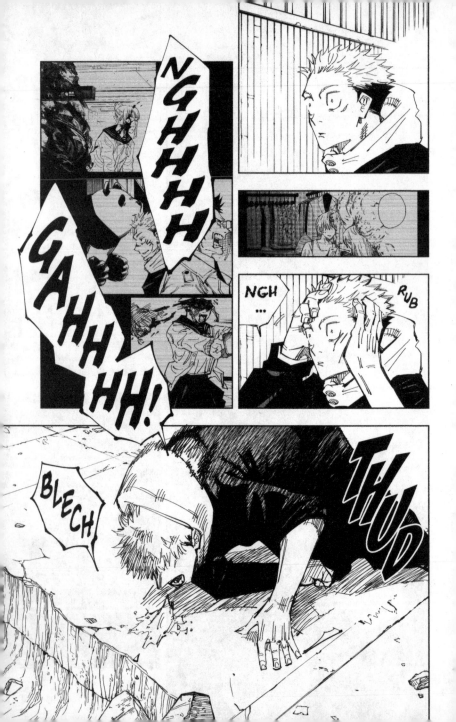

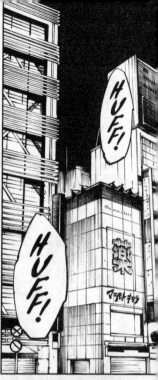

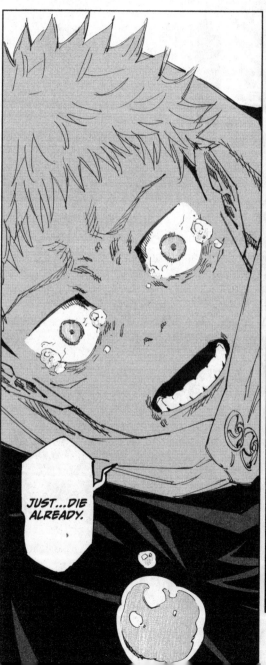

HUFF!

HUFF!

JUST...DIE ALREADY.

"I'M WONDERING WHY THE HECK I HAVE TO BE EXECUTED."

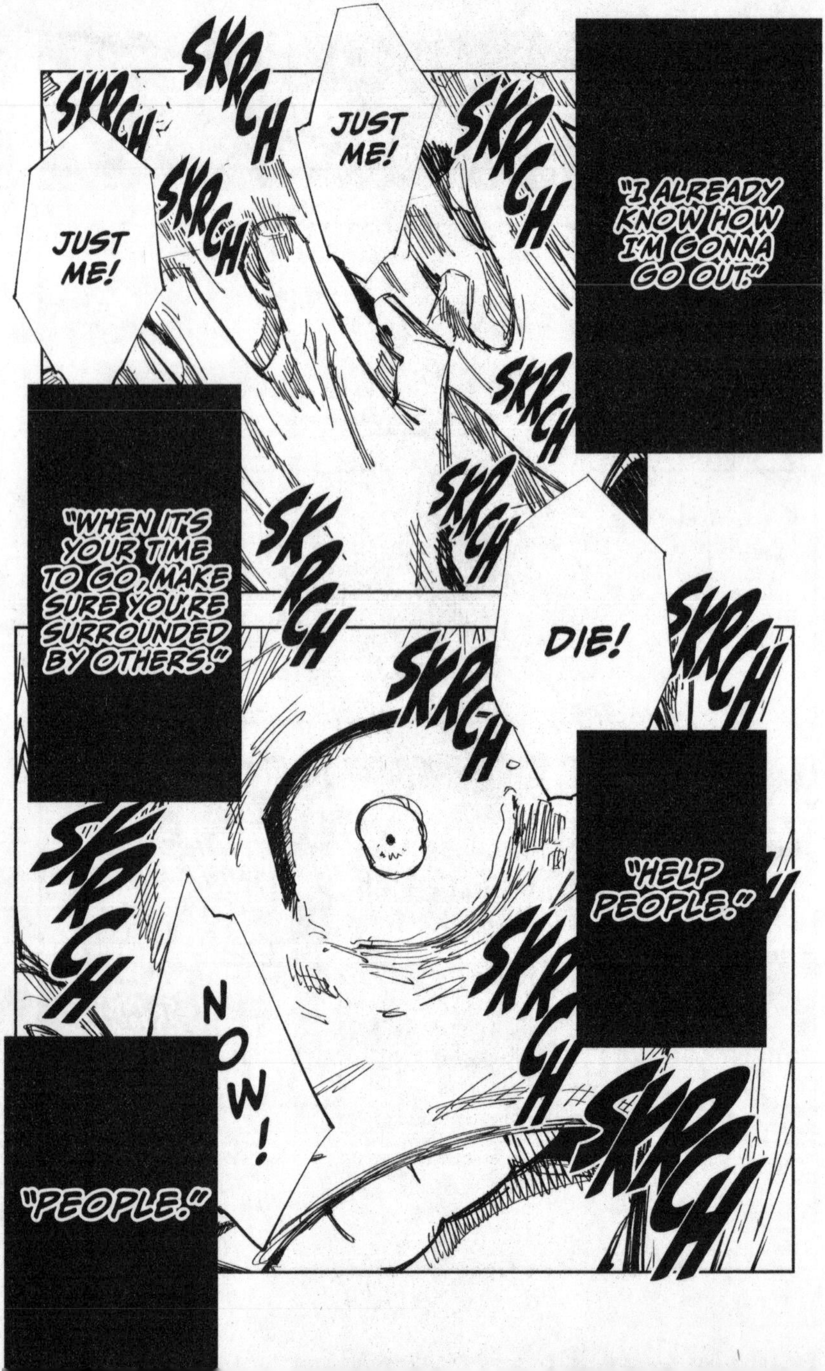
"I ALREADY KNOW HOW I'M GONNA GO OUT."
SKRCH
SKRCH
JUST ME!
SKRCH
SKRCH
JUST ME!
SKRCH
SKRCH
"WHEN IT'S YOUR TIME TO GO, MAKE SURE YOU'RE SURROUNDED BY OTHERS."
SKRCH
DIE!
SKRCH
"HELP PEOPLE."
SKRCH
SKRCH
NOW!
SKRCH
"PEOPLE."

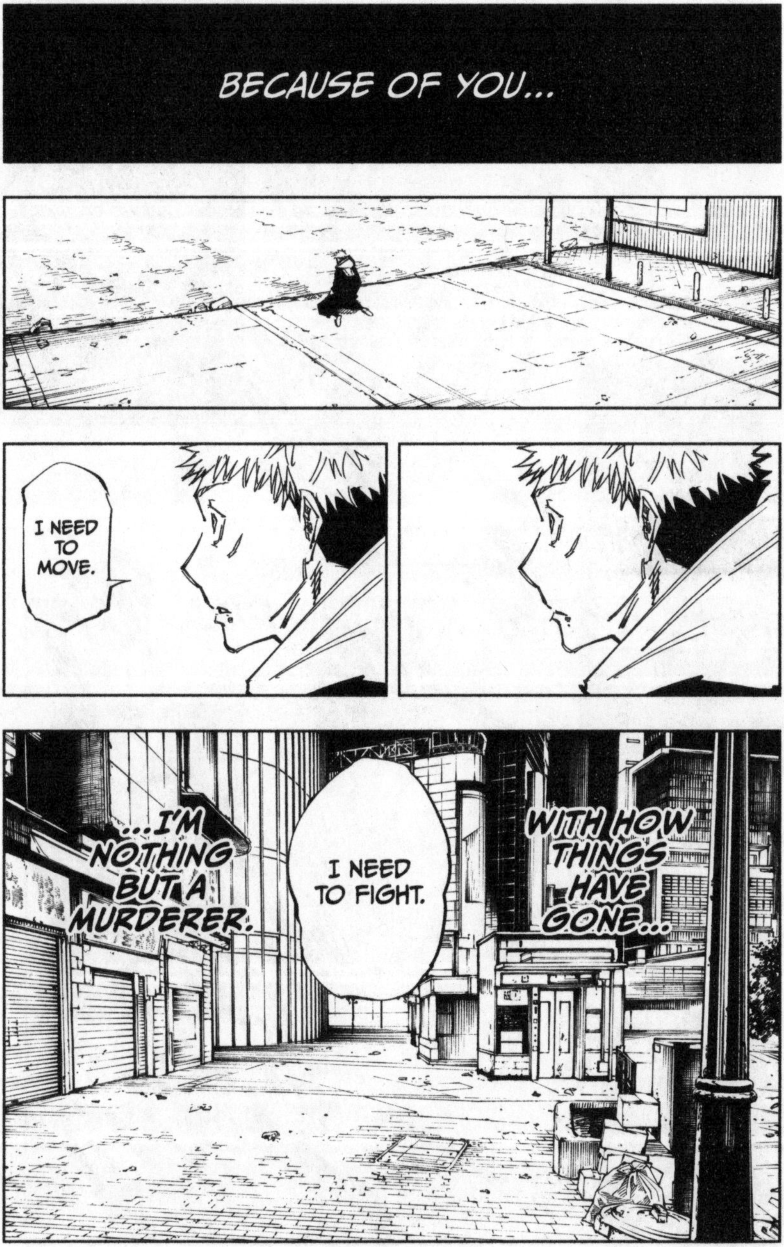
BECAUSE OF YOU...
I NEED TO MOVE.
WITH HOW THINGS HAVE GONE...
I NEED TO FIGHT.
...I'M NOTHING BUT A MURDERER.

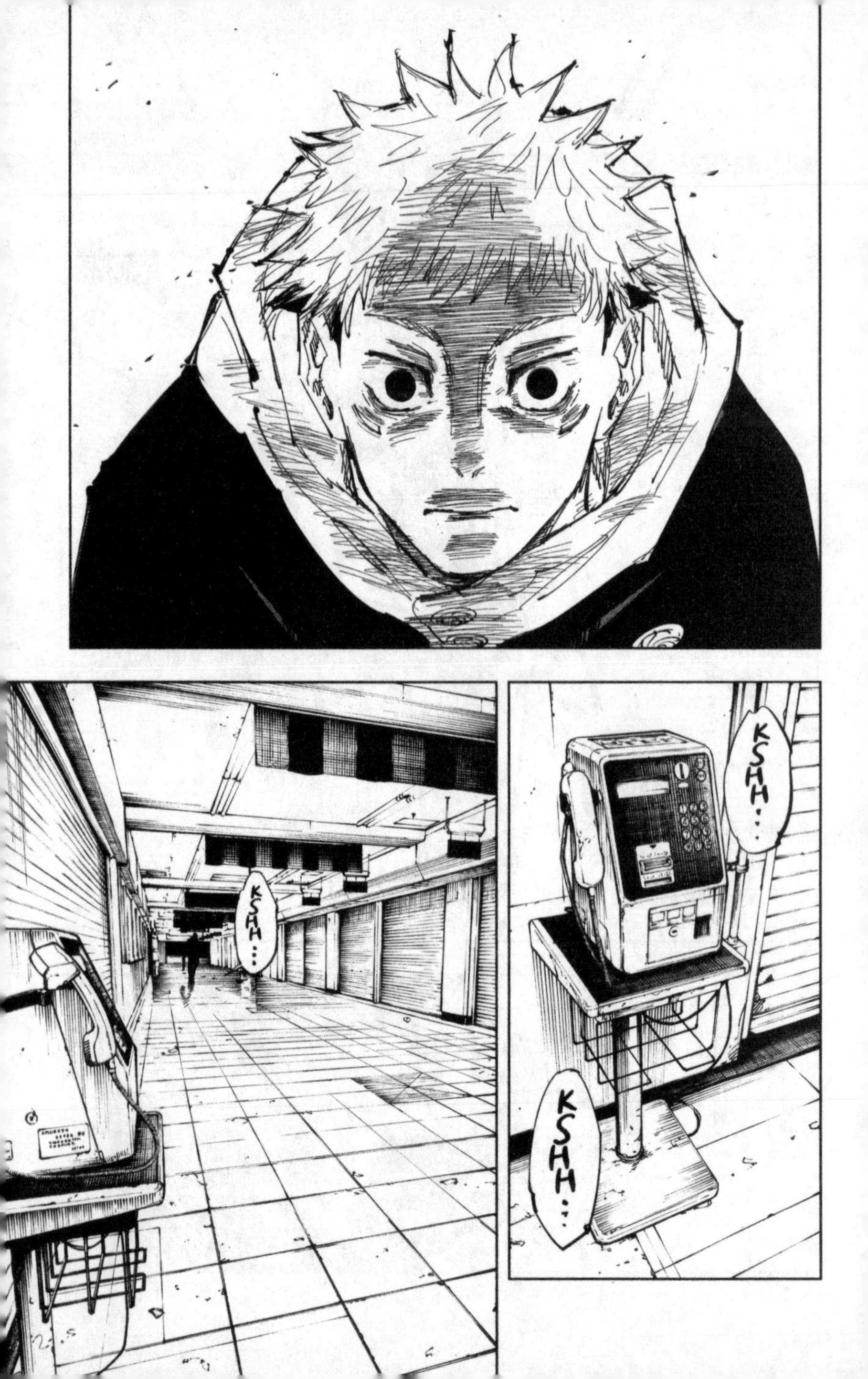
KSHH...
KSHH...
KSHH...

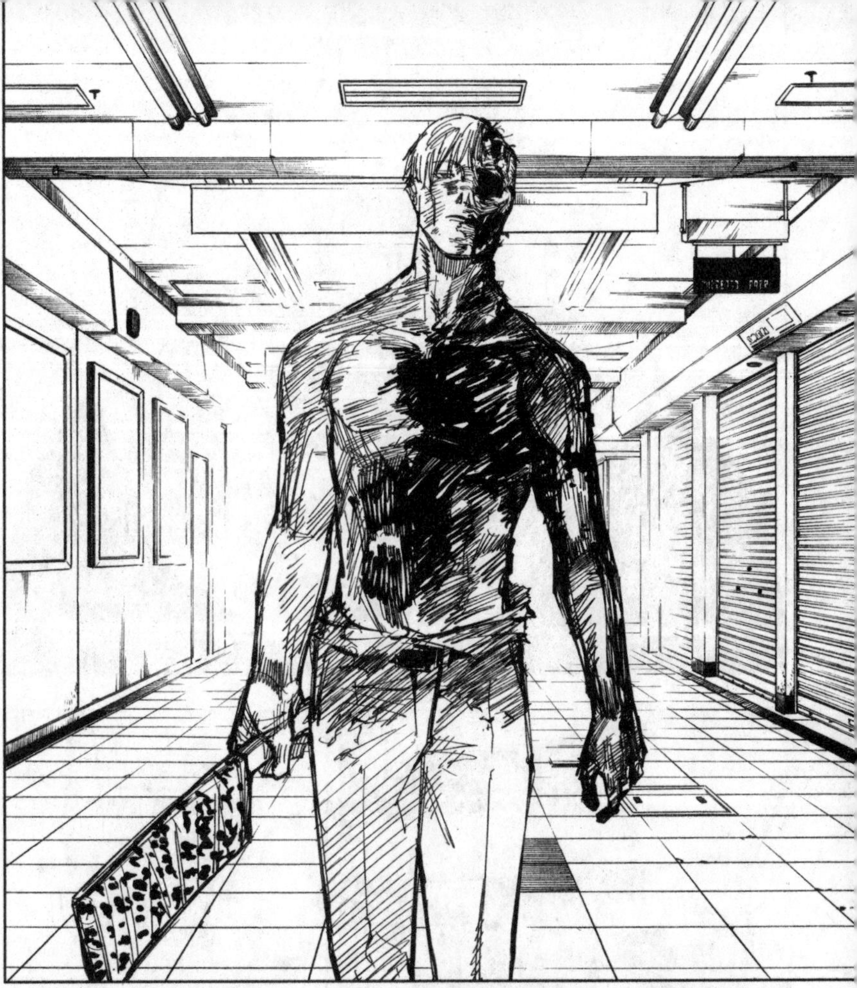
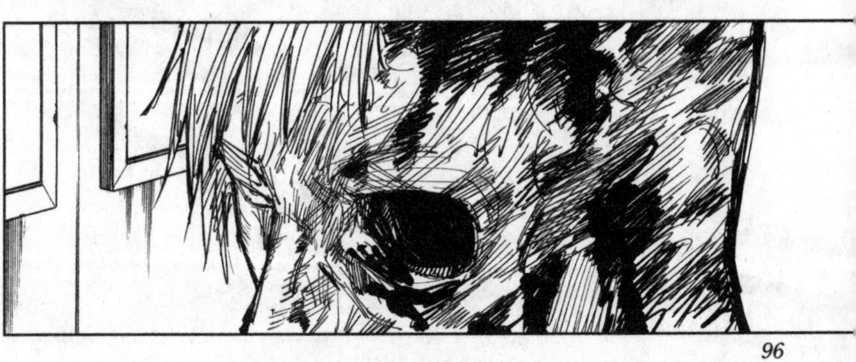

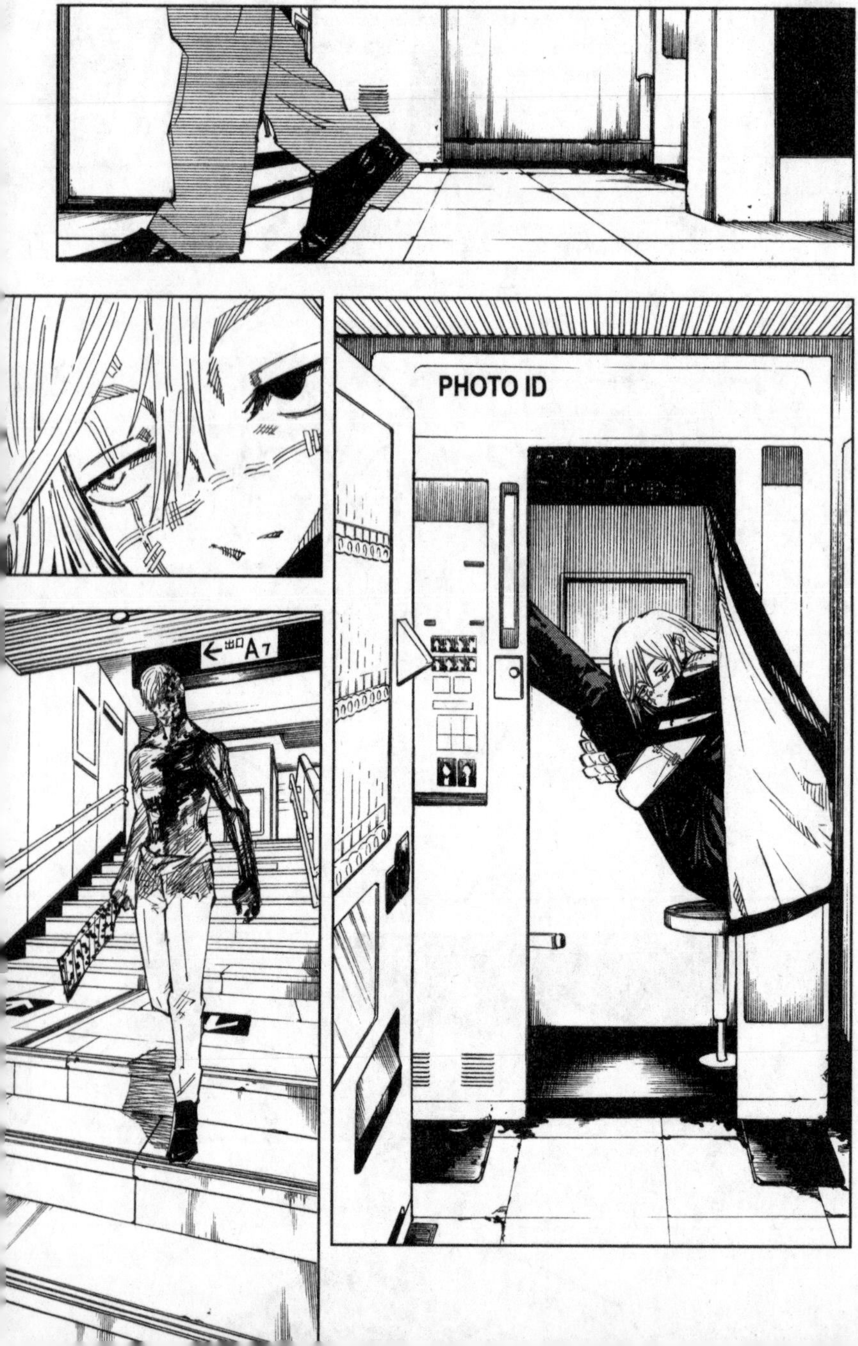
PHOTO ID
←出口A7

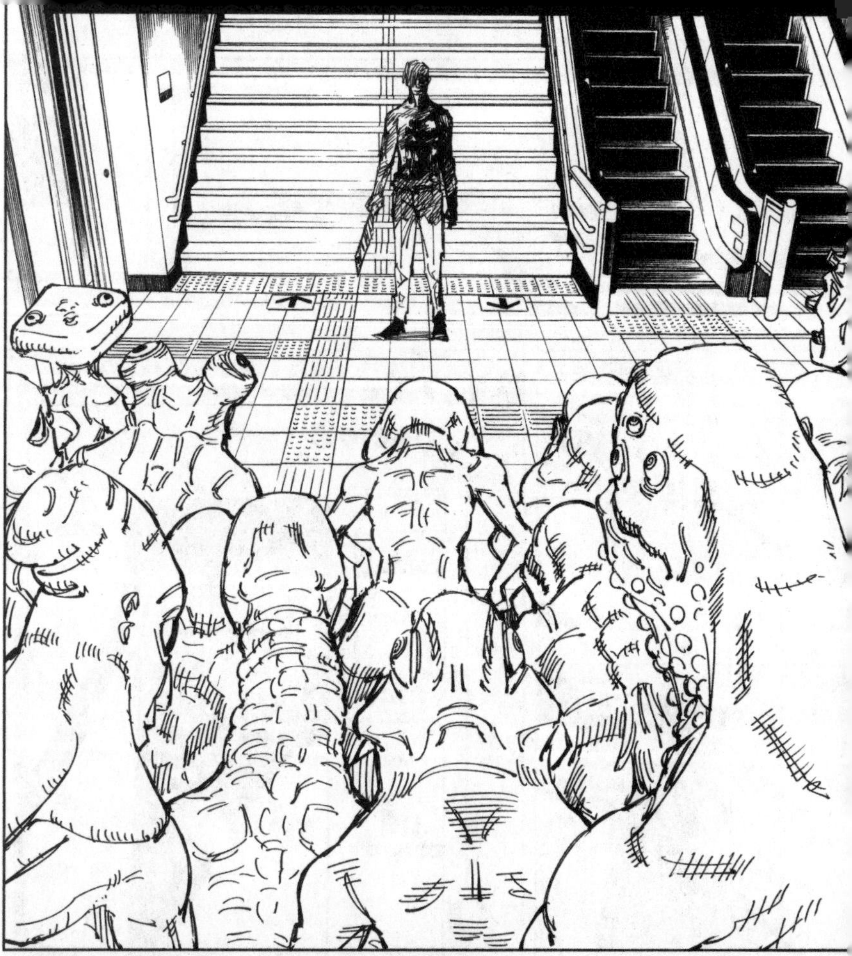

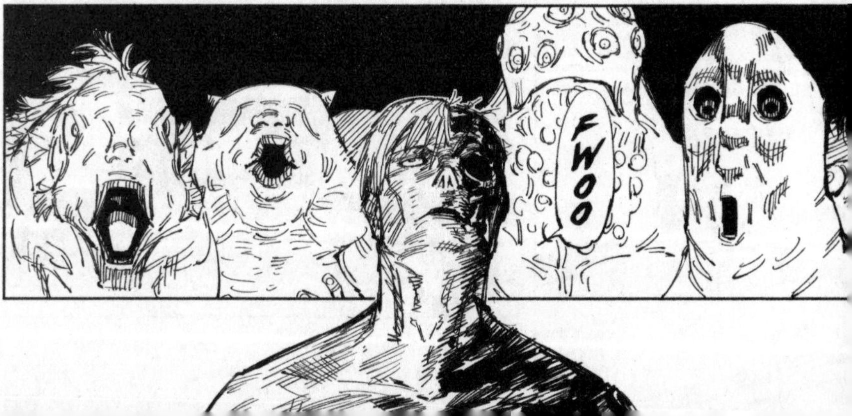
FWOO

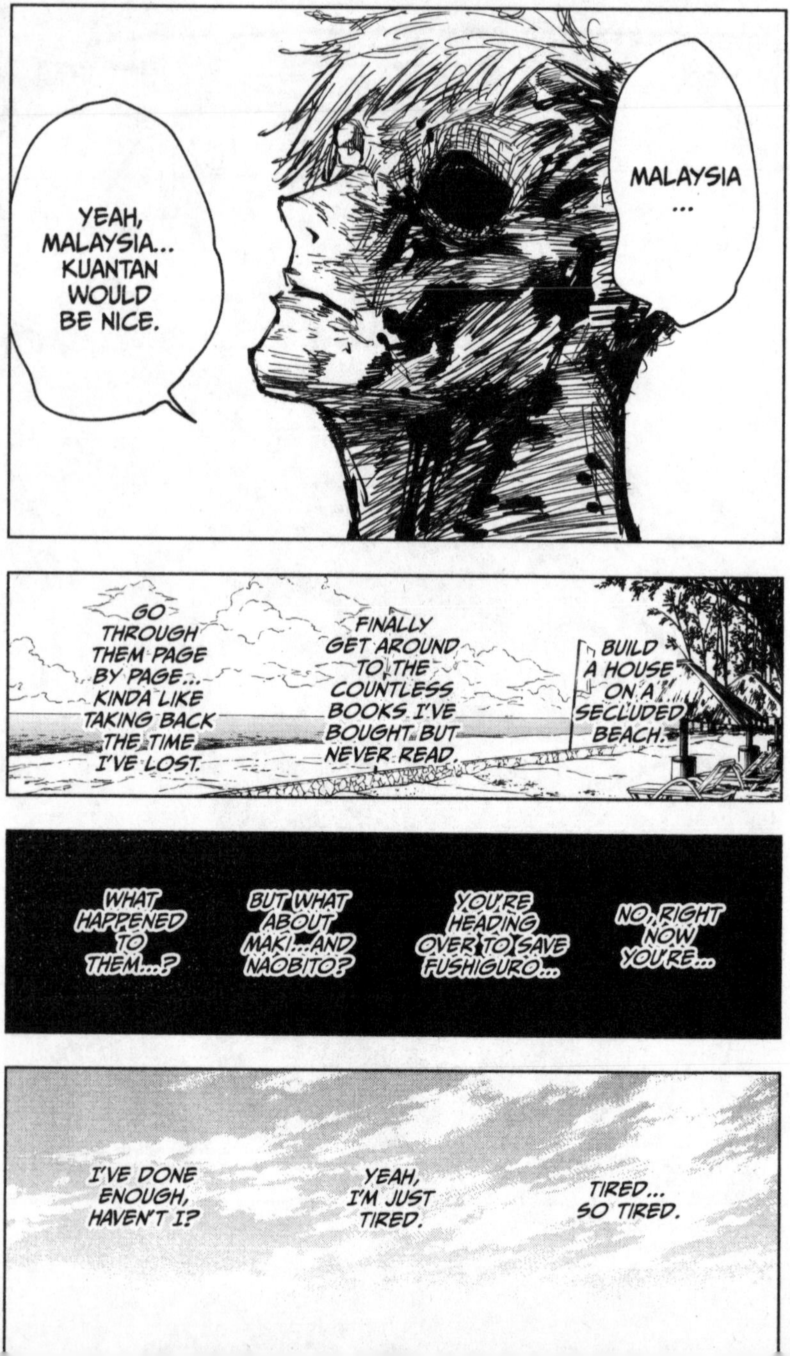
MALAYSIA ...
YEAH, MALAYSIA... KUANTAN WOULD BE NICE.
BUILD A HOUSE ON A SECLUDED BEACH.
FINALLY GET AROUND TO THE COUNTLESS BOOKS I'VE BOUGHT BUT NEVER READ.
GO THROUGH THEM PAGE BY PAGE... KINDA LIKE TAKING BACK THE TIME I'VE LOST.
NO, RIGHT NOW YOU'RE...
YOU'RE HEADING OVER TO SAVE FUSHIGURO...
BUT WHAT ABOUT MAKI...AND NAOBITO?
WHAT HAPPENED TO THEM...?
TIRED... SO TIRED.
YEAH, I'M JUST TIRED.
I'VE DONE ENOUGH, HAVEN'T I?

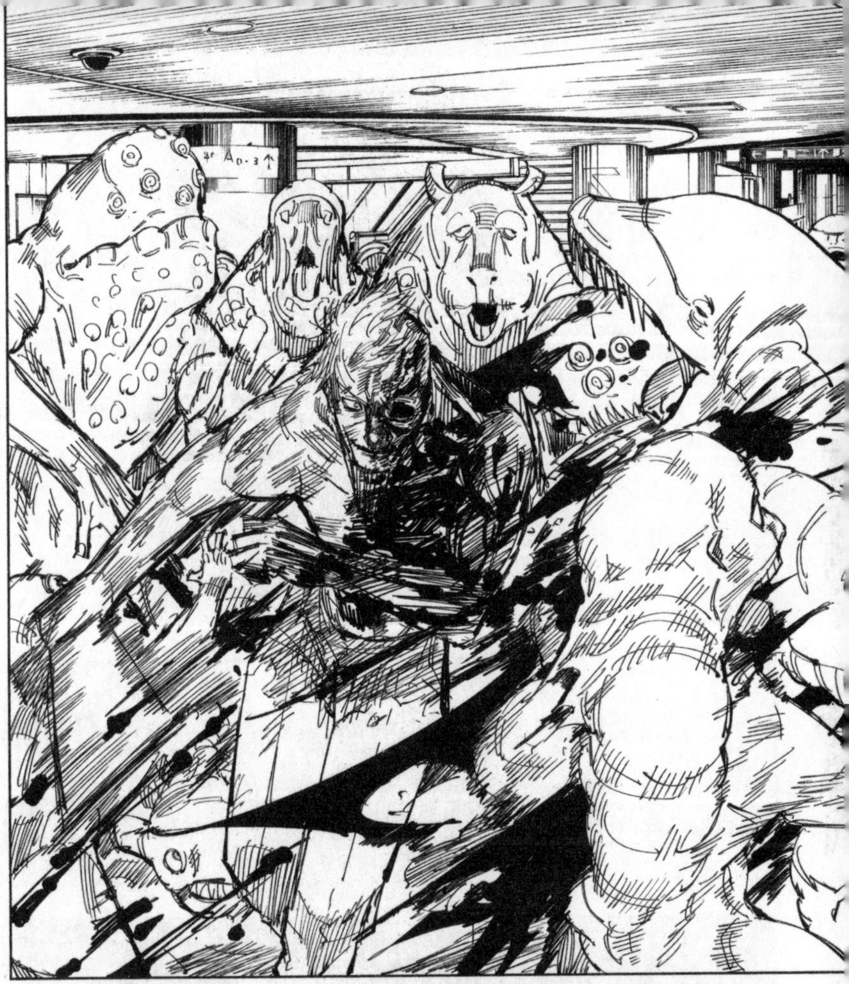
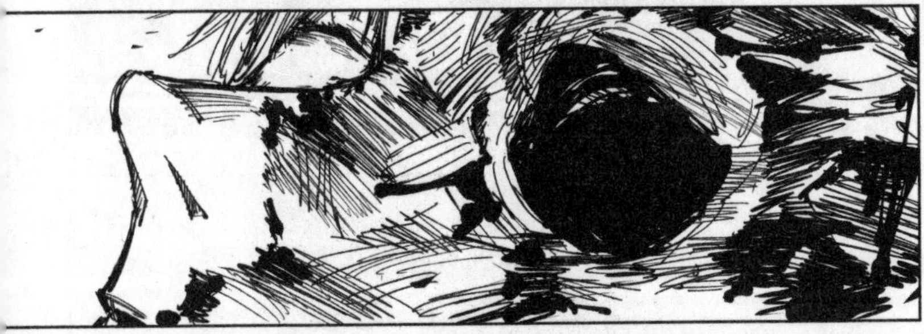

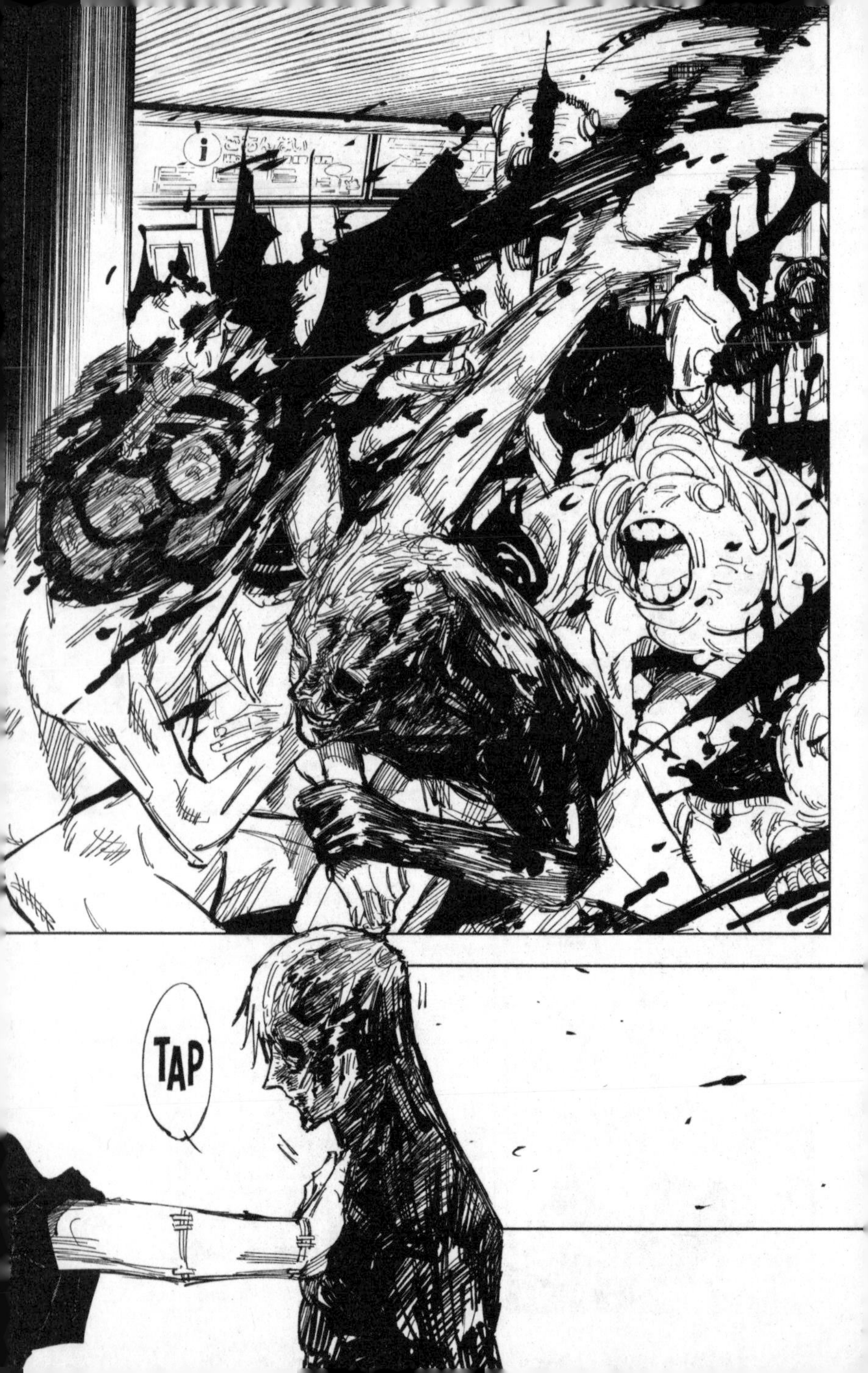
TAP

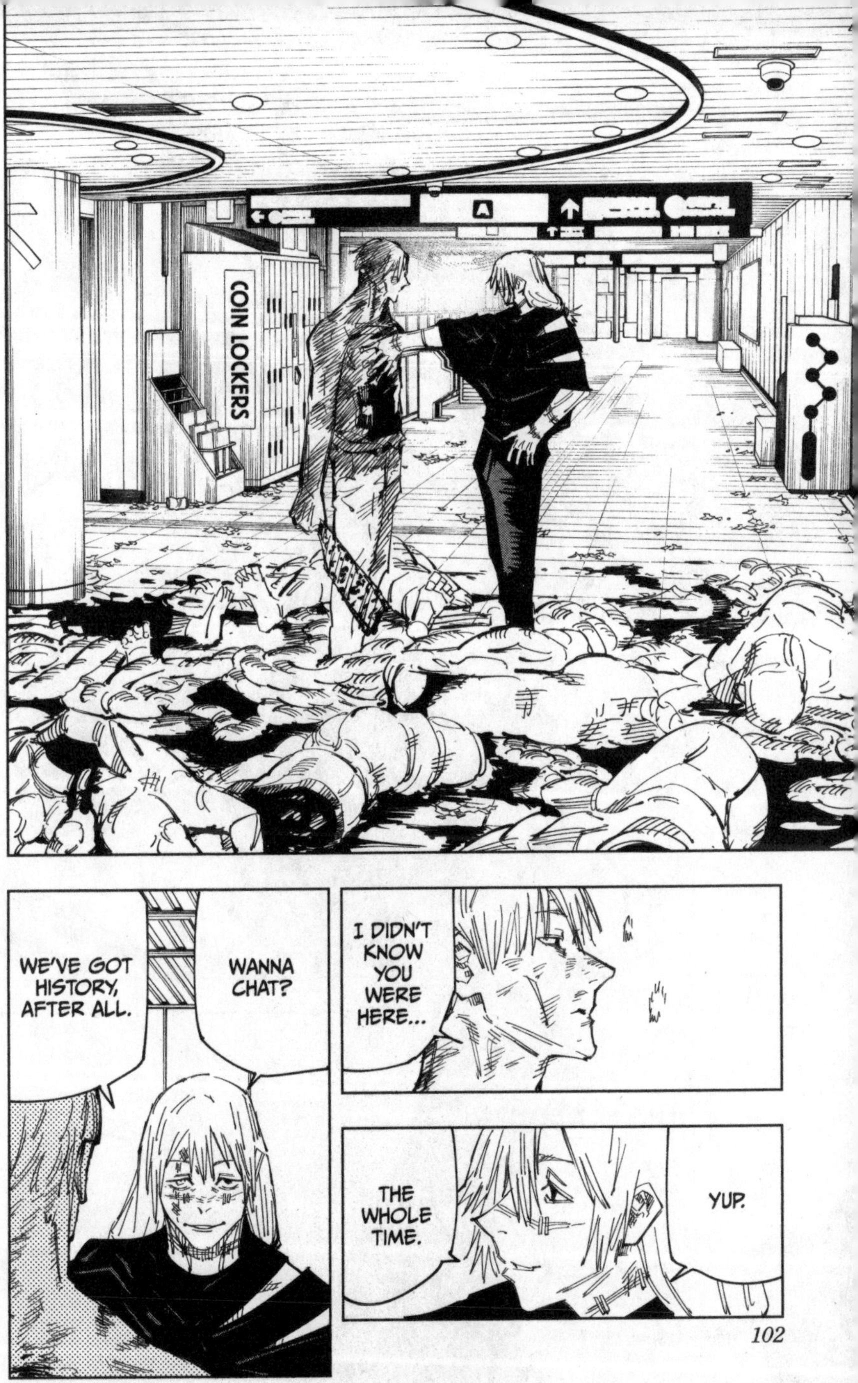
COIN LOCKERS
A
I DIDN'T KNOW YOU WERE HERE...
YUP.
THE WHOLE TIME.
WANNA CHAT?
WE'VE GOT HISTORY, AFTER ALL.

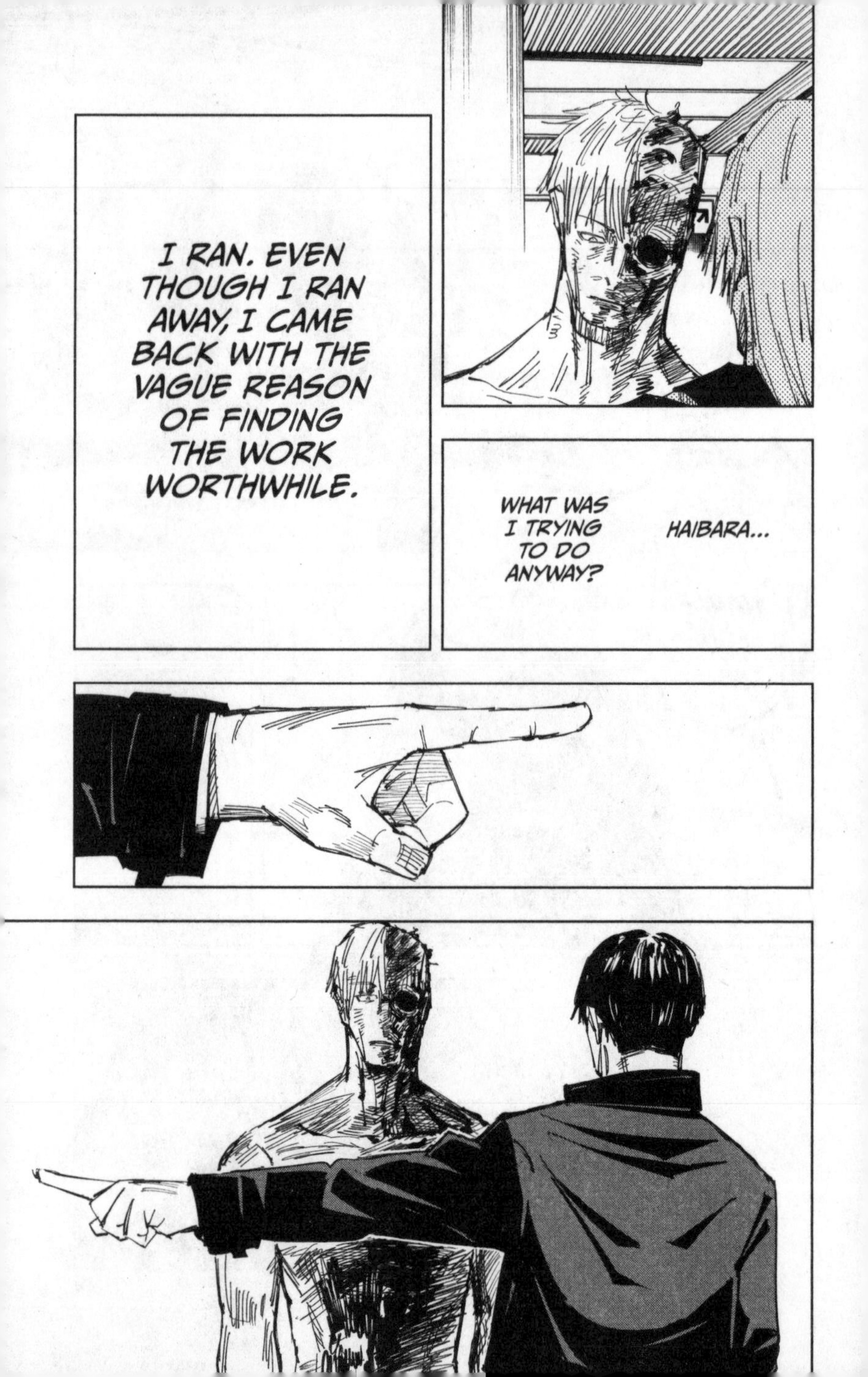
HAIBARA...
WHAT WAS I TRYING TO DO ANYWAY?
I RAN. EVEN THOUGH I RAN AWAY, I CAME BACK WITH THE VAGUE REASON OF FINDING THE WORK WORTHWHILE.

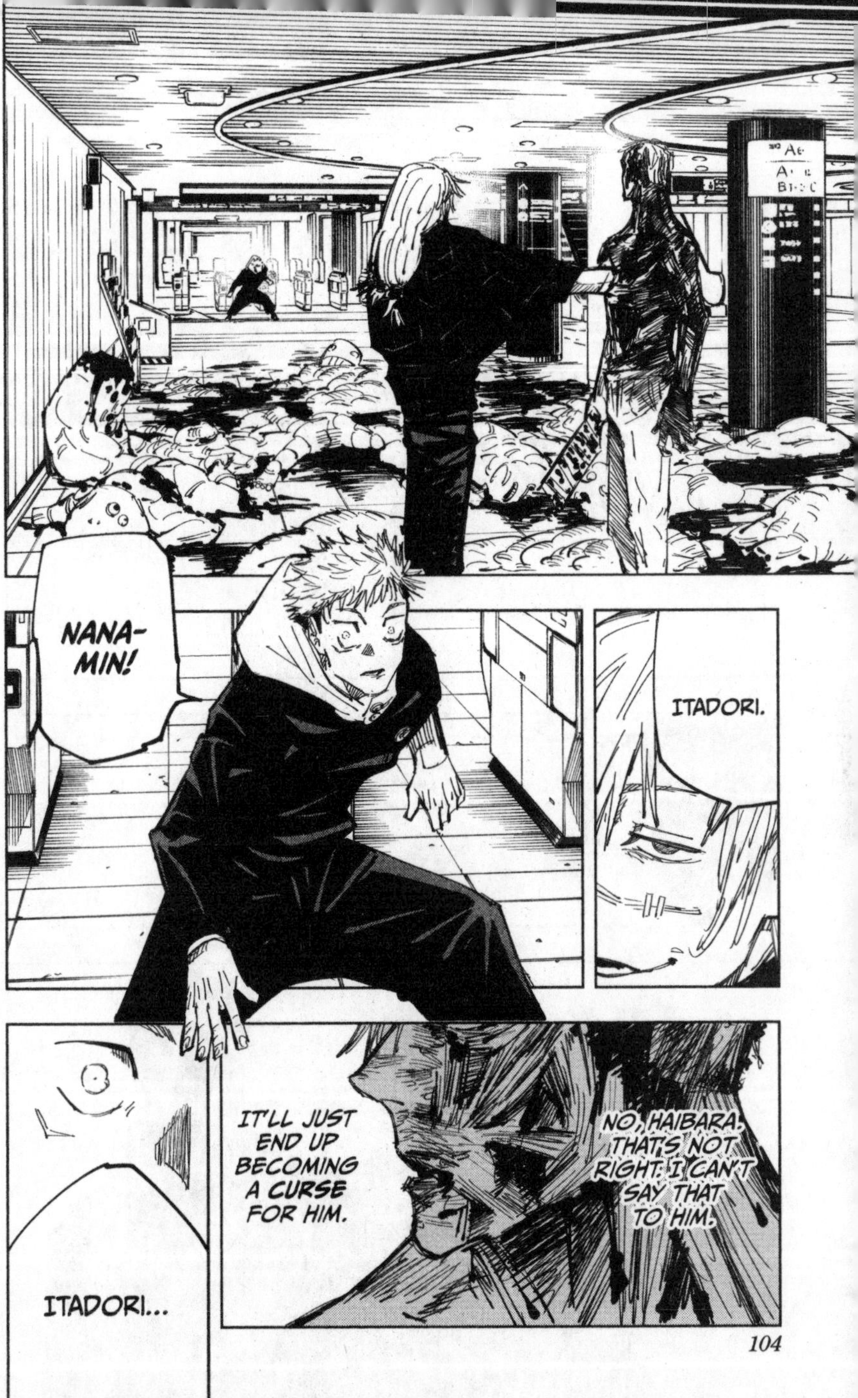
ITADORI.
NANA-MIN!
NO, HAIBARA. THAT'S NOT RIGHT. I CAN'T SAY THAT TO HIM.
IT'LL JUST END UP BECOMING A CURSE FOR HIM.
ITADORI...

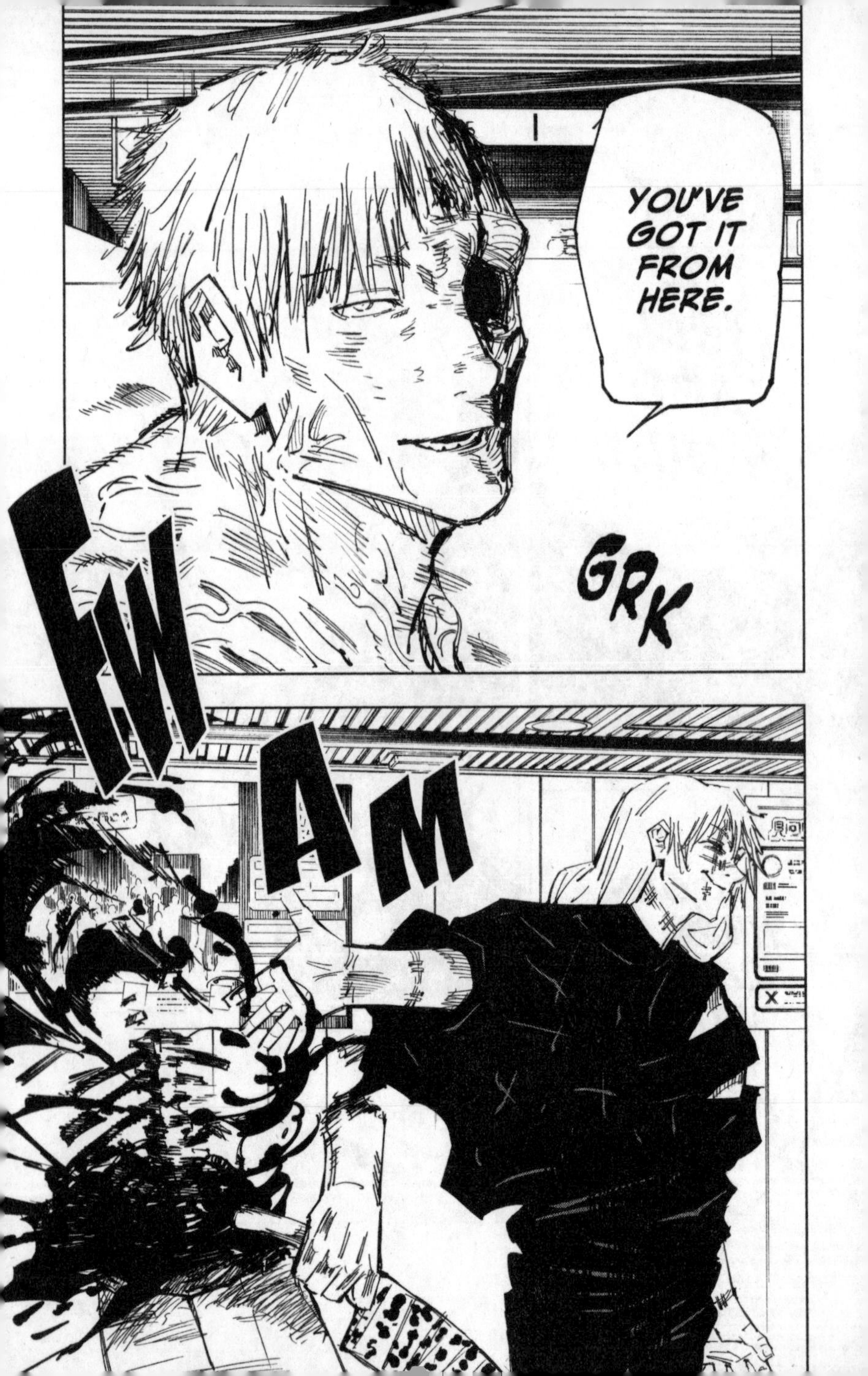
YOU'VE GOT IT FROM HERE.
GRK
WHAM

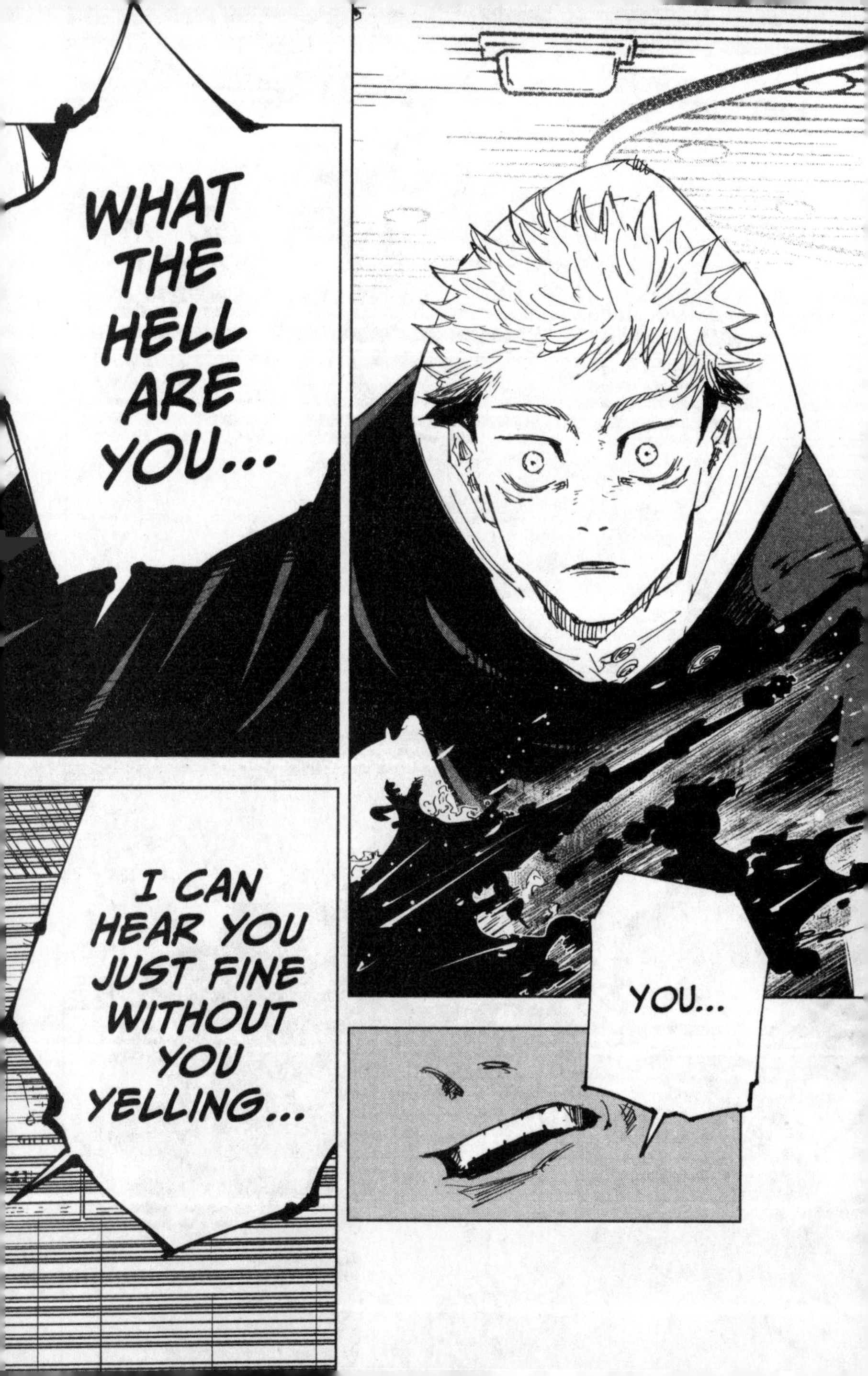
WHAT THE HELL ARE YOU...
YOU...
I CAN HEAR YOU JUST FINE WITHOUT YOU YELLING...

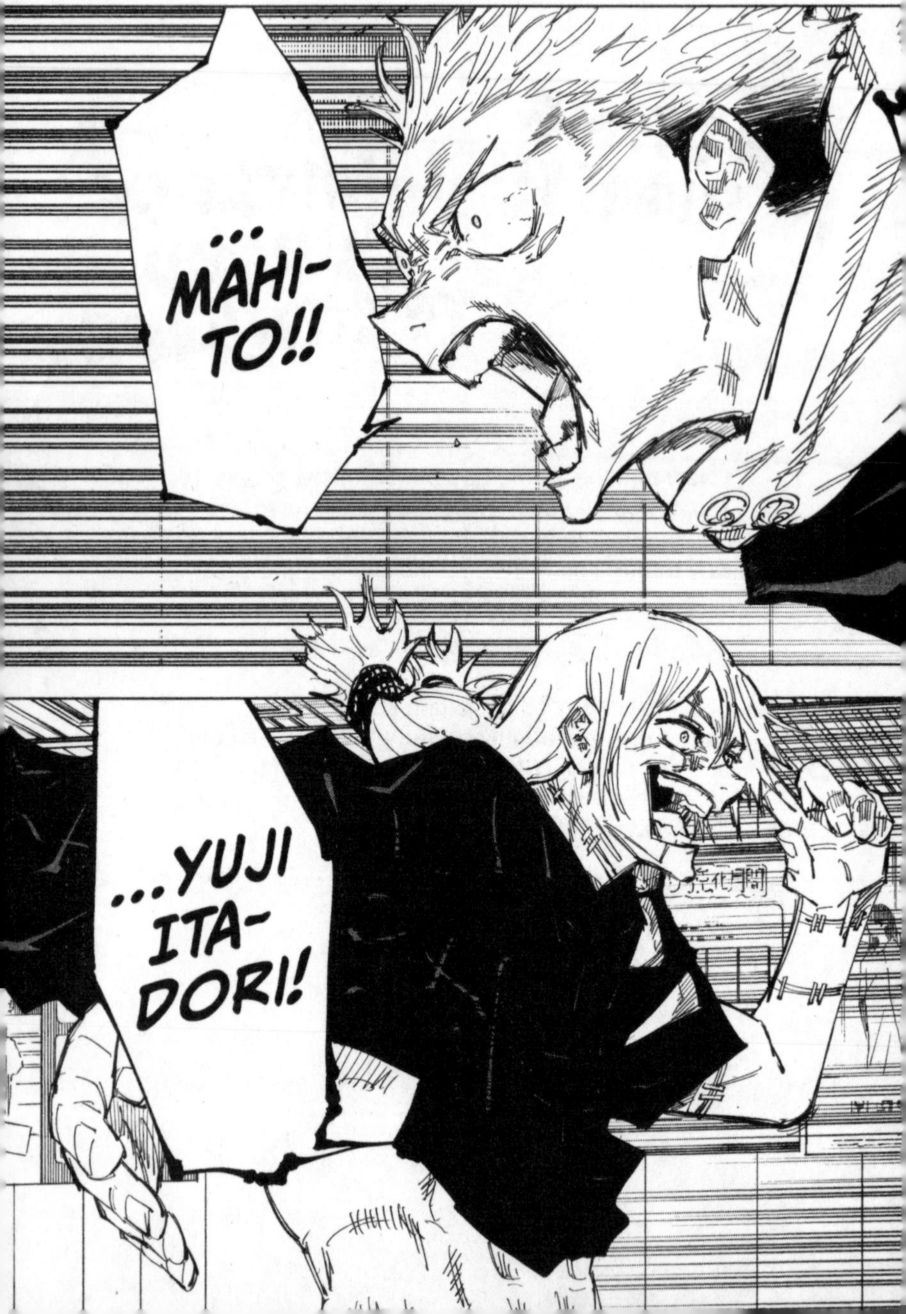
...MAHI-TO!!
...YUJI ITA-DORI!

GETTING IT RIGHT!! LIMITLESS CURSED TECHNIQUE

• Now that the anime has begun, more people in Japan and overseas will check out *Jujutsu Kaisen*. Because of that, I can't keep bluffing my way through stuff. Yes, I'm talking about Gojo's cursed technique.

• So I asked my editor to find someone knowledgeable about mathematics for their input, and the inquiry in the *Jump* editorial staff turned up T-san, who has a master's degree in engineering (information geometry)!!

• I hope to share what I've learned in this volume and the next.

• I should've done this from the start!!

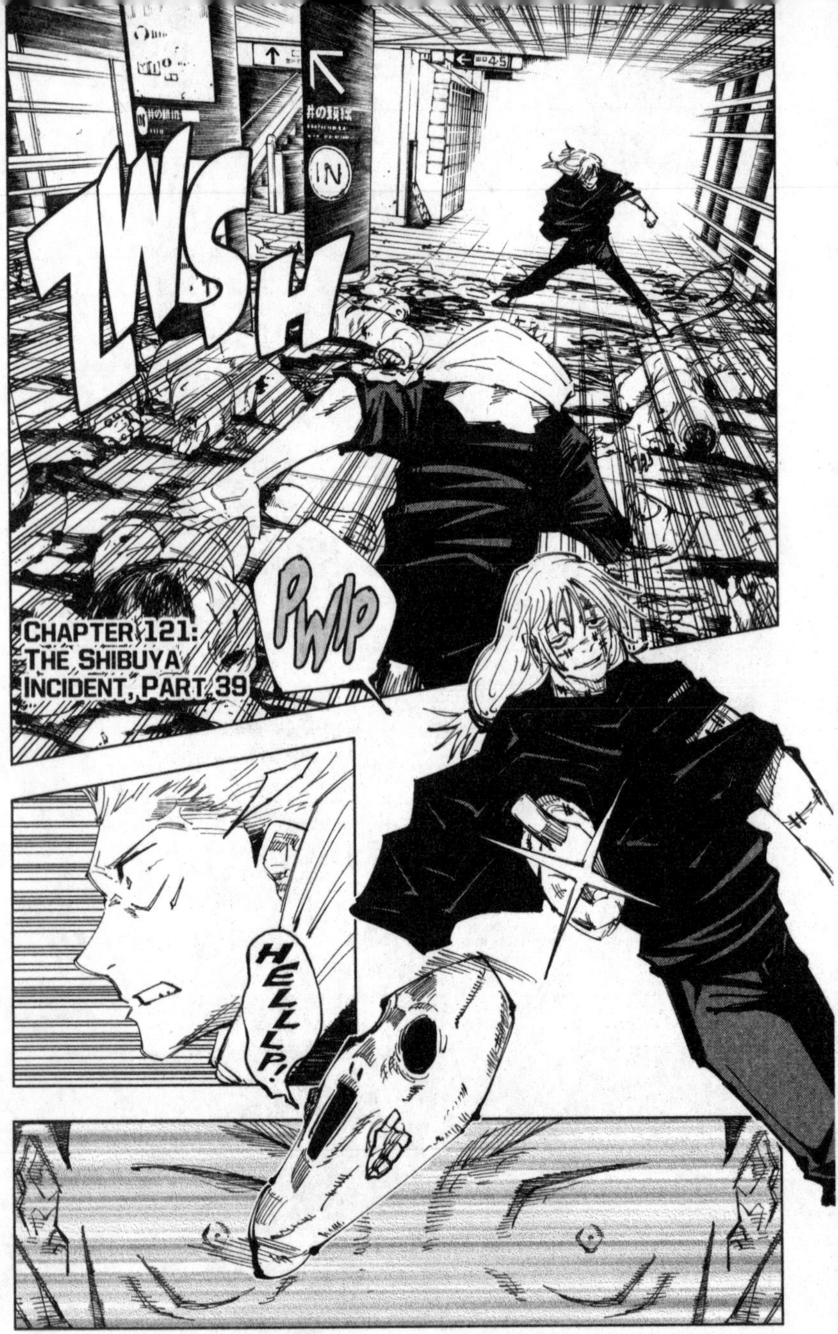
ZWSH
PWIP
CHAPTER 121: THE SHIBUYA INCIDENT, PART 39
HELLLP!

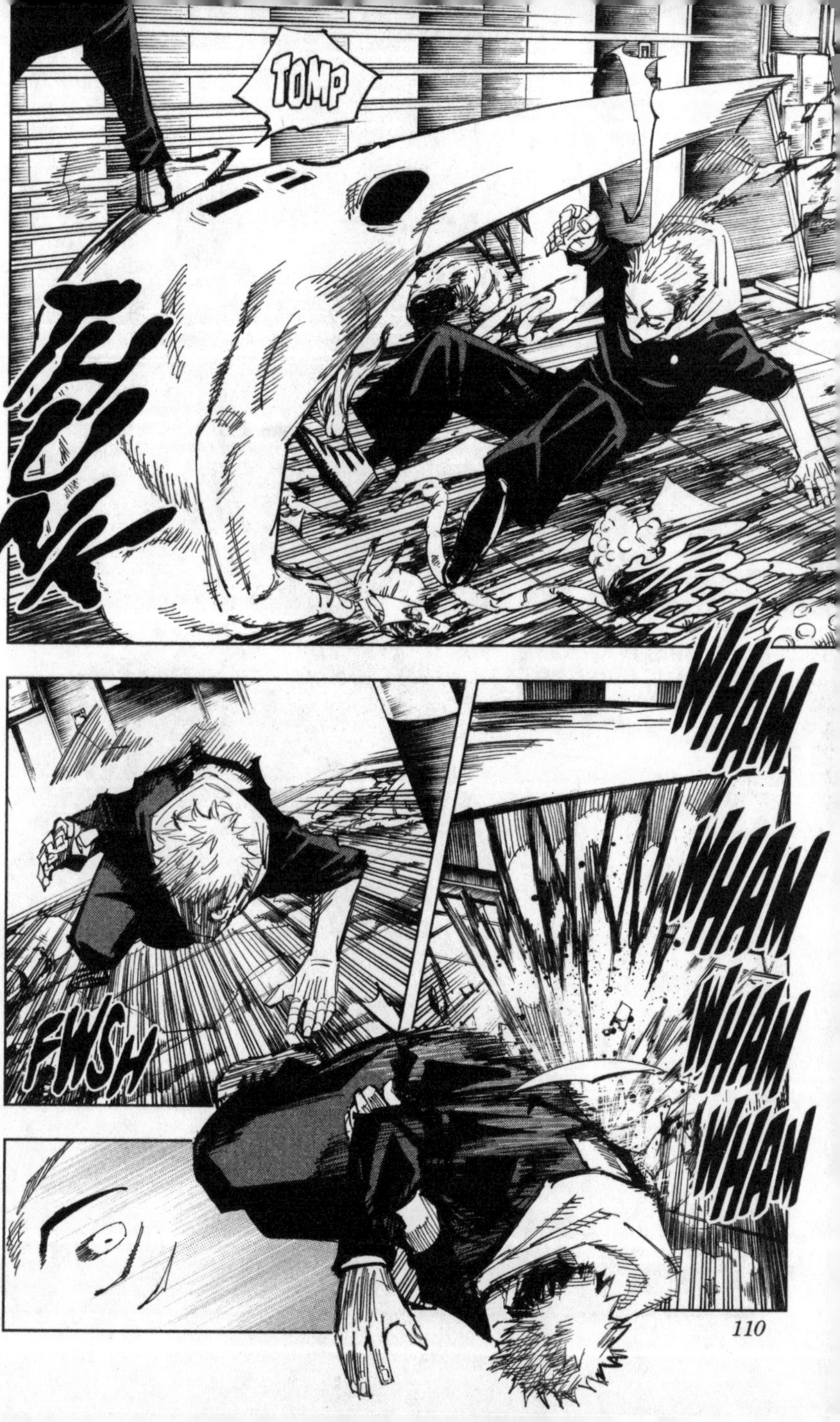
TOMP
THUNK
WHAM WHAM WHAM WHAM WHAM WHAM
FWSH

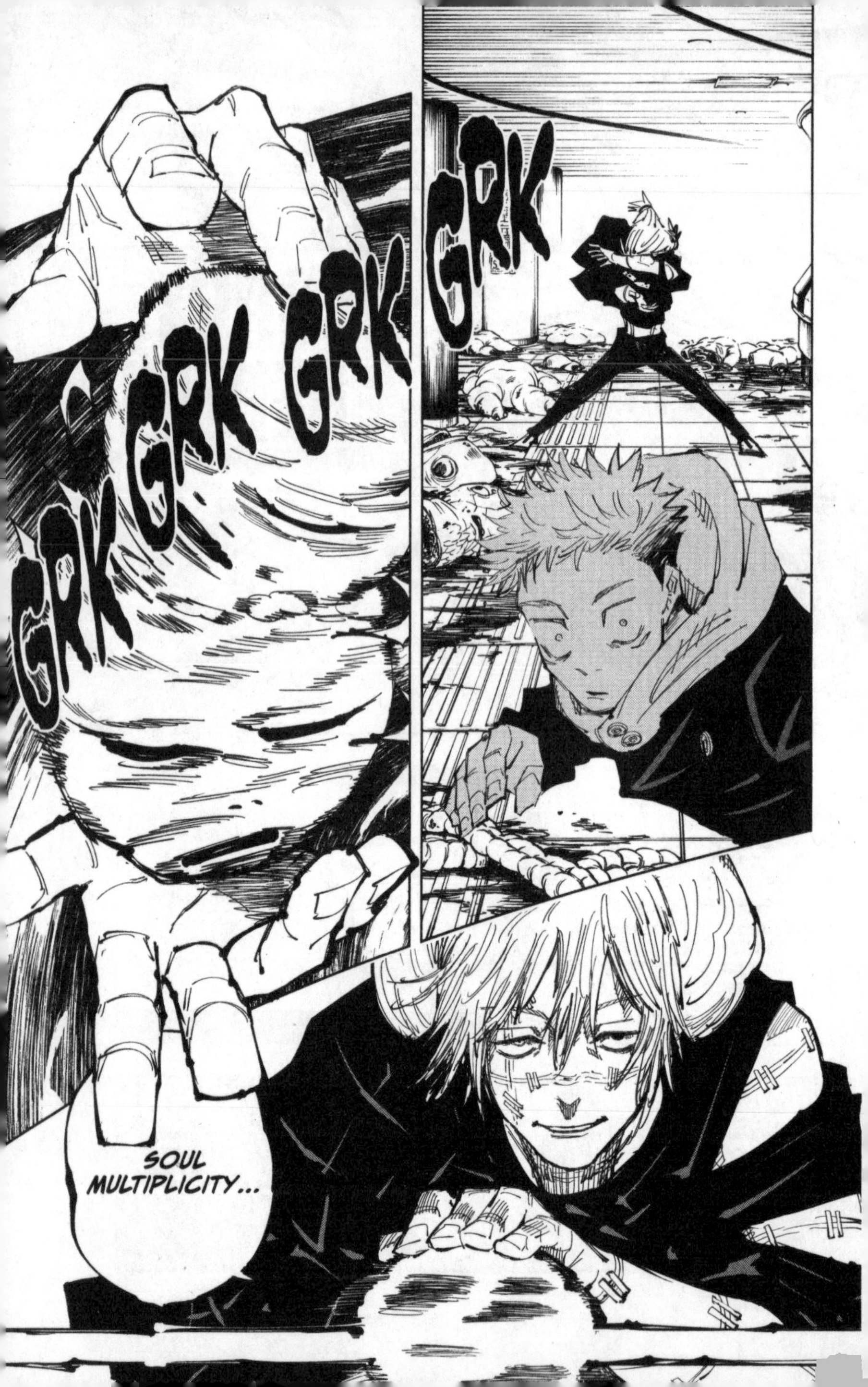
GRK
GRK
GRK
GRK
GRK
SOUL MULTIPLICITY...

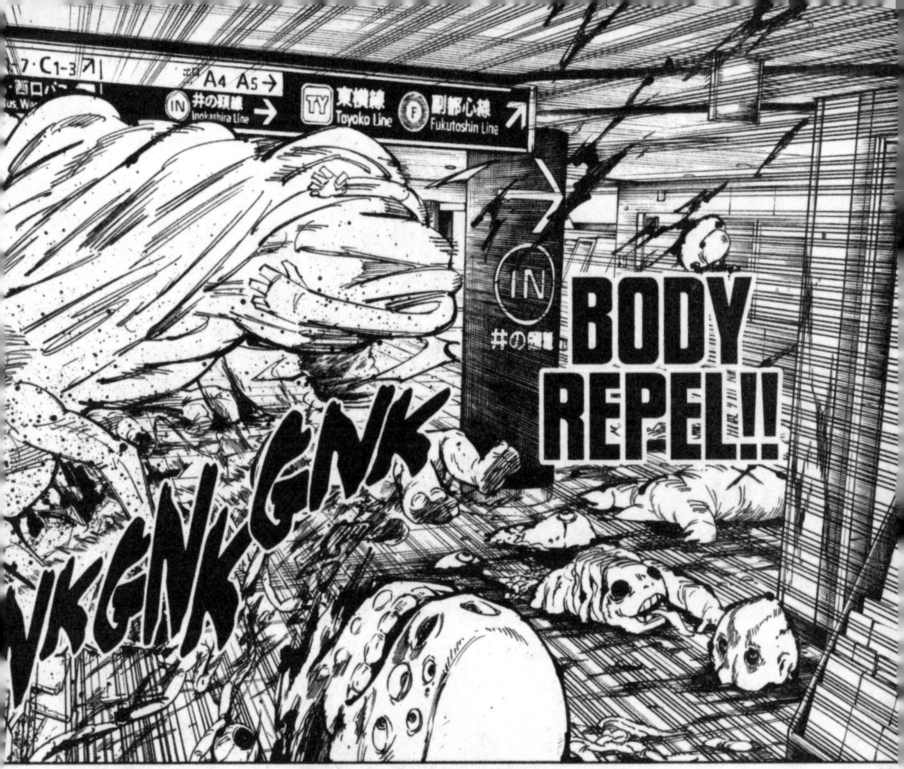
Inokashira Line
Toyoko Line
Fukutoshin Line
BODY REPEL!!
GNK GNK GNK
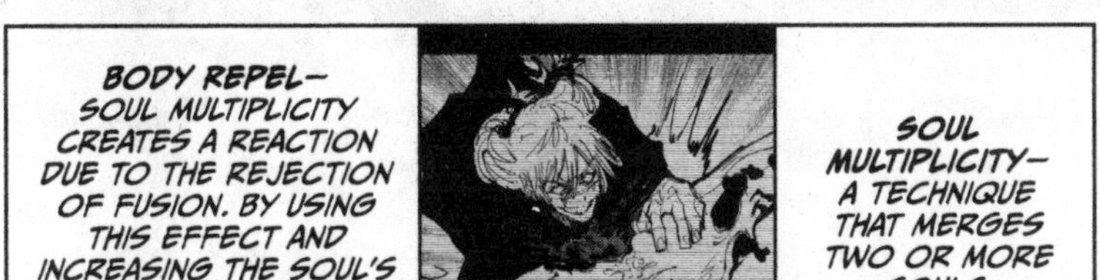
SOUL MULTIPLICITY—A TECHNIQUE THAT MERGES TWO OR MORE SOULS.
BODY REPEL—SOUL MULTIPLICITY CREATES A REACTION DUE TO THE REJECTION OF FUSION. BY USING THIS EFFECT AND INCREASING THE SOUL'S ENERGY, THE OVER-WHELMING OUTPUT CAN BE DIRECTED AT AN OPPONENT.
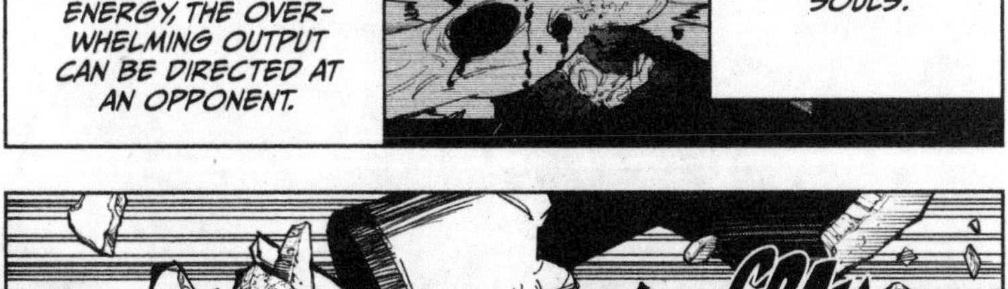
GRAK GRAK GRAK GRAK

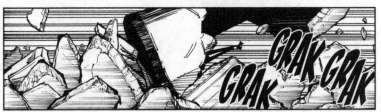

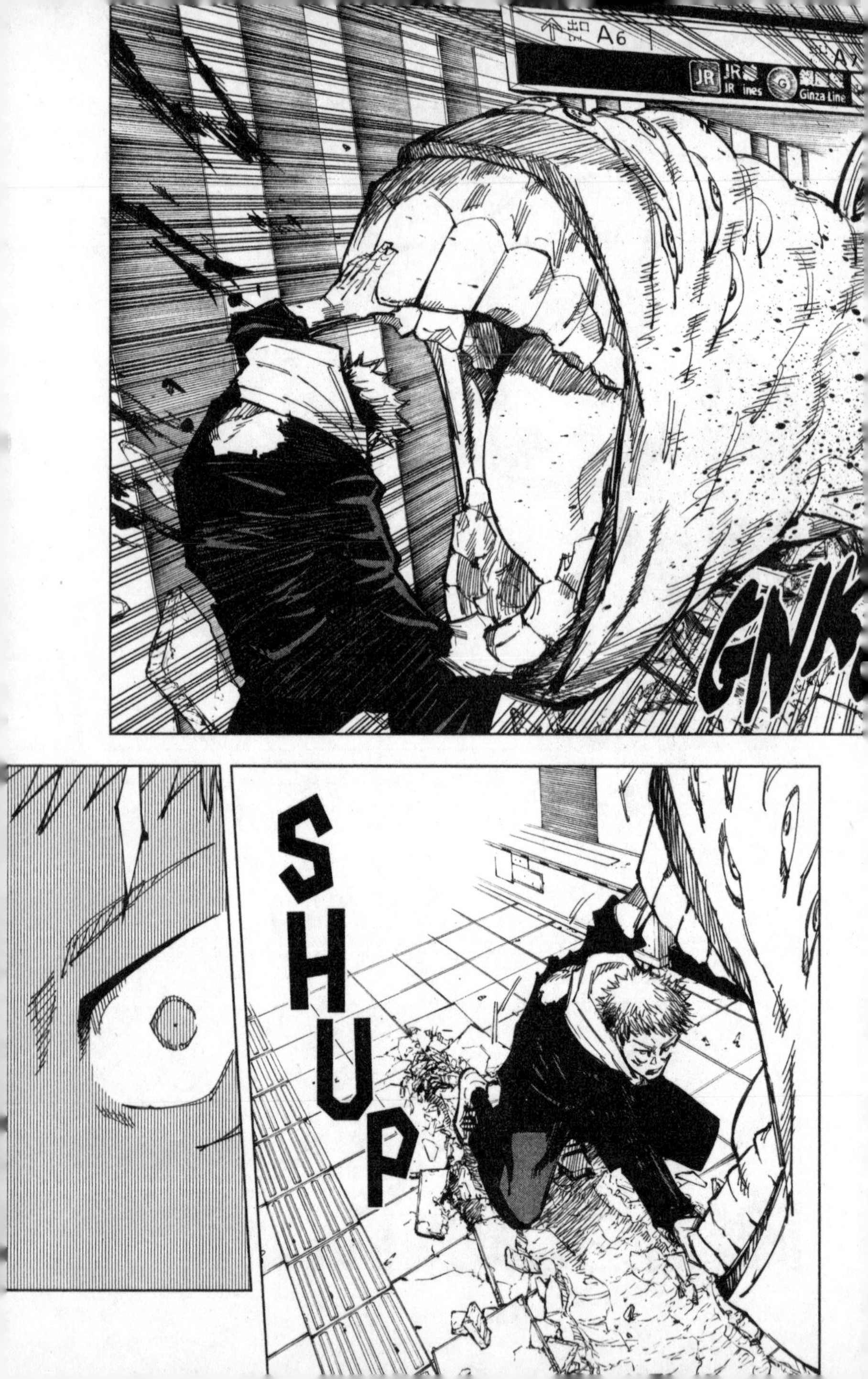

出口 A6
Ginza Line
GNK
SHUP

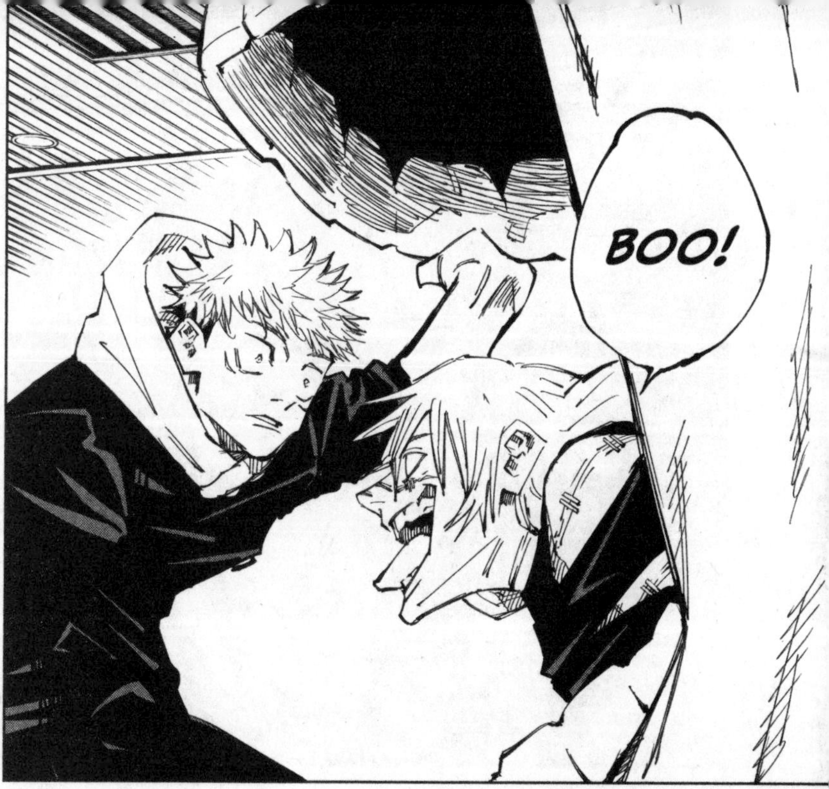
BOO!
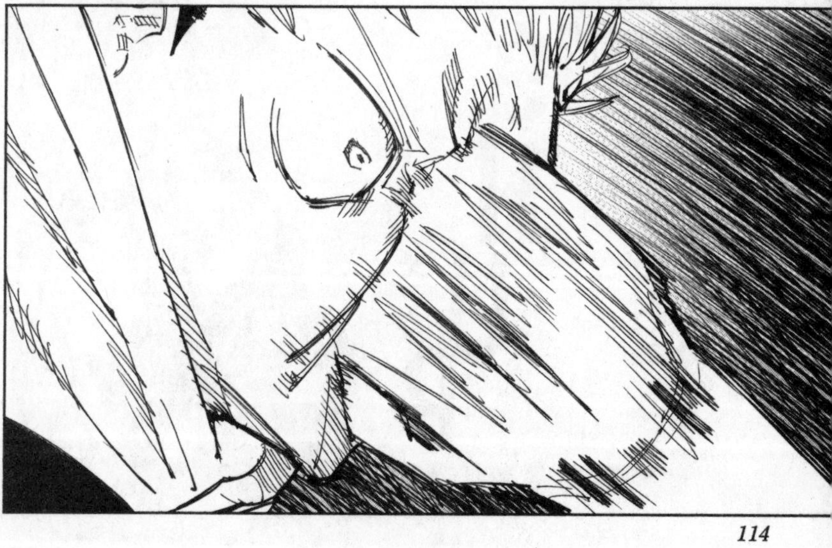

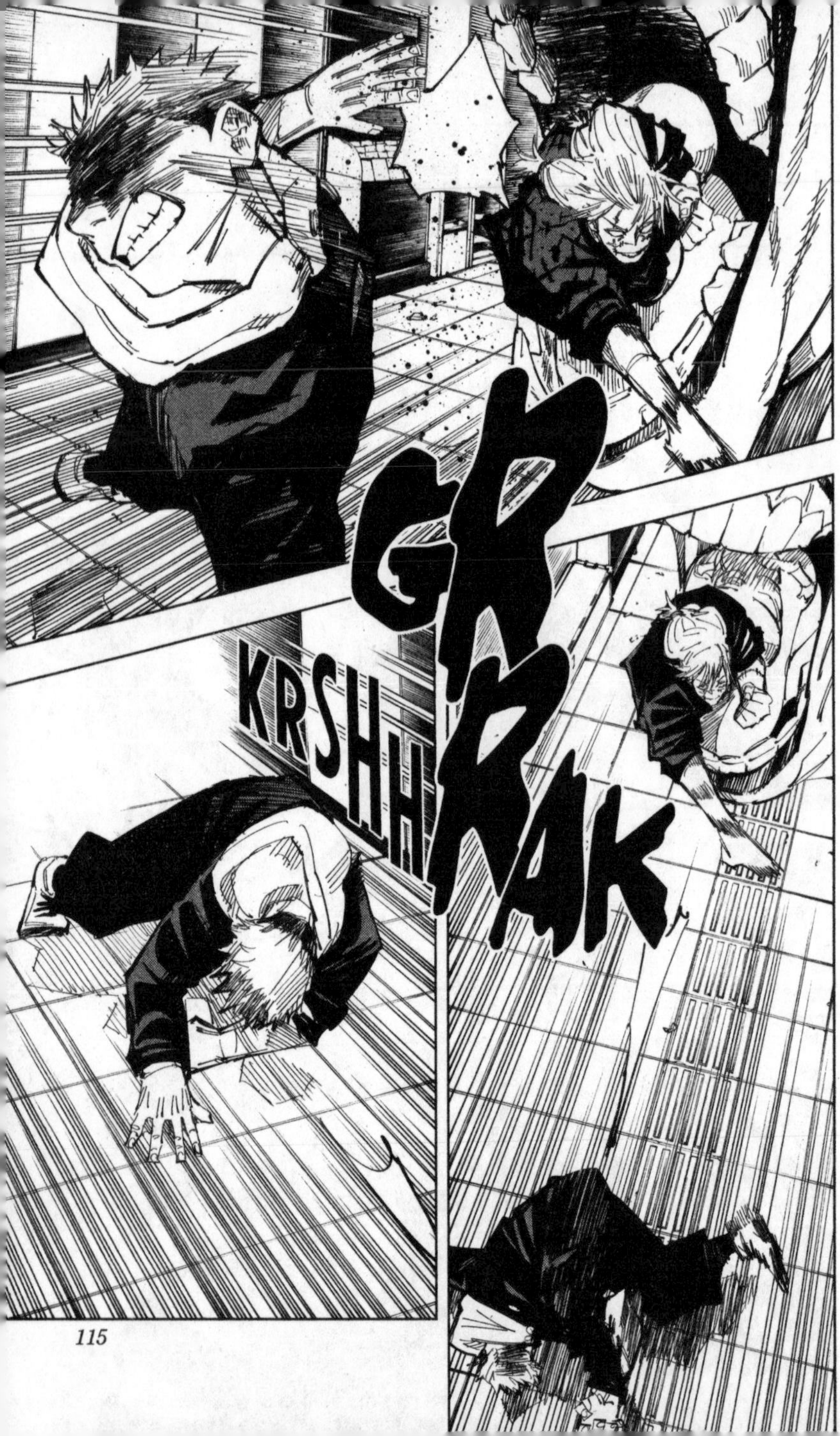
GRRAK
KRSHH

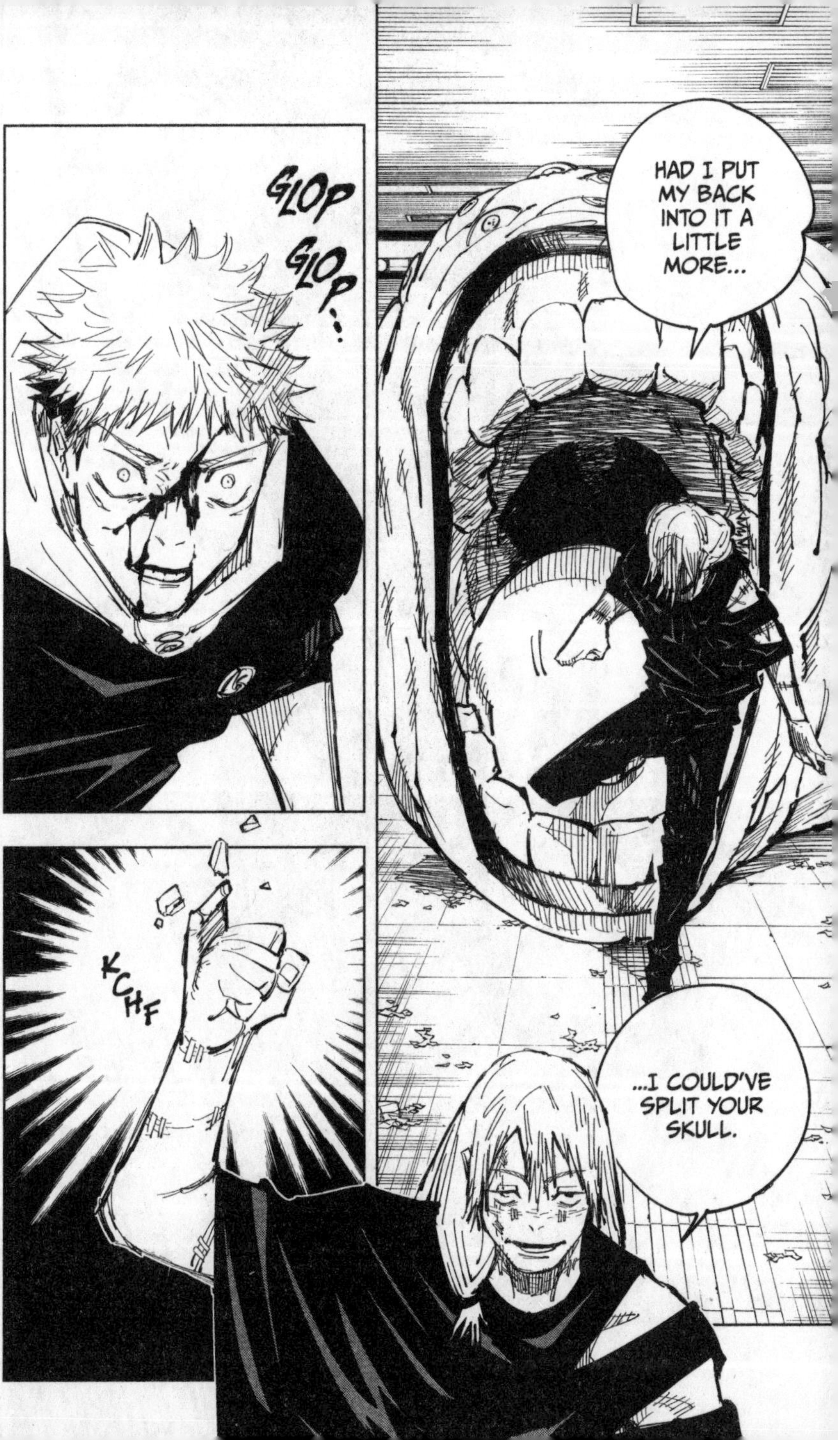
HAD I PUT MY BACK INTO IT A LITTLE MORE...
...I COULD'VE SPLIT YOUR SKULL.
GLOP
GLOP...
KCHF

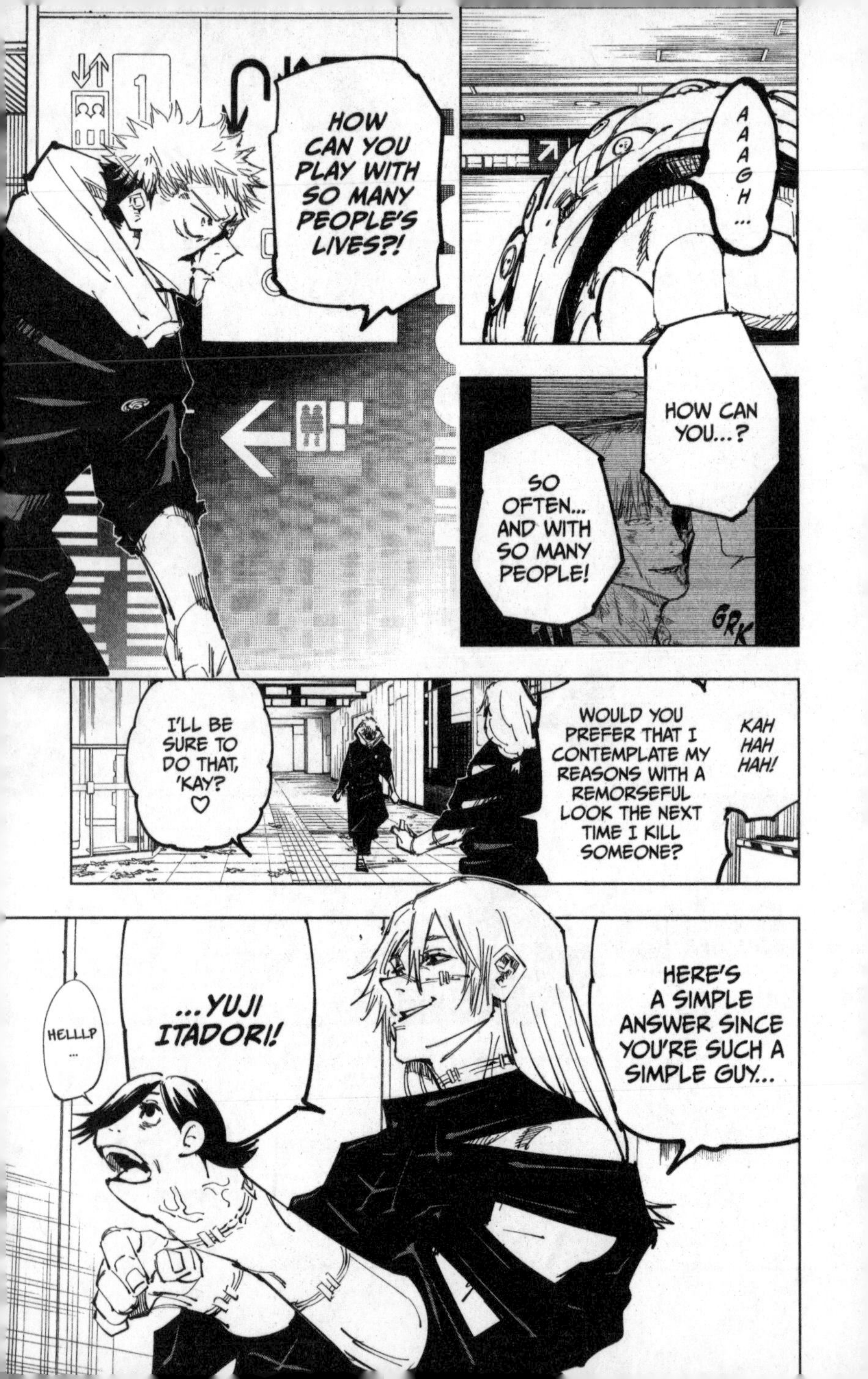
AAAAGH...
HOW CAN YOU...?
SO OFTEN... AND WITH SO MANY PEOPLE!
GRK
HOW CAN YOU PLAY WITH SO MANY PEOPLE'S LIVES?!
KAH HAH HAH!
WOULD YOU PREFER THAT I CONTEMPLATE MY REASONS WITH A REMORSEFUL LOOK THE NEXT TIME I KILL SOMEONE?
I'LL BE SURE TO DO THAT, 'KAY? ♡
HERE'S A SIMPLE ANSWER SINCE YOU'RE SUCH A SIMPLE GUY...
...YUJI ITADORI!
HELLLP...

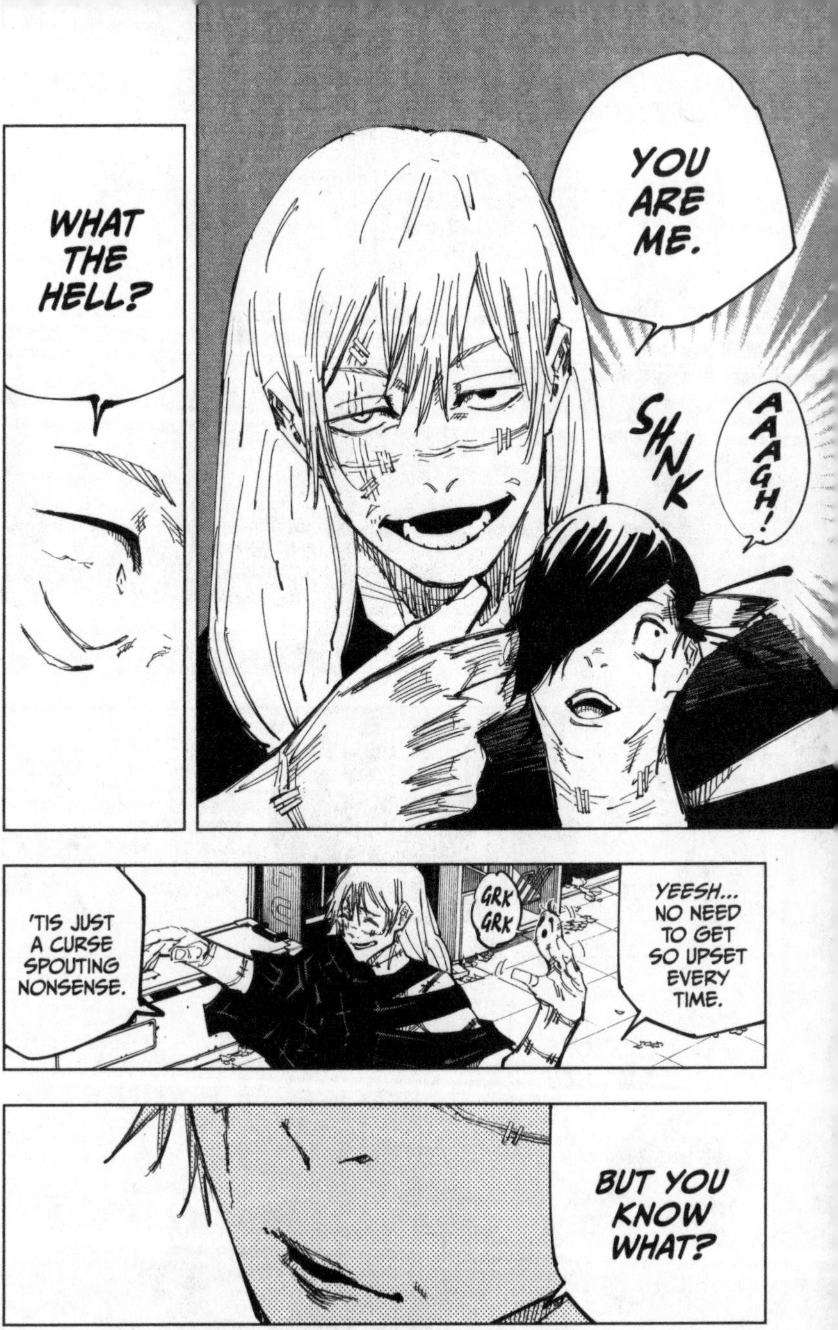
YOU ARE ME.
SHNK
AAAGH!
WHAT THE HELL?
YEESH... NO NEED TO GET SO UPSET EVERY TIME.
GRK GRK
'TIS JUST A CURSE SPOUTING NONSENSE.
BUT YOU KNOW WHAT?

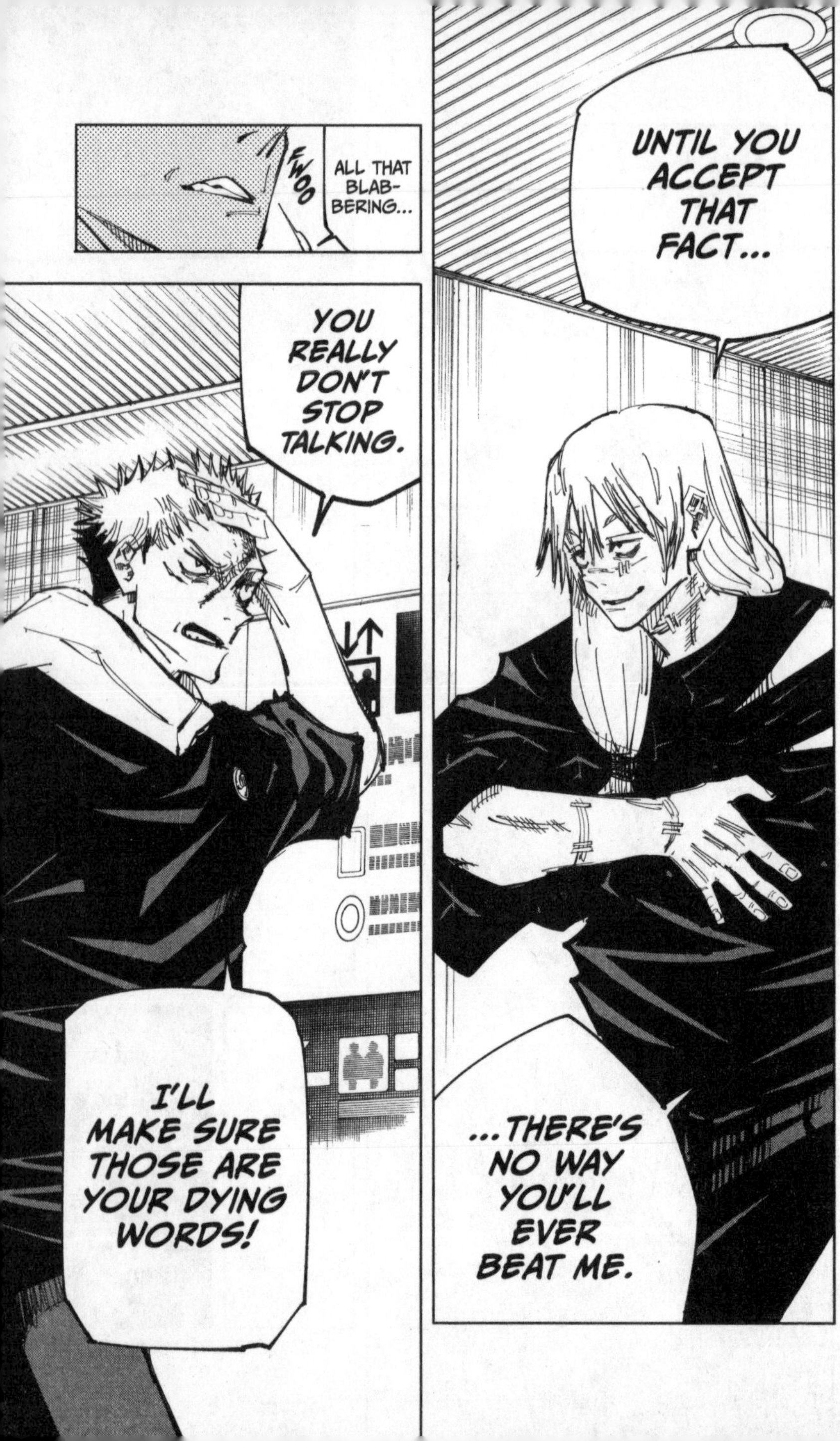
UNTIL YOU ACCEPT THAT FACT...
...THERE'S NO WAY YOU'LL EVER BEAT ME.
FWOO
ALL THAT BLAB-BERING...
YOU REALLY DON'T STOP TALKING.
I'LL MAKE SURE THOSE ARE YOUR DYING WORDS!

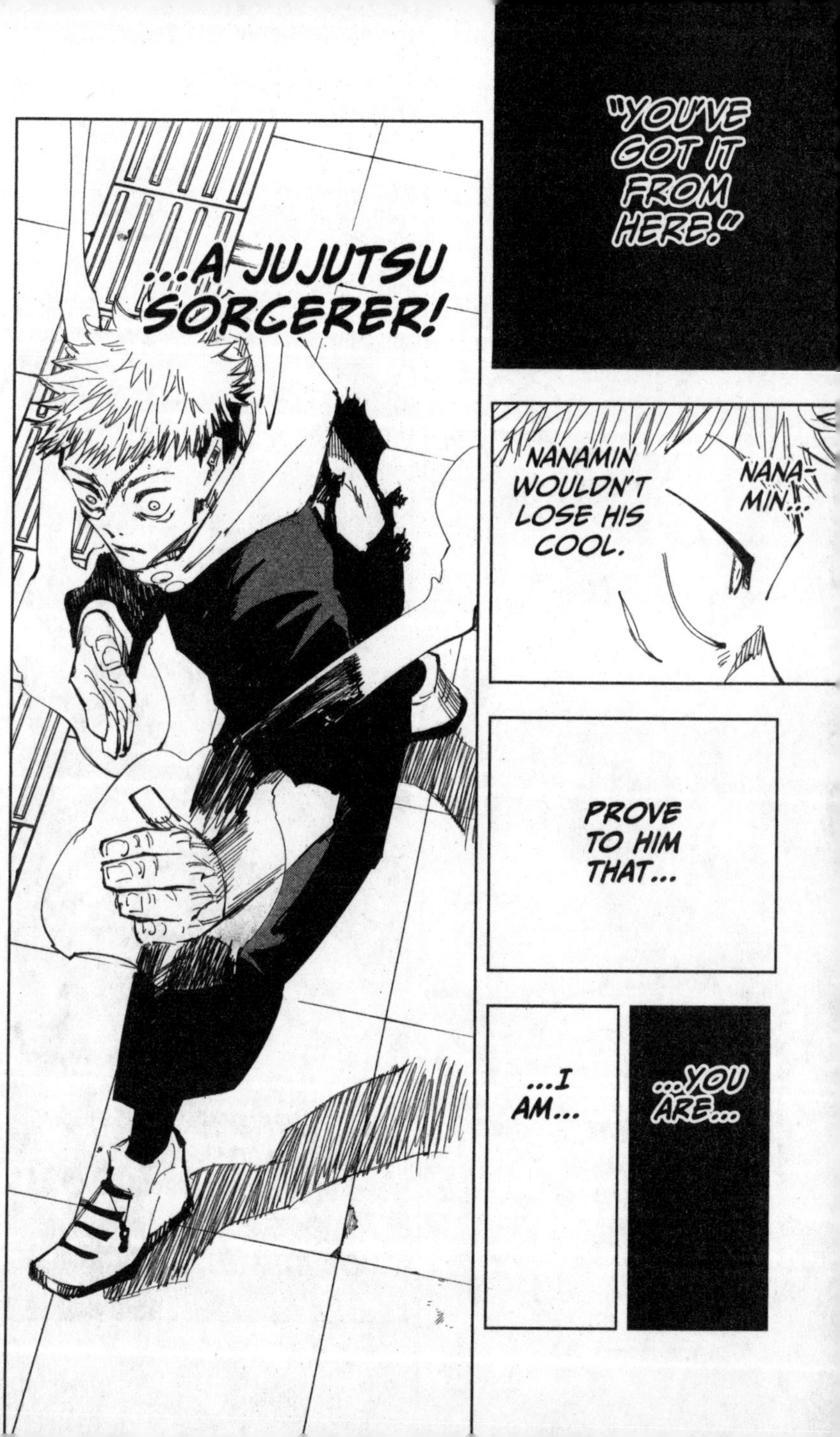
"YOU'VE GOT IT FROM HERE."
NANA-MIN...
NANAMIN WOULDN'T LOSE HIS COOL.
PROVE TO HIM THAT...
...YOU ARE...
...I AM...
...A JUJUTSU SORCERER!

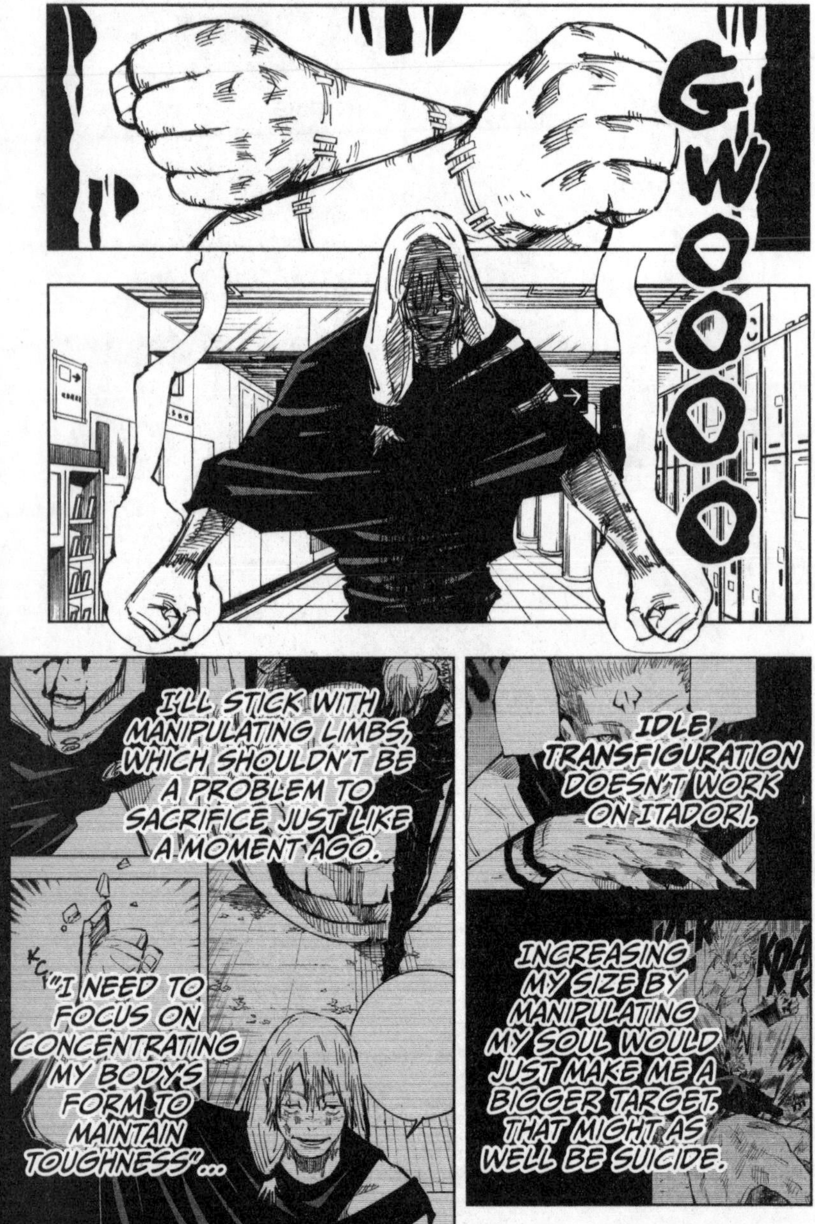
GWOOOOO
IDLE TRANSFIGURATION DOESN'T WORK ON ITADORI.
INCREASING MY SIZE BY MANIPULATING MY SOUL WOULD JUST MAKE ME A BIGGER TARGET. THAT MIGHT AS WELL BE SUICIDE.
I'LL STICK WITH MANIPULATING LIMBS, WHICH SHOULDN'T BE A PROBLEM TO SACRIFICE JUST LIKE A MOMENT AGO.
"I NEED TO FOCUS ON CONCENTRATING MY BODY'S FORM TO MAINTAIN TOUGHNESS"...

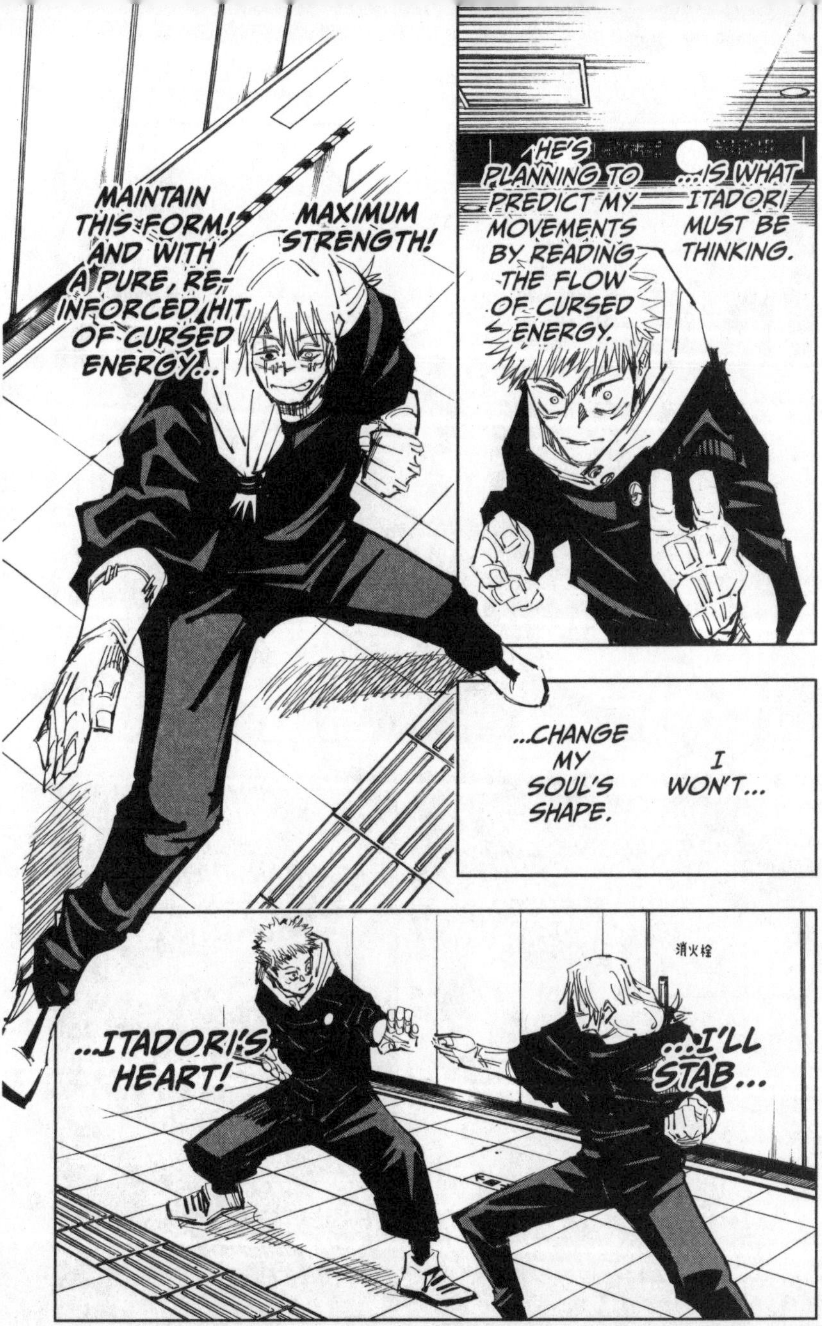
HE'S PLANNING TO PREDICT MY MOVEMENTS BY READING THE FLOW OF CURSED ENERGY.
...IS WHAT ITADORI MUST BE THINKING.
I WON'T...
...CHANGE MY SOUL'S SHAPE.
MAXIMUM STRENGTH!
MAINTAIN THIS FORM! AND WITH A PURE, RE-INFORCED HIT OF CURSED ENERGY...
消火栓
...I'LL STAB...
...ITADORI'S HEART!

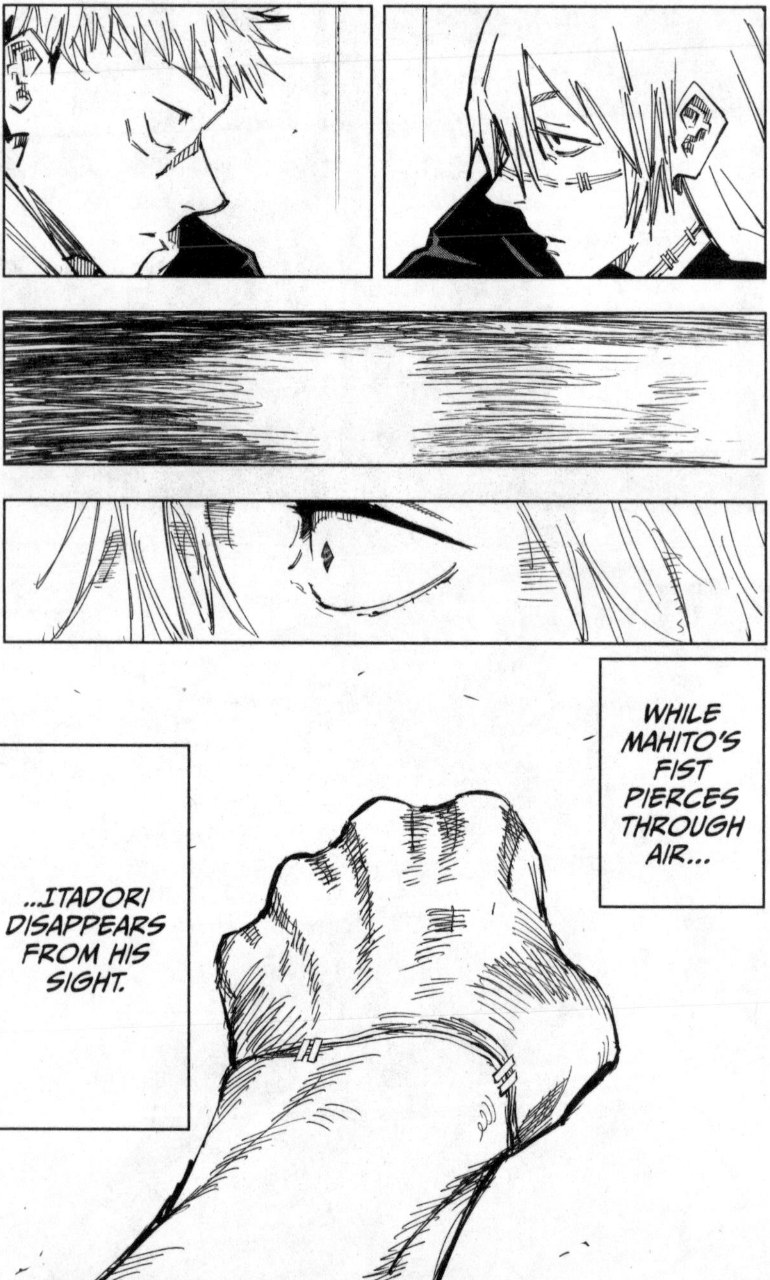
WHILE MAHITO'S FIST PIERCES THROUGH AIR...
...ITADORI DISAPPEARS FROM HIS SIGHT.

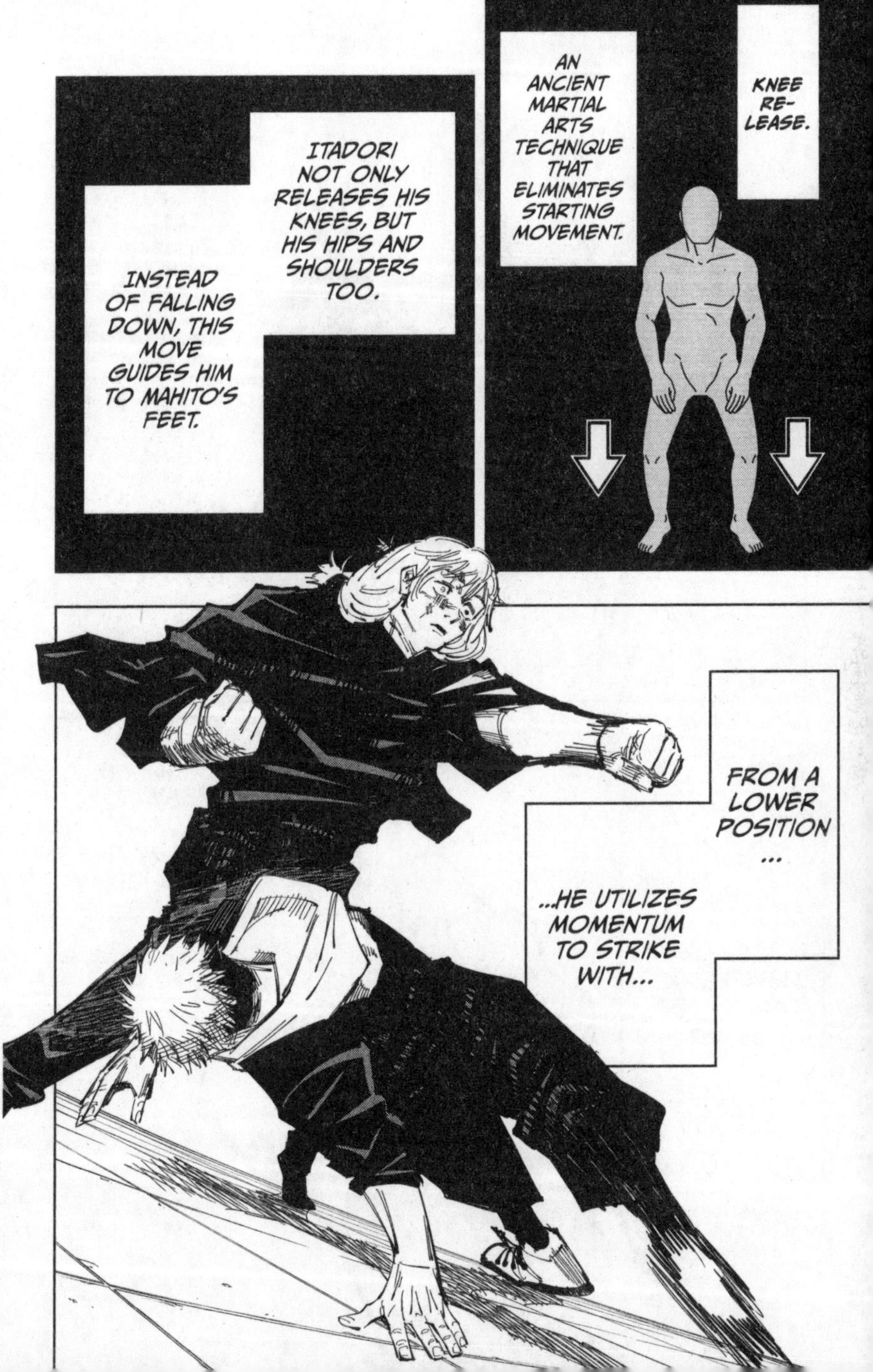
KNEE RE-LEASE.
AN ANCIENT MARTIAL ARTS TECHNIQUE THAT ELIMINATES STARTING MOVEMENT.
ITADORI NOT ONLY RELEASES HIS KNEES, BUT HIS HIPS AND SHOULDERS TOO.
INSTEAD OF FALLING DOWN, THIS MOVE GUIDES HIM TO MAHITO'S FEET.
FROM A LOWER POSITION ...
...HE UTILIZES MOMENTUM TO STRIKE WITH...

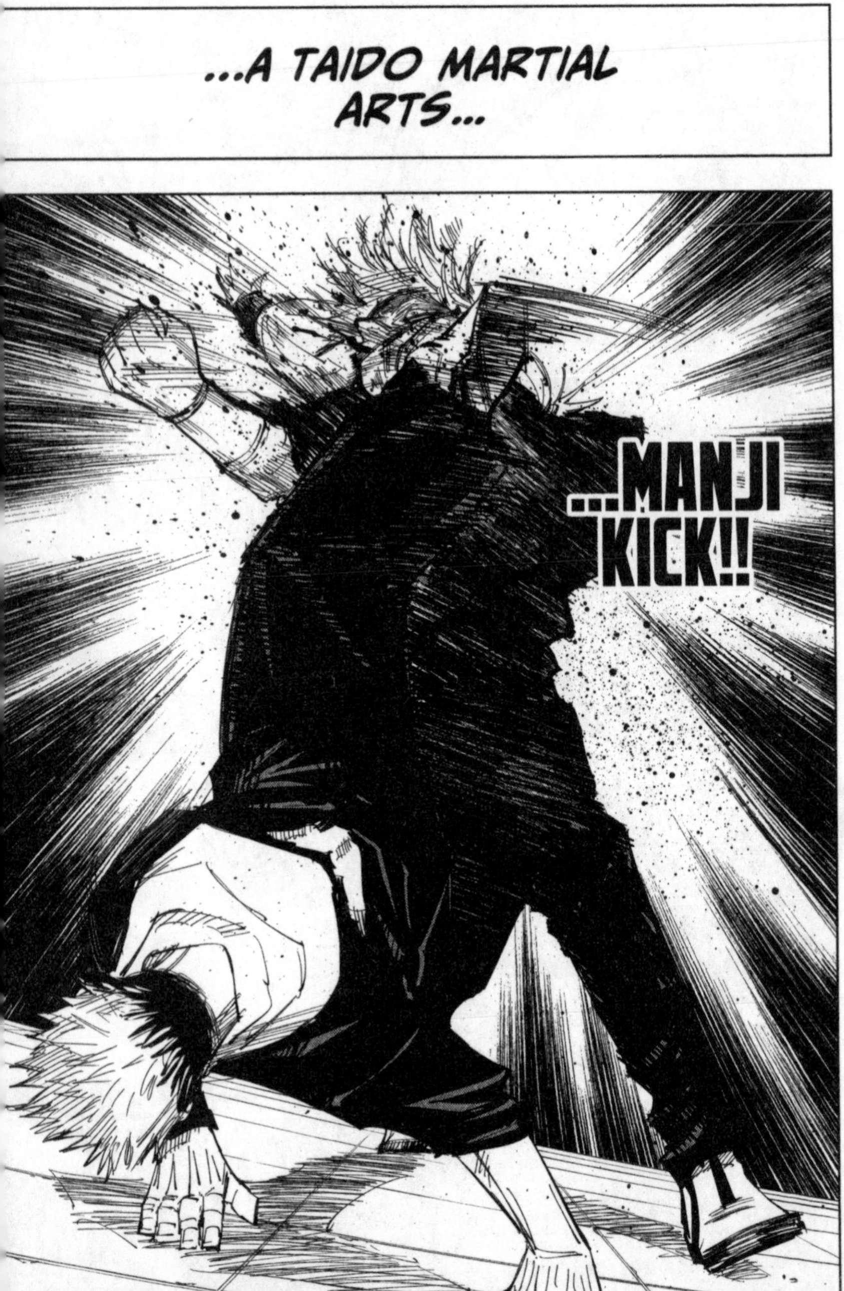
...A TAIDO MARTIAL ARTS...
...MANJI KICK!!

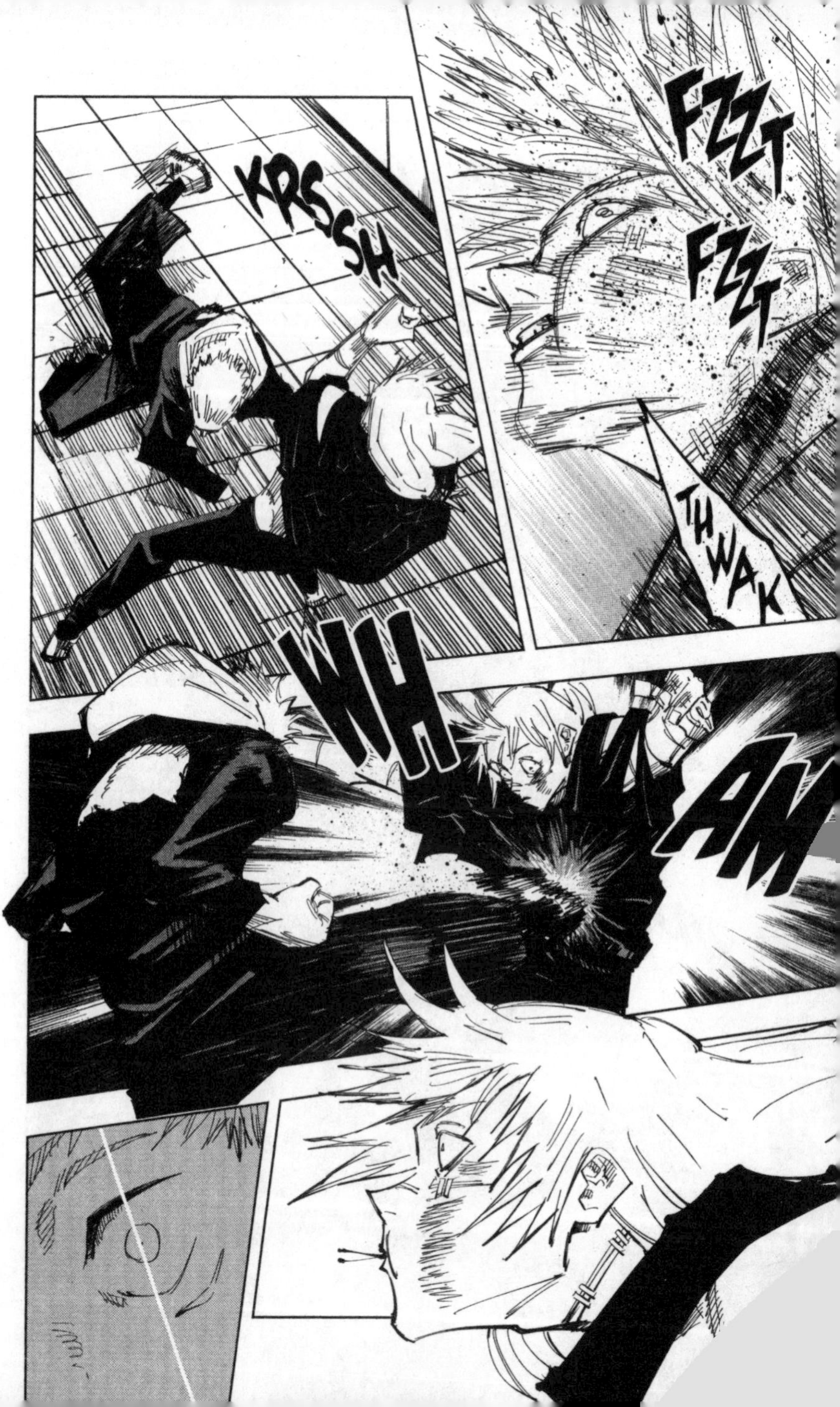
FZZT
FZZT
THWAK
KRSSSH
WHAM

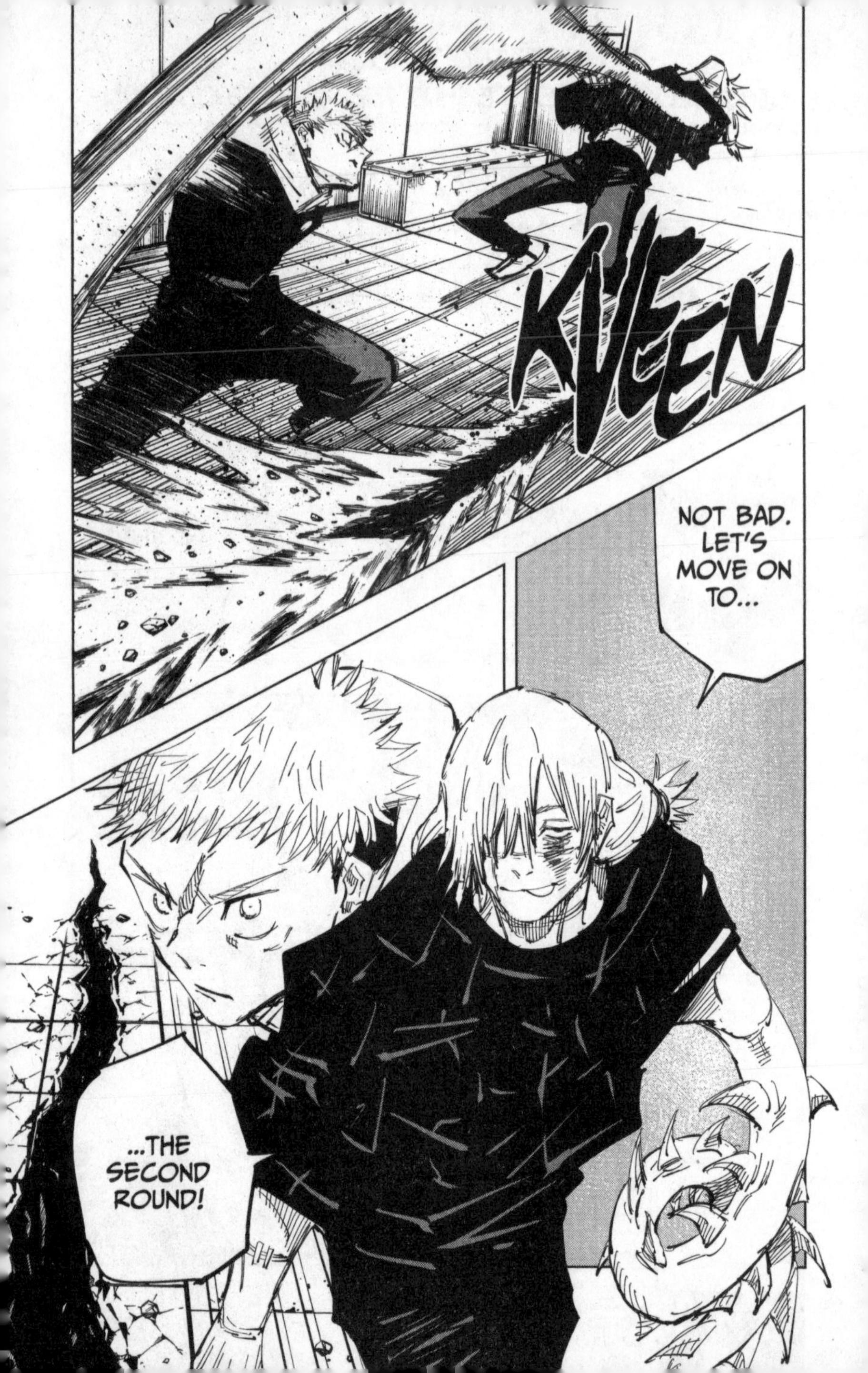
KVEEN
NOT BAD. LET'S MOVE ON TO...
...THE SECOND ROUND!

GETTING IT RIGHT!!
LIMITLESS CURSED TECHNIQUE ~INTRODUCTION~

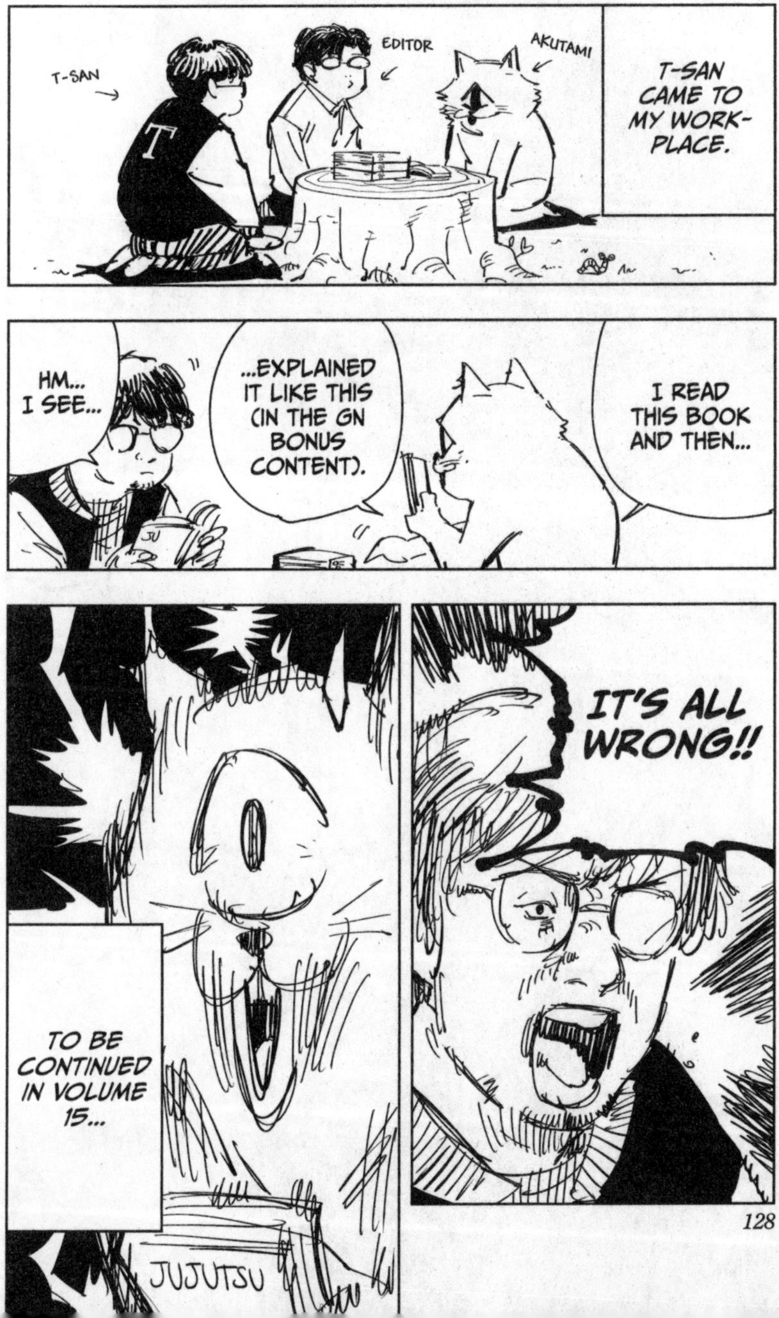

T-SAN CAME TO MY WORK-PLACE.
AKUTAMI
EDITOR
T-SAN
I READ THIS BOOK AND THEN...
...EXPLAINED IT LIKE THIS (IN THE GN BONUS CONTENT).
HM... I SEE...
IT'S ALL WRONG!!
TO BE CONTINUED IN VOLUME 15...
JUJUTSU

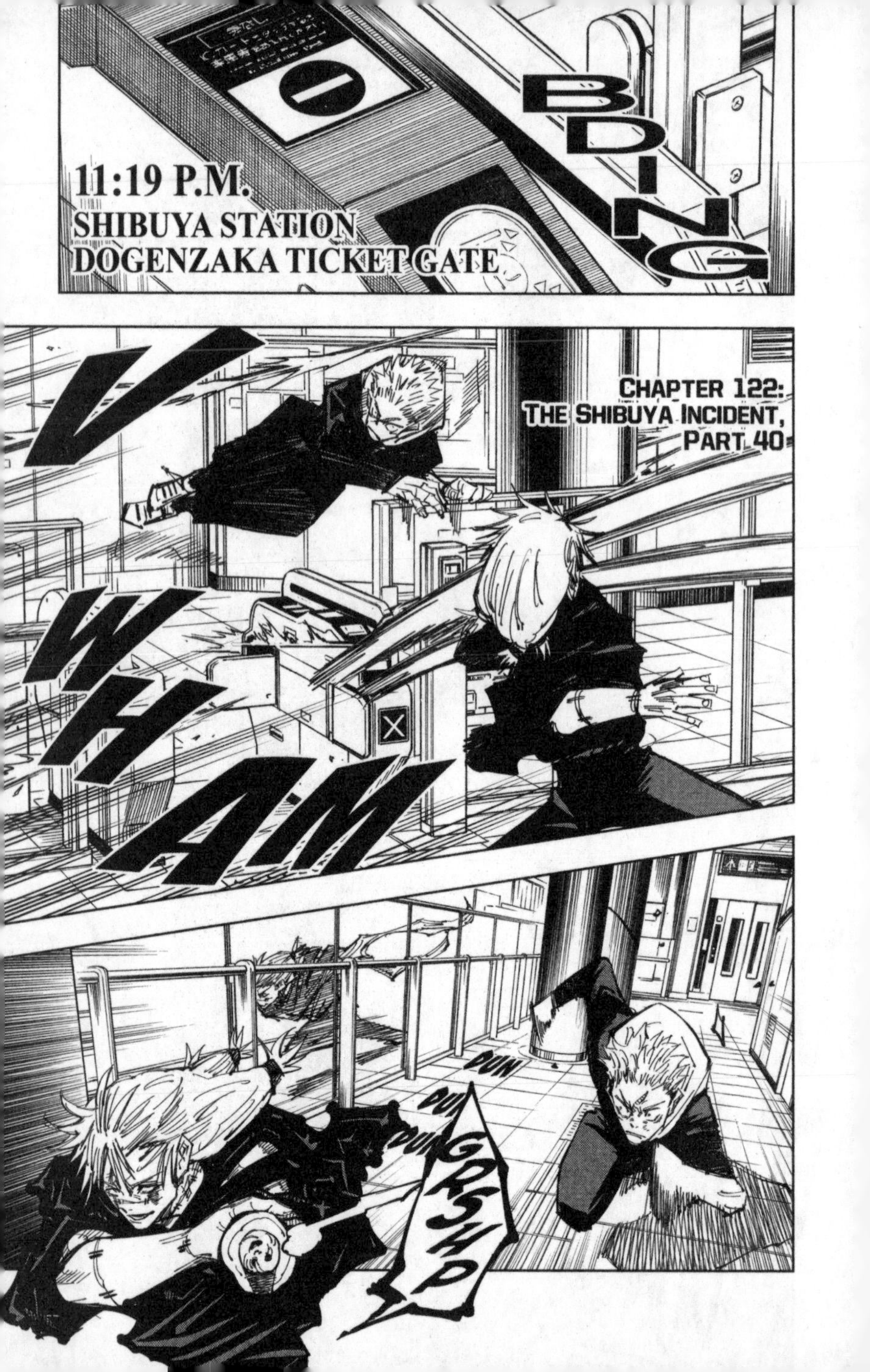
11:19 P.M.
SHIBUYA STATION
DOGENZAKA TICKET GATE
BDING
CHAPTER 122:
THE SHIBUYA INCIDENT,
PART 40
VWHAM
DUN
DUN
DUN
GRSHP

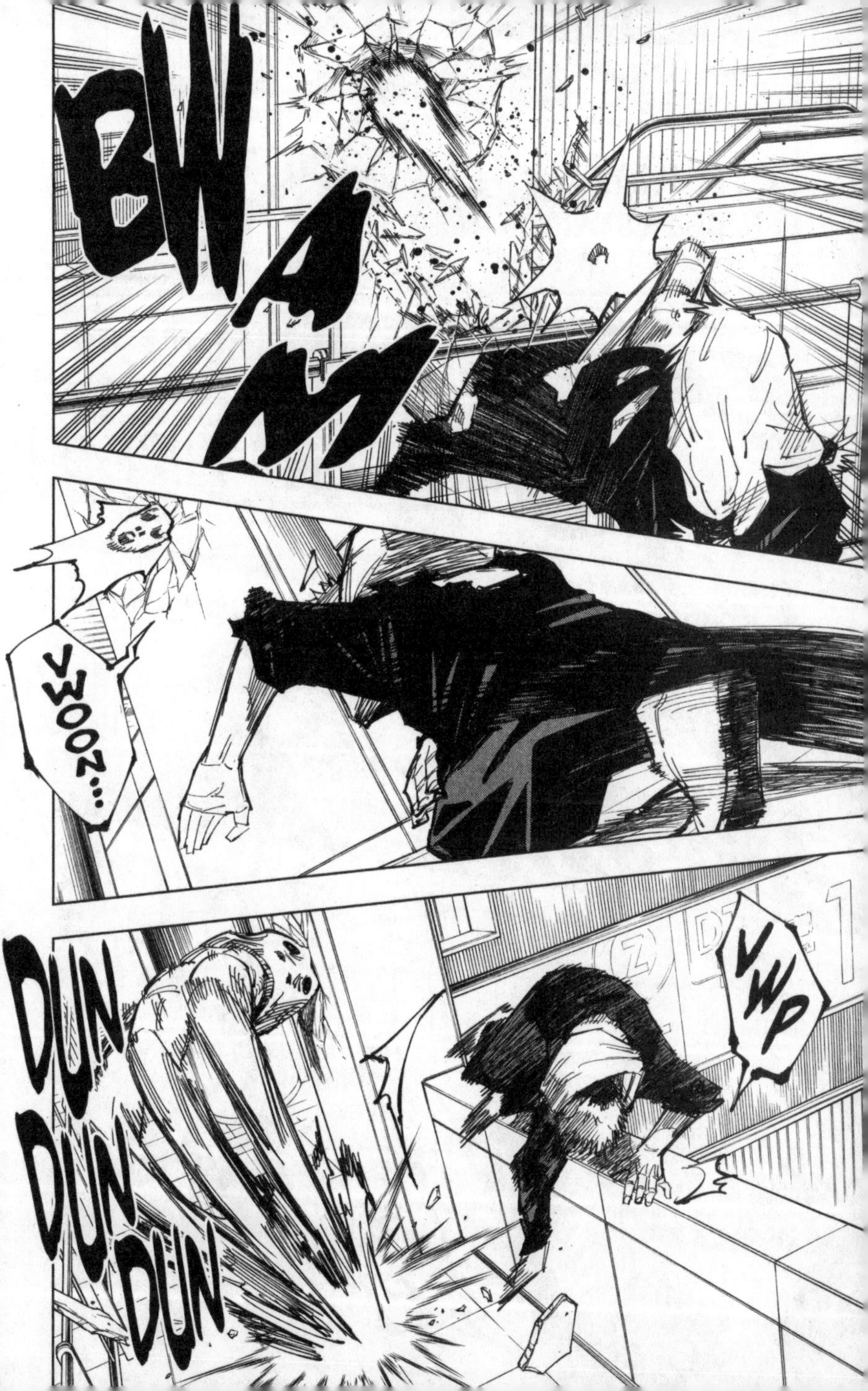
BWAM
VWOON...
VWP
DUN DUN DUN DUN

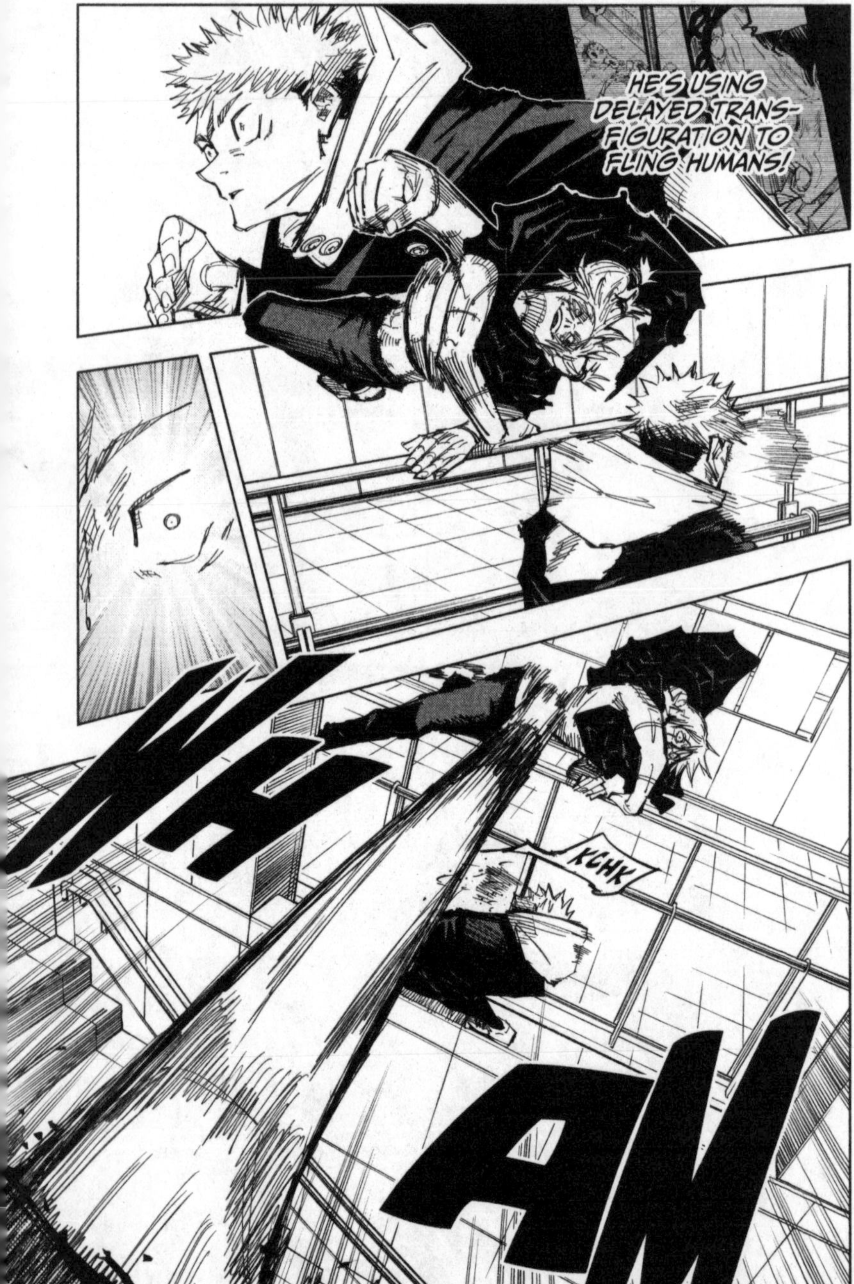
HE'S USING DELAYED TRANS-FIGURATION TO FLING HUMANS!
WHAM
KCHK

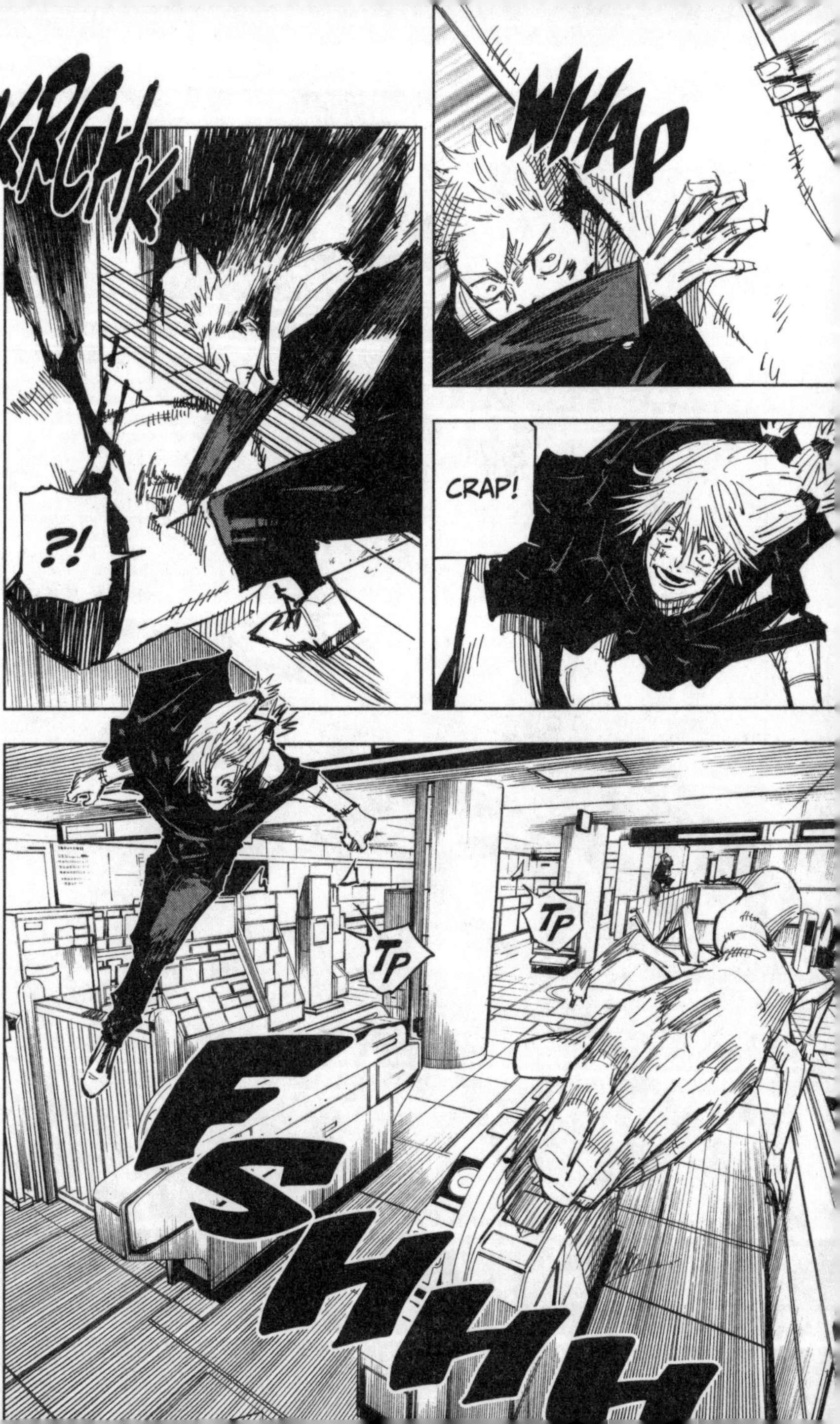
WHAP
CRAP!
KRCHK
?!
TP
TP
FSHHHH

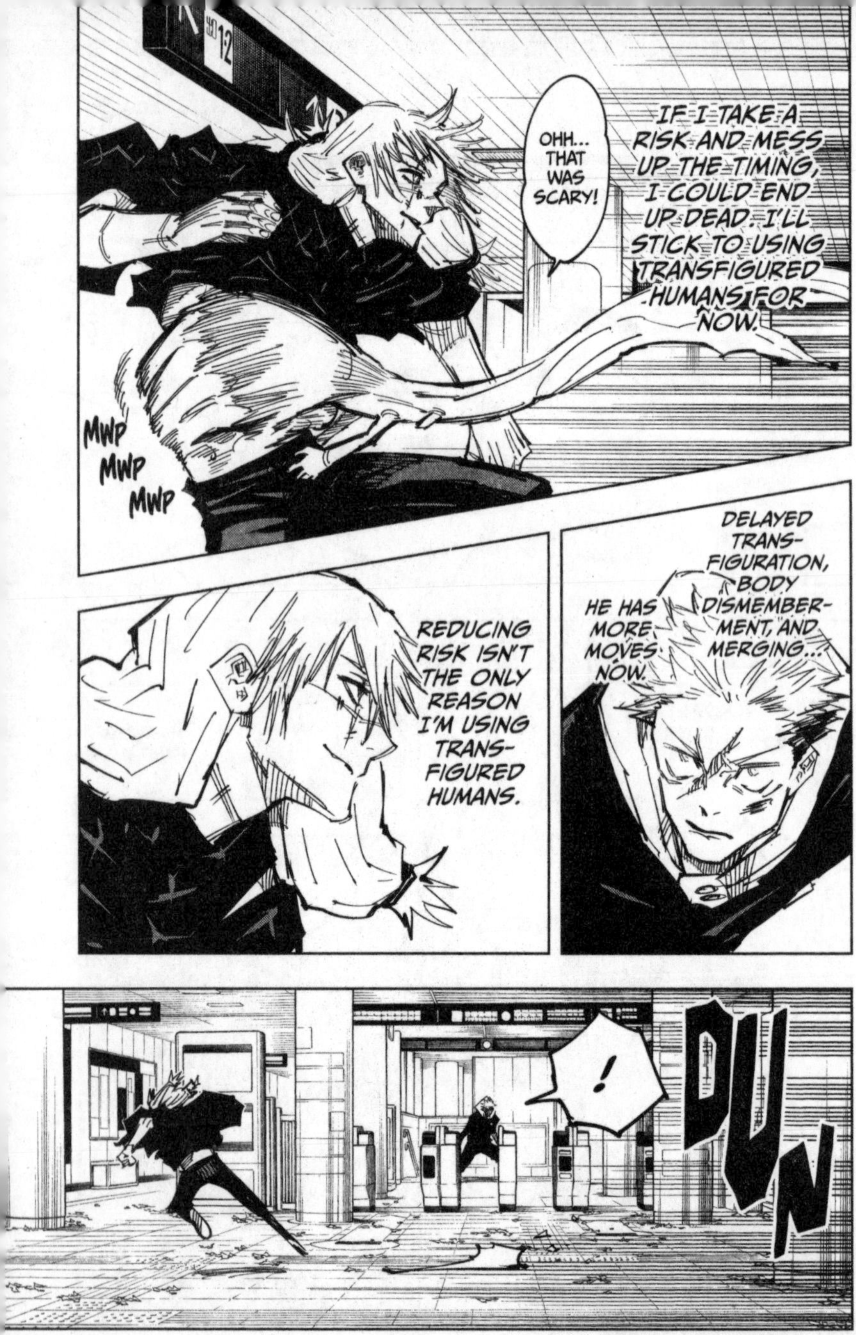
OHH... THAT WAS SCARY!
IF I TAKE A RISK AND MESS UP THE TIMING, I COULD END UP DEAD. I'LL STICK TO USING TRANSFIGURED HUMANS FOR NOW.
MWP MWP MWP
DELAYED TRANS-FIGURATION, BODY DISMEMBER-MENT, AND MERGING...
HE HAS MORE MOVES NOW.
REDUCING RISK ISN'T THE ONLY REASON I'M USING TRANS-FIGURED HUMANS.
DUN
!

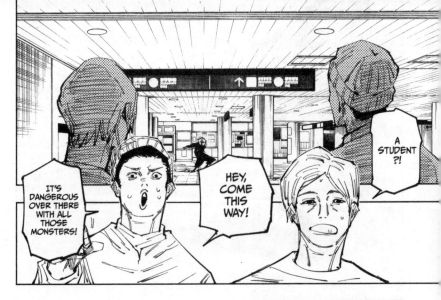

IT'S DANGEROUS OVER THERE WITH ALL THOSE MONSTERS!

HEY, COME THIS WAY!

A STUDENT?!

SORRY, BUT NOWHERE'S SAFE IN SHIBUYA.

TRY TO STAY SOMEW—

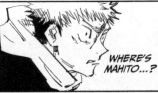

WHERE'S MAHITO...?

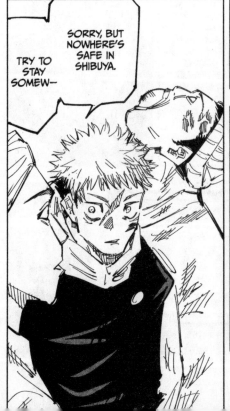

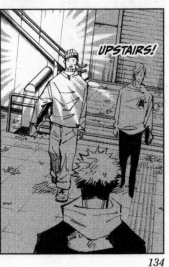

UPSTAIRS!

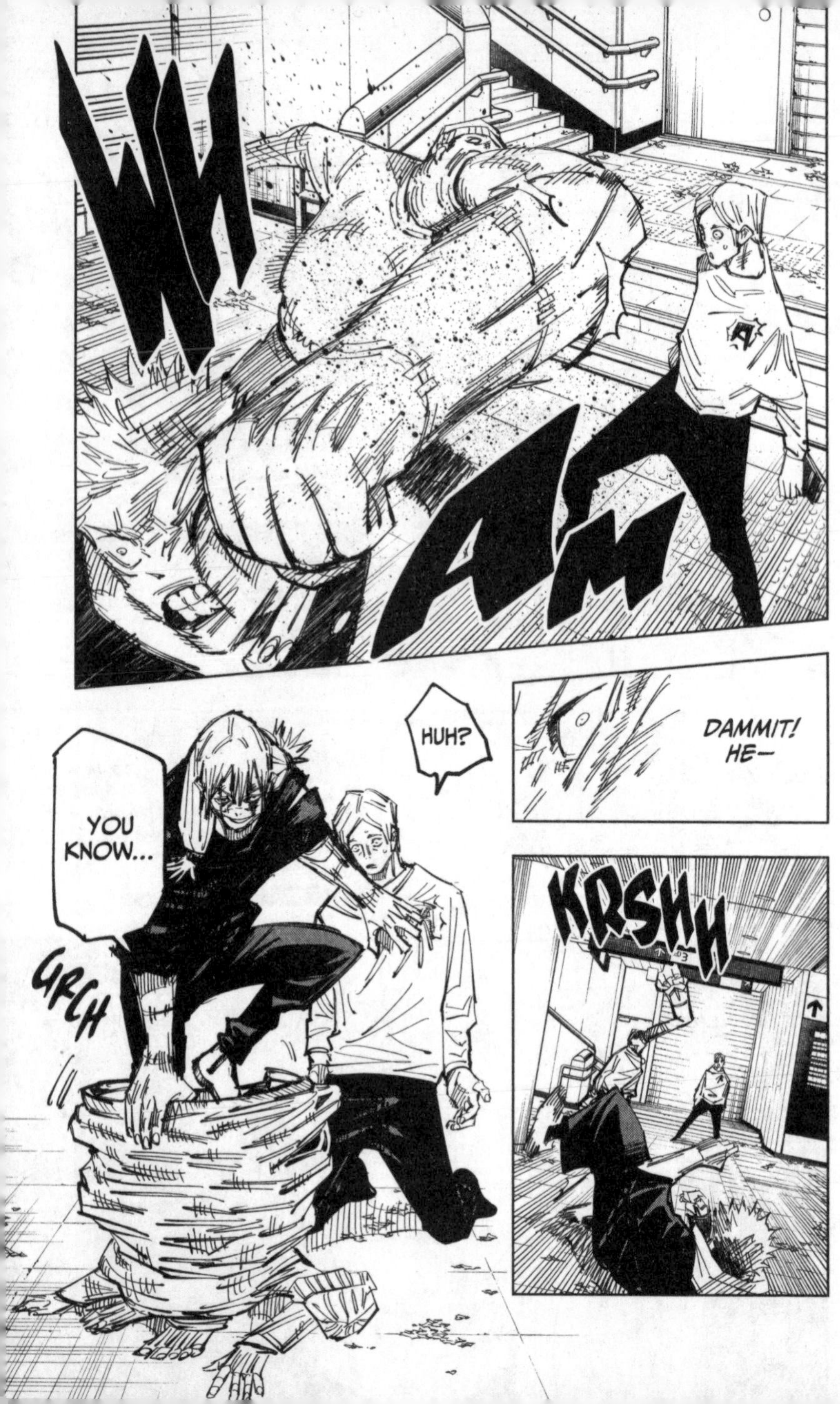
WHAM
DAMMIT! HE—
KRSHH
HUH?
YOU KNOW...
GRCH

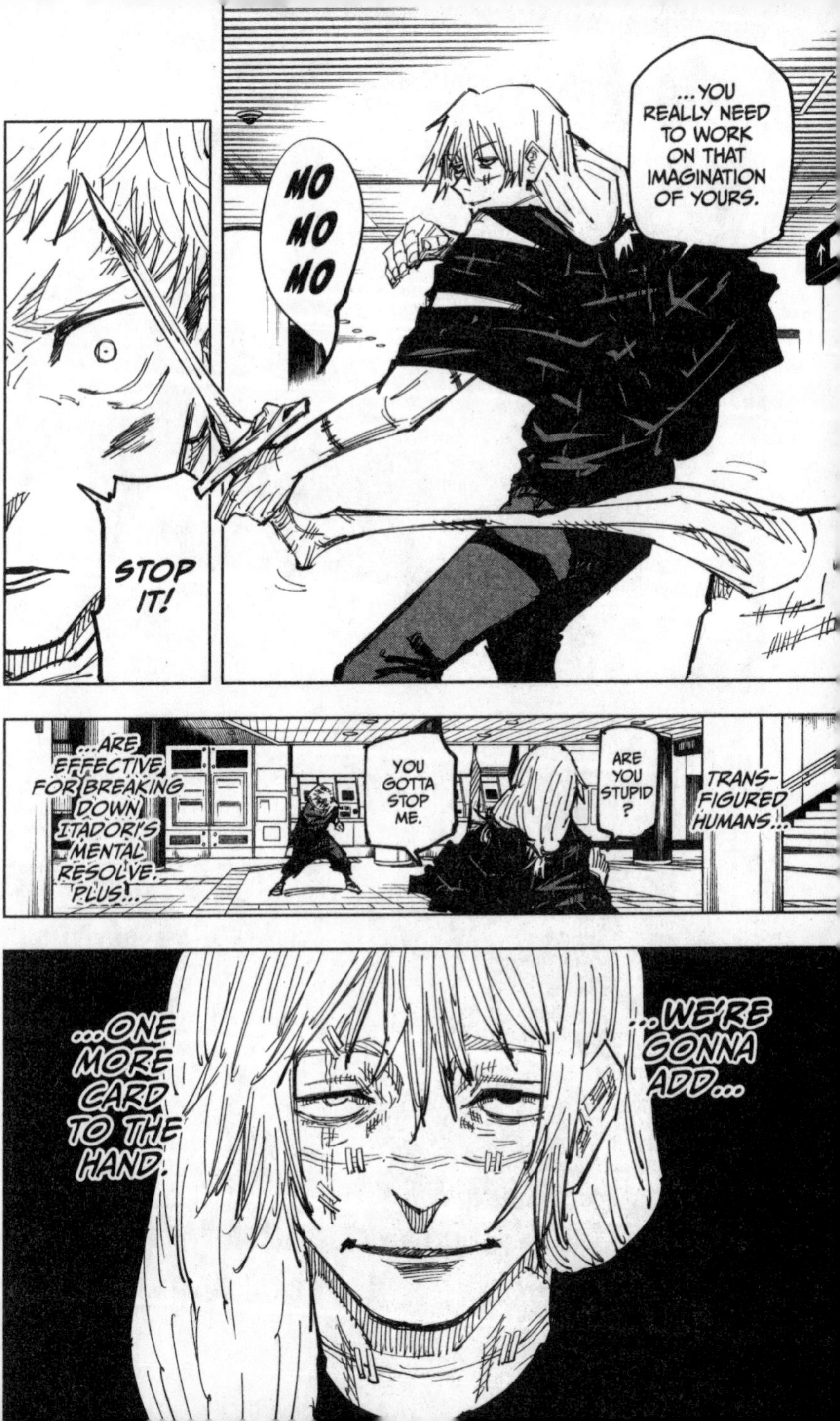
...YOU REALLY NEED TO WORK ON THAT IMAGINATION OF YOURS.
MO MO MO
STOP IT!
TRANS-FIGURED HUMANS...
ARE YOU STUPID?
YOU GOTTA STOP ME.
...ARE EFFECTIVE FOR BREAKING DOWN ITADORI'S MENTAL RESOLVE. PLUS...
...WE'RE GONNA ADD...
...ONE MORE CARD TO THE HAND.

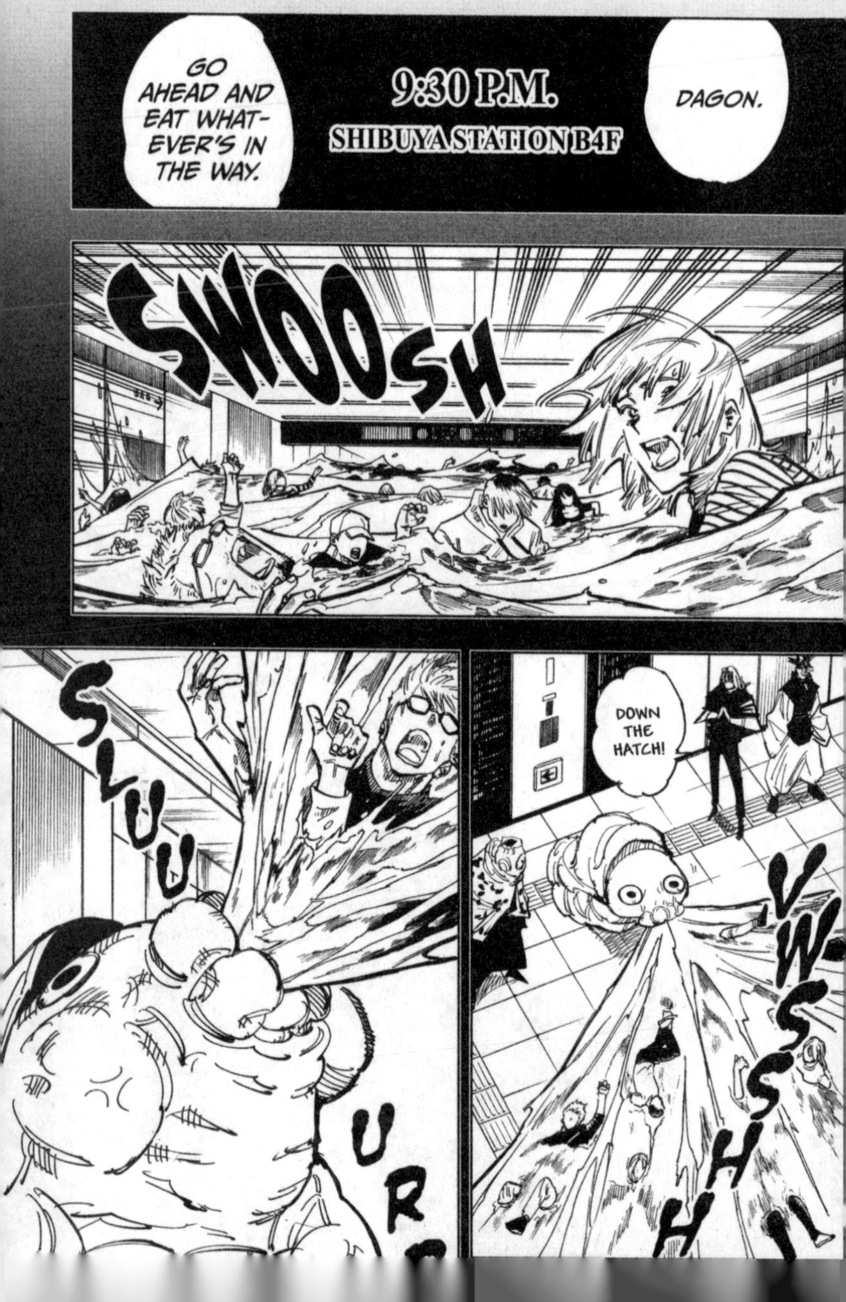
DAGON.
9:30 P.M.
SHIBUYA STATION B4F
GO AHEAD AND EAT WHAT-EVER'S IN THE WAY.
SWOOSH
DOWN THE HATCH!
VWSSHHH
SLUUU
URR

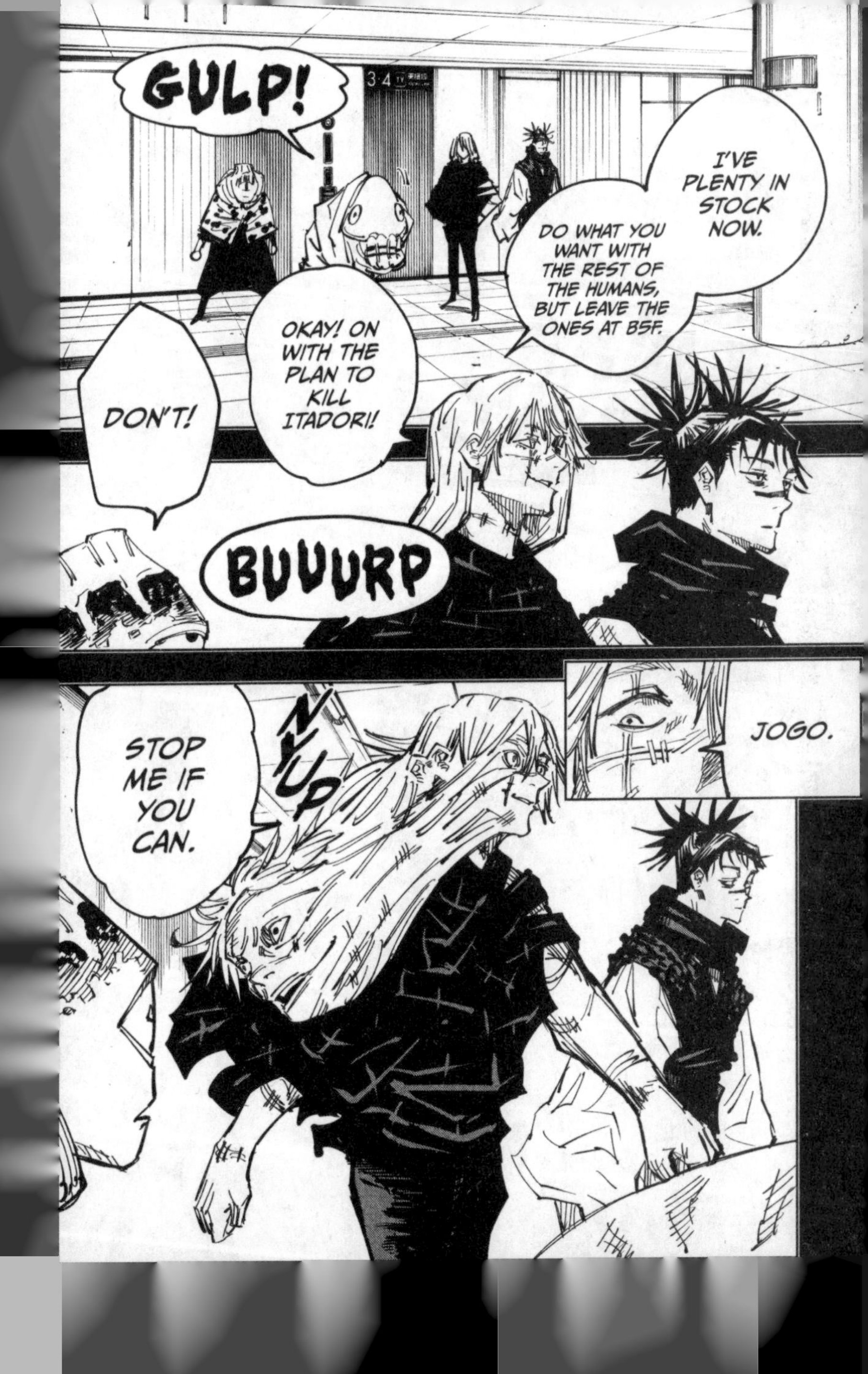
I'VE PLENTY IN STOCK NOW.
DO WHAT YOU WANT WITH THE REST OF THE HUMANS, BUT LEAVE THE ONES AT B5F.
GULP!
OKAY! ON WITH THE PLAN TO KILL ITADORI!
DON'T!
BUUURP
JOGO.
STOP ME IF YOU CAN.
NYUP

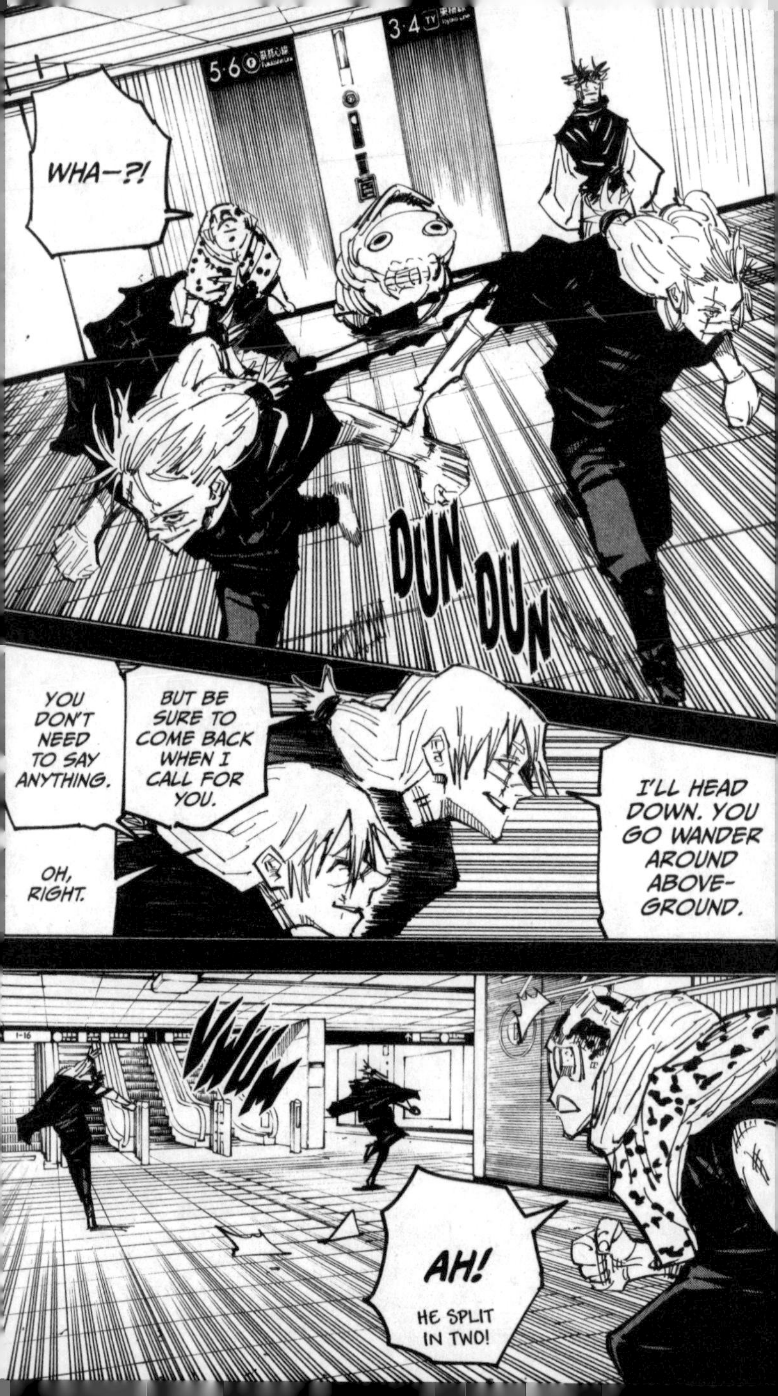
WHA—?!
DUN DUN
I'LL HEAD DOWN. YOU GO WANDER AROUND ABOVE-GROUND.
BUT BE SURE TO COME BACK WHEN I CALL FOR YOU.
YOU DON'T NEED TO SAY ANYTHING.
OH, RIGHT.
VWUM
AH!
HE SPLIT IN TWO!

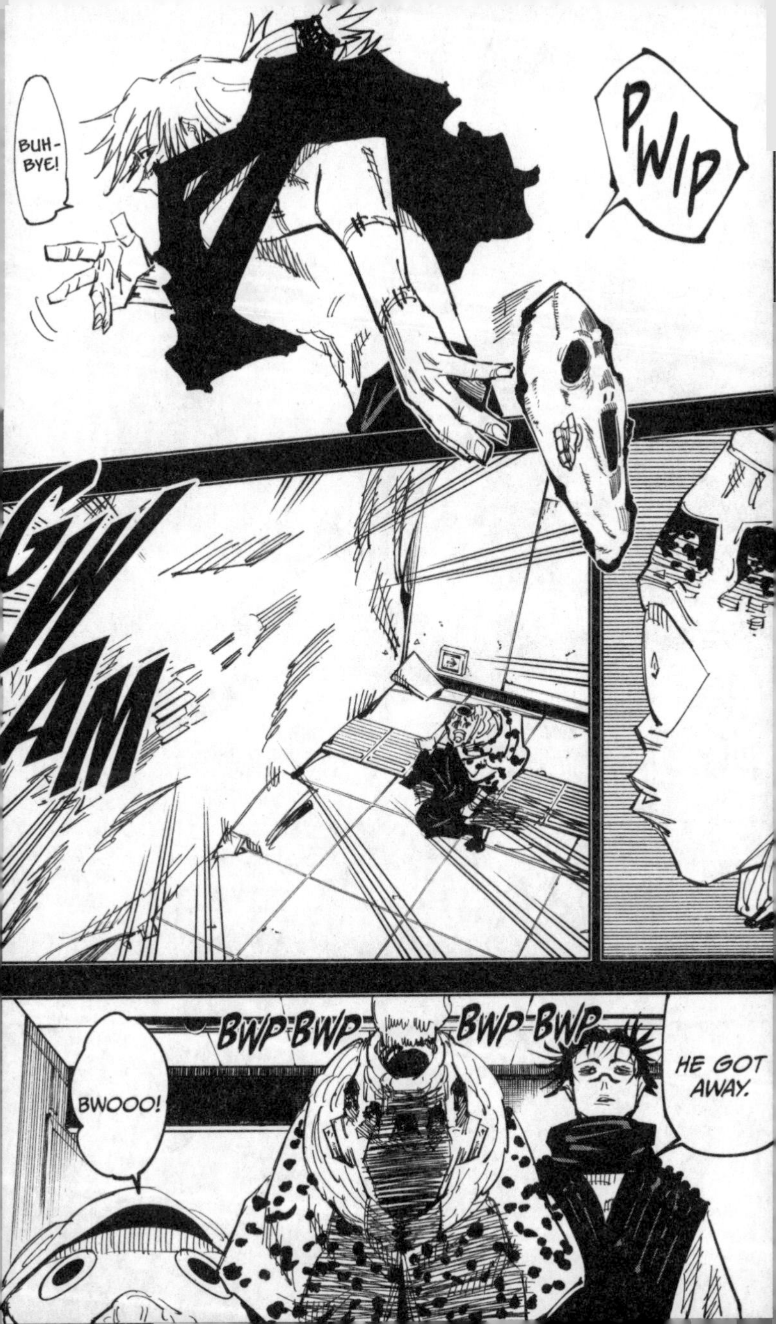
PWIP
BUH-BYE!
GWAM
HE GOT AWAY.
BWP BWP BWP BWP
BWOOO!

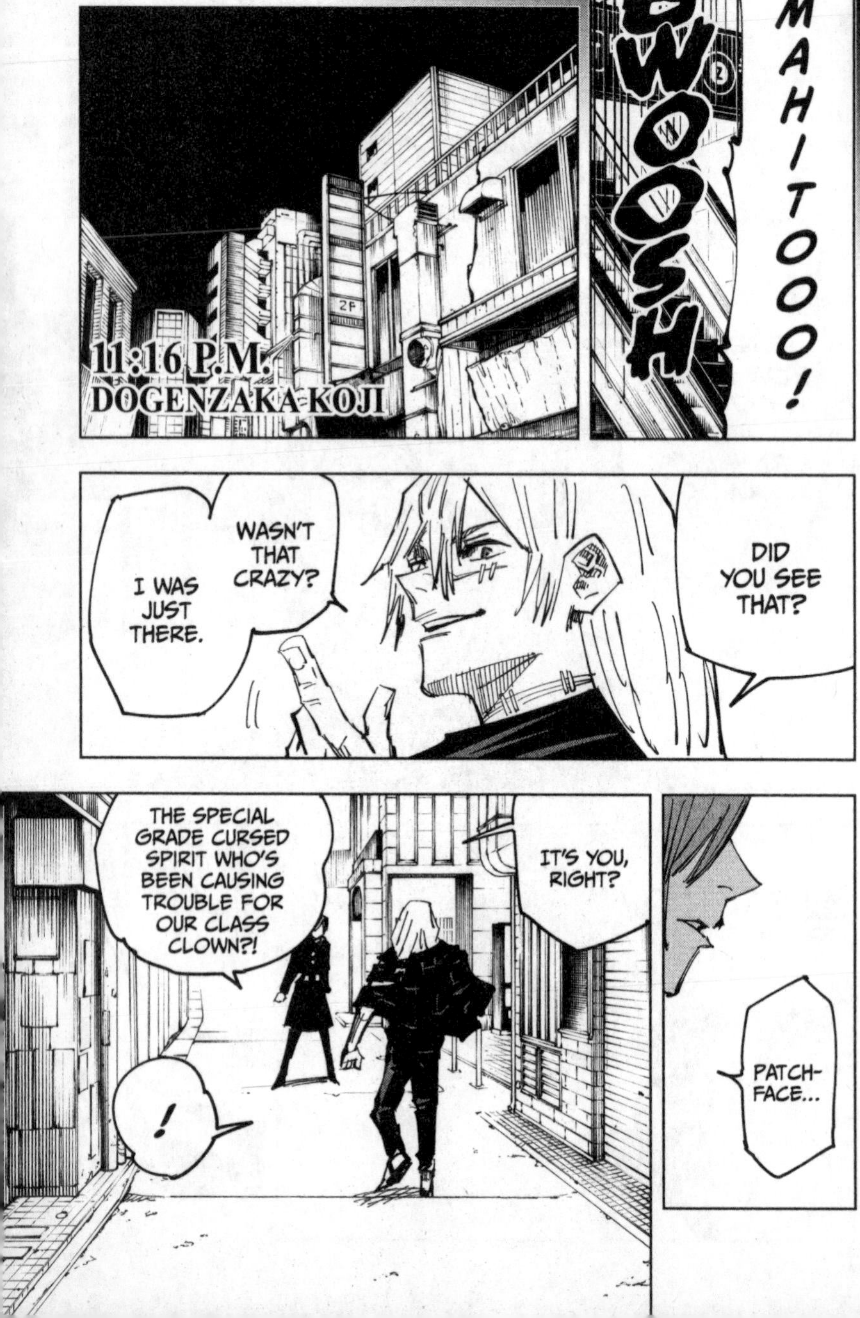

MAHITOOO!
BWOOSH
11:16 P.M.
DOGENZAKA KOJI
DID YOU SEE THAT?
WASN'T THAT CRAZY?
I WAS JUST THERE.
PATCH-FACE...
IT'S YOU, RIGHT?
THE SPECIAL GRADE CURSED SPIRIT WHO'S BEEN CAUSING TROUBLE FOR OUR CLASS CLOWN?!
!

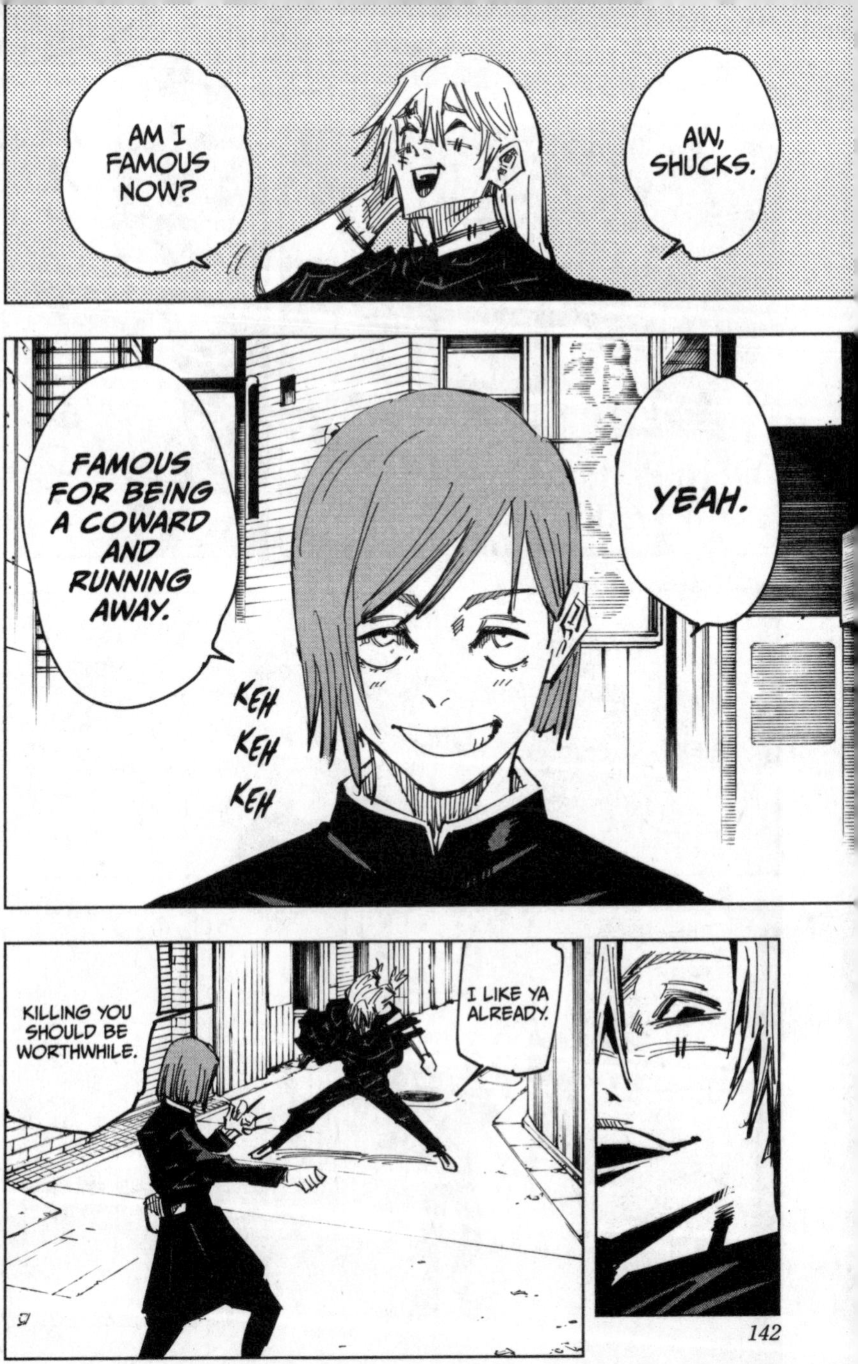
AW, SHUCKS.
AM I FAMOUS NOW?
YEAH.
FAMOUS FOR BEING A COWARD AND RUNNING AWAY.
KEH KEH KEH
I LIKE YA ALREADY.
KILLING YOU SHOULD BE WORTHWHILE.

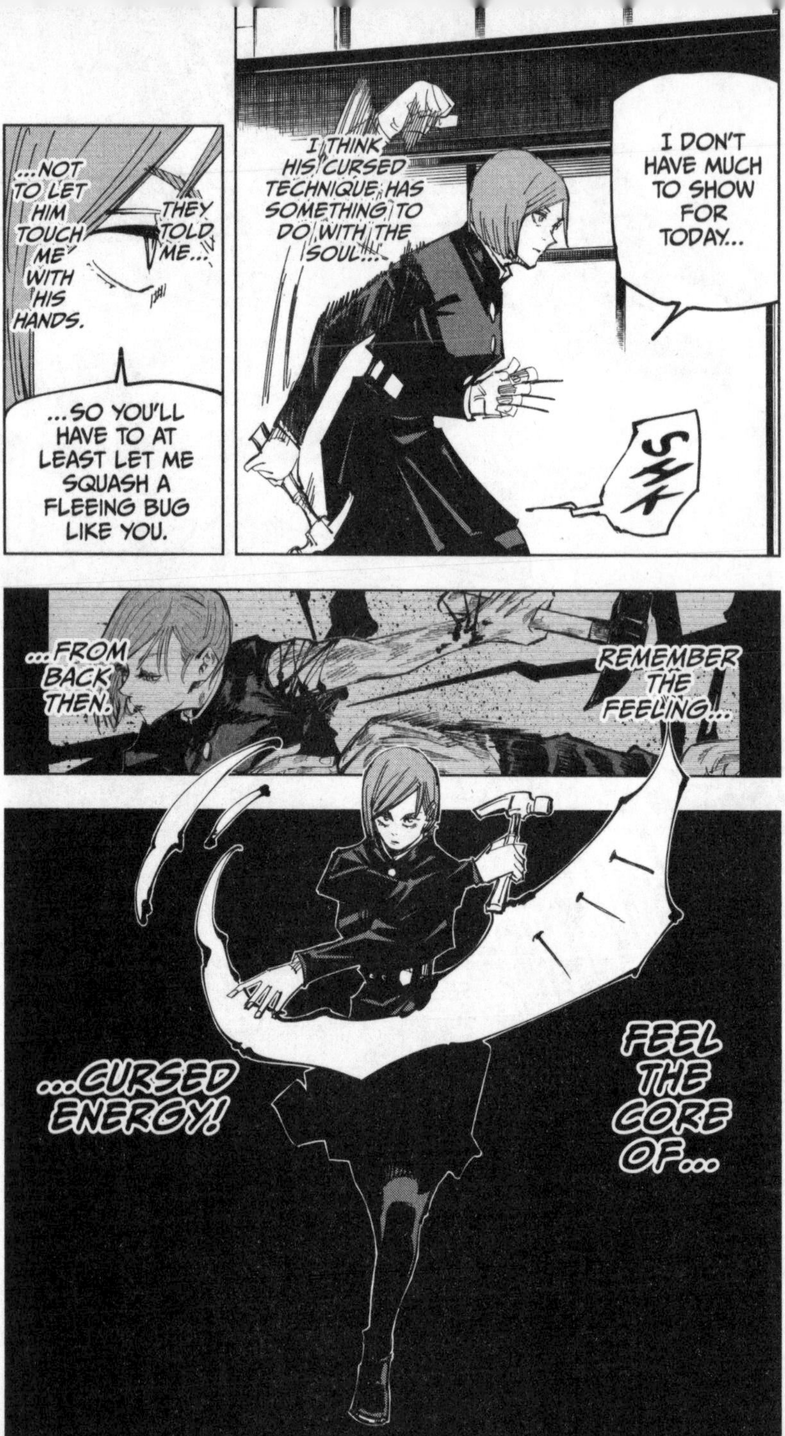
I DON'T HAVE MUCH TO SHOW FOR TODAY...
I THINK HIS CURSED TECHNIQUE HAS SOMETHING TO DO WITH THE SOUL...
SHK
THEY TOLD ME...
...NOT TO LET HIM TOUCH ME WITH HIS HANDS.
...SO YOU'LL HAVE TO AT LEAST LET ME SQUASH A FLEEING BUG LIKE YOU.
REMEMBER THE FEELING...
...FROM BACK THEN.
FEEL THE CORE OF...
...CURSED ENERGY!

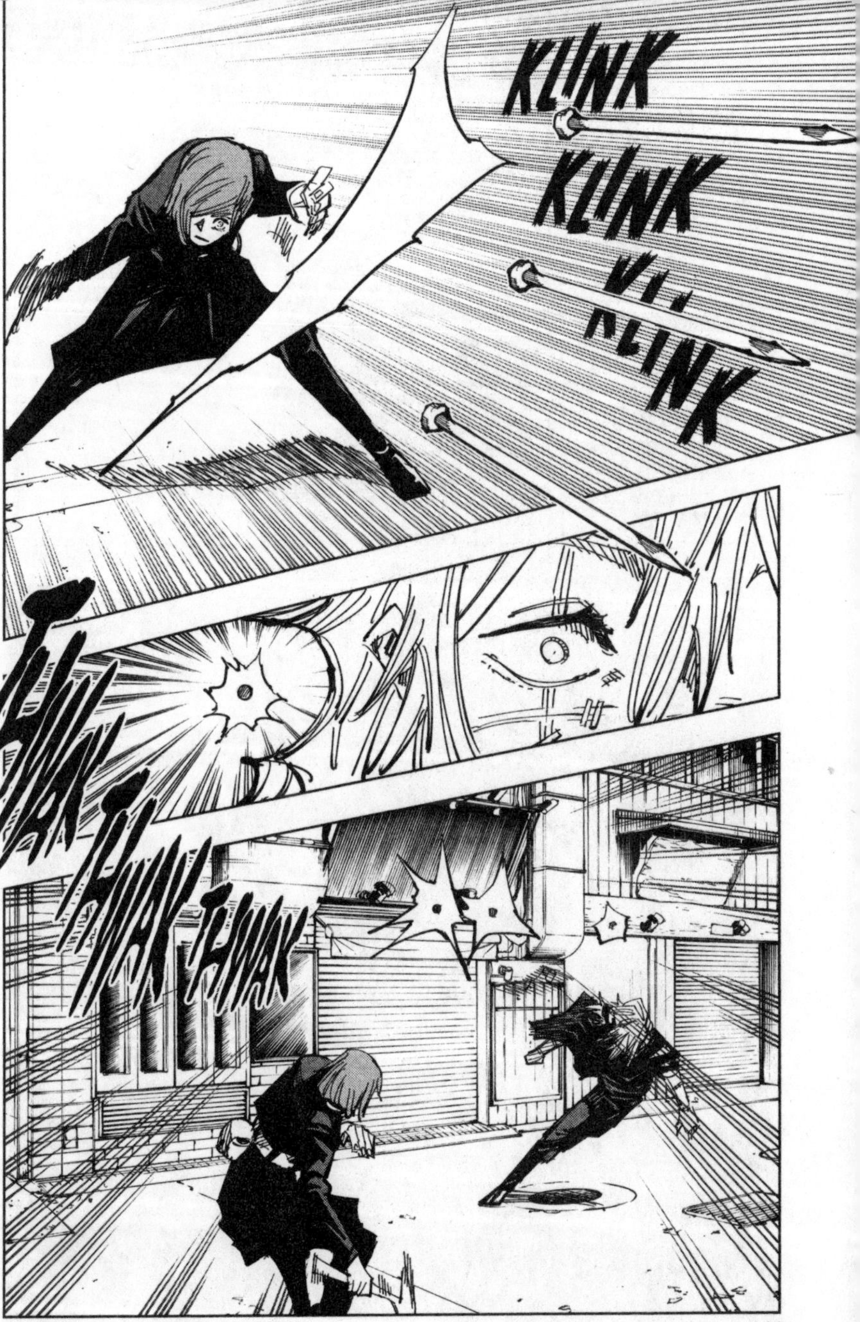
KLINK
KLINK
KLINK
THWAK
THWAK
THWAK

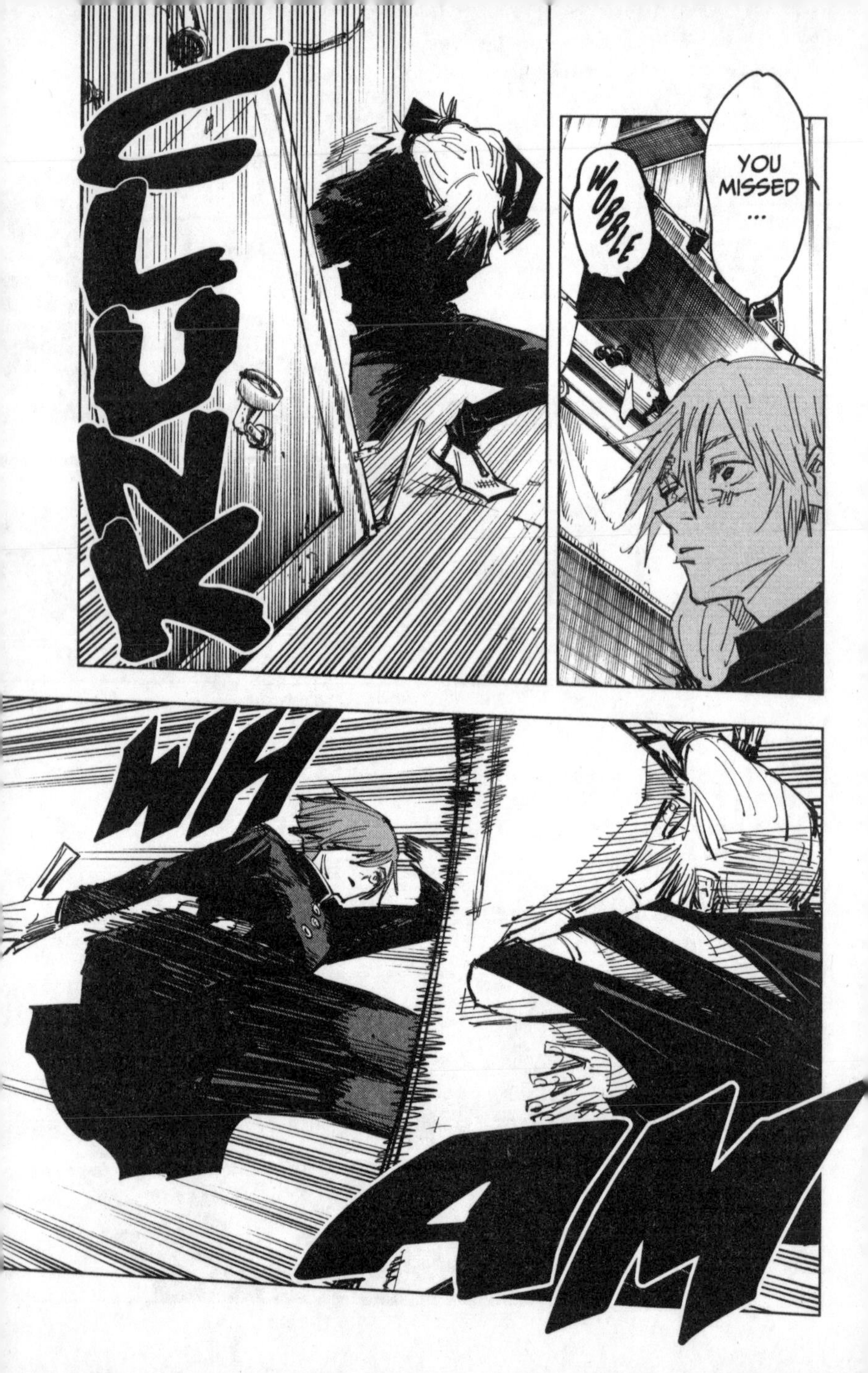
YOU MISSED ...
WOBBLE
WHAM

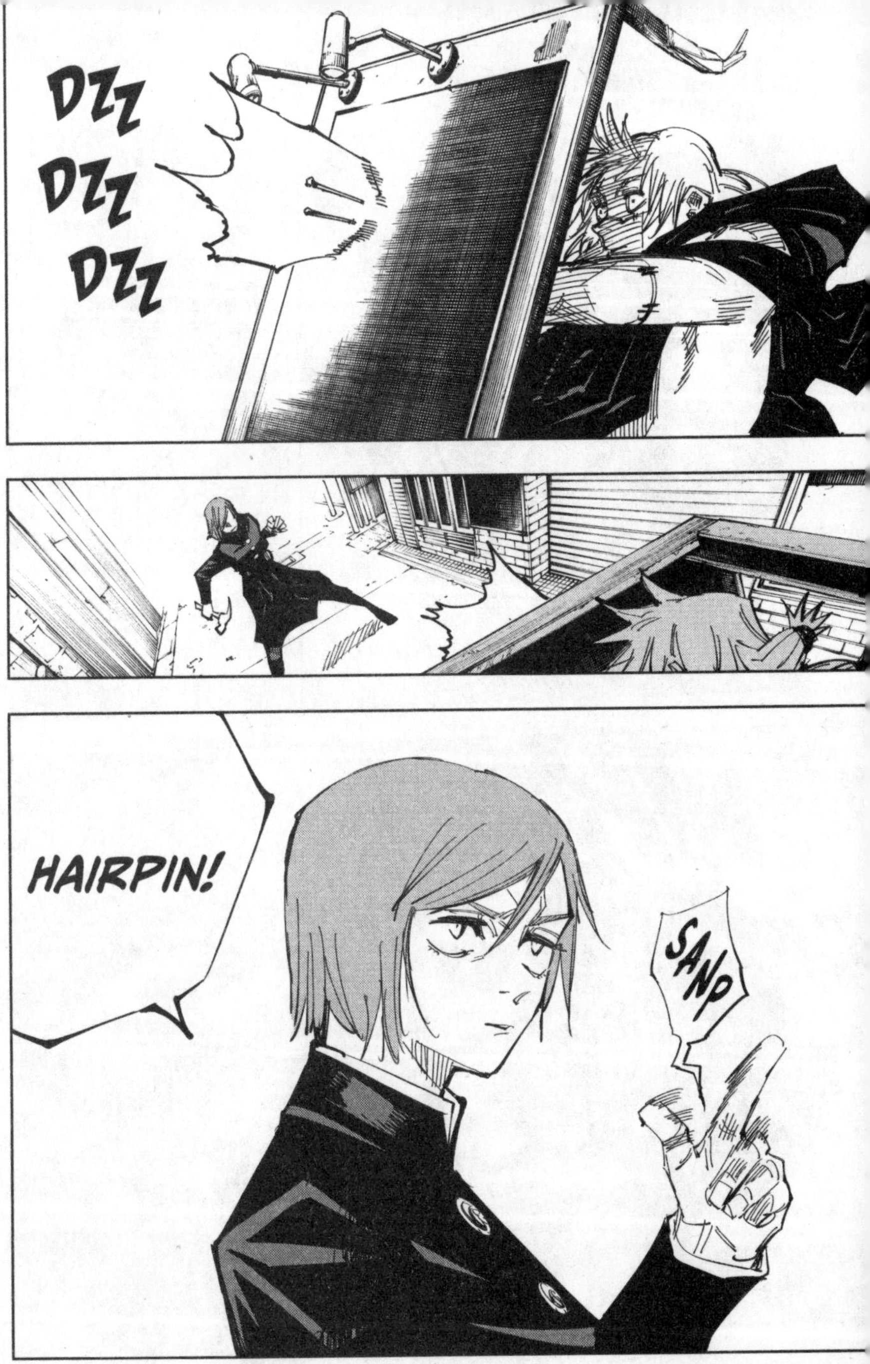
DZZ
DZZ
DZZ
HAIRPIN!
SNAP

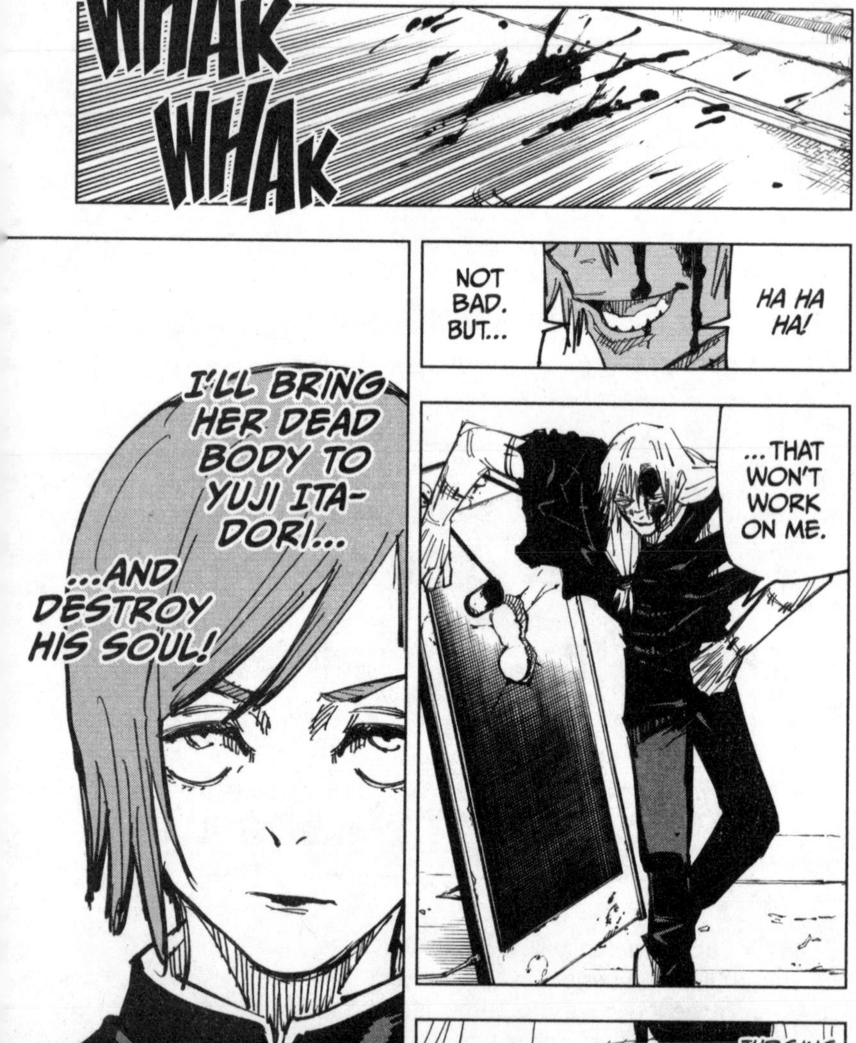
WHAK WHAK
HA HA HA!
NOT BAD. BUT...
...THAT WON'T WORK ON ME.
JUDGING BY THE WAY SHE TALKS...
...I'D SAY SHE'S A FRIEND OF HIS.
I'LL BRING HER DEAD BODY TO YUJI ITA-DORI...
...AND DESTROY HIS SOUL!

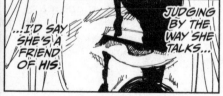

Extra Info

KRRK
VWAM
WHAM
WHAM
WHAMHAM

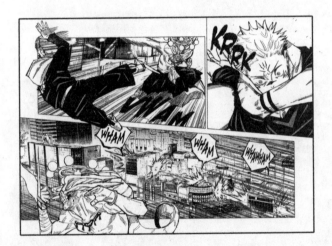

• Sukuna actually flew all the way outside the curtain in this scene.
• Since there was no particular effect on either Sukuna or Mahoraga and visually it had no particular bearing on the fight, I left it out.

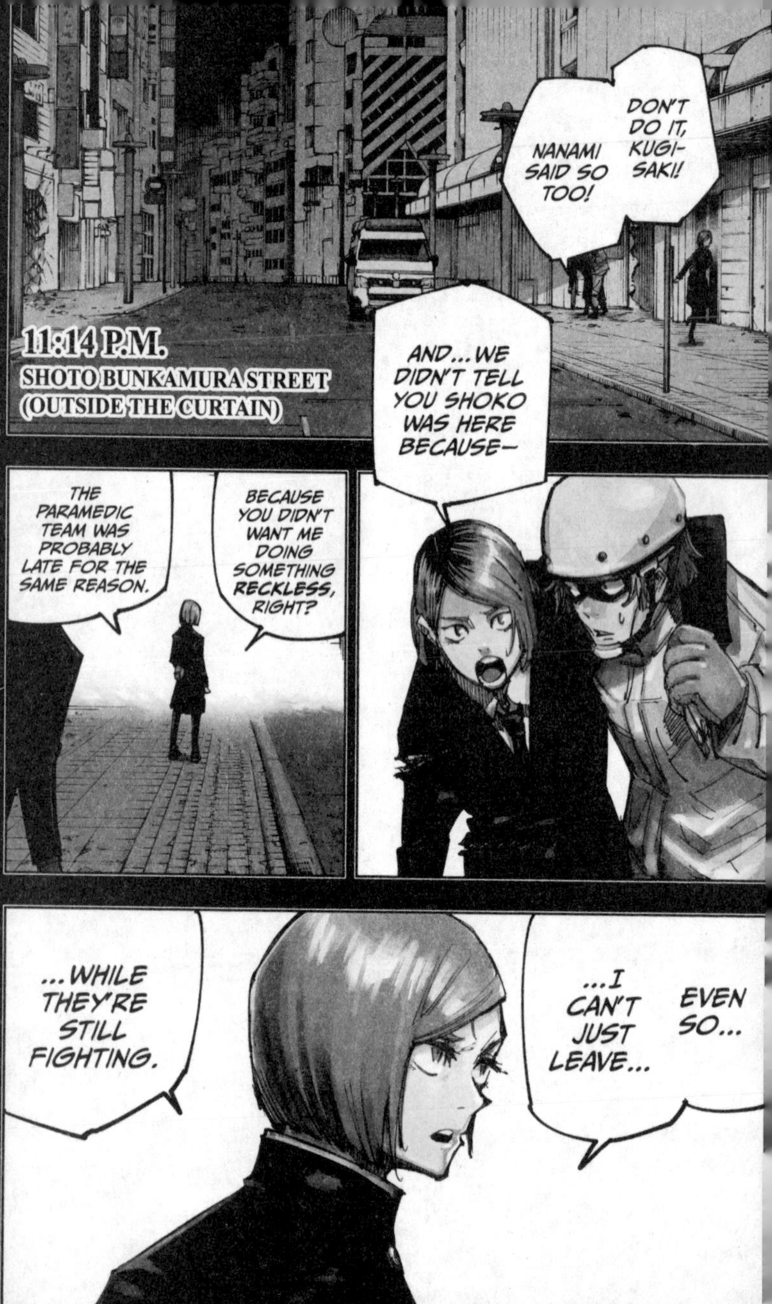
DON'T DO IT, KUGI-SAKI!
NANAMI SAID SO TOO!
11:14 P.M.
SHOTO BUNKAMURA STREET (OUTSIDE THE CURTAIN)
AND...WE DIDN'T TELL YOU SHOKO WAS HERE BECAUSE—
BECAUSE YOU DIDN'T WANT ME DOING SOMETHING RECKLESS, RIGHT?
THE PARAMEDIC TEAM WAS PROBABLY LATE FOR THE SAME REASON.
EVEN SO...
...I CAN'T JUST LEAVE...
...WHILE THEY'RE STILL FIGHTING.

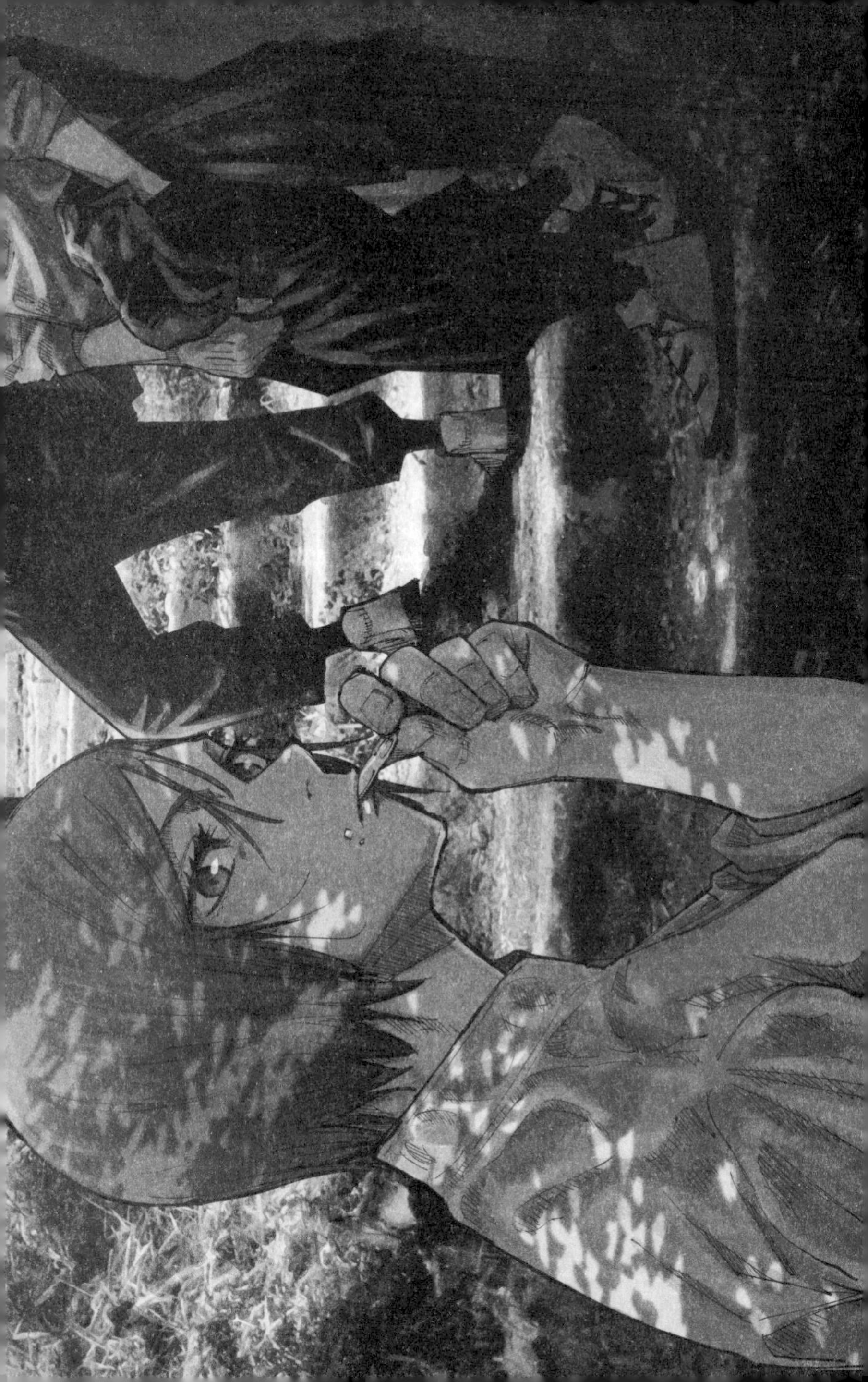

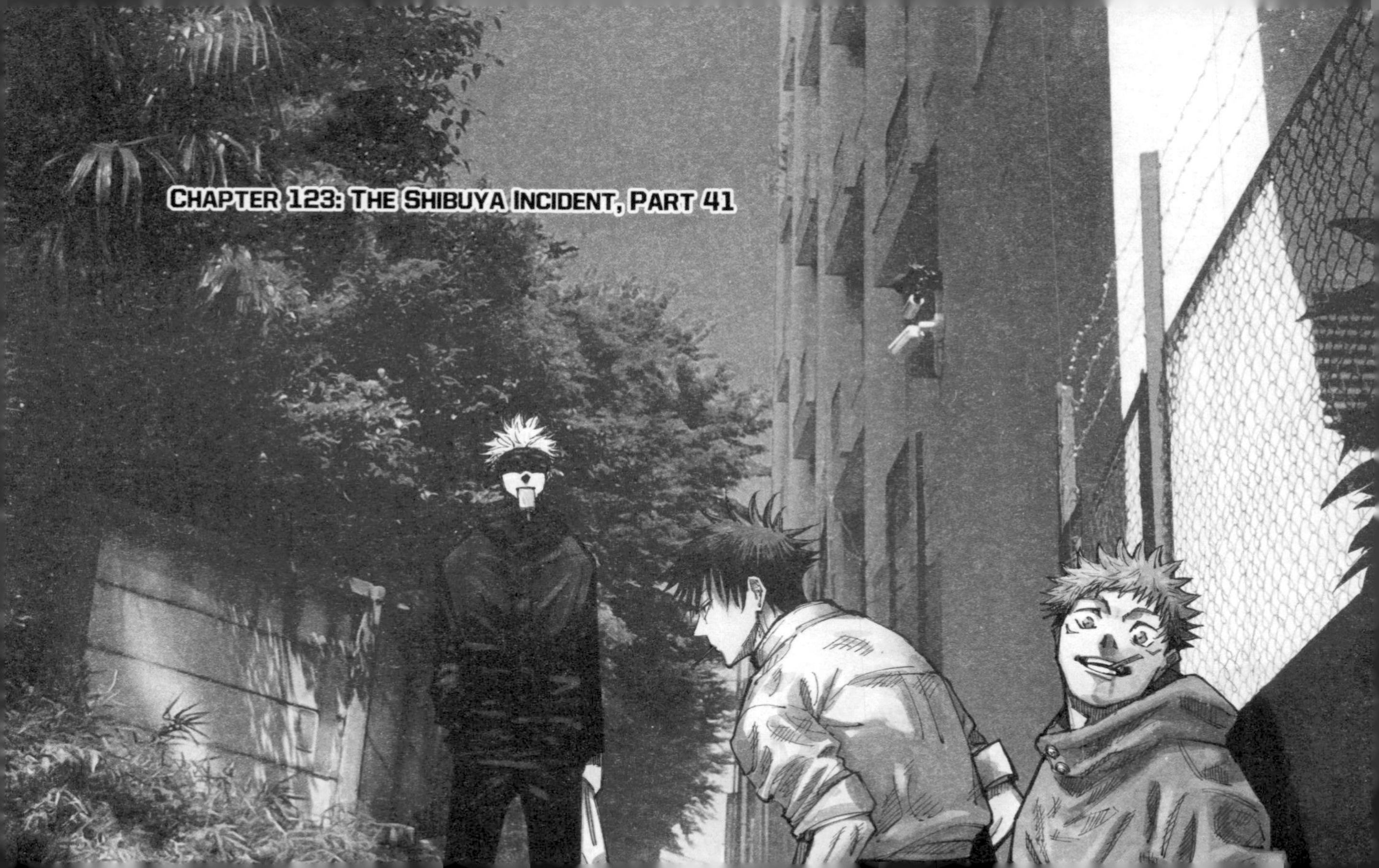
CHAPTER 123: THE SHIBUYA INCIDENT, PART 41

JUJUTSU KAISEN

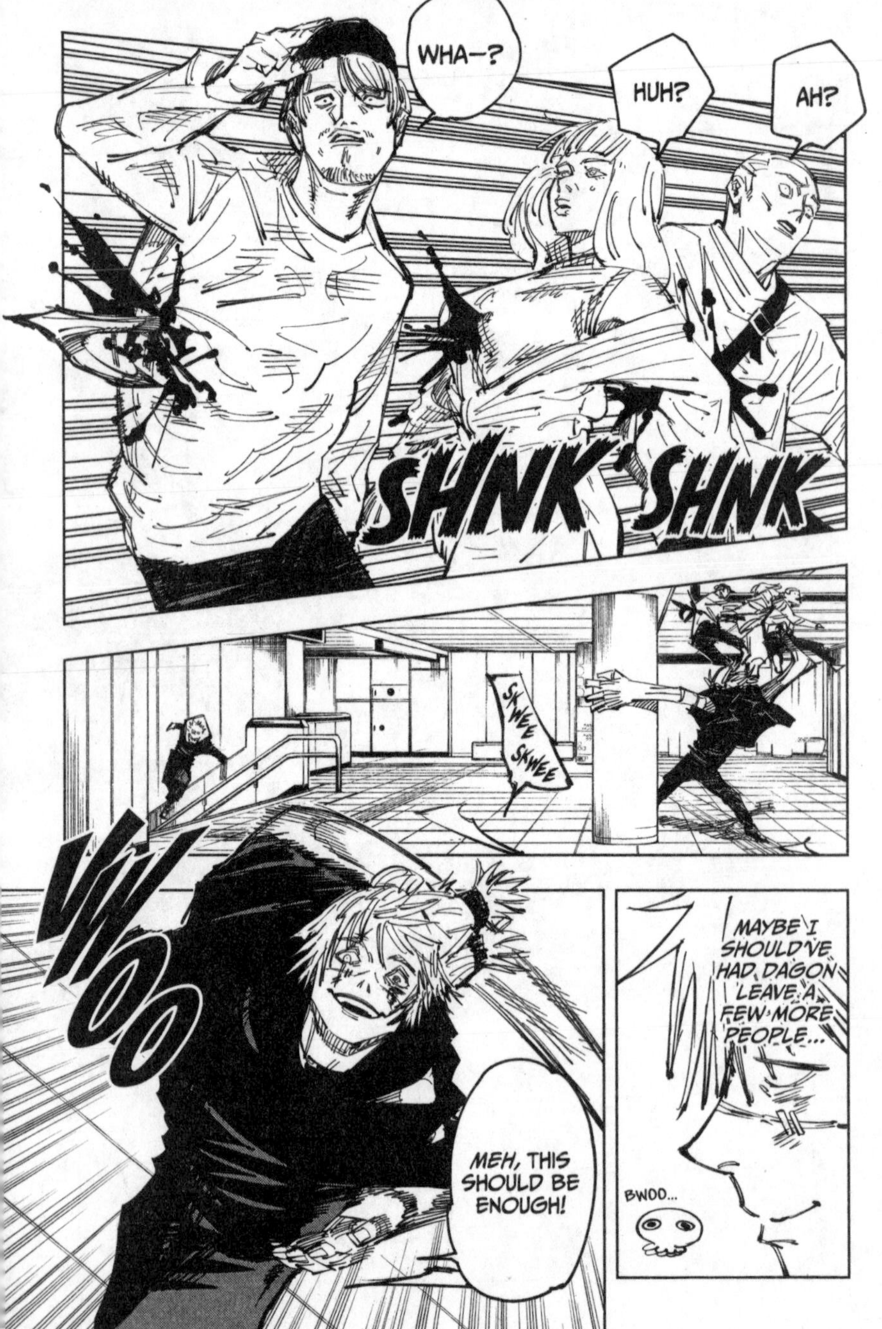
AH?
HUH?
WHA-?
SHNK SHNK
SKWEE SKWEE
MAYBE I SHOULD'VE HAD DAGON LEAVE A FEW MORE PEOPLE...
BWOO...
MEH, THIS SHOULD BE ENOUGH!

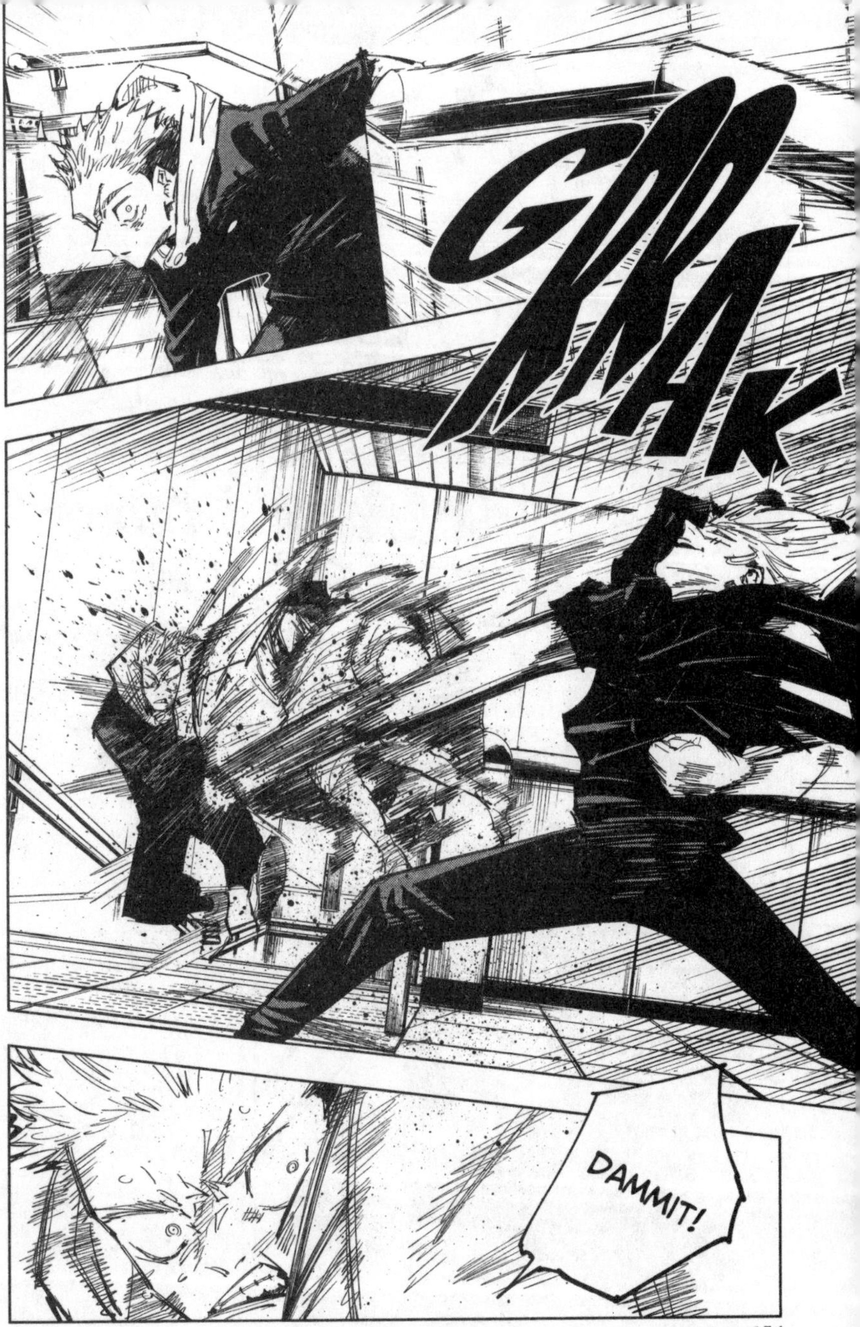
GWAAK
DAMMIT!

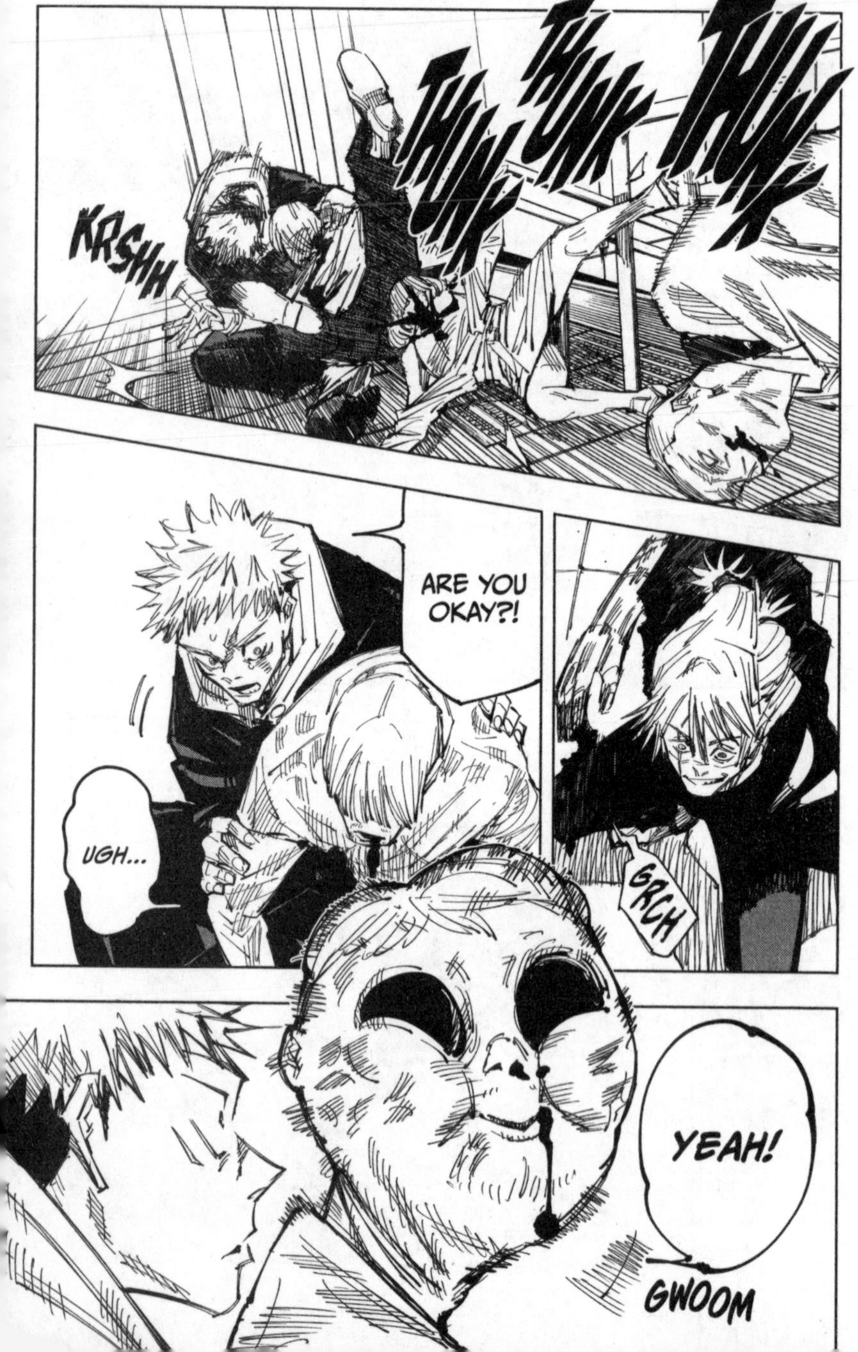
THUNK
THUNK
THUNK
KRSHH
GRCH
ARE YOU OKAY?!
UGH...
YEAH!
GWOOM

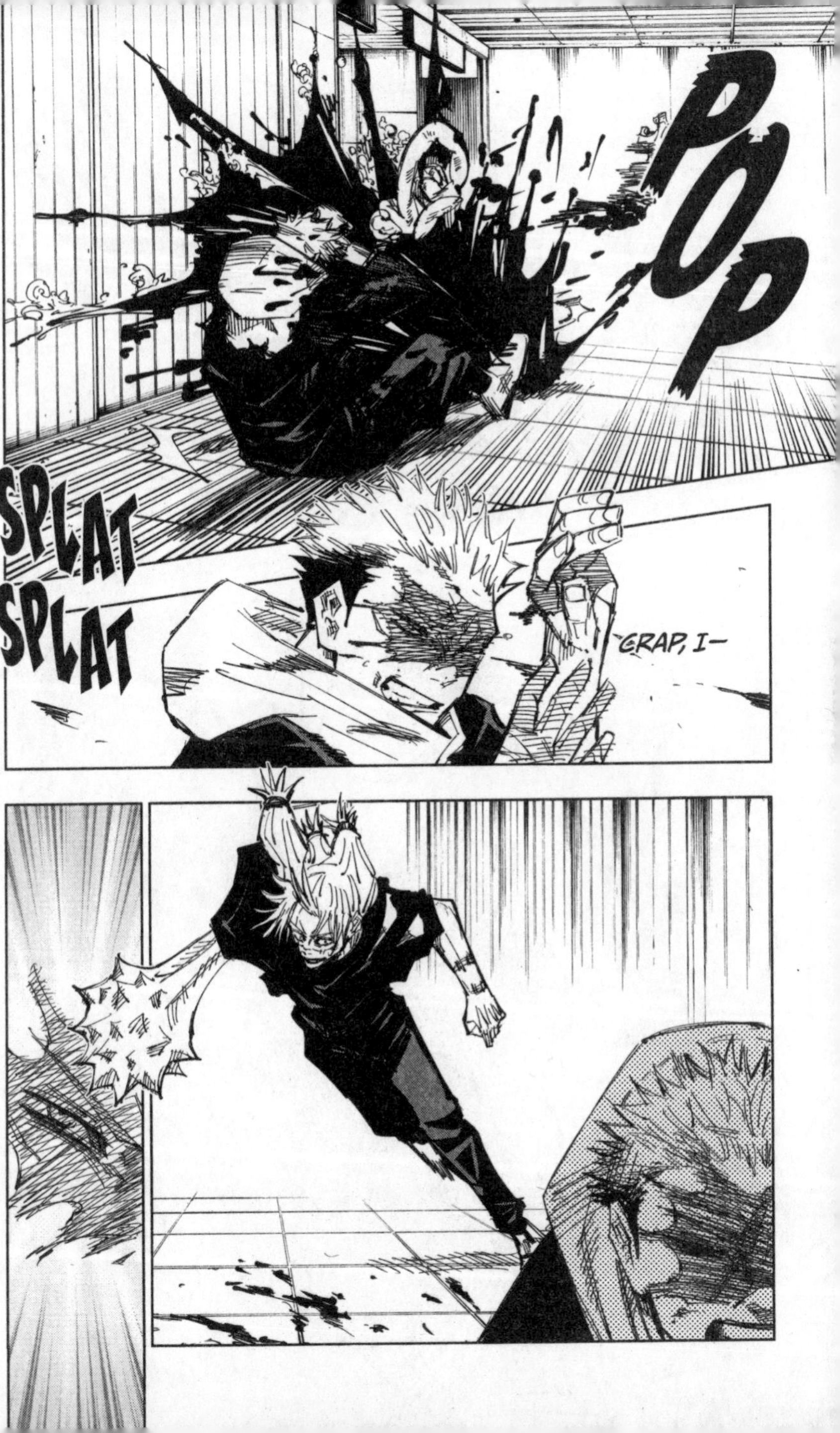
POP
SPLAT
SPLAT
CRAP, I—

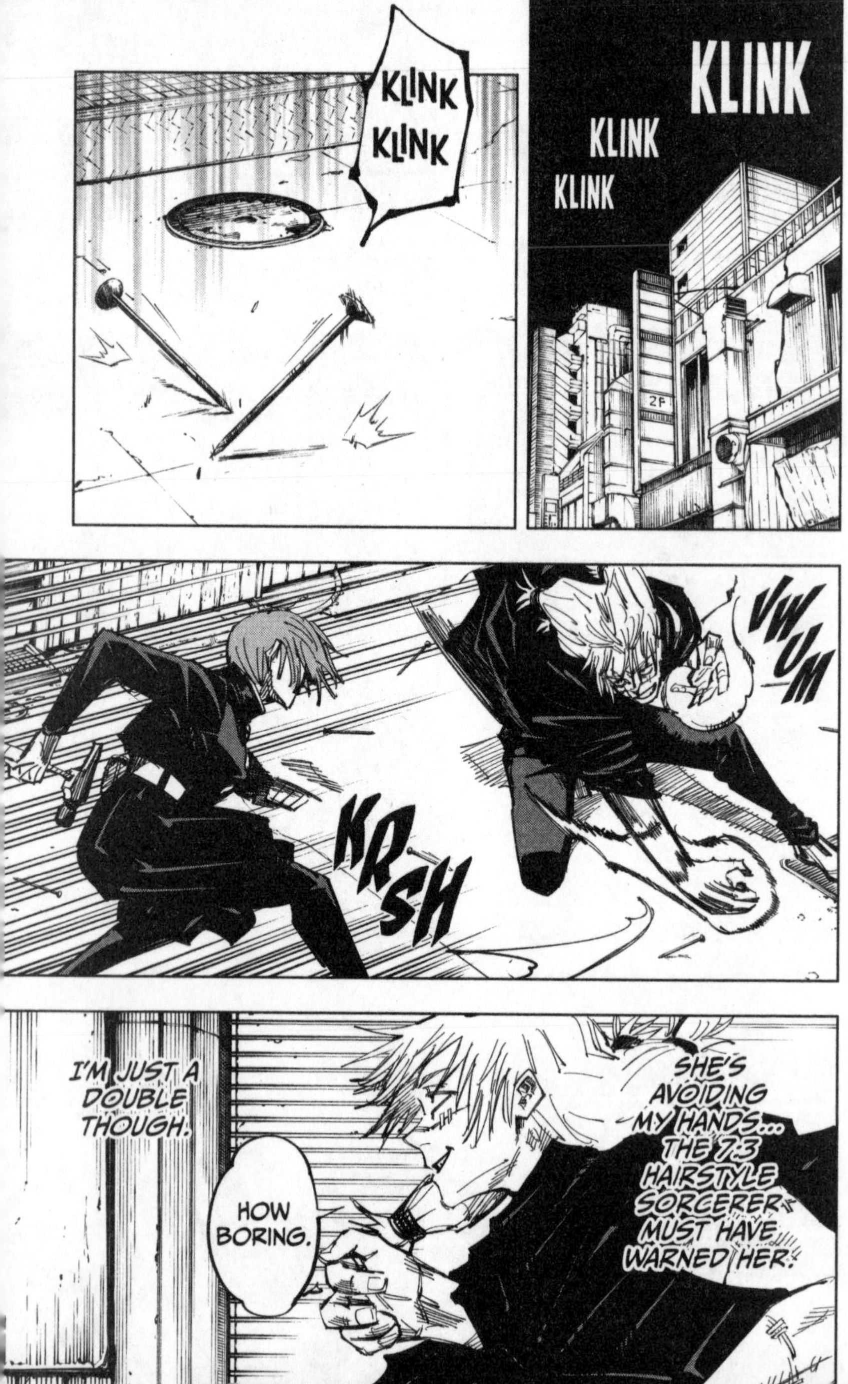
KLINK
KLINK
KLINK
KLINK KLINK
VWUM
KRSH
SHE'S AVOIDING MY HANDS... THE 7:3 HAIRSTYLE SORCERER MUST HAVE WARNED HER.
I'M JUST A DOUBLE THOUGH.
HOW BORING.

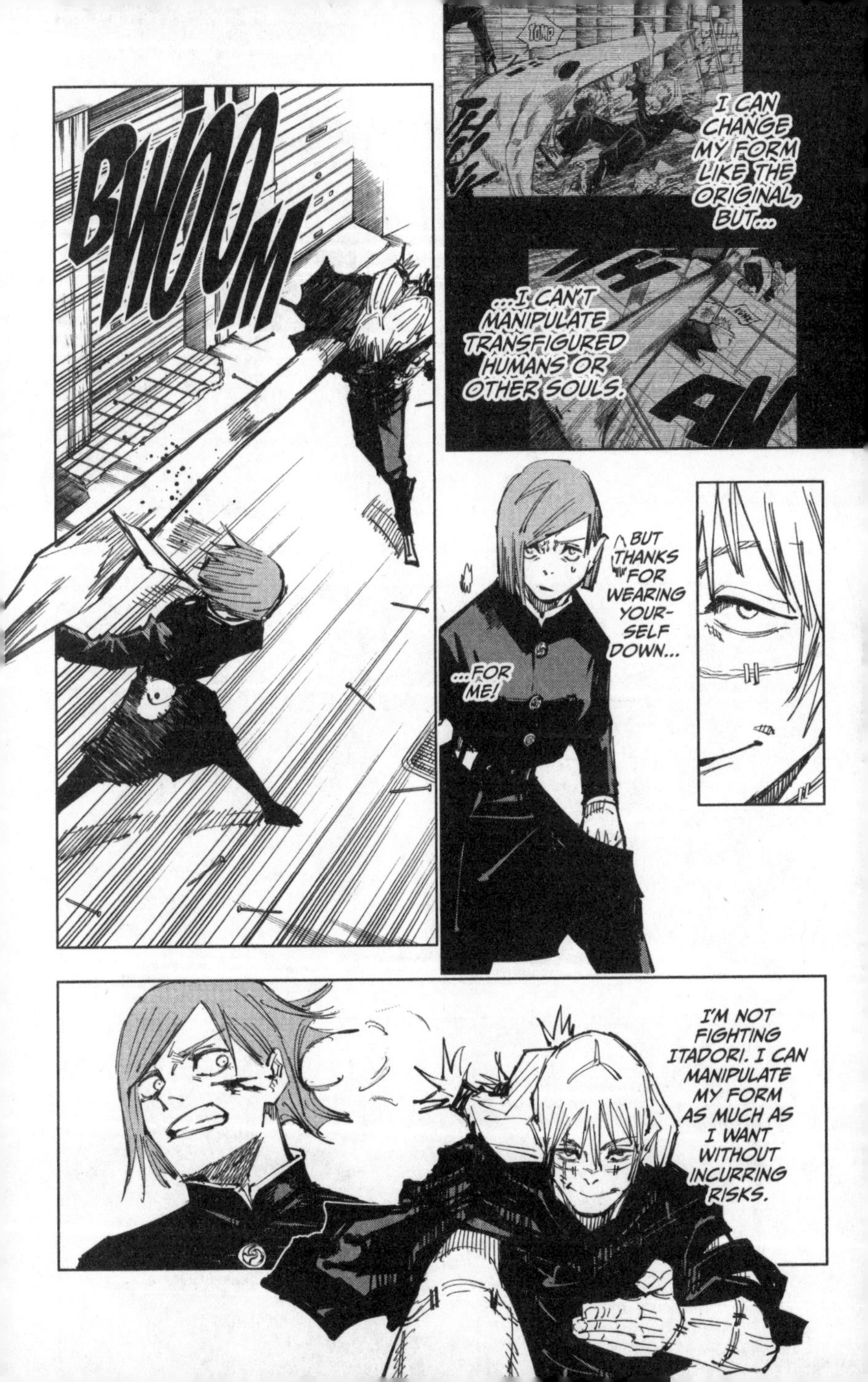
I CAN CHANGE MY FORM LIKE THE ORIGINAL, BUT...
...I CAN'T MANIPULATE TRANSFIGURED HUMANS OR OTHER SOULS.
BWOOM
BUT THANKS FOR WEARING YOURSELF DOWN...
...FOR ME!
I'M NOT FIGHTING ITADORI. I CAN MANIPULATE MY FORM AS MUCH AS I WANT WITHOUT INCURRING RISKS.

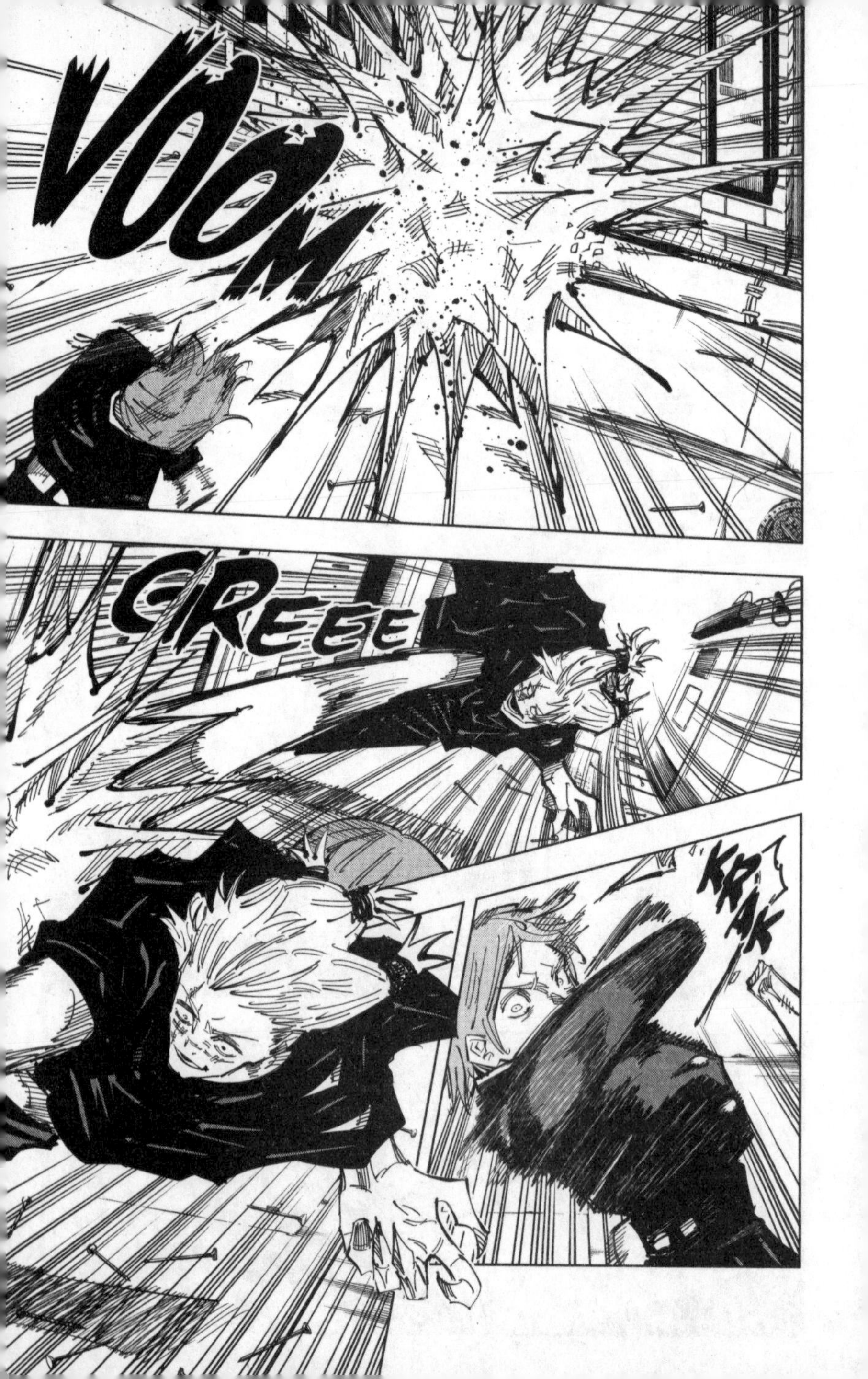
VOOM
GREEEE
KRAK

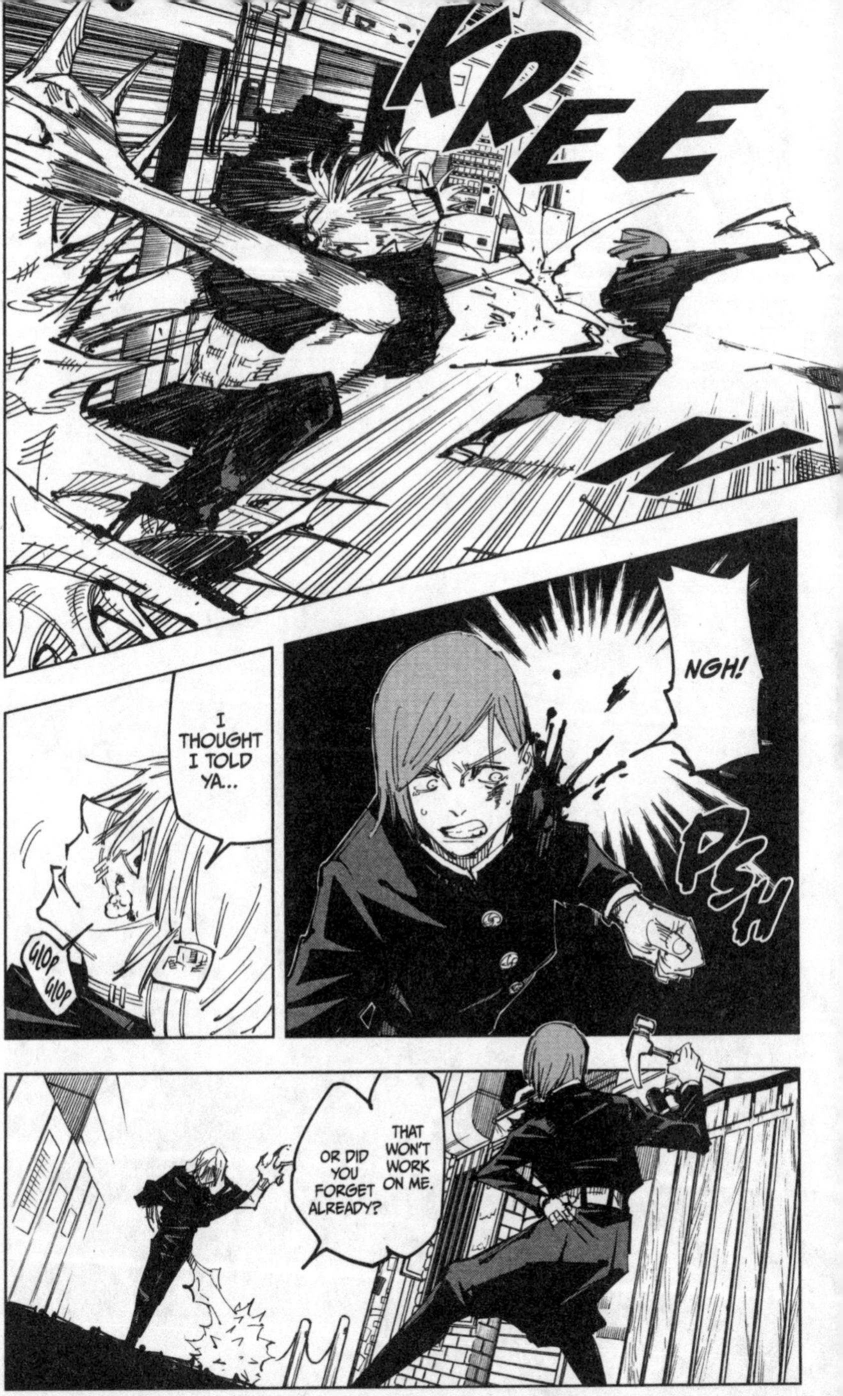
KREEN
NGH!
PSH
I THOUGHT I TOLD YA...
GLOP GLOP
THAT WON'T WORK ON ME.
OR DID YOU FORGET ALREADY?

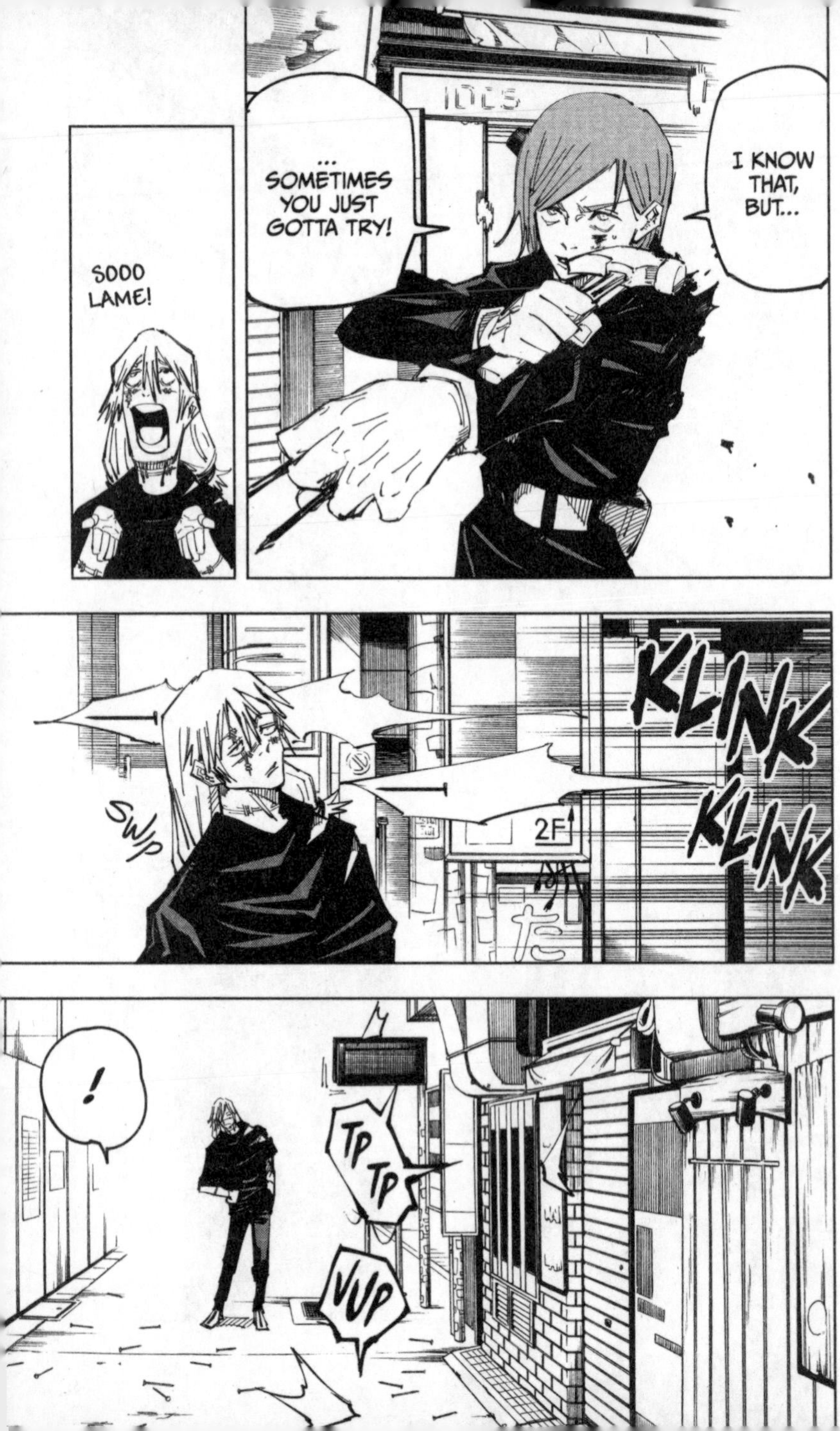
I KNOW THAT, BUT...
... SOMETIMES YOU JUST GOTTA TRY!
SOOO LAME!
KLINK
KLINK
2F
SWIP
!
TP TP
VUP

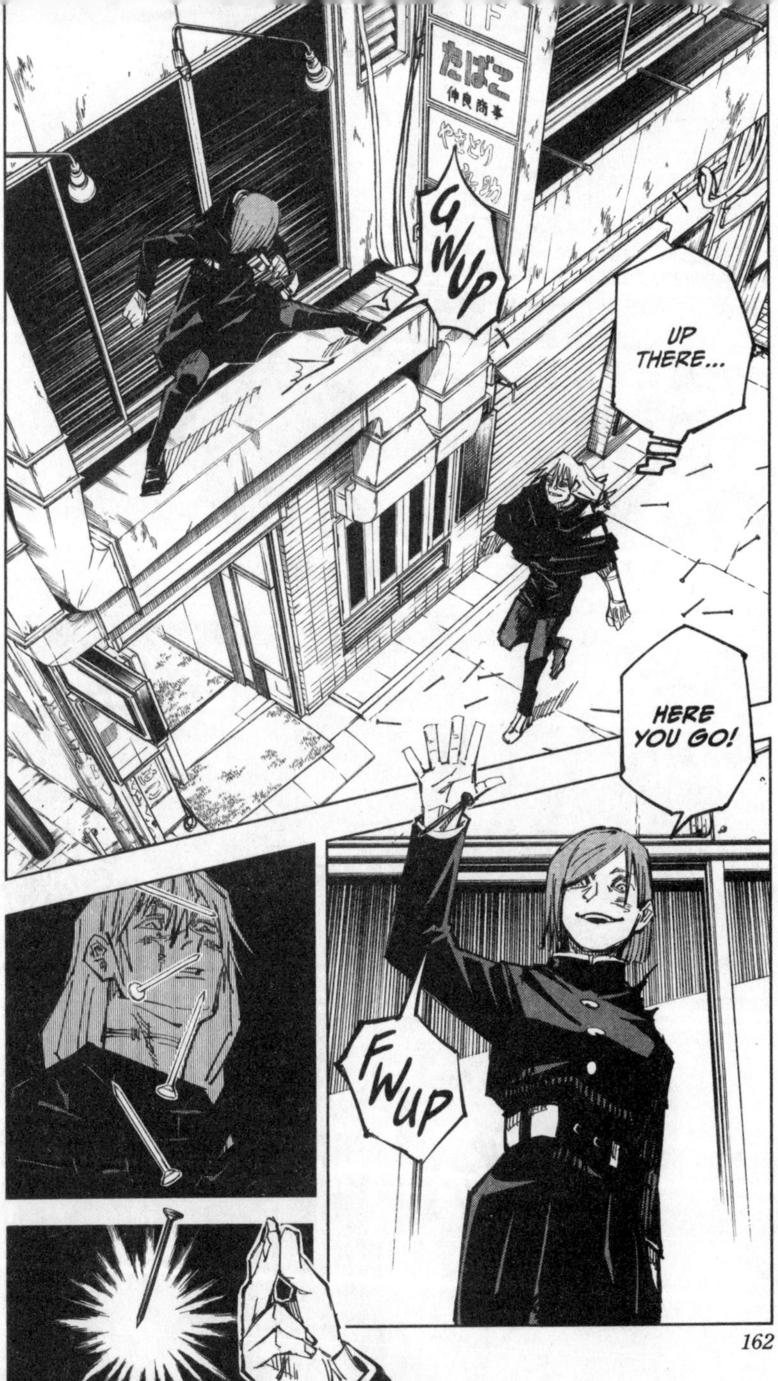
UP THERE...
GWUP
HERE YOU GO!
FWUP

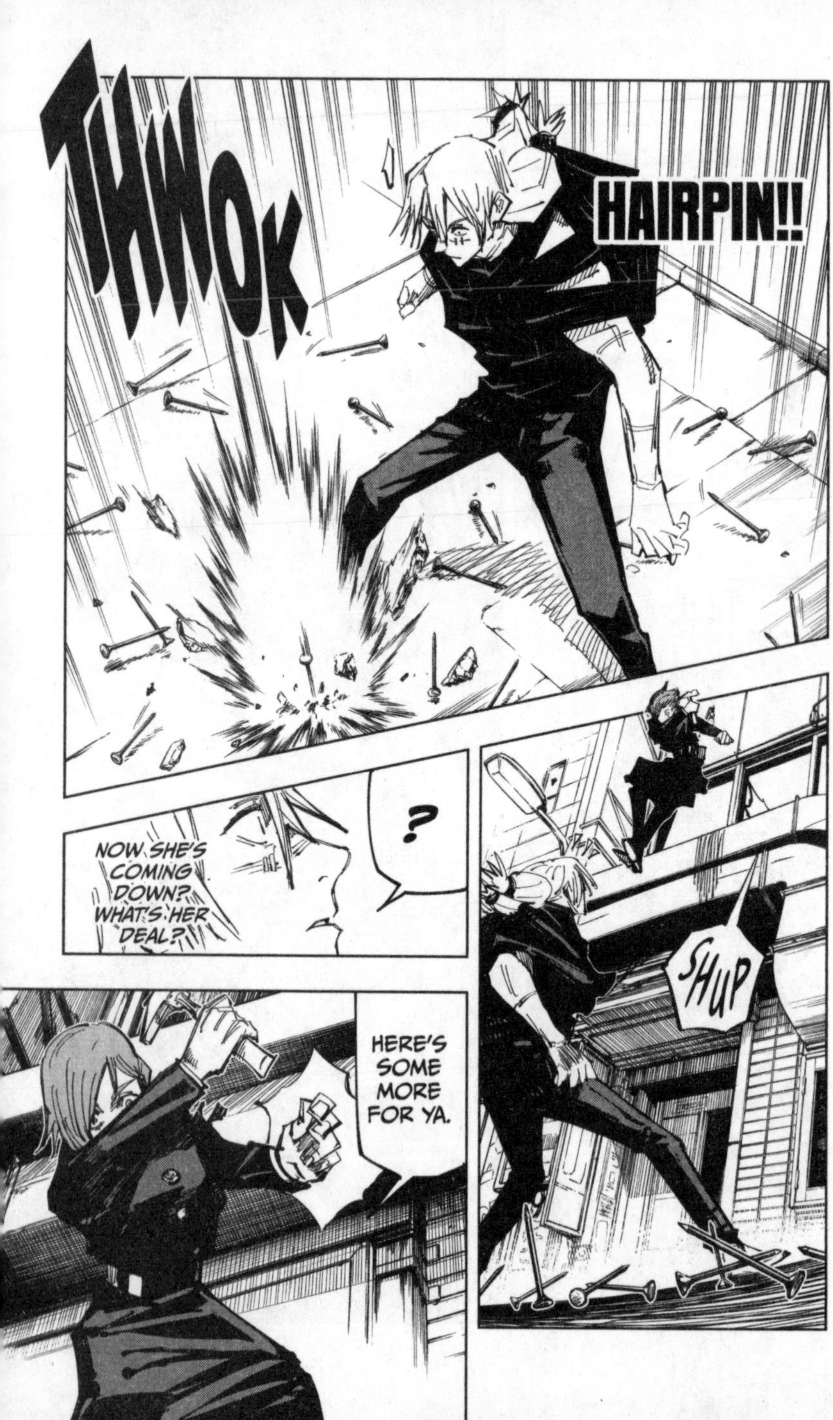
HAIRPIN!!
THWOK
SHUP
?
NOW SHE'S COMING DOWN? WHAT'S HER DEAL?
HERE'S SOME MORE FOR YA.

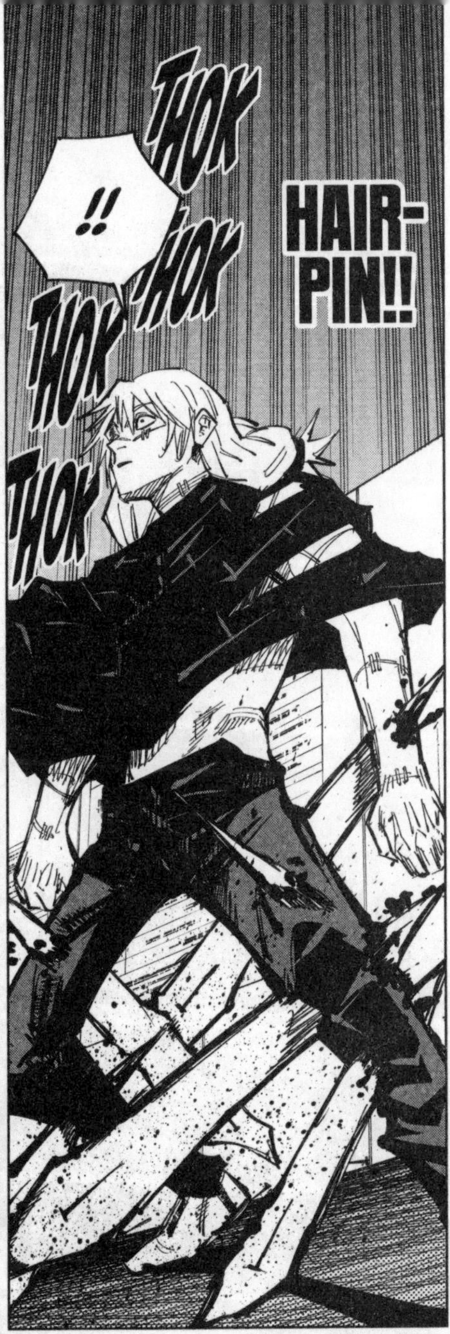
HAIR-PIN!!
THOK
THOK
THOK
THOK
!!

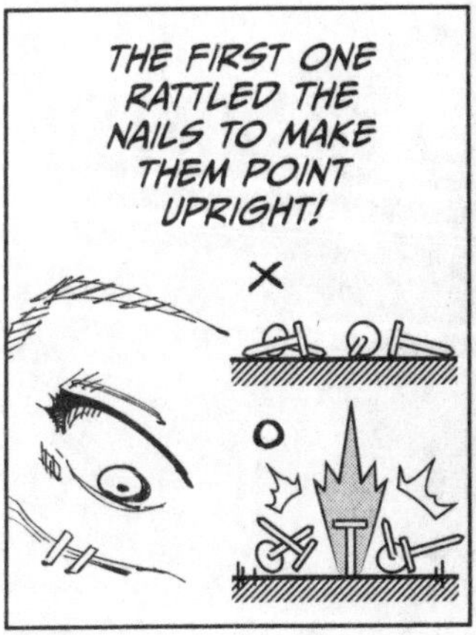
THE FIRST ONE RATTLED THE NAILS TO MAKE THEM POINT UPRIGHT!

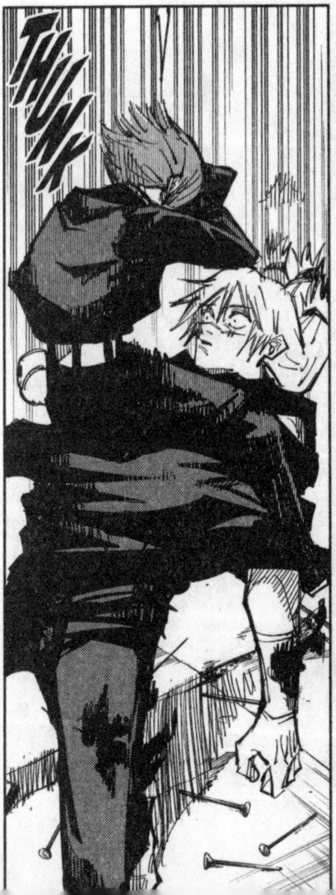
THUNK

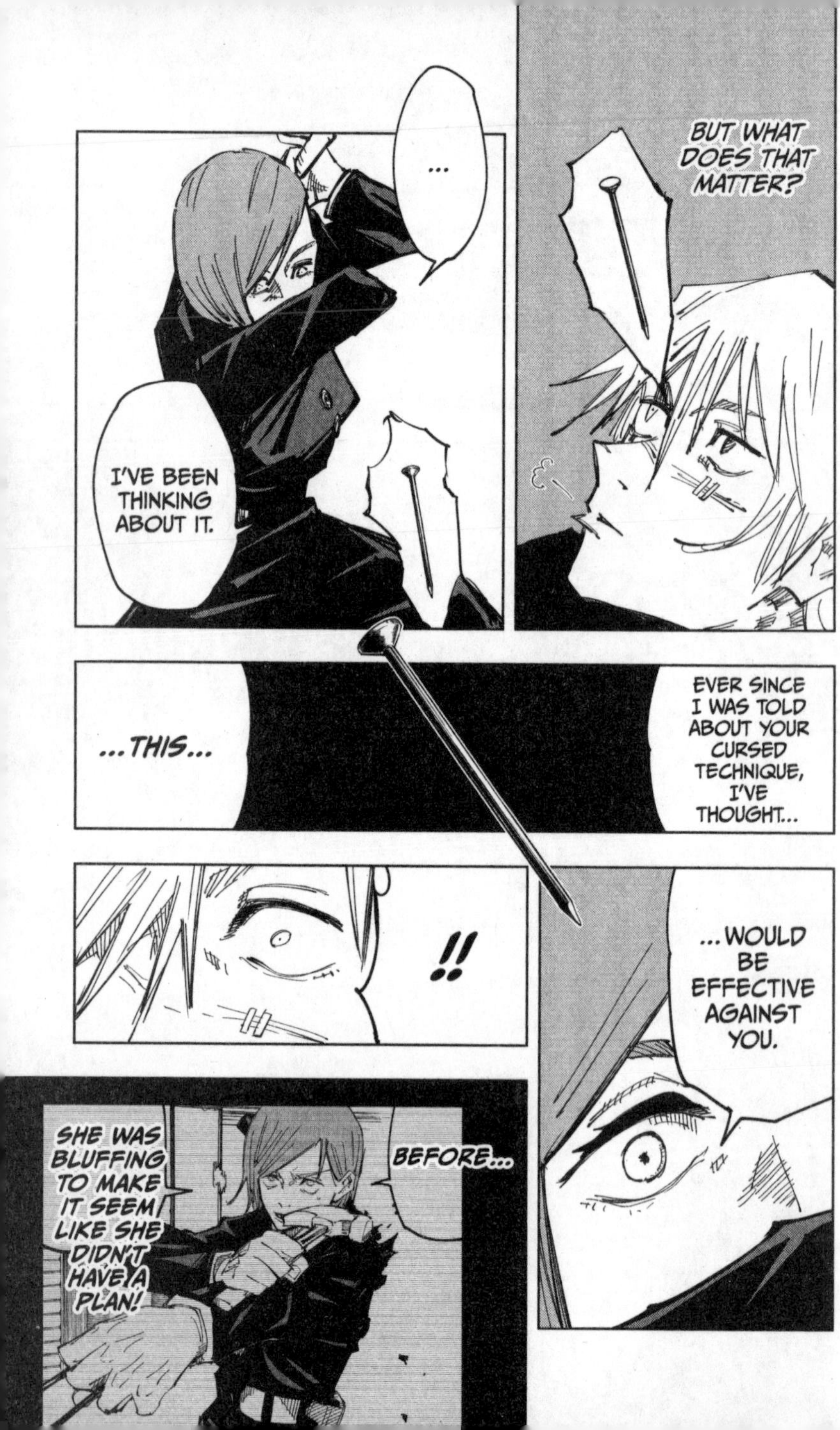
BUT WHAT DOES THAT MATTER?
...
I'VE BEEN THINKING ABOUT IT.
EVER SINCE I WAS TOLD ABOUT YOUR CURSED TECHNIQUE, I'VE THOUGHT...
...THIS...
...WOULD BE EFFECTIVE AGAINST YOU.
!!
BEFORE...
SHE WAS BLUFFING TO MAKE IT SEEM LIKE SHE DIDN'T HAVE A PLAN!

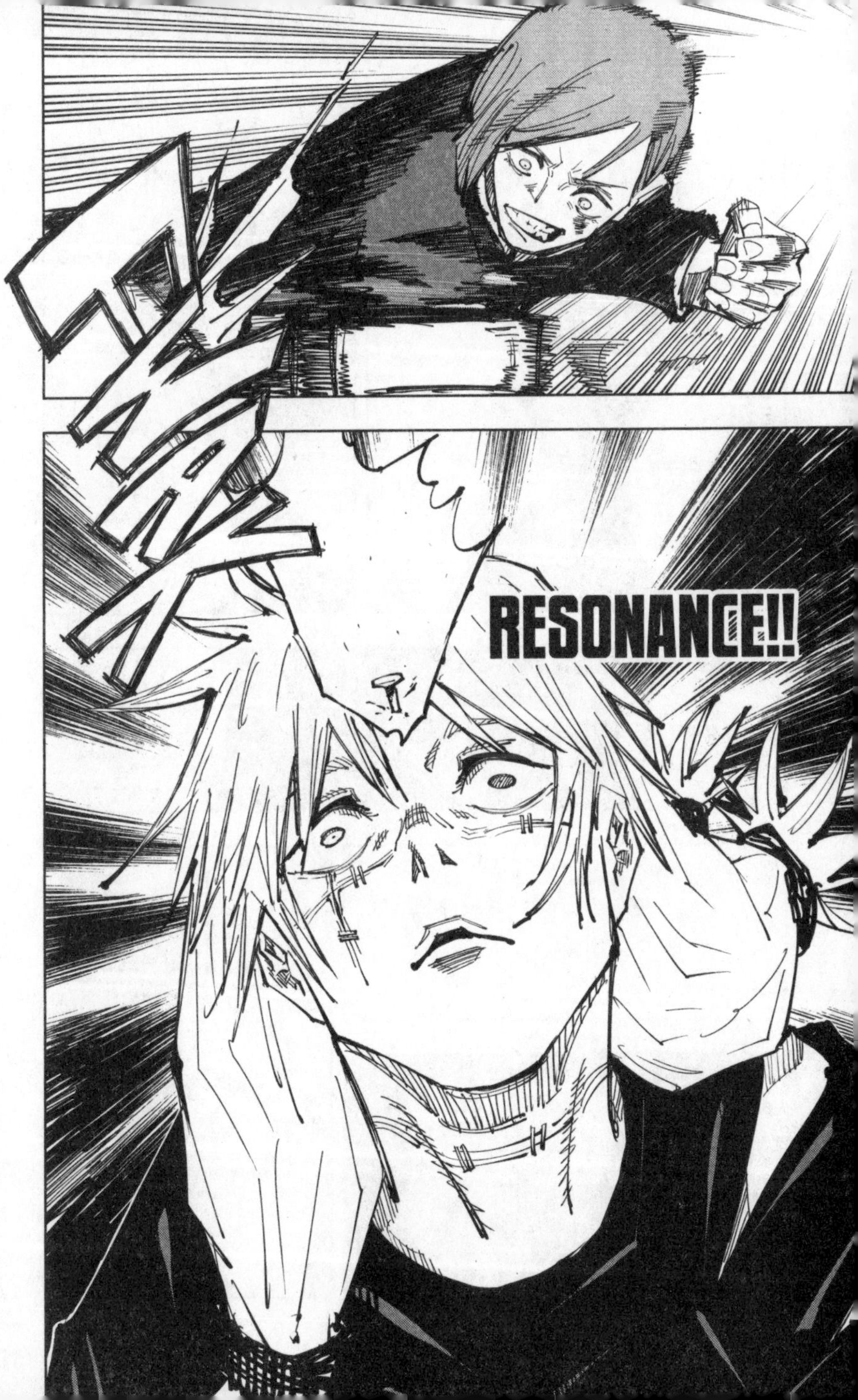
RESONANCE!!

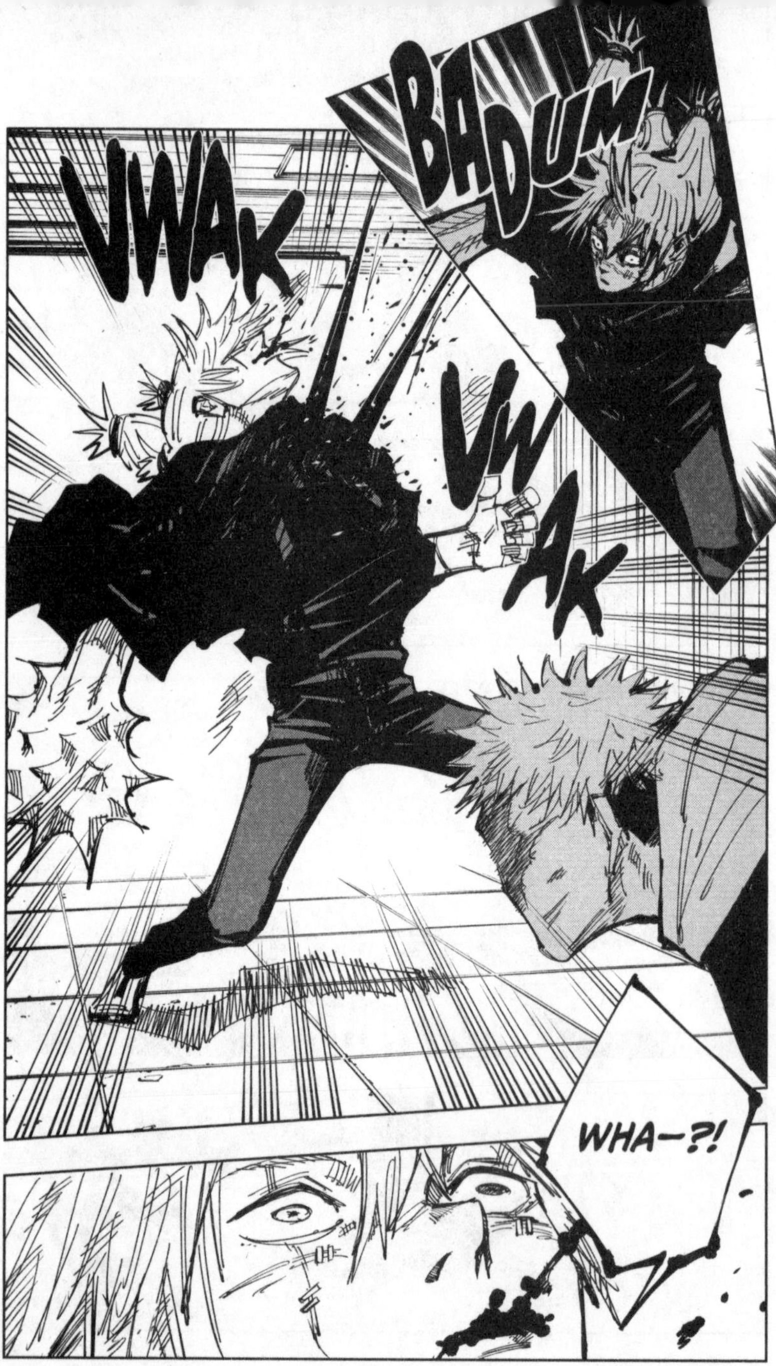
BADUM
VWAK
VWAK
WHA-?!

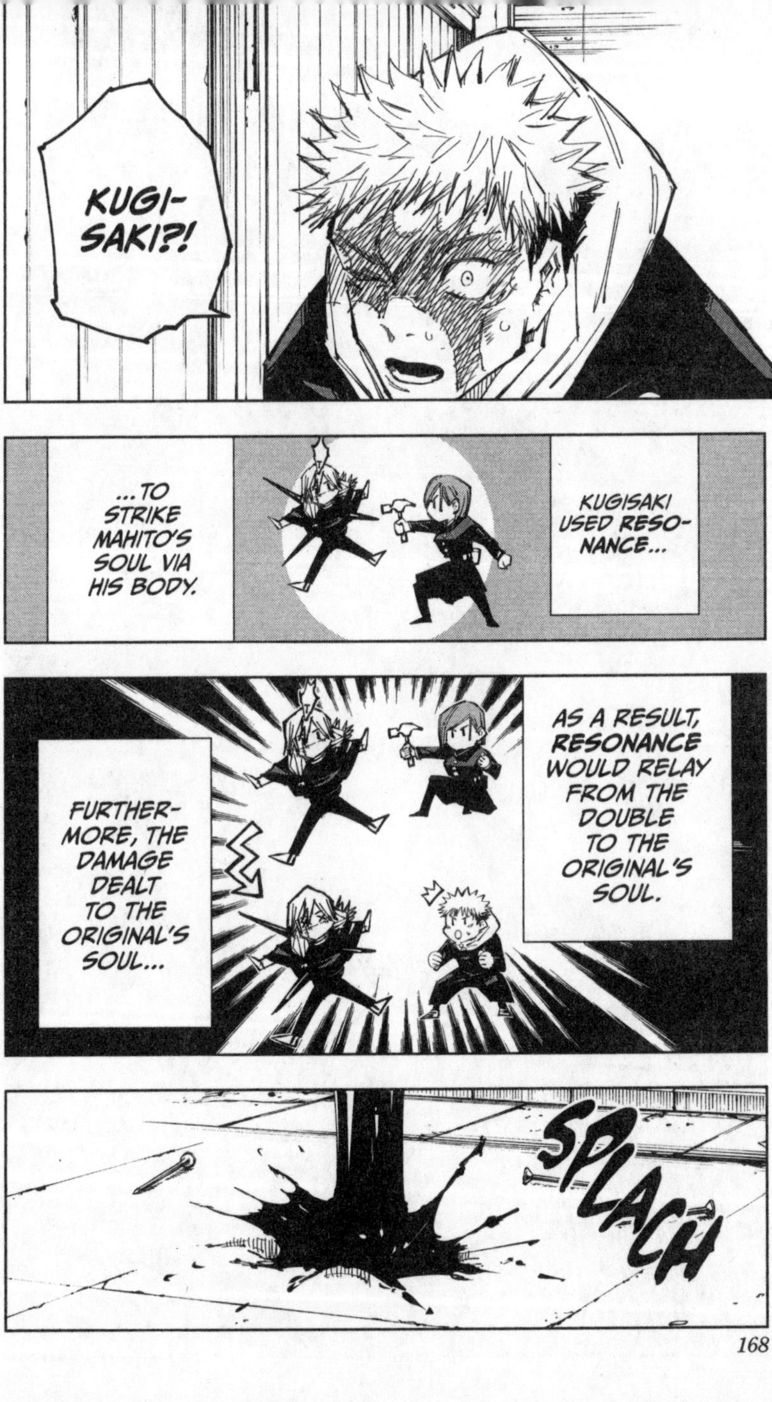
KUGI-SAKI?!
KUGISAKI USED RESO-NANCE...
...TO STRIKE MAHITO'S SOUL VIA HIS BODY.
AS A RESULT, RESONANCE WOULD RELAY FROM THE DOUBLE TO THE ORIGINAL'S SOUL.
FURTHER-MORE, THE DAMAGE DEALT TO THE ORIGINAL'S SOUL...
SPLACH

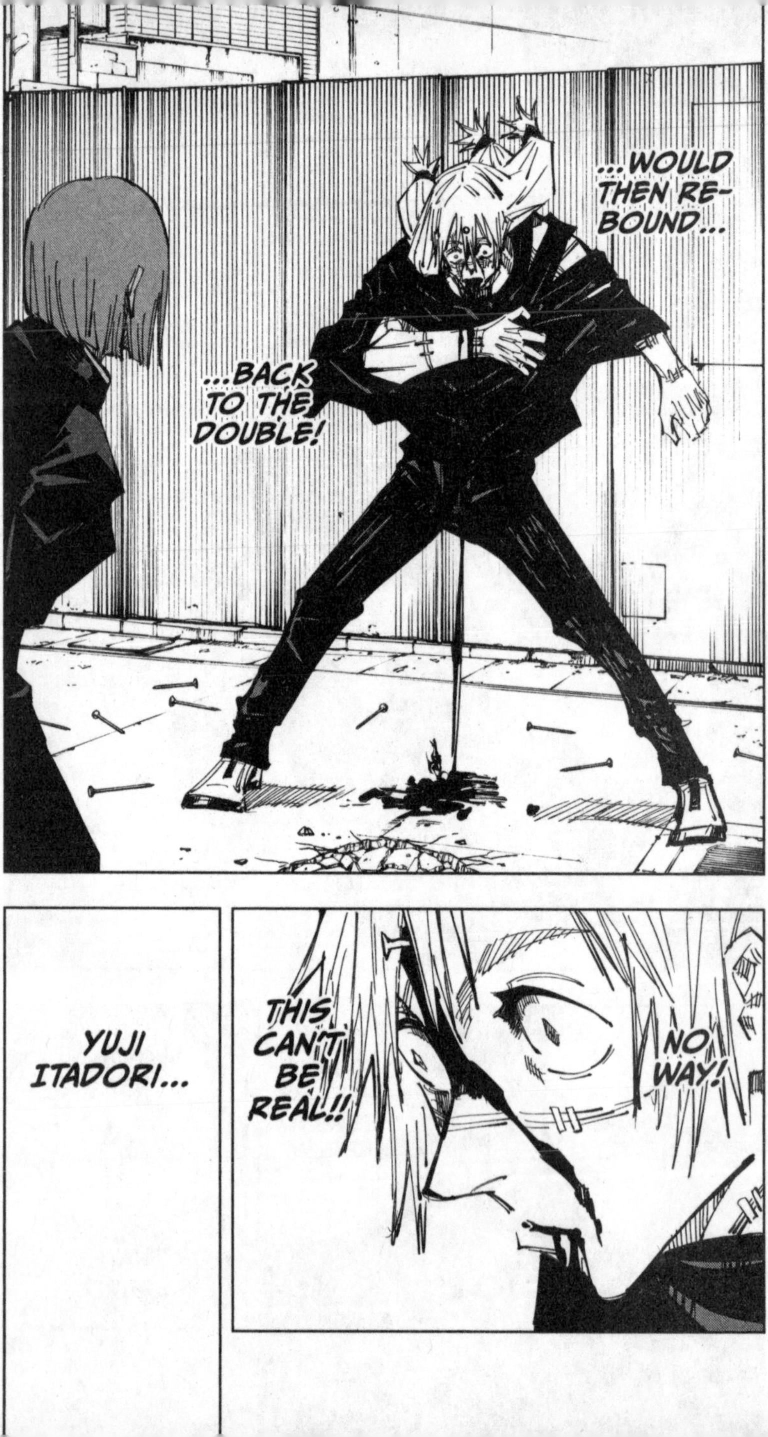
...WOULD THEN RE-BOUND...
...BACK TO THE DOUBLE!
NO WAY!
THIS CAN'T BE REAL!!
YUJI ITADORI...

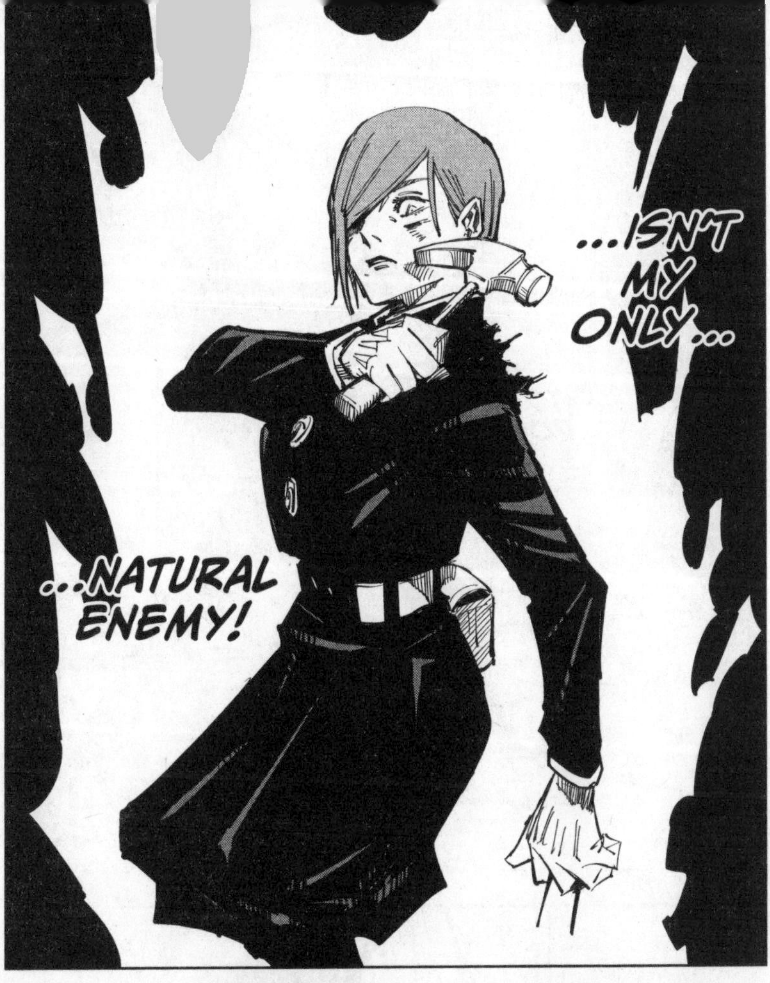
...ISN'T MY ONLY...
...NATURAL ENEMY!

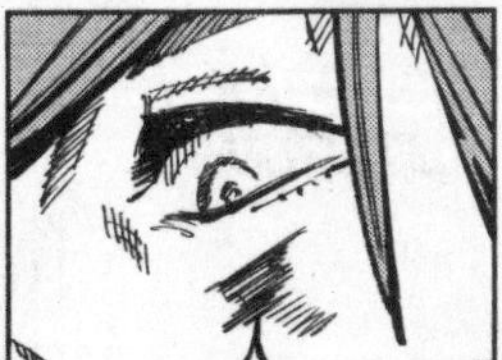
HM... THAT'S WEIRD.

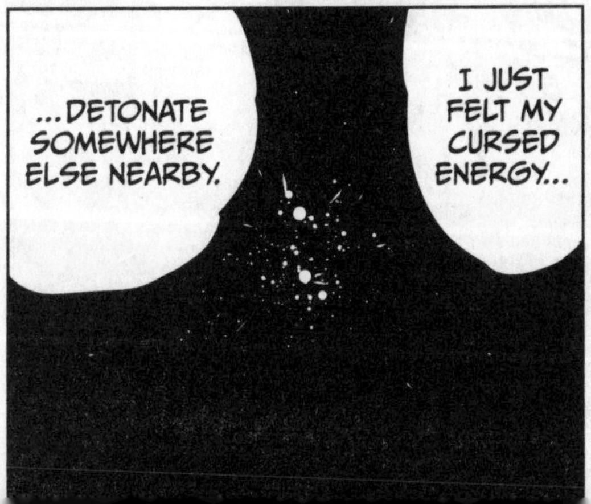
I JUST FELT MY CURSED ENERGY...
...DETONATE SOMEWHERE ELSE NEARBY.

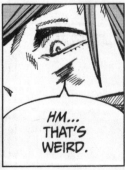

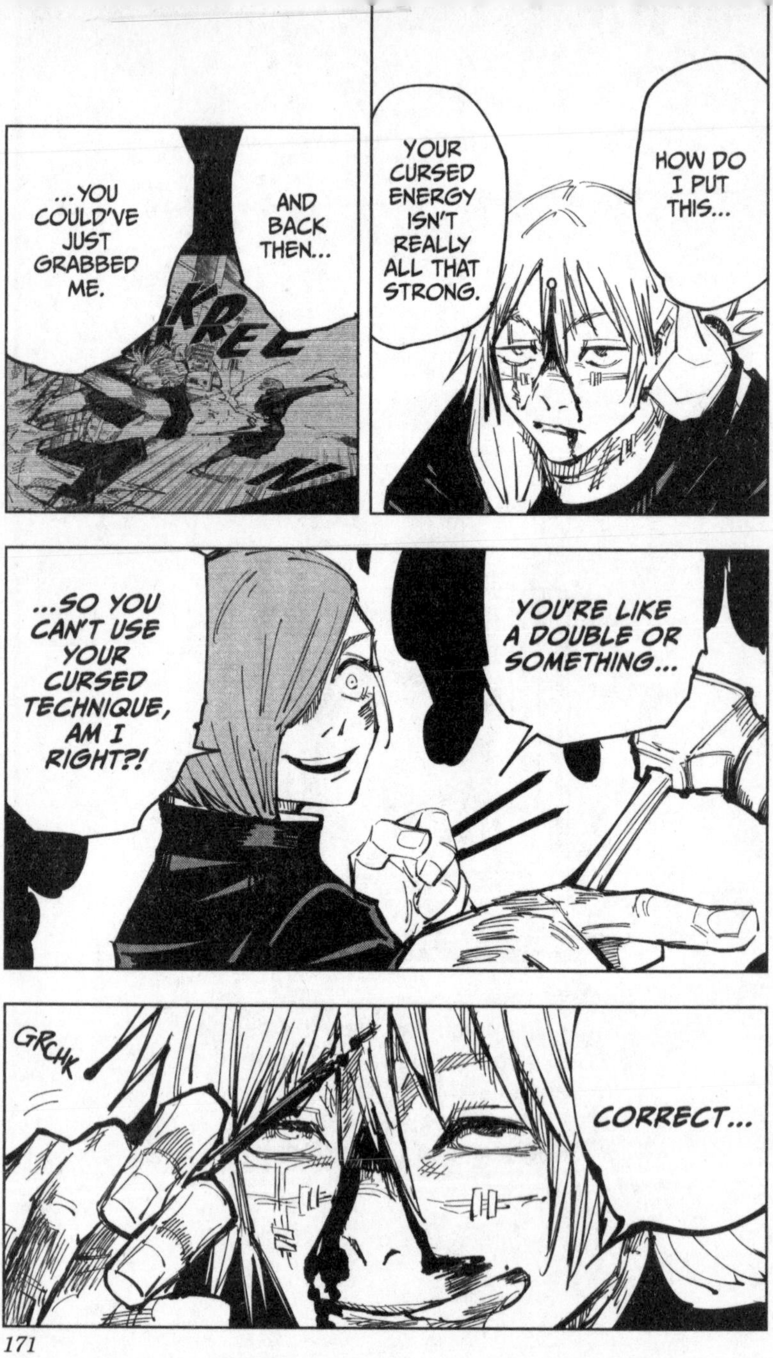
HOW DO I PUT THIS...
YOUR CURSED ENERGY ISN'T REALLY ALL THAT STRONG.
AND BACK THEN...
...YOU COULD'VE JUST GRABBED ME.
KREEN
YOU'RE LIKE A DOUBLE OR SOMETHING...
...SO YOU CAN'T USE YOUR CURSED TECHNIQUE, AM I RIGHT?!
CORRECT...
GRCHK

A Nice Story

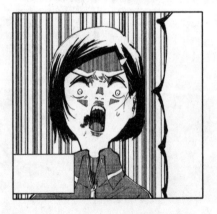

• Hiramatsu-san drew this design
of a young Kugisaki for the anime,
and I used it in the manga too.
• When Hiramatsu-san draws
Kugisaki, she's actually cute.

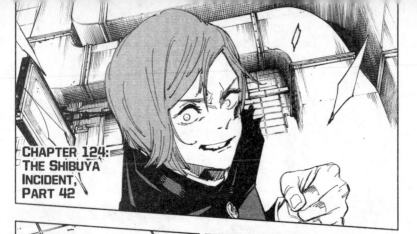

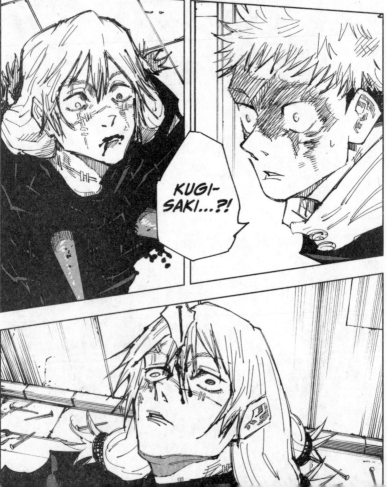

KUGI-
SAKI...?!

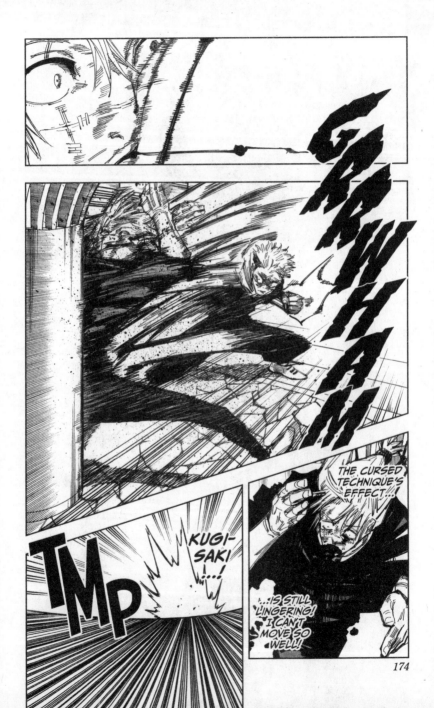

174

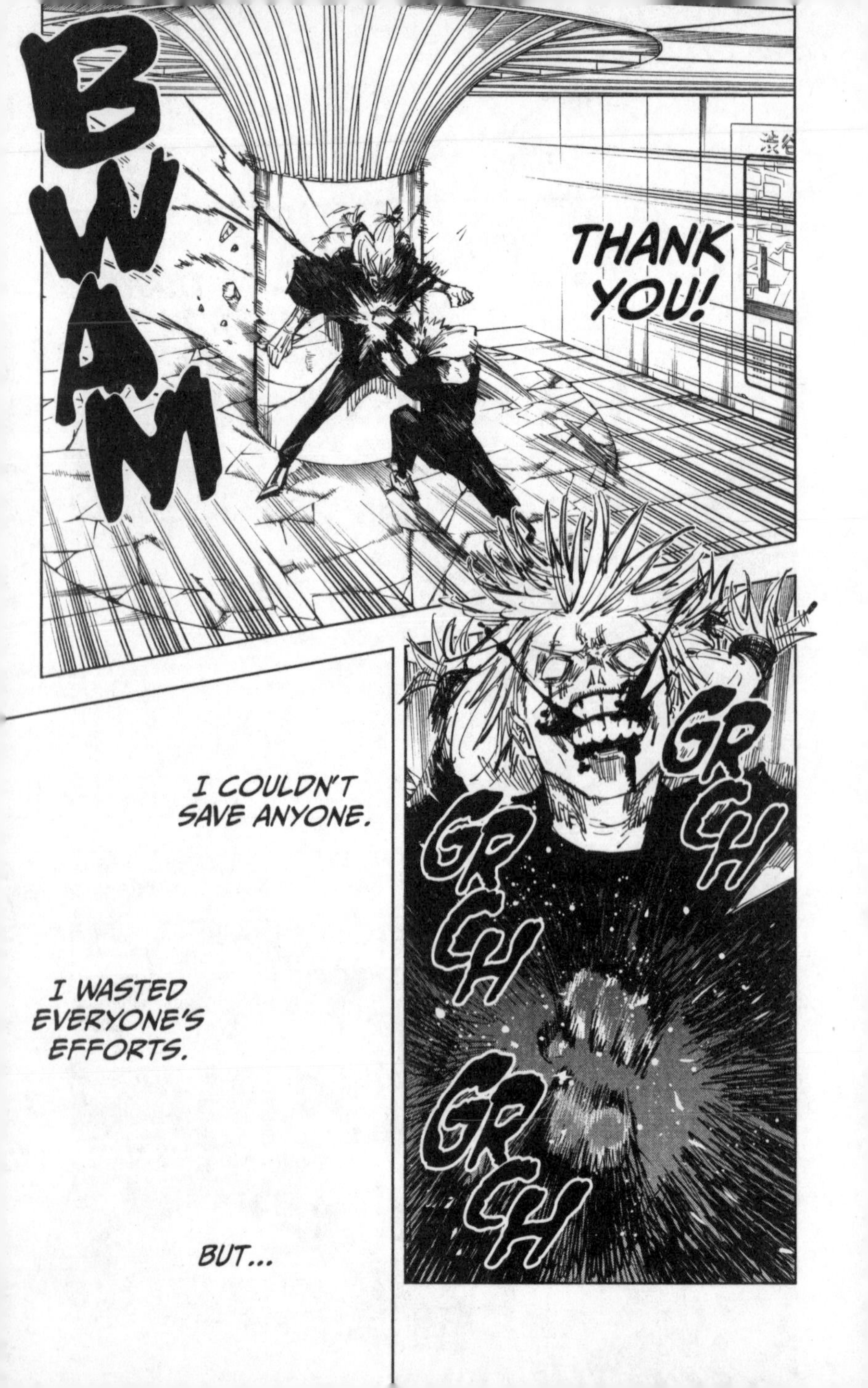
THANK YOU!
BWAM
GRCH
GRCH
GRCH
I COULDN'T SAVE ANYONE.
I WASTED EVERYONE'S EFFORTS.
BUT...

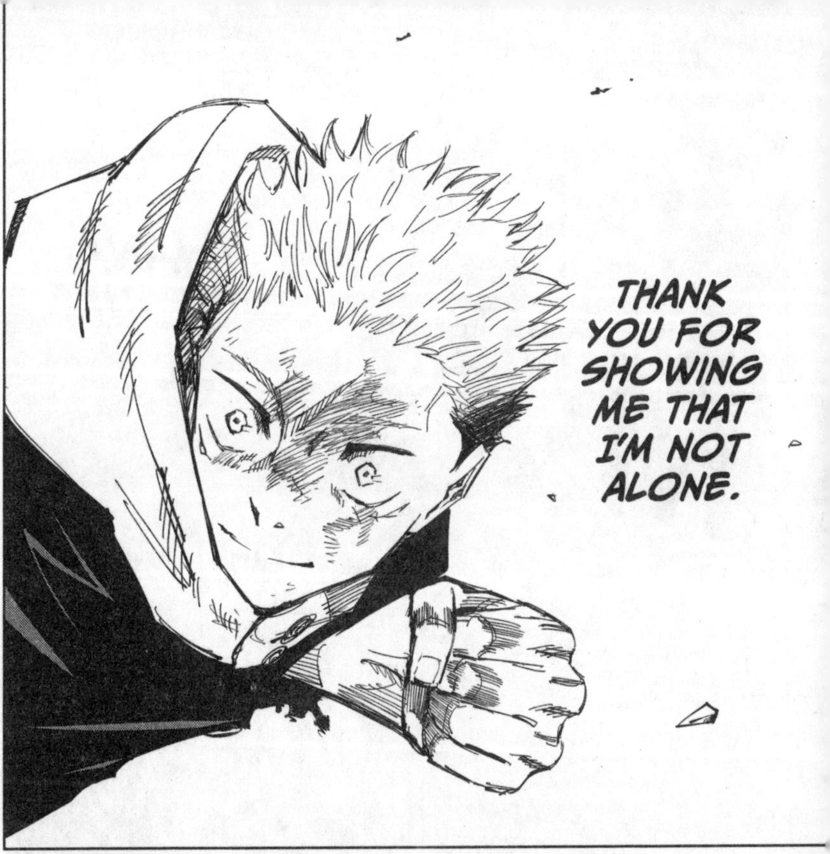
THANK YOU FOR SHOWING ME THAT I'M NOT ALONE.

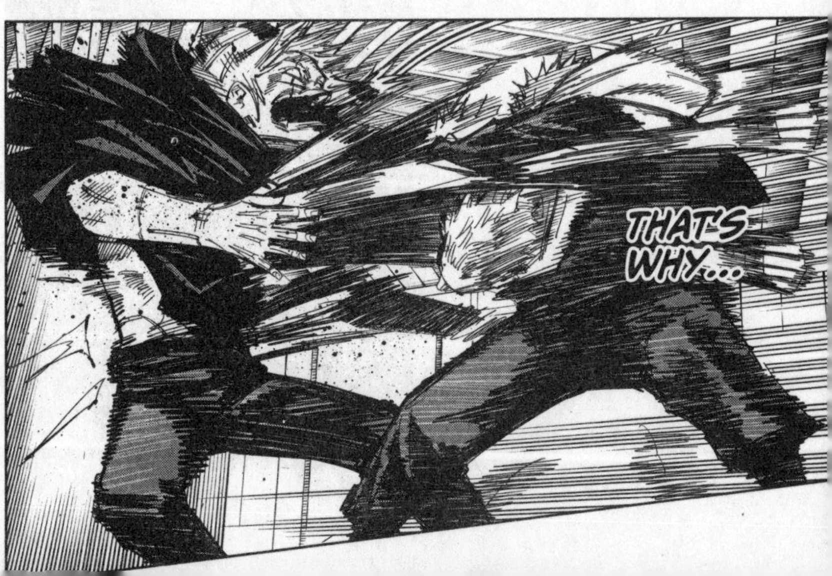
THAT'S WHY...

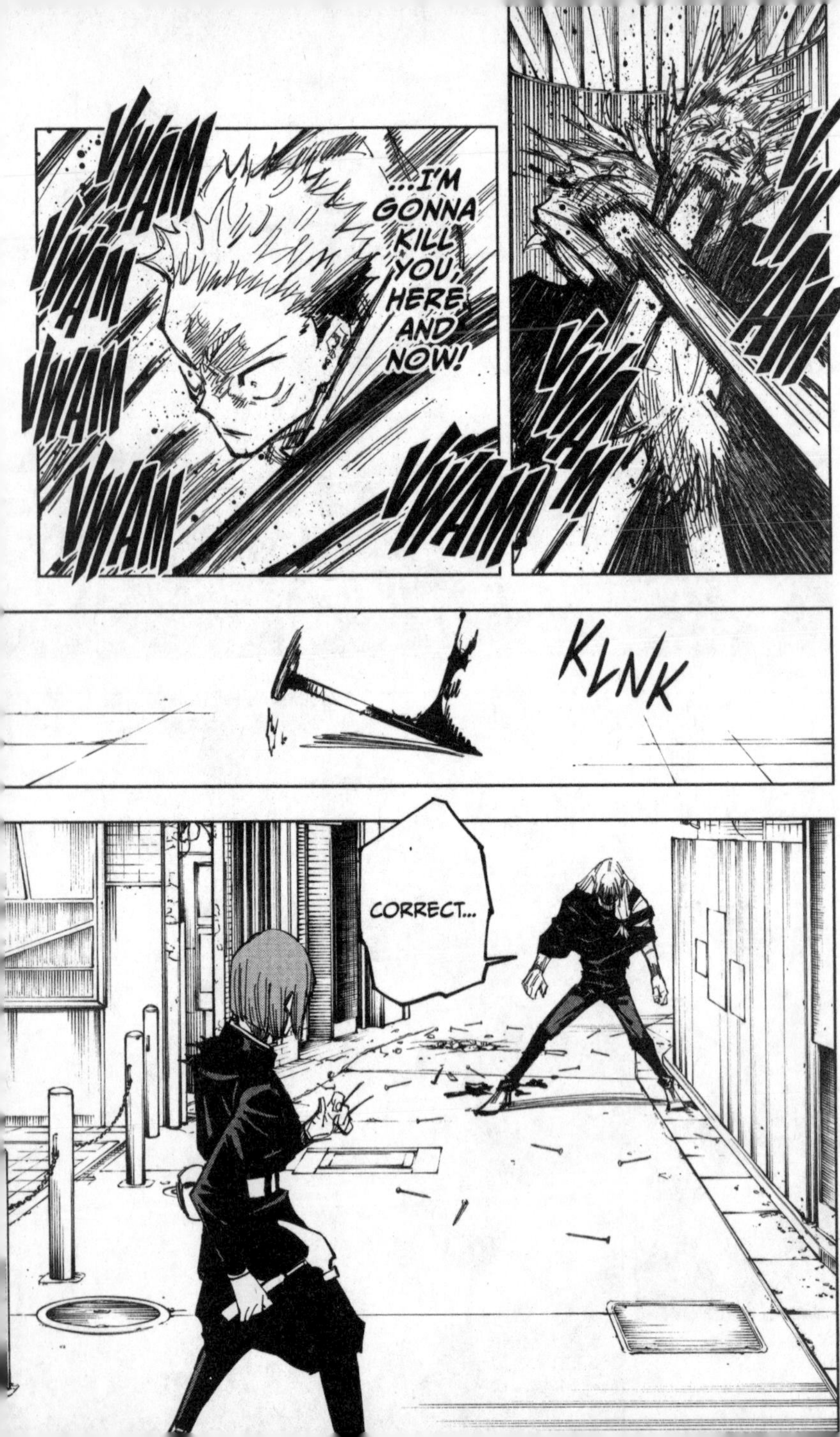
VWAM
VWAM
VWAM
...I'M GONNA KILL YOU, HERE, AND NOW!
VWAM
VWAM
VWAM
VWAM
VWAM
KLNK
CORRECT...

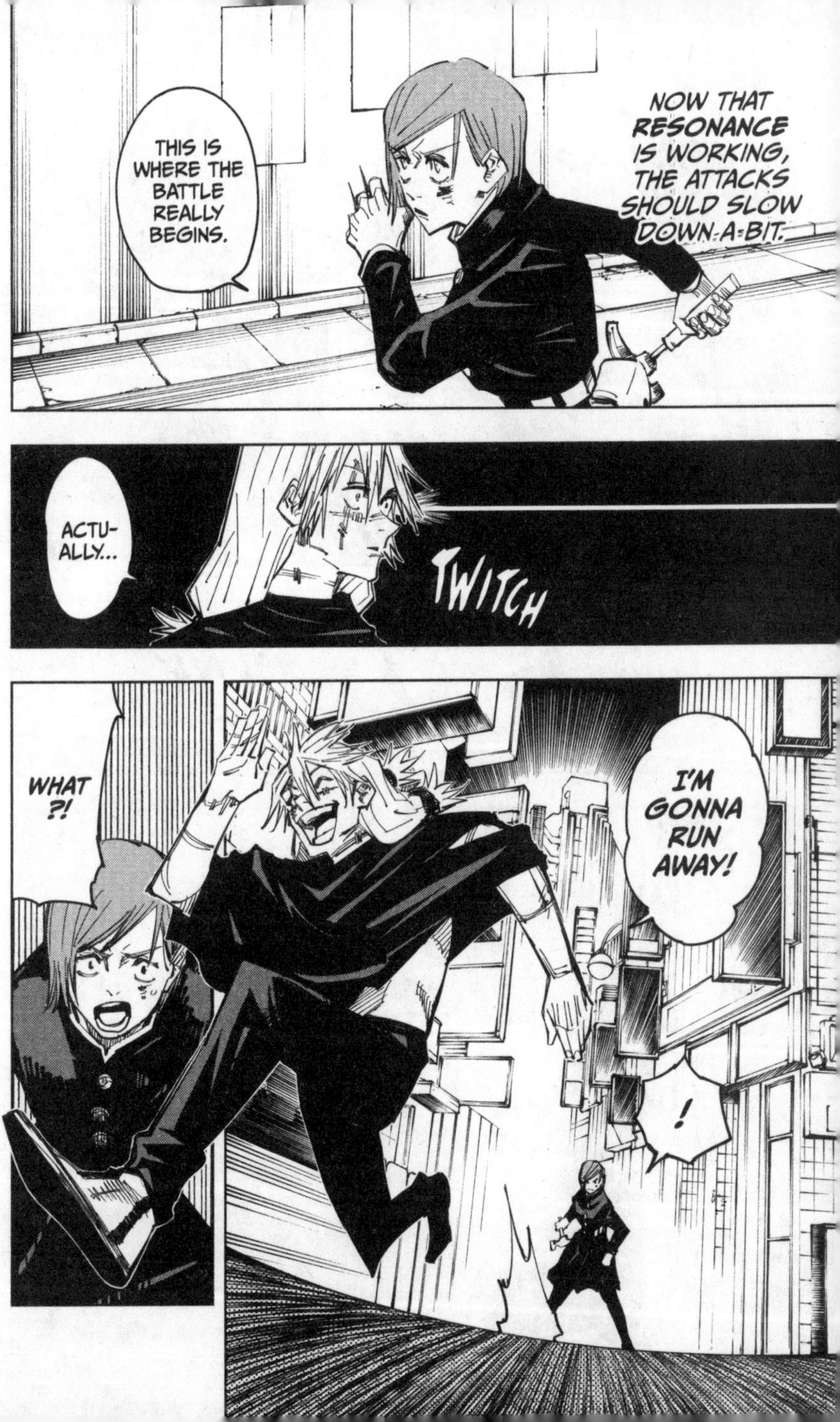
NOW THAT RESONANCE IS WORKING, THE ATTACKS SHOULD SLOW DOWN A BIT.
THIS IS WHERE THE BATTLE REALLY BEGINS.
TWITCH
ACTU-ALLY...
I'M GONNA RUN AWAY!
!
WHAT ?!

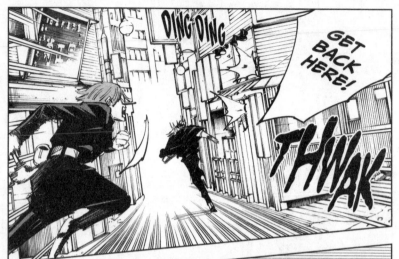

DING-DING

GET BACK HERE!

THWAK

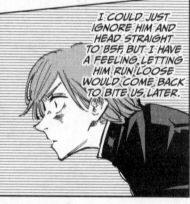

I COULD JUST IGNORE HIM AND HEAD STRAIGHT TO BSF, BUT I HAVE A FEELING LETTING HIM RUN LOOSE WOULD COME BACK TO BITE US LATER.

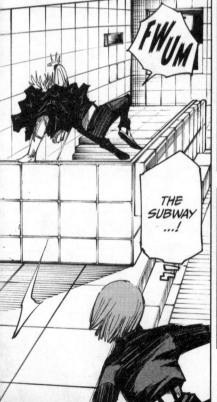

FWUM

THE SUBWAY ...!

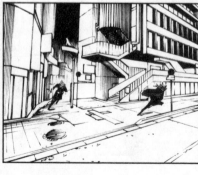

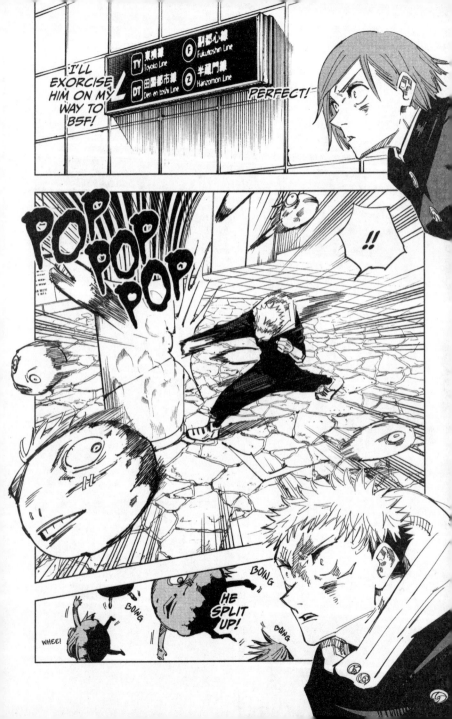

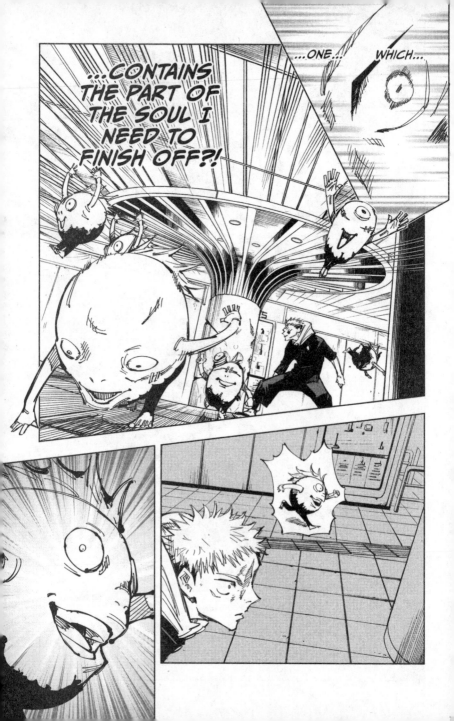

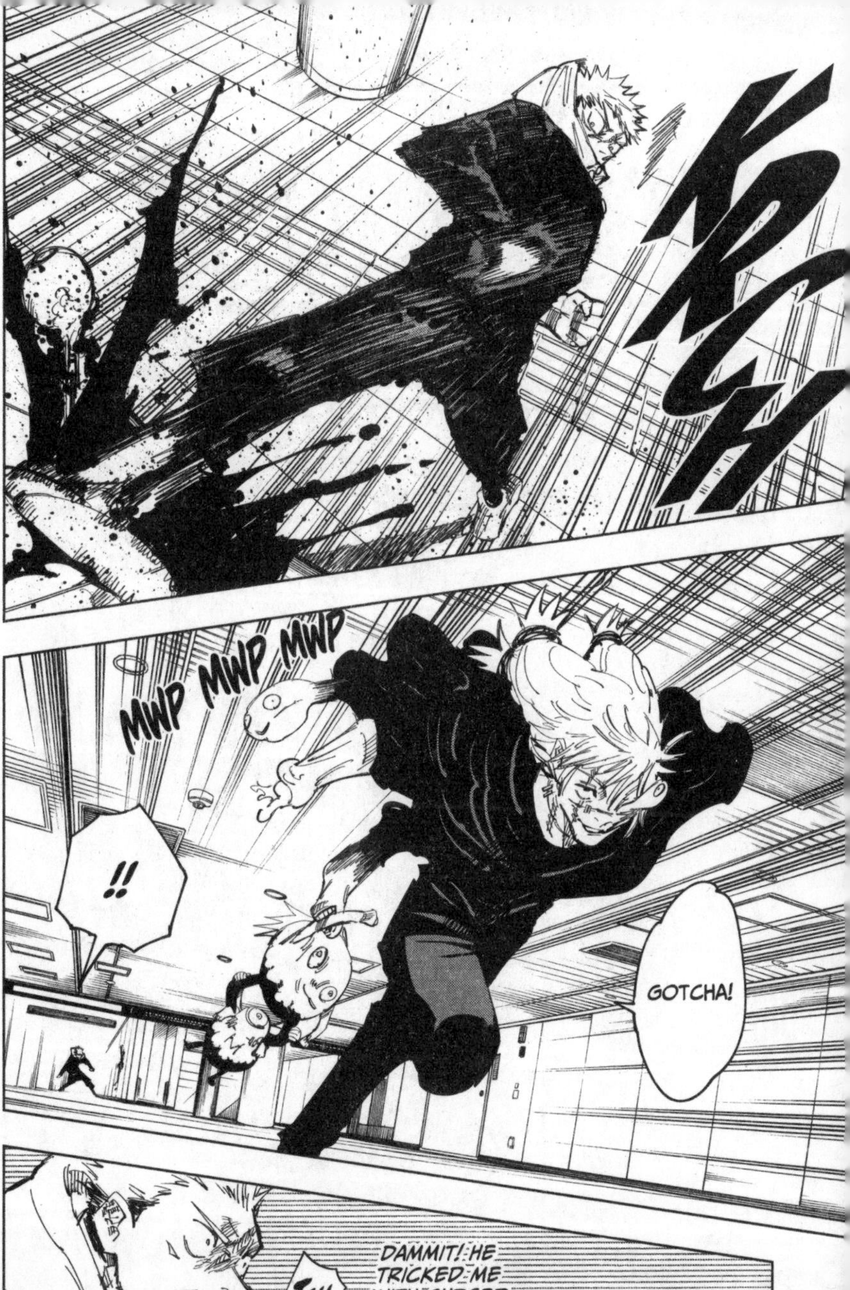
KRSH
MWP MWP MWP
GOTCHA!
!!
DAMMIT! HE TRICKED ME WITH CURSED ENERGY!
TCH!

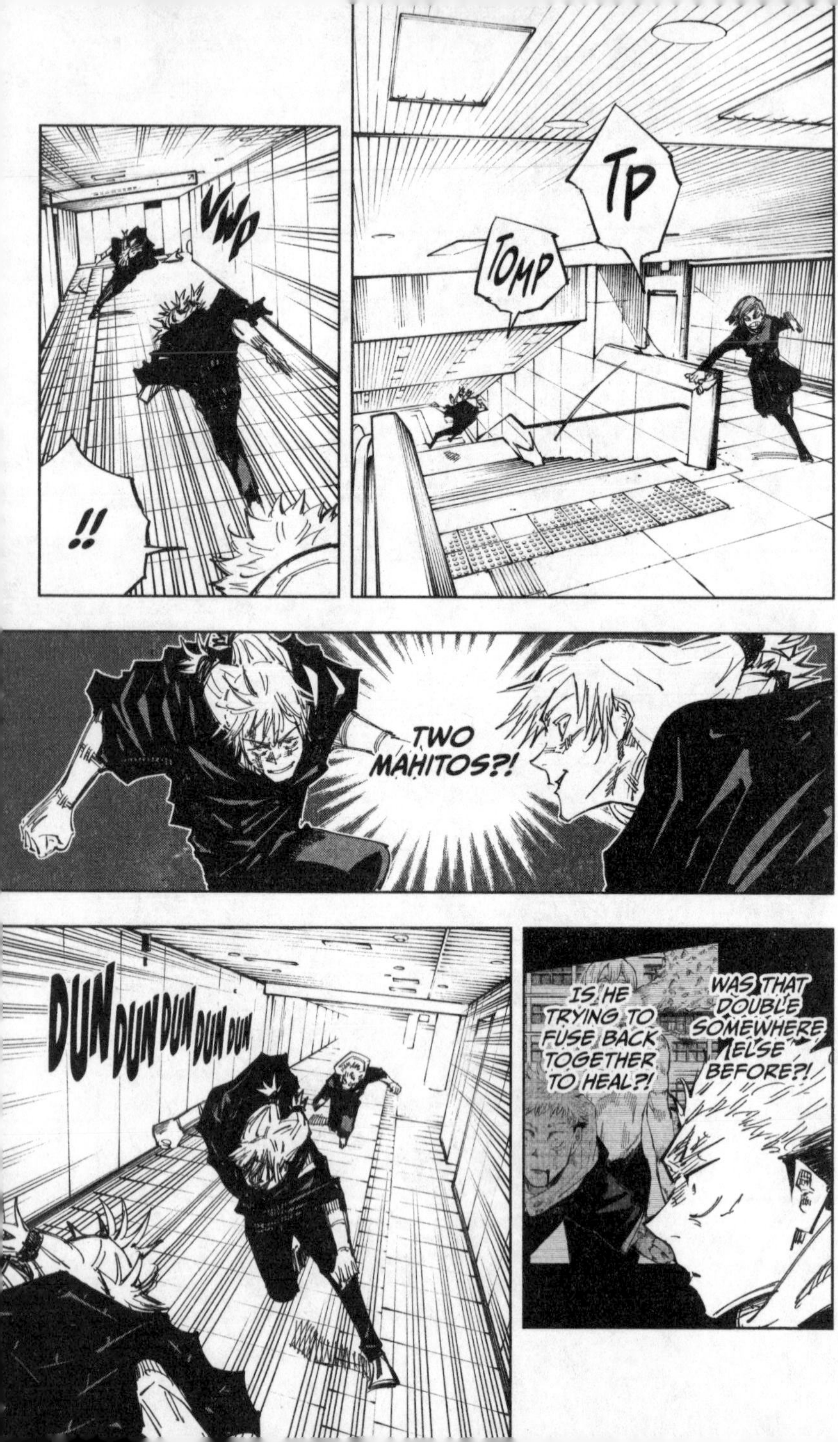
TP
TOMP
VWP
!!
TWO MAHITOS?!
WAS THAT DOUBLE SOMEWHERE ELSE BEFORE?!
IS HE TRYING TO FUSE BACK TOGETHER TO HEAL?!
DUN DUN DUN DUN DUN

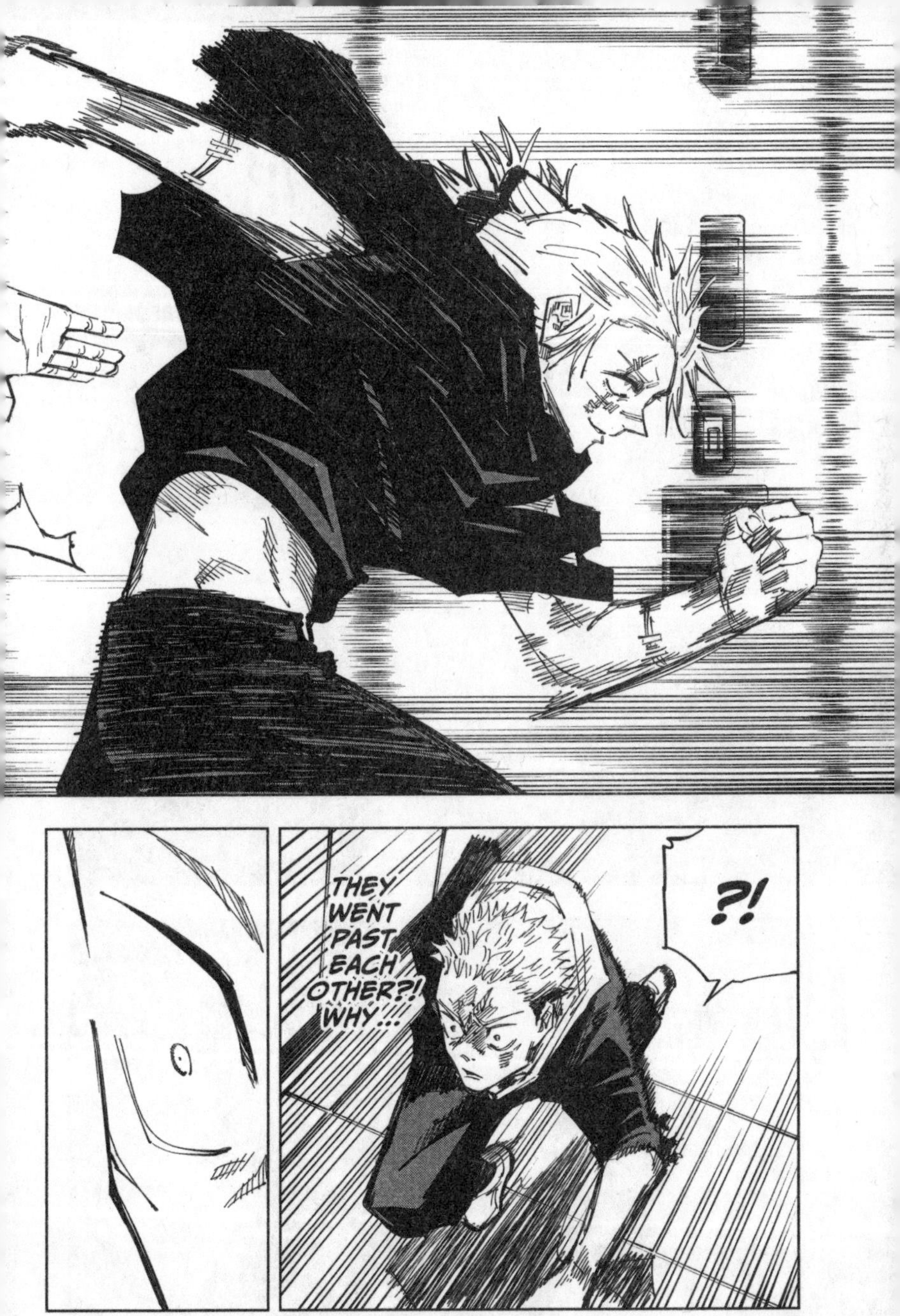
?!
THEY WENT PAST EACH OTHER?! WHY...

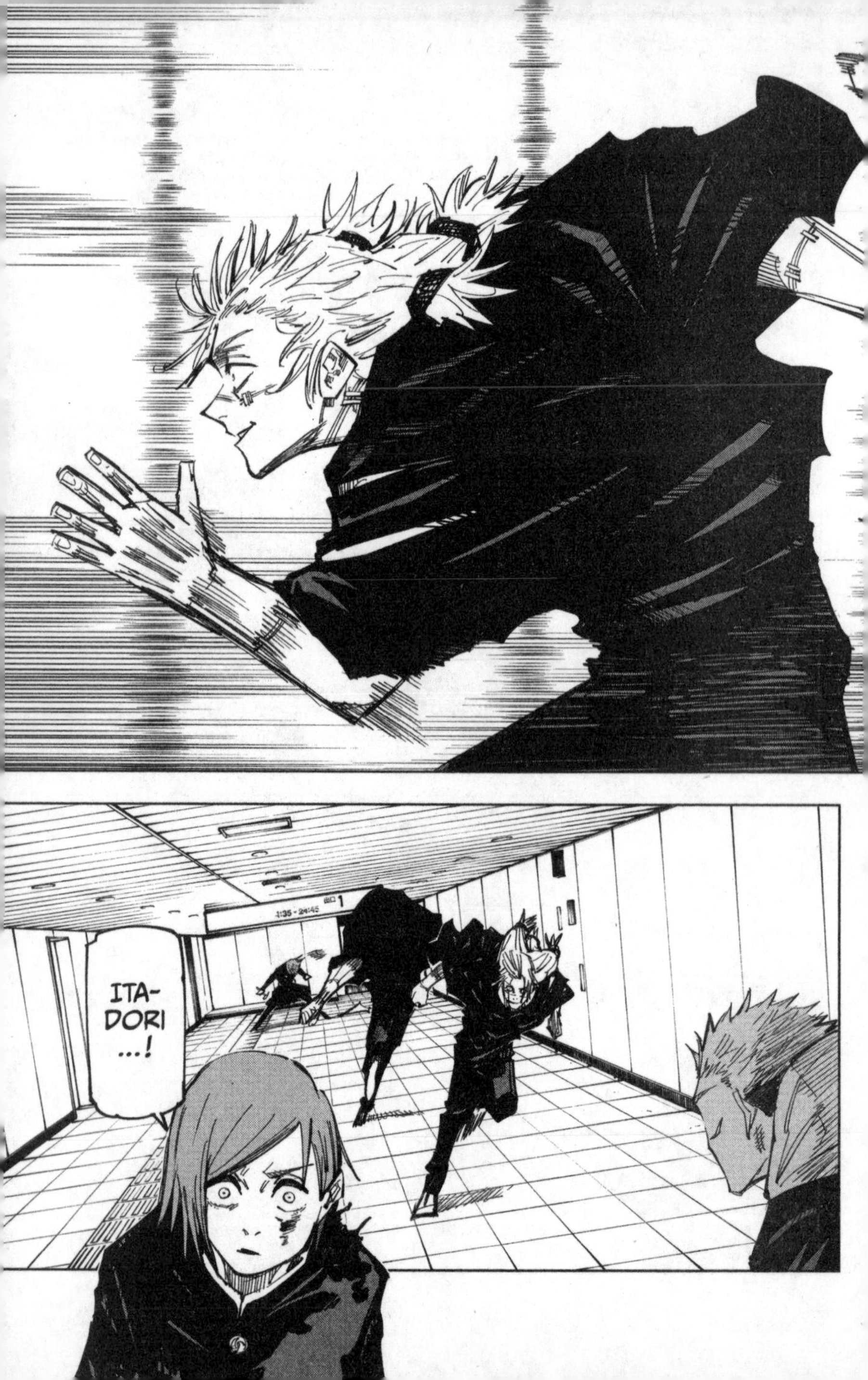
ITA-
DORI
...!

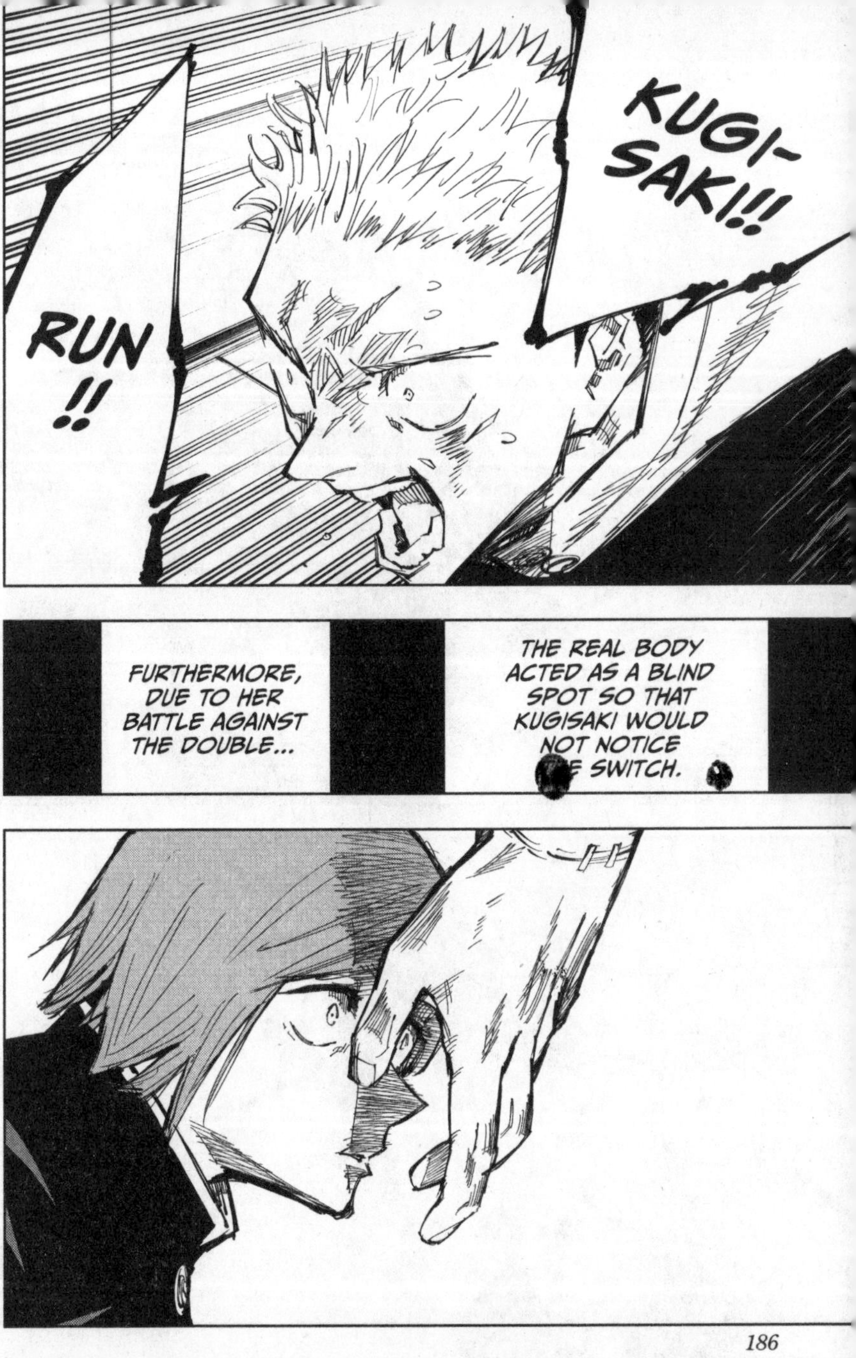
KUGI-SAKI!!!
RUN!!
THE REAL BODY ACTED AS A BLIND SPOT SO THAT KUGISAKI WOULD NOT NOTICE THE SWITCH.
FURTHERMORE, DUE TO HER BATTLE AGAINST THE DOUBLE...

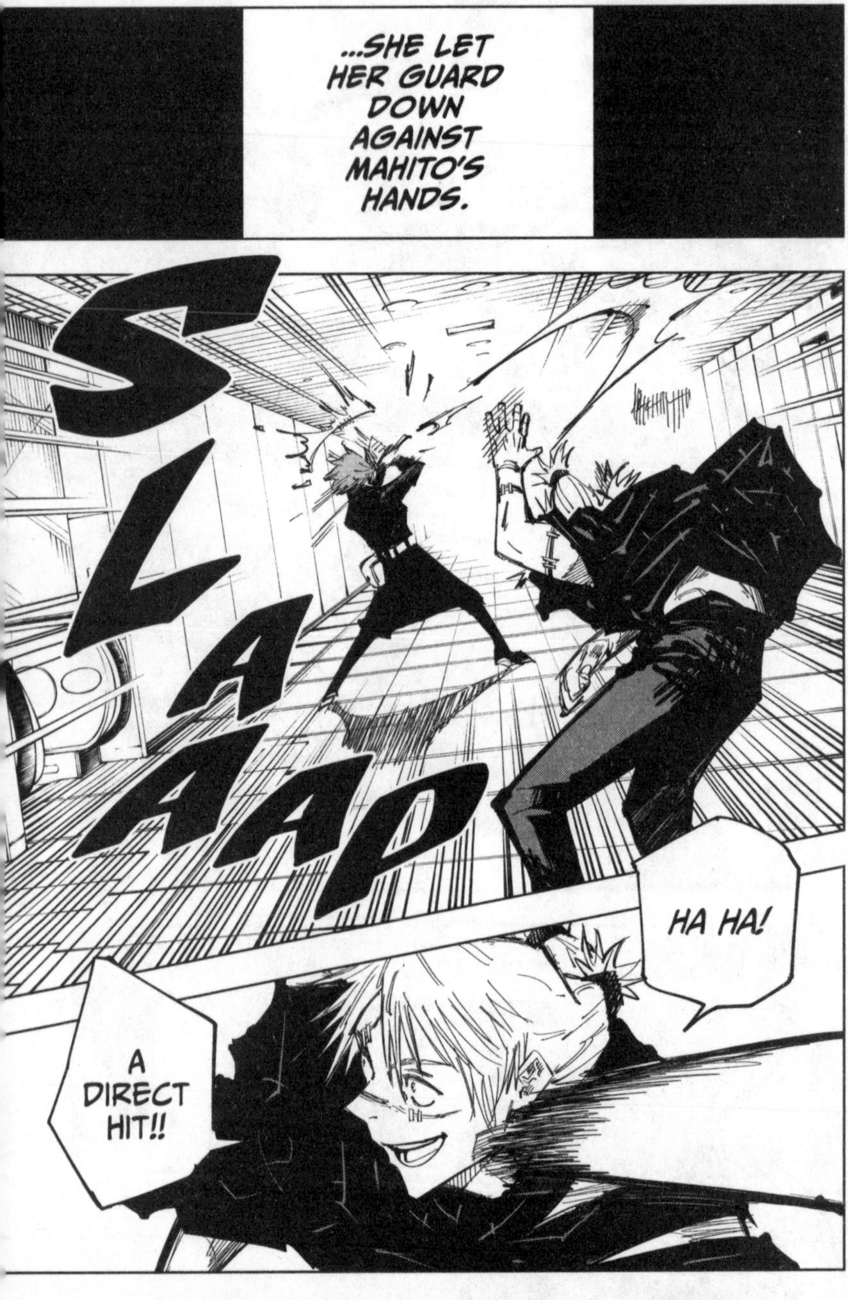
...SHE LET HER GUARD DOWN AGAINST MAHITO'S HANDS.
SLAAAP
HA HA!
A DIRECT HIT!!

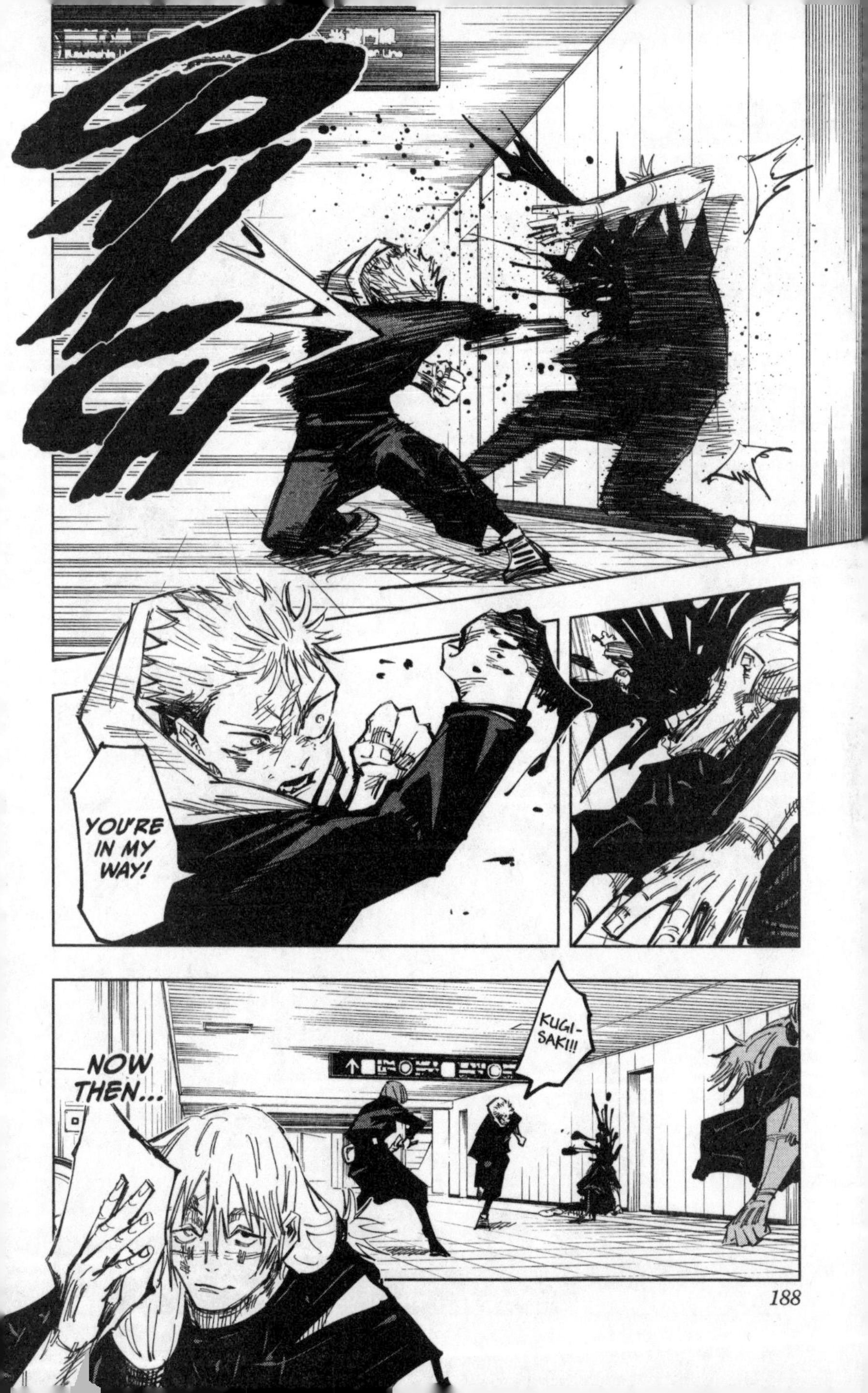
YOU'RE IN MY WAY!
KUGI-SAKI!!
NOW THEN...

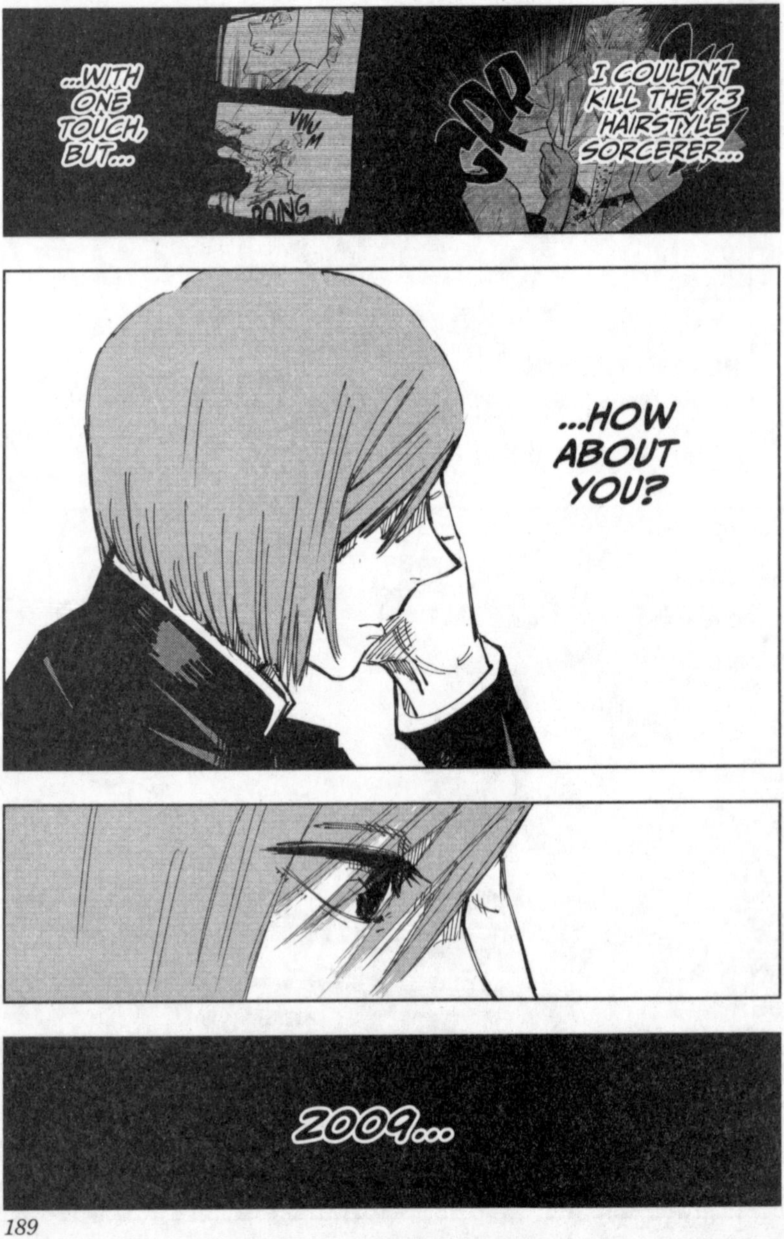
I COULDN'T KILL THE 7:3 HAIRSTYLE SORCERER...
BOING
...WITH ONE TOUCH, BUT...
...HOW ABOUT YOU?
2009...

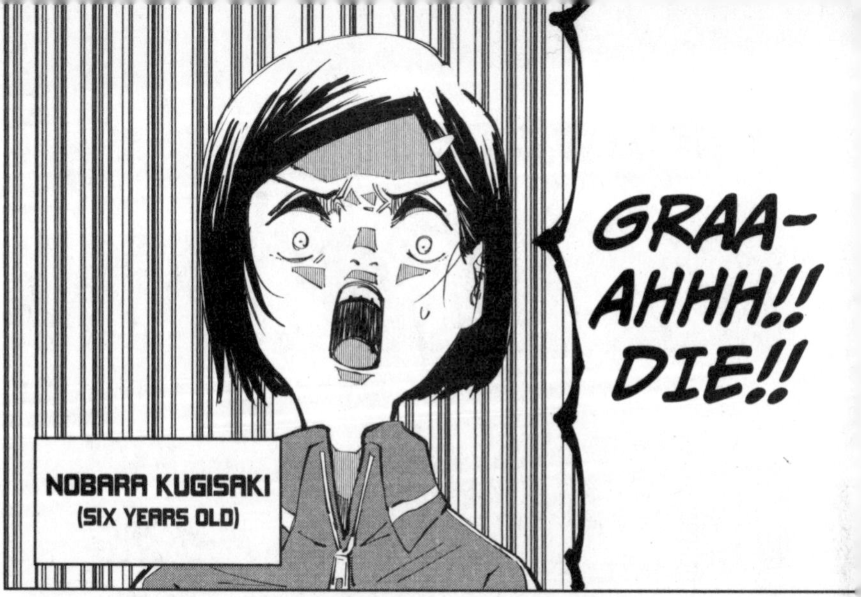
GRAA-AHHH!! DIE!!
NOBARA KUGISAKI (SIX YEARS OLD)

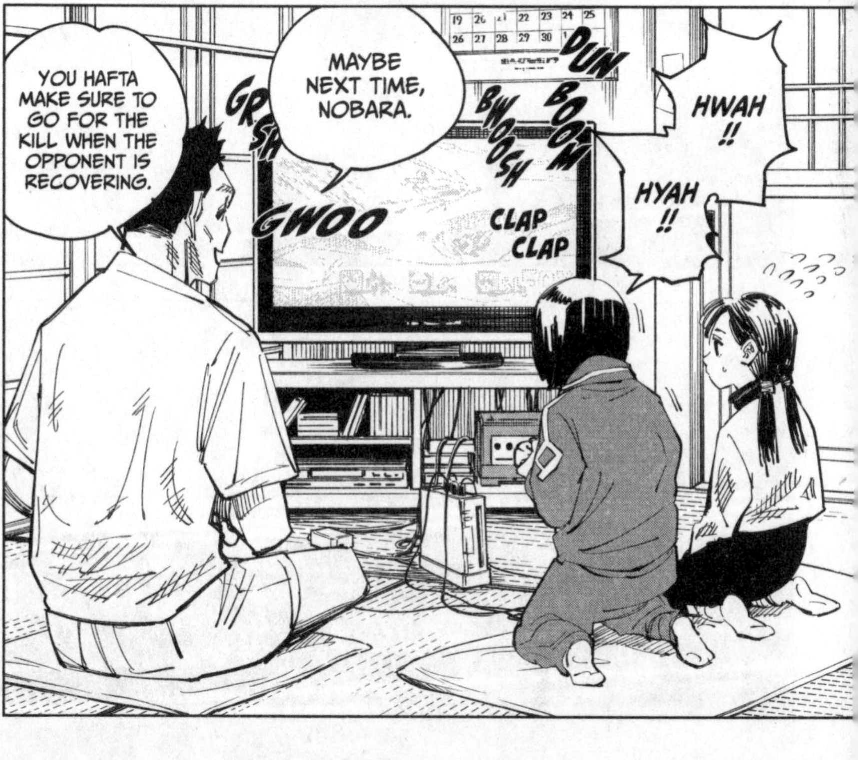
HWAH!!
HYAH!!
DUN BOOM
BWOOSH
CLAP CLAP
MAYBE NEXT TIME, NOBARA.
GWOO
GRSH
YOU HAFTA MAKE SURE TO GO FOR THE KILL WHEN THE OPPONENT IS RECOVERING.

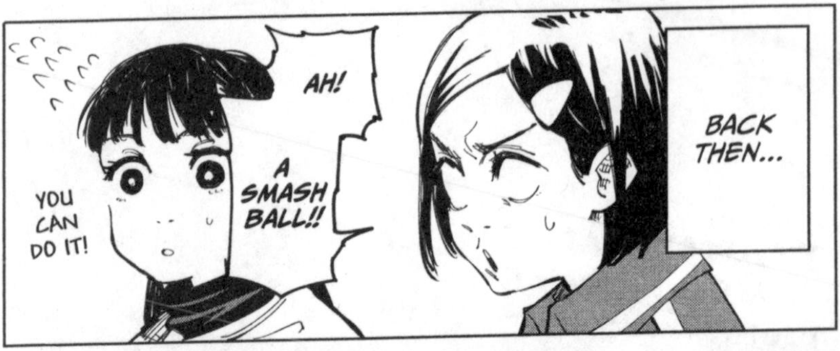
BACK THEN...
AH!
A SMASH BALL!!
YOU CAN DO IT!

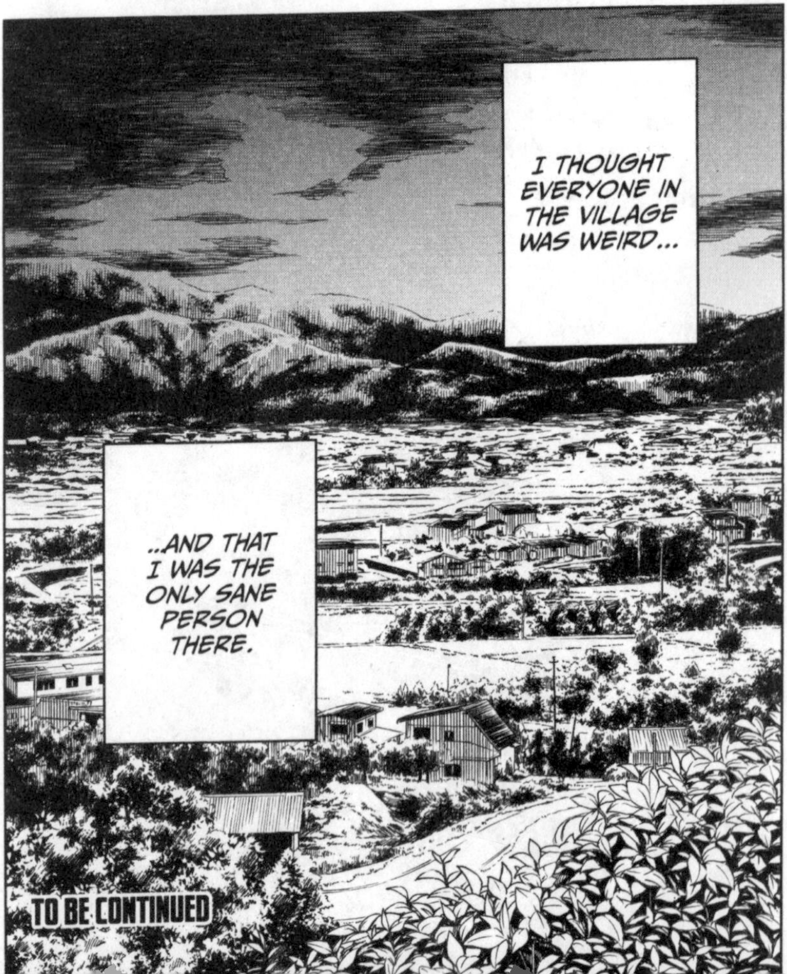
I THOUGHT EVERYONE IN THE VILLAGE WAS WEIRD...
...AND THAT I WAS THE ONLY SANE PERSON THERE.
TO BE CONTINUED

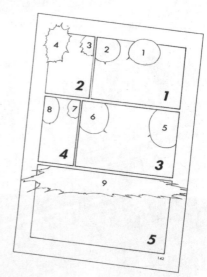

JUJUTSU KAISEN

reads from right to left, starting in the upper-right corner. Japanese is read from right to left, meaning that action, sound effects, and word-balloon order are completely reversed from English order.

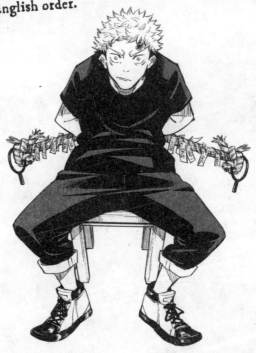

JUJUTSU KAISEN

VOLUME 14
SHONEN JUMP MANGA EDITION

BY GEGE AKUTAMI

TRANSLATION Stefan Koza
TOUCH-UP ART & LETTERING Snir Aharon
DESIGN Joy Zhang
EDITOR John Bae
CONSULTING EDITOR Erika Onabe

Printed in Italy

Published by VIZ Media, LLC
P.O. Box 77010
San Francisco, CA 94107

10 9 8 7 6 5
First printing, February 2022
Fifth printing, August 2024

VIZ MEDIA
viz.com

SHONEN JUMP

ratings.viz.com
RATED T+ OLDER TEEN

PARENTAL ADVISORY
JUJUTSU KAISEN is rated T+ for Older Teen and is recommended for ages 16 and up. This volume contains fantasy violence.

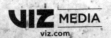

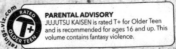

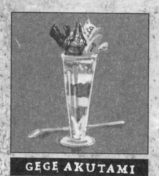

GEGE AKUTAMI

Hamburger!!!

GEGE AKUTAMI published a few short works before starting *Jujutsu Kaisen*, which began serialization in *Weekly Shonen Jump* in 2018.